The Four Domains of Mental Illness

Adolf Meyer
(1866–1950)

Karl Jaspers
(1883–1969)

The Four Domains of Mental Illness

An Alternative to the DSM-5

A Guide to Diagnosing Pathological Alterations in Mental Life Based on Adolf Meyer's Psychobiology, the Johns Hopkins Perspectives of Psychiatry and the Existentialists' Avowal of the Self as Active Agent

René J. Muller, PhD

Routledge
Taylor & Francis Group
LONDON AND NEW YORK

First edition published 2018
by Routledge
711 Third Avenue, New York, NY 10017

and by Routledge
2 Park Square, Milton Park, Abingdon, Oxon, OX14 4RN

Routledge is an imprint of the Taylor & Francis Group, an informa business

Permission to use the photograph of Adolf Meyer was given by the Alan Mason Chesney Medical Archives of the Johns Hopkins Medical Institutions. Getty Images authorized our reproduction of the Karl Jaspers photograph.

Library of Congress Cataloging-in-Publication Data
A catalog record for this book has been requested

ISBN: 978-1-138-30813-8 (hbk)
ISBN: 978-1-138-30814-5 (pbk)
ISBN: 978-1-315-14282-1 (ebk)

Typeset in Sabon
by Keystroke, Neville Lodge, Tettenhall, Wolverhampton

Contents

Foreword

Of the many criticisms of contemporary psychiatric thought and practice—which include claims that psychiatry is "unscientific," "elitist," "sectarian"—the most just and telling criticism—"confused"—derives from the absence of any profession-wide agreement about the nature of mental illnesses, particularly about their provenance. Nowhere else in medicine do doctors propose and provide treatments for conditions they acknowledge to be mysterious in nature and cause.

Trust us, the psychiatrists seem to say. But others can wonder, on the basis of what psychiatrists claim today, whether they've moved far from Polonius's view: "to define true madness, What is it but to be nothing else but mad?" (*Hamlet*, Act 2, Scene 2)

All criticisms and complaints about psychiatry reduce to a sense that psychiatrists use mostly rule-of-thumb treatments, which have underpinnings no stronger than those captured in such common contemporary psychiatric expressions as "this depression is due to a sort of chemical imbalance that responds to medication" or "this patient meets official criteria for this disorder, hence, we believe, he should be treated as others have been treated."

At the moment, most psychiatrists practice under the rules of *The Diagnostic and Statistical Manual of Mental Disorders*, put out by the American Psychiatric Association and now in its 5th edition, which prides itself on being "atheoretical." Actually the DSM-5 is a description-based field guide burdened by the same theoretical presumptions (things that look alike are alike, things that look different are different) as field guides that name birds, wild flowers, trees, etc. Most psychiatrists today suppose that neuroscience will eventually provide all needed explanations for the origin of mental illnesses; all they need do is wait patiently for neuroscientists to make sense of their patients.

The dialogue within the leadership of the discipline remains preoccupied with epistemologic ("how we know") themes as expressed in arguments about the reliability and validity of their methods of diagnosis. They reject, and may even despise, the development of the simplest ontologic themes ("what might exist") that excite most doctors and derive from judicious assumptions about what, on the basis of more fundamental psychological knowledge, might be the intelligible nature of a mental illness and what those assumptions imply for programs of practice and investigation.

The result of all this imprecision is a great dissatisfaction of many patients with their treatment and with psychiatric services in general. The main complaint, heard over and over, is that their psychiatrists no longer try to understand them. Doctors prescribe medicines but seem uninterested in trying to make sense of their illnesses as emerging in some way from who they are and what they have faced.

Such an unsatisfactory situation could have been, and in fact was, predicted if a single perspective were to be employed to assess all the vicissitudes of human conscious experience, as is being done now with the medical model of mental illness. In *Psychiatric Polarities: Methodology and Practice* (1987, reprinted 2016), Phillip R. Slavney and I pointed to several fundamental "polarities" within psychiatry including the brain/mind dichotomy. Psychiatry, we noted, is a discipline bridging the biological sciences and the humanities. It needs to take from both realms in attempting to understand patients and in resolving that old question, "What is madness?" We comfort ourselves about the neglect of our treatise (even as what it predicted has come so vividly to pass) by leaning on the lame, rather self-serving claim that it was "ahead of its time."

Maybe yes, maybe no. Others will decide.

But here in this book before us, René J. Muller, an informed scientist, clinician and philosopher, who struggled for many years to improve the services psychiatric patients receive, has returned to these themes. His aim is to enlarge the scope of psychiatric practice and investigation. His book brings forth a comprehensive body of sound knowledge about the nature of mental illnesses, addressing their ultimate meanings and essences.

Of particular and compelling interest is that the body of knowledge he reviews is embedded and leavened by a set of values. These values, fundamentally existential in nature, derive from recognizing patients as persons who can incur mental illnesses, some generated from objective brain dysfunction, others from subjective conflicts in personal life, after not authentically fulfilling their calling as active agents in their own self-creation. These different understandings of cause do not conflict but enrich one another in Muller's presentation.

Among the pleasing features of this book is its thoughtful description, and thus justification, of the origins of its opinions. Here, for example, the reader finds described Adolf Meyer's contributions to psychiatric thought and a coherent assessment of just how to view those contributions today. With Muller's help, the reader can understand why Meyer would find the contemporary DSM system of clinical diagnosis unsatisfactory as it repeats, in a prideful fashion, the mistakes and misunderstandings Meyer found embedded in the presumptions of Kraepelin's diagnostic approach back in the 1920s.

I, of course, easily find reasons to be pleased with how Muller builds on our *Perspectives of Psychiatry* (McHugh and Slavney, 1998) in interesting, debatable ways such as replacing our metaphor "perspectives" with his metaphor "domains." What praise do authors relish more than engaging seriously with the next generation of contributions to the field, who take their original ideas in different, fruitful directions? Muller enlarges the scope of his contribution by bringing a rich appreciation of the patient's plight, vitally felt, heavily burdening and so personally hard to resolve. He is greatly helped in this endeavor by his understanding of existential philosophy and psychiatry.

By providing a scientifically heuristic and philosophically rich approach to the diagnosis of mental illnesses, Muller opens much wider horizons for thought and practice. Confronting as he does the superficial approach of the DSM diagnostic schema and the neurocentric orientation of the National Institute of Mental Health's "Research Diagnostic Criteria" (RDoC), he awakens all to what could make psychiatry an interesting and challenging medical discipline.

Perhaps the most essential point made in *The Four Domains of Mental Illness* is just how much of the truth about mental illness is being overlooked in official psychiatric circles today. Let the FDMI push us all toward a better day when psychiatry will come of age as a coherent, collaborative, actively scientific clinical discipline.

Paul R. McHugh, MD

University Distinguished Service Professor of Psychiatry,
Johns Hopkins University School of Medicine

Preface

Simply put, psychiatry does not have—and never has had—a valid and reliable method for classifying and diagnosing the pathological alterations in mental life, in spite of claims made to the contrary for the *Diagnostic and Statistical Manual of Mental Disorders* (DSM), through its five editions. Our intention is to fill this void with *The Four Domains of Mental Illness: An Alternative to the DSM-5*. The approach followed here is simple and direct but requires a backward turn that may seem, at first, ironic, even anachronistic.

From 1910 to 1941, while Adolf Meyer was chief of psychiatry at the Johns Hopkins University School of Medicine—long before the DSM became the cynosure of clinical treatment and research in mental health—he was the preeminent psychiatrist in North America. During those three decades, and for some time after, the way Meyer thought about mental illness, worked with patients and taught psychiatric residents was the standard.

The commonest explanation for Meyer's failure to perpetuate his psychobiological approach is that he made no effort to formalize and systematize the method he originated. He wrote no books, and our chances to learn directly from him now are limited to collections of his numerous journal articles and public addresses compiled and edited by others. Meyer appears to have had no interest in creating any document that would have encapsulated his vision and perpetuated his legacy.

A major step in resuscitating Meyer from the limbo that he and psychobiology had fallen into was taken by Paul R. McHugh and Phillip R. Slavney in *The Perspectives of Psychiatry*. Written partly as a response to Freudian psychoanalysis, biological psychiatry and the 3rd and 4th editions of the DSM, these authors parsed the varieties of mental illness from four different perspectives. Each mental illness was viewed from the perspective that best accounted for its origin, and the meaning of its symptoms. Meyer's vision was conserved here, but shaped into an approach that is far more detailed and specific than the inchoate diagnostic formulations he left us.

The Four Domains of Mental Illness—the FDMI—extends the reach of *The Perspectives of Psychiatry* by characterizing the *domains* corresponding to each of the four perspectives: the lived space that someone in the grip of a mental illness inhabits. This elaboration entailed further emphasizing the contribution of existential psychiatry, already important in *The Perspectives*, which draws heavily from Karl Jaspers's *General Psychopathology*. Meyer and Jaspers, a German psychiatrist, looked at the world we live in and through in similar ways. It is no accident that they are the most revered figures in the Johns Hopkins pantheon of psychiatry.

Other existential psychiatrists, including Ludwig Binswanger, Medard Boss and R. D. Laing, as well as several existential philosophers, principally Jean-Paul Sartre, Martin Heidegger and Friedrich Nietzsche, were brought in to help lay the ontological groundwork for the dynamic formulation of what Meyer called *maladaptive reactions* that, he believed, underlie most mental illnesses. These reactions are pathological *choices* people make—defenses they invoke—as they face challenges they cannot or will not work through authentically. The DSM's *mental disorder* signifies only that something is wrong, while Meyer's *maladaptive reaction* provides some notion of what went wrong and why, and implies the active agency of the individual in the process. Extending *perspective* to *domain*, and replacing *disorder* with *reaction* were key steps in creating the classification and diagnostic system that became the FDMI.

The overarching beliefs that spawned the FDMI include these three points: we already know enough now about mental illness not to misdiagnose patients and reflexively prescribe medication that has been shown to be less efficacious than originally believed; the patient under our care comes first, not some theory about mental illness, even if that theory is correct; and psychiatric research should be directed toward understanding the *lived experience* of those who are mentally ill and not pursued on a track parallel to and removed from that reality in the name of a science which exists mainly to promote the careers of its practitioners, fill journal space and swell the coffers of pharmaceutical companies. These points were first made by the author in *Doing Psychiatry Wrong*.

For those who practice and do research according to the diagnostic guidelines of the DSM-5, with the conviction that all mental illnesses are brain diseases, ultimate success is defined as identifying the biological cause of each illness. In spite of a century and a half of hard work by medical scientists, no specific cause of any primary mental illness has been uncovered. Yet attempts to find these "causes," and the search for drugs and other ways to "fix" a putative damaged brain substrate continue, as biological psychiatrists leverage their patients' treatment on discoveries that may never be made.

In contrast, the paradigm that seeds the FDMI offers a common sense assurance, gleaned from the clinical outcomes of many patients and empirical studies, that most mental illnesses can be understood and treated psychodynamically.

Composers, conductors and soloists, when they write, direct or play music, struggle to get what they call the "long line"—a continuous unfolding that allows every note to contribute, from start to finish, to the final result. This means seeing each part of the score in its proper relation to every other part, and every part to the whole. Writers of descriptive and analytical prose also chase the long line, and I have tried to do so in creating the FDMI.

To write—anything—means making choices about what to put in the budding text and what to leave out. In the FDMI, no attempt was made to include every mental illness ever designated or to cite every clinician whose insight has contributed to understanding the illnesses characterized. Literature citations are limited to instances when the addition of another voice seemed to significantly enlarge the discussion. This selectivity made it possible to focus on the phenomena being explored and keep the text to a reasonable length. This said, it is anticipated that some readers will consider the selection—and the omissions—arbitrary and wanting.

The reader is asked to trust the author's synthesis of at least some of the best that has been thought and said about mental illness. In this age of biological psychiatry and the DSM-5, it is not at all certain that most psychiatrists have absorbed or even been exposed to this legacy, a good deal of which appears to have been purposely excluded from psychiatry residency programs and fellowship training. An earnest effort has been made here to provide a philosophical anthropology, a formal sounding term that simply means a sense of what the world is, and what it means to live as a "normal" human being—ultimately a vague and somewhat arbitrary notion—so that mental illness can become comprehensible as the difference between this "normalcy" and the pathological domain a patient inhabits.

It is one thing to think and write about the current state of psychiatry from within or slightly outside the current paradigm. It is something quite different to come at this topic from a radically different point of view as is being done here. Most clinician-writers take a polite stance toward the professional culture in which they were raised. Whether realizing it or not, they think and write through a persona of accommodation to that culture while seeking its improvement.

I myself once took that stance. But as I continued to see patients who were misdiagnosed and ineffectively treated, and, in many instances, damaged, my thinking about the profession changed radically, and I dropped the accommodating persona. Doing this allowed me to think and speak more directly about what I believed was wrong, and to pursue the elements of a different, valid paradigm more actively. In so doing, I became engaged—what Jean-Paul Sartre called *engagé*—in a project to expose the failures of a false paradigm and replace it with a valid one. No doubt, my several years' study of existential philosophy with Ralph Harper at Johns Hopkins, which culminated in my first book, *The Marginal Self*, primed me for pursuing, as both theorist and advocate, the project that became the FDMI.

In spite of being immersed in psychiatry's current paradigm, some clinicians have found ways to authentically and effectively meet their patients' needs. This is usually the case because they have had at least one teacher or mentor who thought and practiced outside the paradigm, or because their natural inclinations and talents took them beyond the limitations of their training. Some of these clinicians have added to psychiatry's knowledge base with new intuitions about the nature and provenance of mental illness, and with new therapeutic techniques. And it must be acknowledged that, while no drug in the psychopharmacology's armamentarium fulfills the claim of correcting a causative "chemical imbalance" or fixing a "broken brain part," there is no question that some patients owe their lives to drugs that control certain *symptoms* of their illness, which, left unmedicated, could have proven fatal.

To be effective, the clinician's approach need not be correct in all its details. Often, being good enough—like Donald Winnicott's "good enough" mother—can get the job done. But not all clinicians who see the weakness in psychiatry's current paradigm are willing or able to step out of the mold. In fact, most continue to follow the path that has led to their certification and remuneration as mental health professionals. This inertia has contributed to a dumbing down and corruption of the profession.

Our ultimate goal as clinicians is to get our patients better, to persuade them to exchange a life that does not work well for them for one that works better. To do that, we must grasp the essence of what it means to be a person, in health and in sickness. The DSM-III, DSM-IV and DSM-5 ultimately fail because these materialist systems endorse a way of diagnosing mental illness that denies the radical essence of every person's life: freedom.

To deny freedom is to deny responsibility. Grounded in these denials, the DSM-5 is a veritable invitation for clinicians to get a diagnosis wrong. Purposely ignoring etiology, and taking symptoms at face value, no provision is made for holding patients (or anyone else) accountable for a mental illness they develop.

What most differentiates the FDMI from the DSM-5 is the notion that, to a considerable degree, the person we become emerges from the sum of the choices we make in the process of exercising our freedom. Originating in what is surely one of the great philosophical insights of the 20th century, Sartre declared that "we are condemned to be free." We have no choice in the matter, only in how we *use or misuse* our freedom. Being condemned to freedom is the ur-paradox of human existence!

Even while we are denying our freedom, which we all do at times, especially under pressure or when things go badly, we are using that freedom to construct this denial: refusing to choose *is* a choice. In the Meyerian and existential formulations of psychic pathology, most mental illnesses are thought to originate in a person's self-deceiving, maladaptive misuse of freedom. In the FDMI, freedom and its misuse play out across all four domains, though in different ways in each domain, and to different degrees.

While acknowledging the limits of what we know about how and why people become mentally ill, the FDMI offers clinicians an approach to parsing the varieties of mental illness that affords both human freedom and biology their due, so that patients can receive their due. If we are to do justice to the growing number of patients who are seeking help, our profession will have to alter the paradigm that shapes its practice.

I had hoped never to write a sentence saying that a book of mine is divided into two parts. Nonetheless, that is the case here. A few words of explanation will help the reader to see how this text evolved. In Part I, the first two chapters are given to explaining, at some length, why the DSM-5 and the two editions of the DSM that preceded it are invalid—and why the current paradigm of biological psychiatry, constituted as this medical model is mostly by the DSM-5 and the unsubstantiated assertion that all mental illnesses are brain diseases, is invalid as well.

In the three remaining chapters of Part 1, the groundwork is laid for understanding both Meyerian psychobiology and existential psychiatry. It is demonstrated how, ultimately, these two seemingly different approaches to mental illness are alike, and draw from similar notions of what it means to be a human being, in sickness and in health. The McHugh-Slavney four *perspectives* of psychiatry are introduced, followed by the concept of the four *domains*, which are existential elaborations of their mainly analytical perspectives.

The range and reach of the four domains is spelled out in Part 2. We believe that parsing mental illness in this way is phenomenologically sound and valid, and would be in synchrony with any future psychobiological advances made in understanding and explaining the pathological alterations in mental life.

The approach taken here presupposes that the most irreducible property of the human spirit is freedom and that most of the alterations in mental life that have come to be known as mental illness are best understood as a misuse of that freedom. The centrality of freedom is a leitmotif in Adolf Meyer's psychobiology, the Johns Hopkins perspectives of psychiatry and the thinking and clinical work of existential philosophers and psychiatrists, which, taken together, constitute the theoretical foundation of the FDMI.

The FDMI is a bet on the future. Having argued that the medical model of mental illness is inauthentic and invalid, I am not so naïve as to believe that the DSM-5 will be discarded any time soon. Mistakes—delusions—of this magnitude have remained embedded in cultures for decades. Eventually, though, it becomes easier to tell the truth than to prop up the lie. That will happen with psychiatry's medical model of mental illness. In fact, it is already happening. To recall Nietzsche, if from a very different context, in psychiatry we are caught now between two worlds: one dying, the other struggling to be born.

As this process moves toward completion, the FDMI offers what I believe will eventually be seen as an authentic and valid alternative to the DSM-5, an iteration of the so-called "third way": not the unconsciousness-dominated model of Freud, and not our current neurocentric biological psychiatry, but something else entirely. The FDMI is ultimately an attempt to reboot a false psychiatric paradigm. Eyeing the bottom line, mental health practitioners and those who supply them with the medications they prescribe may come to see the FDMI as what economists call a "disruptive innovation" that portends a significant change in how clinical services are remunerated and how widely drugs are used.

Acknowledgments

Two people contributed mightily to the project that became *The Four Domains of Mental Illness.*

Paul R. McHugh, University Distinguished Service Professor of Psychiatry at the Johns Hopkins School of Medicine and coauthor with Phillip R. Slavney of *The Perspectives of Psychiatry*, provided a link back to Adolf Meyer and the psychobiology he taught while directing the Department of Psychiatry at Johns Hopkins from 1911 to 1940. After Meyer retired as chairman, the department changed orientation: first to Freudian psychoanalysis, then to biological psychiatry, pretty much following the norms adopted at other American academic centers. When McHugh became chairman in 1975, he reinstated the Meyerian approach, and *The Perspectives of Psychiatry* became the new iteration of Meyerian psychobiology. It was a joy and an honor to work with Professor McHugh, who generously offered his time and counsel. Without the four perspectives of psychiatry, there would be no four domains of mental illness.

Barbara Young, who did her psychiatry residency with John C. Whitehorn, Adolf Meyer's immediate successor as chairman of psychiatry at Johns Hopkins, has been my friend and colleague for many years. We both write, and are both sticklers for getting our sentences and paragraphs right. While I was working on the FDMI, she was writing *The Persona of Ingmar Bergman: Conquering Demons Through Film.* We read and critiqued each other's work, chapter by chapter. Thank you, Barbara, for all those corrections and suggestions, and for passing on so much of the knowledge you accumulated over a lifetime of clinical work and writing.

Many others have influenced, in one way or another, the person I became, and the work I have done and continue to do: William von Eggers Doering, Lawrence H. Knox, Ernest L. Elliel, Alan Schriesheim, Alex Nickon, Walter Koski, John Gryder, Raymond C. Weglein, Laurence J. McGowan, Bruce Q. Ballert, Eugene V. Clark, Edgar Hilliar, Edwin Ryan, Bernard J. McMahon, John F. Lyons, Tony Bill, Frank O'Malley, Philip Hughes, Joseph M. Duffy, James A. Reyniers, Daniel J. O'Neil, Thomas J. Brennan, Elliott Coleman, Ralph Harper, Julian Stanley, Robert Hogan, Phillip J. Cunningham, Donald King, William P. Partridge, Randall Mullin, Ken Brown, Garry Wills, David E. Crossley, Tom Nugent, Harvey Alexander, David L. Smith, Scott D. Churchill, William F. Fischer, Olivia Cherry, Freddy Medora Espy, Ann McNutt, William Dieal, Newman Pettit, Virginia and Gregory Day, Lucile and Francis Barr, Lydia and Arthur Kabus, Carla and Gunther Keil, Edna Mae and Walter Bauman, Ann and Thomas Shields, Mary and Jack Stacey, Carol and Martin Stacey, and, of course, my mother and father, Katherine Hoerrner Muller and René Muller.

The African proverb "It takes a village to raise a child" is only a part of the story: it takes a world to create an adult. Had the people named here, and others, not been my parents, teachers, colleagues, employers, friends, neighbors and financial supporters of my work, things would have turned out differently for me, and surely not as well. Most are gone now, so this list carries intimations of mortality. No one tells you that those who matter most to you won't be around forever.

Between 2011 and 2015, the computer that processed the sentences I typed to make this book confounded me many times, in ways large and small. In every instance, the productivity consultants at Vitalyst, accessible by phone around the clock and all through the year, solved one problem after another, with obvious talent and always good cheer. To all those at Vitalyst who made it possible for me to keep writing after so many computer snafus sent me into a wall, I am deeply grateful. Special thanks to Diego Rosales who took so many of my calls in the middle of the night and never once came up short or showed the slightest impatience, no matter how hard the going got, or how long it took to do the fix.

The Past as Prologue

The text that follows includes excerpts from articles written by the author for *The Humanistic Psychologist*, *Philosophy, Psychiatry & Psychology*, *Hopkins Medicine*, *Psychiatric Times* and *The Baltimore Sun*.

The brief biographical sketch of Adolf Meyer in Chapter 3 was excerpted from the author's entry on Meyer for the *Encyclopedia of Clinical Psychology*. In Chapter 9 the story of Mrs. K was taken from *Doing Psychiatry Wrong*, as was Peter's story in Chapter 17, part of which originated as the epilogue. In Chapter 14 the Elyn Saks text appeared previously in *Psychiatric Times*; Kim's story was taken from *Psych ER* and John Nash's story from *Doing Psychiatry Wrong*. In Chapter 16 Alicia's and Angela's narratives came out first in *Doing Psychiatry Wrong*, along with some commentary on the misdiagnosis of bipolar disorder. The description in Chapter 10 of the "resigned person" is from Karen Horney's *Neurosis and Human Growth*.

Also by René J. Muller

The Marginal Self

Anatomy of a Splitting Borderline

Beyond Marginality

Psych ER

Doing Psychiatry Wrong

The greatest thing a human soul ever does in this world is to see something and tell what it saw in a plain way. Hundreds of people can talk for one who can think, but thousands can think for one who can see.

—John Ruskin (1856)

My experience is what I agree to attend to. Only those items which I notice shape my mind . . .

—William James (1890)

In so much of our world—in the sciences and the humanities, business and politics, medicine and government—there are mistaken beliefs that have survived all this time largely through force of habit. They are spirals of misinformation hiding in plain sight.

—William R. Brody, 132nd Commencement of
The Johns Hopkins University, May 22, 2008

Part I

Where Psychiatry Has Been, Needs to Go, and How to Get There

Chapter 1 Why Psychiatry Needs Another Way to Classify and Diagnose the Pathological Alterations in Mental Life

Between 1994 and 2004, I evaluated over 3,000 psychiatric patients in the emergency rooms at three hospitals in Baltimore. About halfway through this decade of intense clinical work, I came to see that many of my patients with prior psychiatric treatment had been wrongly diagnosed and prescribed medication that was unnecessary and, in some instances, harmful. This was especially true when the diagnosis was bipolar disorder or schizophrenia. It soon became obvious to me that misdiagnosis, rather than the exception, had become the rule and the standard of care in psychiatry.

With the foregoing epiphany came the understanding that the principal reason for this debacle was an essential error in the way diagnoses were being made—using the mostly behavioral criteria specified by the DSM-IV. In 2008 I published a book, *Doing Psychiatry Wrong*, where I showed how the mental health profession had been corrupted by a false and often toxic paradigm, and how patients were being betrayed by clinicians who had taken an oath to help them (Muller 2008).

Consistent with their understanding of mental illness, the creators of the 3rd, 4th and 5th editions of the DSM did not require clinicians to determine or specify the *meaning* of their patients' symptoms. Nor were these innovators interested in trying to identify the psychological structure of any mental illness. Their approach was deliberately atheoretical, taken with the hope of avoiding further dissention among various factions in psychiatry, whose adherents had diverse ideas about the etiology of mental illness—a situation that had already caused a good deal of acrimony within the profession. By 1980, with the DSM-III, psychiatry was ready for an approach that would cut through this confusion and offer unambiguous instructions for diagnosing mental illness.

"We can't live in a state of perpetual doubt [echoes of Descartes here], so we make up the best story possible and we live as if the story were true." So wrote psychologist Daniel Kahneman, as quoted by Mario Livio in *Brilliant Blunders* (2013, p. 140; Else 2011), a collection of essays revealing how some of the best scientists have deceived themselves about an important issue, often missing the truth by mistaking a part for the whole. Though neither Livio nor Kahneman takes on the last three editions of the DSM, their characterization of this kind of blundering applies perfectly here: the DSM-III took behavioral symptoms, without regard for etiology or meaning, as sufficient information to diagnose a mental disorder.

To many mental health professionals, the DSM-III (1980), DSM-IV (1994) and DSM-5 (2013) appeared to offer the best possible story about diagnosing mental illness. Since 1980 psychiatry has pretended that this story is true. Regrettably, there is no "brilliance" in this blunder. Taken together, the DSM and the notion of the biologically "broken brain" constitute a self-deceiving, self-serving and reductive distortion of reality that perpetuates Descartes's *Cogito*. By attempting to remove the "doubt" that inevitably attaches to something as complex as a mental illness—supposedly to achieve "reliability" in diagnosis—psychiatry created a paradigm that is a *reductio ad absurdum*.

The claim that the atheoretical DSM classification system produced valid results could not possibly have been true, and it wasn't. As any experienced clinician knows, different mental illnesses manifest many of the same symptoms. How could counting symptoms of unspecified origin and meaning lead clinicians and investigators to make a valid—or even similar—diagnosis, time after time, particularly in illnesses where criteria could be met with more than one combination of symptoms? It was inevitable that different diagnoses would result from similar symptom sets.

And what was a clinician to do when a patient's symptoms did not quite match the criteria for one mental illness or another? To those who implicitly believed in a diagnosis made with categories defined by certain kinds and numbers of symptoms, the DSM implicitly encouraged "stretching" these symptoms to *fit* the criteria for one diagnosis or another. When all a clinician has to work with are illnesses of unspecified etiology and symptoms of unspecified meaning, this concession to the god of categorical diagnosis does not seem too much.

Initially the DSM-III and DSM-IV were intended for researchers investigating the biological causes of mental illness, and not for clinicians who saw and diagnosed patients. Biological psychiatrists believed that the descriptive checklists, mostly composed of behavioral criteria, coupled with a fast-developing, white-hot neuroscience, would lead to an unearthing of the brain malfunction behind each designated mental disorder. To those who were in thrall to the biological model of mental illness, only time separated this vision from its realization.

In one way, the DSM's 3rd and 4th editions succeeded beyond their creators' expectations. Clinicians, who had not been the primary intended audience for the DSM, found the behavioral criteria easy to apply, and patients were confidently diagnosed using the checklists of symptoms provided for each mental disorder. The public was similarly enthralled. The DSM-III and DSM-IV became publishing phenomena, defining mental illness for the world.

Misdiagnosing Mental Illness with the DSM

Over time, it became increasingly clear that, using criteria based on symptoms with no established meaning, a number of mental illnesses were being misdiagnosed—most frequently attention deficit hyperactivity disorder (ADHD), post-traumatic stress disorder (PTSD) and dissociative identity disorder (DID; formerly multiple personality disorder [MPD]).

In a similar fashion, the diagnosis of bipolar I disorder (BPD) was overtaken by a definitional creep that erroneously extended that label to other conditions marked by mood lability. Many people with personality disorders—and anyone who presents with chronic anger, irritability and the "mood swings" that occur for so many different reasons—now fall under the BPD aegis. This trend was spurred by a number of new tranquilizing drugs that curb anxiety and agitation, common symptoms in many mental illnesses. Pharmaceutical companies aggressively promoted their products.

In the DSM-5, criterion A for a manic episode reads as follows: "A distinct period of abnormally and persistently elevated, expansive, or irritable mood and abnormally and persistently increased goal-directed activity or energy, lasting at least 1 week and present most of the day, nearly every day (or any duration if hospitalization is necessary)" (2013, p. 124).

A truck could be driven through the holes in criterion A. Taken at face value, a clinician would be allowed to substitute *irritable* mood for *elevated* or *expansive* mood—*irritable* being inexplicably conflated with *elevated* or *expansive*—so that an irritable patient would not have to be either "elevated" or "expansive" to the degree that has historically defined mania in psychiatric practice. (Other mental illnesses produce symptoms with different kinds and lesser intensities of mood elevation or expansion.) If an irritable patient is hospitalized, as happens often with patients who come to the ER, the DSM-5 time criterion of one week is suspended, reducing that window to an unspecified lesser time.

Since the DSM-5 plays fast and loose with the meaning of psychiatric symptoms, any sufficiently angry or irritable person, particularly when disruptive or threatening—especially if the clinician does not understand that the emotions described by the adjectives *elevated*, *expansive* and *irritable* are, in their purest forms, *three distinct phenomena*—may fulfill criterion A, the most distinctive behavior of the manic state. Clinicians are provided neither the guidance nor the incentive to identify the unique *phenomenon* of bipolar disorder in patients who present with bimodal mood lability. This phenomenon is vividly elicited by Kay Redfield Jamison in her memoir *An Unquiet Mind* (1995), as she describes her own bipolar I illness.

As if this were not bad enough, the first bipolar phenotype specified by the DSM-5 is Bipolar I Disorder, Single Manic Episode, which, as the name implies, allows the diagnosis to be made after *only one manic episode*—provided there have been no past episodes of major depression and the manic episode is "not better accounted for" by the obvious exclusion criteria. How many patients have been diagnosed as bipolar because they became anxious, angry, agitated or irritated, did not know how to calm themselves down, talked too much and too wildly, lost sleep, bragged to cover their feelings of vulnerability and perhaps even threatened someone? Have the worst day of your life and the bad luck to be evaluated by a clinician who takes the DSM-5 to be the bible of mental illness, literally rather than figuratively, and your name may be added to that list.

Is it any wonder that the DSM-III, DSM-IV and DSM-5 have spurred an epidemic of misdiagnosed bipolar disorder? With the criteria written as they are, could it have turned out any other way?

The DSM-5 Task Force made the same kind of mistakes in creating the criteria for diagnosing schizophrenia. Because the context and meaning of psychotic symptoms are usually now ignored (except when a medical cause is identified), many patients walk the earth diagnosed with schizophrenia who do not have this illness, but some lesser disturbance of mind or brain involving distortions of reality, which goes unrecognized and unaddressed.

Simply put, these various misdiagnoses are, to adapt the legal metaphor, fruit of the DSM's poisonous tree, the consequence of what amounts to a clinician's invitation to get a diagnosis wrong. The unquestioned enthusiasm originally felt for the DSM classification system overlooked the obvious fact that only a valid psychiatric diagnosis could lead to valid psychiatric research. Inevitably, wrong diagnoses generate invalid data and conclusions, which in turn wrongly influence clinical treatment. For this reason, a good deal of the literature based on diagnoses made using the DSM-III, DSM-IV and DSM-5 criteria must be considered suspect (Ross & Pam 1995). Many who do research now have come to accept this reality and compensate for it by focusing on the professional rewards that publication brings, independent of any salutary effect their findings might or might not have on those affected by mental illness. It is not an exaggeration to say that the work of some research groups amounts to a shell game.

According to the Gestalt psychologist Kurt Lewin, "There is nothing more practical than a good theory" (Lewin 1952, p. 169). Conversely, history offers strong evidence that there is nothing so destructive as a *bad* theory, whether it originates in politics, economics, social science, physical science or psychiatry. The idea that clinicians could take a patient's symptoms at face value, without regard to *why* these symptoms occurred at a certain time and under certain circumstances will, I suspect, eventually be counted as one of the worst ideas in the history of Western thought. The DSM-5 cannot be fixed because it is not broken, a characterization that implies a former condition of wholeness and utility. The fact is that the 3rd, 4th and 5th editions of the DSM *never* worked, and were always *wrong!* Their "success" falls under the heading of what the economist Paul Krugman, in another context, has called the "triumph of bad ideas" (Krugman 2013).

In a book titled *A Research Agenda for DSM-V* (2002), the Task Force editors acknowledged the anguish they must have been feeling about their mission a full 11 years before the 2013 publication of this 5th edition: "All these limitations in the current diagnostic paradigm suggest that research exclusively focused on refining the DSM-defined syndromes may never be successful in uncovering their underlying etiologies. For that to happen, an as yet unknown paradigm shift may need to occur" (Kupfer, First & Regier 2002, p. xix).

Such a "paradigm shift" did not emerge in the DSM-5 because it could not, and not just because there is as yet no biological explanation for *any* mental illness. In the DSM diagnostic system of symptoms, without known etiology or known meaning, the concept of mental illness is implicitly grounded in the false belief that a human being is primarily determined by brain biology and chemistry. But the best evidence, to say nothing of common sense, suggests that a person—the self as active agent—*emerges* from a brain biological substrate, which, in turn, is altered, for better or worse, by thoughts, feelings and actions permitted by a (relative) freedom that a biologically facilitated consciousness makes possible.

Any future valid paradigm for psychiatry will have to recognize the dialectical interaction between what we have come to call mind and brain. This integration is not a part of the agenda for the DSM-5, guided as it is by biological determinism, which takes every mental illness to be a biological disease. At the most basic level, the DSM has failed to incorporate in its approach what it means to be a human being.

The DSM-5

Days before the official unveiling of the DSM-5, during the annual meeting of the American Psychiatric Association in Los Angeles on May 22, 2013, a number of psychiatrists who were closely associated with the project scrambled to do some preemptory damage control, mostly by lowering expectations for what was to come.

Michael B. First, professor of psychiatry at Columbia, acknowledged on NPR that there was still no empirical method to confirm or rule out any mental illness. "We were hoping and imagining that research would advance at a pace that laboratory tests would have come out. And here we are 20 years later and we still unfortunately rely primarily on symptoms to make our diagnoses" (Hamilton 2013). Speaking to the *New York Times*, Thomas R. Insel, director of the National Institute of Mental Health (NIMH), insisted that this failure had not been for lack of effort. "We've tried. You know we've actually looked—using brain imaging, using various endocrine tests, looking at a range of other kinds of biomarkers. So far that has been found wanting" (Belluck & Carey 2013). In the same *Times* article, David J. Kupfer, chairman of the DSM-5 Task Force, admitted "a failure of our neuroscience and biology to give us the level of diagnostic criteria, a level of sensitivity and specificity that we would be able to introduce into the diagnostic manual." Kupfer, Insel and First agree that the new paradigm envisioned for psychiatry—the reason the new edition was undertaken—remains elusive. Nonetheless, four months after publication, the DSM-5 had sold 382,000 copies and brought in $33.7 million. Over the previous ten years, the 5th edition had cost the American Psychiatric Association (APA) about $22 million to produce.

Two years before the DSM-5 was scheduled to appear, Kupfer and Rieger (2011), recognizing that the 5th edition would not bring about the expected paradigm shift, attempted to align their failing effort with the newly launched National Institutes of Health Research Domain Criteria (RDoC) project. (The use of "domain" here has nothing in common with the domains defined in the *Four Domains of Mental Illness*.) Led by Thomas Insel, the NIMH director, the RDoC was billed as a "new classification framework for research on mental disorders." This "new" approach shifts the focus from symptoms and syndromes to what Insel believes are the aberrant neural circuits that underlie *each symptom of each mental illness* (Insel, Cuthbert, Garvey, et al. 2010). Instead of attempting to find biomarkers for DSM syndromes and diagnostic categories—one justification for creating "categorical" psychiatric diagnosis in the first place—the RDoC project will try to identify biomarkers that correspond to the distinct disturbances of emotion, thought and behavior that are common to all mental illnesses. The term *paradigm shift* hovers over the claims made for the RDoC approach.

Is this "new" strategy likely to succeed, or are we being offered, to recall a cloying metaphor, "old wine in new bottles?" This will probably turn out to be the case since the basic tenet of the medical model—that all mental illnesses are brain diseases initiated and sustained by some abnormality in the brain's neural substrate—is conserved. Oddly, the RDoC is not mentioned in DSM-5.

The RDoC is an attempt by its creators to further situate psychiatry under the aegis of medicine. In an article in *Science* titled "Brain Disorders? Precisely," Insel and Cuthbert try to make the case that their approach to psychiatric research follows the lead of investigators who have been able to identify subtypes of several medical diseases, including cancer. This is how they envision "precision medicine," sometimes called "individual medicine" coming to fruition in psychiatry: "As new diagnostics will be redefining 'mental disorders' as 'brain circuit disorders,' new therapeutics will likely focus on tuning these circuits. What is the best way to tune a negative valence or social processing circuit? Medications might be useful, but recent attention has focused on devices that invasively (deep brain stimulation) or noninvasively (transcranial magnetic stimulation) alter brain circuit activity." As a sop to those who do not accept the medical model of mental illness, Insel and Cuthbert immediately added to the just-quoted text:"Paradoxically, one of the most powerful and precise interventions to alter such activity may be targeted psychotherapy, such as cognitive behavioral therapy, which uses the brain's intrinsic plasticity to alter neural circuits and as a consequence, deleterious thoughts and behavior."

Paradoxically? Do Insel and Cuthbert really believe that CBT "targets" brain circuitry in a way that allows a "mistuned" brain to become "tuned" directly from the dialogue that occurs between clinician and patient? And that a "retuned" brain will rid someone of the negative thoughts, feelings and behavior that cause and sustain the "brain disease" they are allegedly being treated for? This would require that each "unit" of negative *thought-feeling-behavior* be linked to a *specific mistuned brain circuit*. No empirical evidence of this psychobiological phenomenon exists. Proposing that it does amounts to a *reductio ad absurdum* of what precision medicine actually has achieved, as in the therapeutically probative subtyping of breast cancer based on the presence or absence of certain cell-surface receptors (Onitilo, Engle, Greenlee & Mukesh 2009).

Cognitive behavioral therapy most likely works because the patient-clinician dialogue directly addresses the psychodynamic issues that *are* the patient's mental illness.

It is noteworthy that adherents to the medical model of mental illness believe that psychotherapy can "retune" brain circuitry while simultaneously denying that the manner in which a person adapts or fails to adapt to life circumstances can itself initiate and sustain a mental illness and its biological correlatives. These psychobiological changes are often observed in brain scans and incorrectly credited as the biological *cause* of the illness.

Ultimately, the 3rd, 4th and 5th editions of the DSM failed—as the RDoC will most likely fail—because its creators, focusing primarily on the brain, do not understand that a human being is, in essence, freedom, who may, under pressure, deny or misuse that freedom in ways that incline emotion, thought and behavior to fall outside the boundaries that have been consensually defined as "normal." Because freedom is our essence, we do not just *have* freedom, we *are* freedom. This ontological property of the self is always limited by our psychobiological constitution, our circumstances at any given moment and our will to act authentically when the chips are down.

The Pseudoscience of Biological Psychiatry

In 2005 John P. A. Ioannidis, MD, PhD, professor of medicine at Stanford, published an article in *PLoS Medicine* titled "Why Most Published Research Findings Are False." His conclusion should come as no surprise to anyone who follows medical research, in the journals, or in the media. Brian Williams, formerly NBC's top anchor, routinely added this tag to many of his reports about the results of "new" medical research: And if you don't like what this study says, wait six months, and we'll have another result for you.

In his article, Ioannidis offers several sobering take-home messages: "Simulations show that for most study designs, it is more likely for a research claim to be false than true. Moreover, for many current scientific fields, claimed research findings may often be simply accurate measures of the prevailing bias" (Ioannidis 2005). He argued that the results of one research group should not be taken as the final word on a medical question, and that different groups researching the same question should share their data before any group publishes a conclusion.

According to David Healy, a psychiatrist and psychopharmacologist who is professor of psychological medicine at Cardiff University, in Wales, "It is controlled trials, an invention that was designed to restrict the use of unnecessary treatments and tests . . . that has been medicine's undoing" (Healy 2012, p. 94). And psychiatry's undoing. Factors contributing to the failure of controlled trials to reveal the truth about a mental illness, and the drugs used to treat it include invalid diagnostic criteria for the illness; bias that inevitably comes with the financial support of, and personal gifts to clinicians and researchers from pharmaceutical companies; suppression of data in trials that do not support the efficacy of a drug, device or procedure by companies sponsoring the trials; and disregard of evidence of what happens in the lives of those who become mentally ill and receive psychiatric treatment that is easily read by anyone with common sense, and without obvious bias. Healy insists that some components of this toxic mix mar most trials of psychotropic drugs. He calls the terrible upshot "pharmageddon."

It is often heard that research in science is self-correcting, which is to say that if a published result is wrong, someone will eventually come up with the right answer, or at least a better answer. This is what eventually happened with the Women's Health Initiative (WHI) study, sponsored by the National Institutes of Health (NIH), published in 2002. Prior to that study, it was widely believed that hormone replacement therapy (HRT) for postmenopausal women reduced cancer, cardiovascular disease and osteoporosis.

But when a large cohort of women was followed for a long period of time, the results told a very different story. Depending on the hormones used—estrogen alone or estrogen "opposed by" progesterone—and the age of the women, breast cancer, endometrial cancer, heart attack and stroke could either increase *or* decrease with HRT. Because of the WHI study, the widespread use of relatively high-dose prophylactic hormones after menopause was discontinued in favor of lower doses of these drugs, taken as needed to control postmenopausal symptoms, especially hot flashes. Some of the conclusions of this study did not withstand the test of later, more targeted studies, and further changes were made in the recommendations given to women about using hormones after menopause that took into account their age, health history and current health status.

The issues involved in the HRT study in menopausal women cut across a number of medical specialties including: gynecology, endocrinology, cardiology, oncology, orthopedics, internal medicine and pharmacology. In many ways, the story of HRT is the story of medical research—a major research effort indicates that an established treatment protocol leads to bad outcomes, and clinical practice is changed accordingly. Much the same thing happened with the prostate specific antigen (PSA) test that cut its own arc through the recent history of prostate cancer diagnosis and treatment. For many diseases, the iterative process of clinical trial, and observation of clinical outcome over time, followed by a revision of clinical practice based on this observation may be the best that medicine can do (Groopman 2007).

There is a core of more or less established medical science and praxis, some component of which is always being exposed as erroneous, and then corrected. This can happen because medicine is grounded in natural science, essentially biology and chemistry, while psychiatry is not. For a century and a half, psychiatry has strained to find the biological causes of mental illness, without success, though many clinicians and researchers would vigorously argue that they are fast approaching the time when these causes will be known.

The fact is that biological psychiatry lacks a ground that would permit the kind of exploration, through trial and error, followed by more trial and more error, which has allowed medicine to advance to its present level. This paradigm—comprising the DSM, the "broken brain part," the "chemical imbalance" and the statistical manipulation of data derived from behavior—has lost itself in a tail-chasing effort to explain what cannot be explained by biology, chemistry or statistics. Truth cannot emerge directly from error or without an external reference point of truth. Error has no way to correct itself. Psychiatry writhes now in its own self-made trap.

A decade before the Ioannides article appeared, psychiatrist Colin A. Ross and psychologist Alvin Pam co-edited a book titled *Pseudoscience in Biological Psychiatry* (1995). By the time their book was published, the DSM-III (1980) had been widely used for 15 years. During this decade and a half, many clinicians and researchers recognized that the reductive biologism of this new approach was not leading to valid diagnoses or facilitating valid research. In one particularly memorable chapter, Alvin Pam argued that many of the articles published in psychiatric journals that had come to define biological psychiatry were marred by poor thinking and invalid statistical analysis, and that the conclusions drawn in these articles were wrong. This criticism goes far beyond the usual objections raised against empirical studies and the data produced—"flawed" is a criticism often made—and leads ineluctably to the word "pseudoscience," the first word of this chapter's title. These were not just flawed studies, Pam insists, but *invalid* studies that stood—and mostly still stand—as pillars of a false paradigm.

How do ostensibly sound scientific experiments lead to pseudoscience? In biological psychiatry, some experiments may produce valid data. But because of the fallacious meanings assigned to, and the erroneous inferences drawn from these data, the *conclusions* are invalid. It is as if one were trying to construct a story from elements that did not add up to the story, simply because it was advantageous to tell this story.

Chapter 2 The Initial Promises of Biological Psychiatry Do Not Look So Promising Now

As biological psychiatry continued to betray its patients, while simultaneously dumbing-down and corrupting the mental health profession, an increasing number of articles and books appeared highlighting different facets of this betrayal.

In 1991 Peter Breggin came out with *Toxic Psychiatry*, in which he questioned the biological basis of any mental illness and the need for any psychotropic medication. He insisted that "the only biochemical imbalances that we can identify with certainty in the brains of psychiatric patients are the ones produced by psychiatric treatment itself" (Breggin 1991, p. 12).

Citing Nancy Andreasen's *The Broken Brain*, Breggin conveys the core concept of biological psychiatry: "*The major psychiatric illnesses are diseases*. They should be considered medical illnesses, just as diabetes, heart disease, and cancer are" (Andreasen 1984, p. 29; original emphasis). Thirty years after Andreasen's book first appeared—she was editor in chief of the *American Journal of Psychiatry* from 1993 to 2005—biology is still the operative center of psychiatry's paradigm, even as the evidence steadily chips away at the belief that most mental illnesses are medical diseases. As of this writing, Breggin's claim that no solid evidence exists for a "chemical imbalance" in any mental illness is as true as the day he made it. In the course of using brain scans in the hope of uncovering the biological causes of mental illness, many *correlations* have been established between aberrant mood and behavior and changes in brain activity. But correlations are not causes, and the search for causes continues.

Breggin doubts that even schizophrenia originates as a primary brain disease. Rather, he sees the illness as a psychodynamic response a person makes to overwhelming anxiety in an effort to be spared from psychic annihilation, or, as he calls it, "schizophrenic overwhelm." His take on schizophrenia reminds us of R. D. Laing and Adolf Meyer, as will become evident when, further on, schizophrenia is considered both as a 1st domain illness (maladaptive reaction)—with a correlative brain substrate that may be more the result of a patient's psychodynamic alteration than its cause—and as a primary psychiatric disease of the 4th domain.

Breggin's criticism of biological psychiatry includes these now widely accepted, if hard-won truths: drugs used to treat anxiety, depression, mania, schizophrenia and other illnesses can cause or worsen symptoms of these illnesses; withdrawal of some psychotropic drugs can lead to rebound symptoms that are worse than the original symptoms, an outcome that may convince a clinician that the drug was working and needs to be restarted, or even that the symptoms are due to a more serious mental illness.

The argument is made in *Toxic Psychiatry* that biological psychiatry is based on self-serving pseudoscience and that its practice damages many patients, leading Breggin (1991) to recommend that the present paradigm be stripped of what he sees as its "legal but illegitimate powers" (p. 408).

In 2000, almost a decade after the debut of Breggin's *Toxic Psychiatry*, Joseph Glenmullen (2000), a clinical instructor in psychiatry at Harvard Medical School, published a book titled *Prozac Backlash*. During that decade, millions of prescriptions for Prozac and SSRIs (selective serotonin reuptake inhibitors, at that time mainly Zoloft, Paxil and Luvox) were written for patients with depression and other psychiatric illnesses. Gradually, it became clear that these new drugs were not as benign as was first believed. The "backlash" of SSRI side effects is the subject of Glenmullen's book.

Like Breggin, Glenmullen does not believe that depression is caused by a "chemical imbalance," or that depression is a "medical disease" as Nancy Andreasen insists in *The Broken Brain*. He sees SSRIs functioning as "serotonin boosters," stimulants and mood brightening agents, but not as antidepressants that reboot a "depressed" brain substrate. (He does not, however, explain how a stimulant drug that calms people and helps them to focus can also make them feel numb and unreal.) Glenmullen reprises many stories of patients who were prescribed SSRIs, for a variety of complaints, and came to harm because of these drugs.

Glenmullen's principal issue with SSRIs is what he sees as both the short- and long-term neurotoxicity of these drugs. The Parkinson-like tremors, tics and akathisia (which has been counted as a contributing factor in suicides) observed in some patients imply damage to brain cells. These disturbances are more commonly seen in those taking neuroleptics and atypical antipsychotics that are known to effect dopamine cells, which SSRIs may ultimately influence indirectly in spite of their vaunted "selectivity" for serotonin. No one knows if the neurotoxicity of these drugs may predispose users, especially long-term users, to developing Parkinson's and Alzheimer's in their advancing years.

Besides believing that SSRSs act as stimulants, rather than directly as antidepressants, Glenmullen recognized the importance of the placebo effect in the pharmacological treatment of depression. In so-called double-blind studies, where neither patients nor clinicians are told which patients are in the drug and placebo arms, the "blind" is often effectively breached *during* the study as patients and clinicians identify the side effects of the active drug. There is good empirical evidence that mental illnesses and medical diseases respond to patients' expectations and hopes that a drug or other intervention may help to correct their malady. Those who know they are taking a "real" drug are more likely to believe they will improve than those who are not certain about this, thus increasing the *placebo effect of the active drug.*

A decade after the appearance of Glenmullen's *Prozac Backlash*, Irving Kirsch (2010), a clinical psychologist who had studied the placebo affect for many years, came out with *The Emperor's New Drugs: Exploding the Antidepressant Myth.* Kirsch had already undertaken a meta-analysis of published journal articles reporting on the effectiveness of many drugs used to treat depression (Kirsch 2010, p. 21). He ends Chapter 1, which he titles "Listening to Prozac, but Hearing Placebo," with this summary:

1. Antidepressants produce significantly more side effects than inert placebos.
2. Most patients in clinical trials are able to figure out whether they have been assigned to the drug group or the placebo group before being told.
3. There are relatively small but significant differences between active drugs and inert placebos, and these differences are independent of the type of active drug that is used. Indeed, the active drug need not even be an antidepressant.
4. Although a drug need not be an antidepressant to be more effective than a placebo, it does seem to need sufficient side effects that patients can figure out that they have not been given a placebo.
5. When antidepressants are compared to active placebos [drugs that produce side effects but have no antidepressant action], differences in outcome are substantially harder to find.
6. The more side effects that depressed patients experience on the active drug, the more they improve.
7. When you control for differences in side effects, drug-placebo differences in improvement are not statistically significant.

Kirsch acknowledges the clinical effectiveness of antidepressants but sees these agents working as "active placebos"—placebos with side effects that alert patients that they are taking a real drug rather than an inert placebo—not as antidotes to a "chemical imbalance" caused by the deficiency of a neurotransmitter associated with the modulation of mood. This "active" placebo effect is different from, and considerably larger than, the one historically believed to occur with antidepressants and other types of medication.

The term "response expectancy" was coined by Kirsch to help characterize the essence of this placebo effect: "Although placebo effects are generally referred to as nonspecific, there is also a sense in which they are very specific. The effect of the placebo is specific to the beliefs that people have about the substance they are ingesting. Placebo morphine, for example, reduces pain, whereas placebo antidepressants reduce depression. Even the side effects that people report when given a placebo tend to be the same side effects that are produced by the real drug. In other words, the effect of a placebo is specific to the effect that the person expects it to have" (pp. 136–137). It is common knowledge, in psychiatry and in medicine, that drugs having vastly different chemical structures often remediate the same illness. Kirsch cites studies showing that patients who did not respond to one SSRI and were switched to another SSRI, an SNRI (selective norepinephrine uptake inhibitor) or bupropion (which targets norepinephrine and dopamine receptors) all had approximately the same response rate (25%–27%).

Kirsch sees this result as further evidence for an active placebo effect: "[T]he rate of improvement did not depend on the kind of drug to which the patient had been switched. Simply changing from one SSRI to another was as effective as changing to a completely different type of antidepressant. Once again we have the strange 'coincidence' of virtually identical effects produced by chemically different drugs. This indicates that it is not the specific chemical action of the drug that alleviates the person's depression. Instead, it may simply be the idea of changing treatment" (pp. 61–62).

Taken together, the work of Peter Breggin, Joseph Glenmullen, Irving Kirsch and a number of other investigators seems to drive a stake through the heart of the claim that antidepressant drugs alleviate depression by correcting the kind of "chemical imbalance" that has been used to explain this mental illness since the tricyclic antidepressants came to market in the early 1950s.

As was the case with many psychotropic drugs, tricyclic antidepressants were discovered serendipitously. Iproniazid, the first commercially sold antidepressant, was not a tricyclic but an MAO (monoamine oxidase) inhibitor and was also found fortuitously. The drug was originally an anti-tubercular agent produced in 1951 by Hoffmann-La Roche. Unexpectedly, iproniazid brightened the mood of some patients who had taken it. In 1957, Nathan Kline published the results of a trial on non-tubercular depressed patients and found an approximate two-thirds response rate (Loomer, Saunders & Kline 1957). Iproniazid was withdrawn after it was found to cause hepatitis.

Kline's study did not include a control group; neither did the first study of imipramine, which *was* the first tricyclic, published by Roland Kuhn (1958). Kuhn was using imipramine to treat psychotic patients when three psychotically depressed patients showed a marked improvement in their mood. He then tried the drug on patients with depression alone and found a rapid, significant response. Imipramine was widely used, considered to be highly effective and continues to be prescribed.

Kirsch says it is not surprising that the iproniazid and imipramine trials were not placebo controlled, since the power of the placebo was just beginning to be recognized in the 1950s and 1960s, and few trials employed it during that time. Taking into account what has been learned since about the placebo effect, these "positive" results are no longer used to support the catecholamine hypothesis of depression.

In 1965 Joseph Schildkraut, then at the National Institute of Mental Health (NIMH), published an overview of the literature on catecholamines and mood disorders in the *American Journal of Psychiatry* titled "The Catecholamine Hypothesis of Affective Disorders: A Review of Supporting Evidence." Schildkraut's claim, made cautiously, was that depression was caused by a deficiency of norepinephrine in the synapses that connect neurons in the brain. It is ironic that this article, though reserved in its tone and assertions, is generally credited with launching the catecholamine hypothesis of depression and giving cachet to the "chemical imbalance," which is still invoked by many clinicians as the cause of depression and other mental illnesses.

Schildkraut (1965) emphasized the "heuristic value" of the hypothesis, which, he acknowledged, was "at best a reductionistic oversimplification of a very complex biological state." And, he cautioned, "A rigorous extrapolation from pharmacological studies to pathophysiology clearly cannot be made. . . . It is not possible, therefore, to confirm definitively or to reject the catecholamine hypothesis on the basis of data currently available." Almost a half-century later, this confirmation is still nowhere near being made. But that has not deterred many psychiatrists, and the entire pharmaceutical industry from claiming the catecholamine hypothesis as an established truth, even as more evidence accumulates against the idea than for it (Lacasse & Leo 2005).

In 2007 Ruhé, Mason and Schene published a meta-analysis of a large cohort of studies that addressed the possible connection between low serotonin and mood. They concluded: "Although previously the monamine systems were considered to be responsible for the development of major depressive disorder (MDD), the available evidence to date does not support a direct causal relationship with MDD. There is no simple direct correlation of serotonin or norepinephrine levels in the brain and mood." As Kirsch sees it: "From the beginning, the chemical-imbalance theory was based on weak and contradictory evidence, and data contradicting it were simply ignored. . . . A half-century of research has produced data indicating that the chemical-imbalance theory must be wrong. Yet it remains the most popular explanation for depression, and most of the data contradicting it continues to be ignored" (Kirsch 2010, p. 83).

Even though the serotonin story did not fit the data, it was a pleasing story, and everyone *wanted* to believe it—pharmaceutical companies who made huge profits from selling tricyclic antidepressants and SSRIs; clinicians prescribing these agents, who made more money than they would doing psychotherapy; patients who took the drugs wanting to believe that their depression was not their fault; and managed-care companies that saved money by avoiding having to pay for more expensive psychotherapy or inpatient treatment.

Kirsch's *The Emperor's New Drugs* was reviewed by Marcia Angell in *The New York Review of Books* along with two other volumes that are highly critical of what psychiatry had become in the era of the 3rd and 4th editions of the DSM and the "chemical imbalance": Robert Whitaker's (2010) *Anatomy of an Epidemic: Magic Bullets, Psychiatric Drugs, and the Astonishing Rise of Mental Illness in America* and Daniel Carlat's (2010) *Unhinged: The Trouble With Psychiatry—A Doctor's Revelations About a Profession in Crisis.*

Angell, who is not a psychiatrist, is a former editor in chief of *The New England Journal of Medicine*, and the author of *The Truth About the Drug Companies: How They Deceive Us and What We Can Do About It* (2004), wrote a long, two-part essay (Angell 2011a; 2011b) that leaves little doubt that psychiatry has betrayed itself and its patients:

> The books by Irving Kirsch, Robert Whitaker, and Daniel Carlat are powerful indictments of the way psychiatry is now practiced. They document the "frenzy" of diagnosis, the overuse of drugs with sometimes devastating side effects, and widespread conflicts of interest. Critics of these books might argue, as Nancy Andreasen implied in her paper on the loss of brain tissue with long-term antipsychotic treatment, that the side effects are the price that must be paid to relieve the suffering caused by mental illness. If we knew that the benefits of psychoactive drugs outweighed their harms, that would be a strong argument, since there is no doubt that many people suffer grievously from

> mental illness. But as Kirsch, Whitaker, and Carlat argue convincingly, that expectation may be wrong (Angell 2011b).

The Andreasen article mentioned by Angell (principal author B.-C. Ho), "Long-term Antipsychotic Treatment and Brain Volumes: A Longitudinal Study of First-episode Schizophrenia," appeared in the *Archives of General Psychiatry* (2011). The conclusions are summarized below:

> Viewed together with data from animal studies, our study suggests that antipsychotics have a subtle but measurable influence on brain tissue loss over time, suggesting the importance of careful risk-benefit review of dosage and duration of treatment as well as their off-label use. . . .
>
> [It is] probable that antipsychotics do not treat the fundamental pathophysiologic mechanism of schizophrenia (i.e., the brain disease). . . .
>
> Antipsychotics are effective medications for reducing some of the target clinical symptoms of schizophrenia: psychotic symptoms. In medicine we are aware of many instances in which improving target symptoms worsens other symptoms. Hormone therapy relieves menopausal symptoms but increases stroke risk. Nonsteroidal anti-inflammatory drugs relieve pain but increase the likelihood of duodenal ulcers and gastrointestinal tract bleeding. It is possible that, although antipsychotics relieve psychosis and its attendant suffering, these drugs may not arrest the pathophysiologic processes underlying schizophrenia [which is referred to as a "brain disease"] and may even aggravate progressive brain tissue volume reductions.

Two years after this article appeared—and in spite of its warnings—patients being treated for depression were still being urged by print and TV ads to add Abilify (an atypical antipsychotic) to their antidepressant!

From all appearances, Andreasen continues to believe that biology causes most psychotic illnesses and that the *shrinking of a human brain*, with all the known and unknown consequences of such a perturbation, is an acceptable price to pay for whatever these drugs—many of which are known to cause the same symptoms as the "diseases" they are supposed to treat—actually do to alleviate the suffering of those with certain mental illnesses.

By 2005 the idea that mental illnesses were medical diseases had caught on to the extent that Andreasen (2005) could title a book *Brave New Brain*. The title was inspired by a line from Shakespeare's play *The Tempest*: "How beauteous mankind is! O brave new world" (Act 5, Scene 1). These words are spoken by Miranda, a young girl who grew up on an isolated island, where her father was the only other human. After a storm (the tempest of the title) wrecks a passing ship, the survivors scurry to the island's shore, and Miranda begins to see that the world consists of more than herself and her father.

Substituting *brain* for *world*, Andreasen equates the discoveries that constituted the growing bubble of brain science with Miranda's awakening to human society, implying that the new science would reveal the mysteries of life itself. Andreasen's subtitle, *Conquering Mental Illness in the Era of the Genome*, acknowledged her high expectations as she told the story of what happens when, as she put it, "mind and molecule meet."

Toward the end of his long career and long life, Leon Eisenberg, a professor of psychiatry at Harvard Medical School, recognized that, during the last half of the 20th century, the "brainlessness" of Freud's psychoanalysis had been replaced by the "mindlessness" of biological psychiatry. In an article that appeared shortly after his death, Eisenberg asked, never doubting the answer: "Were we all asleep at the switch?" (Eisenberg & Guttmacher 2010).

The DSM Is a Mistake That Does Not Want to, or Know How to, Correct Itself

It was with an eye to eventually finding the now largely discredited "chemical imbalance"—not just for depression but for all mental illnesses—that led the creators of the DSM-III, DSM-IV and DSM-5 to come up with checklists of predominantly behavioral symptoms. Matching these symptoms to the biological substrate of a mental illness would render the meaning of patients' symptoms superfluous in diagnosis and treatment. With a biological explanation in hand, there would be no *need* to determine these meanings—all a clinician would have to do is select a drug that would "fix" the biological lesion of each "medical disease."

As Carol Bernstein, president of the American Psychiatric Association from 2010 to 2011, wrote in *Psychiatric News*: "It became necessary in the 1970s to facilitate diagnostic agreement among clinicians, scientists, and regulatory authorities [a stated goal of the DSM-III, DSM-IV and DSM-5 task forces as well] given the need to match patients with newly emerging pharmacologic treatments" (Bernstein 2011). This "matching" occurred at the then-acceptable cost of sacrificing validity for reliability—which, because of the validity sacrificed, was not realized either.

In 2006 at a conference at Sheppard Pratt Hospital in Baltimore, Steven Sharfstein, President and CEO of the Sheppard Pratt Health System and past president of the American Psychiatric Association (which publishes the DSM), was confronted with the prospect that nothing would change for the better in psychiatry until the meaning and context of symptoms were considered in diagnosis. Spontaneously and with conviction, he replied, "That will never happen." Sharfstein's words, heartfelt and unambiguous, revealed how deeply embedded in the consciousness of psychiatry the idea was that mental illness can be diagnosed without taking into consideration what is going on in a patient's life.

An oncologist who misdiagnoses a malignant lesion and treats the patient for that presumed malignancy would very likely be sued for malpractice. Yet a psychiatrist who misdiagnoses schizophrenia or bipolar disorder almost always escapes this fate. The fact is that, using the decontextualized and meaningless symptoms of the DSM, misdiagnosis in psychiatry has become common (Genova 2003). This outcome has not stopped mental health professionals from demanding "parity"—access to services comparable to those provided for medical conditions and diseases—by invoking the unsubstantiated claim that most mental illnesses are caused by an abnormal brain substrate.

Clinicians are reluctant to change an earlier diagnosis, one of their own or someone else's, even if they suspect the diagnosis is wrong. Reasons for this disinclination include the fear that, if the diagnosis of a less serious illness is substituted and medication is reduced or withdrawn and patients later decompensate or harm themselves or others, the clinician could be held responsible by the profession and the law. Better to play it safe in a culture that rewards this kind of self-protective action.

In spite of the DSM's failure to foster a reliable and valid method for diagnosing mental illness, those most responsible for introducing the meaningless symptom have generally escaped serious repudiation (though criticism is growing). At a retirement celebration for Robert L. Spitzer at Columbia University, where he had served in the psychiatry department for 52 years, the driving force behind the DSM-III was lauded as one of the great names in psychiatric diagnosis. His contribution to medicine was placed alongside those of Hippocrates, Galen, Sydenham, Pinel, Kraepelin and Freud! Spitzer's name was added to that list by Allen Frances, Chair of the DSM-IV Task Force, who later wrote an article for *Psychiatric Times* titled "The Most Influential Psychiatrist of Our Time Retires Undefeated" (Frances 2011).

According to Frances, the DSM-III "anchored psychiatry back to medicine and science." To the degree this means that the DSM showed clinicians how to recognize the psychiatric symptoms seen with medical conditions such as delirium due to electrolyte or endocrine imbalance, or to diseases such as tertiary syphilis—so these conditions can be rectified *medically*—this was a valuable contribution.

But when it comes to the unsupported presumption that most mental illnesses originate in a "broken brain part," we might ask: How has this attempt to "anchor" psychiatry in medicine and science compromised the numerous patients who have been wrongly diagnosed? And what about the ludicrous claim, often heard, that the DSM-III, DSM-IV and DSM-5, though perhaps not good for diagnosing patients, made it possible to do clinical research on mental illness? But there is no way that research with wrongly diagnosed patients could yield valid data. Ultimately, the results from this kind of research are used to influence and justify erroneous clinical treatment!

The criticism made here of the 3rd, 4th and 5th editions of the DSM does not imply that the DSM-I (1952) and DSM-II (1968), both significantly shorter than the editions that followed, were satisfactory guides to classification and diagnosis, either. The creators of the DSM, from the 3rd edition on, felt that behavior—assessed as symptoms—was a better portal to psychic life than concepts such as the unconscious, ego, superego and id, which had ruled the DSM-II, and the maladaptive psychodynamic reaction criteria of the DSM-I. This could have turned out better if not for the deliberate omission of provenance and meaning in using these symptoms for diagnosis.

The Illusion of an Autonomous Brain Generated the "Bubble" of Biological Psychiatry

Those who created the DSM-III, DSM-IV and DSM-5, and those who enthusiastically supported this method of doing psychiatric diagnosis—with its implicit promise of eventually providing a biological explanation for all mental illnesses—did so with an evangelical zeal. Around 1980, with the DSM-III freshly published; the engine of neuroscience churning; a pharmaceutical industry that was eager to turn the discoveries of neuroscience into new drugs; and a managed-care system that was just starting its quest to reduce the costs of mental health care at all costs, a "bubble" began to take form that for several decades would determine and limit the thinking and practice of most mental health professionals. The amplifying interaction of these four elements caused a perfect storm that, over time, would remake psychiatry in a way that served many patients poorly. In this process, psychiatry lost its integrity and the ability to help many of those who looked to this profession for help (Taylor 2014).

"Every age has its folly; some scheme, project, or phantasy into which it plunges, spurred on by the love of gain, the necessity of excitement, or the mere force of imitation" (Mackay 1980, p. 369). These are the words of Charles Mackay who, in 1841, put out a book that became a publishing phenomenon: *Extraordinary Popular Delusions & the Madness of Crowds*. From the vantage point of mid-19th-century London, Mackay looked as far back as the Middle Ages and identified a number of widely held delusions that, he believed, had been shaped by a self-deceiving promise of gain. These compromises of reason and judgment included wild financial schemes involving real estate and the sale of tulips; alchemy; fortune-telling; the crusades; witch mania; and the veneration of relics. In the mid-20th century, a delusion took hold—the "bubble" of biological psychiatry that radically altered the way many people understood their thinking, emotions and behavior—which may one day stand alongside Mackay's litany of delusions.

The bubble that psychiatry grew and inhabited did not evolve in a cultural or social vacuum. The primacy of natural science, a hallmark of our time, blindly drove the unproven assumption that a full understanding of a mental illness would come only after that illness was explained at the molecular level.

Psychiatry, like every other human endeavor, is something made—a construct—by individuals who have come to see a certain aspect of the world in a certain way. It should come as no surprise that its errors have the same essential nature as those made in other professions. This is how Colin Negrych, who describes himself as a "macroeconomic and geopolitical strategist disguised as a bond salesman," explained the global economic meltdown that began in the fall of 2008 and led to what eventually became known as the Great Recession: "Financial engineering fills the gap between people's desires and their wherewithal. So what you have is optimism buttressed by pseudo-science and statistical legerdemain" (Paumgarten 2009).

Replace "financial engineering" with "the promises of neuroscience and psychopharmacology" and you get a pretty good idea of what has been driving psychiatry since at least 1980. Read the articles that appear in the best journals and ask if "pseudo-science and statistical legerdemain" have not gotten between the phenomenon being studied and the results and conclusions reported. Wouldn't it be nice to feel that these articles really do explain why our patients have the problems that we try to understand and address? Psychiatry, it seems, is no less subject to self-deception and self-serving delusion than is any other profession.

Here is Paul Krugman, Nobel Prize winner in economics and Princeton professor, assessing the contribution of his profession to the Great Recession of 2008: "As I see it, the economics profession went astray because economists, as a group, mistook beauty, clad in impressive-looking mathematics, for truth" (Krugman 2009). How tempting it is to accept Nancy Andreasen's notion of the "brave new brain," and her belief that its exploration with the latest in scanner technology would finally, after all these centuries of ignorance about the real causes of schizophrenia, reveal the truth about this disease. How impressive those scans are, with their red, orange, yellow, blue, green and violet colors, declaring normal and abnormal brain function. How beautiful.

The question is, do the results and conclusions in the articles Andreasen and her University of Iowa colleagues published over several decades really identify and explain the phenomenon of schizophrenia? Or are these results and conclusions just beautiful? And self-serving to investigators, and to patients who volunteered their brains for these procedures, who all wished to believe that they were participating in a revolution in understanding and treating mental illness? In psychiatry, John Keats aside, truth is not beauty and beauty is not truth.

Psychiatry Created Its Own Version of Reality

What is felt to be "real" is often later discredited by new evidence proving that prior evidence was wrong. It is possible to live for an extended period of time in a "reality" that is not real. Psychiatry, it seems, has been doing that for some time.

The architecture critic Ada Louise Huxtable, in a compilation of her articles for the *New York Times* and other publications titled *On Architecture*, had these words for the efforts of preservationalists who convert architectural treasures of previous centuries into what are essentially theme parks, like Williamsburg:

> I do not know just when we lost our sense of reality or interest in it, but at some point it was decided that reality was not the only option; that it was possible, permissible, and even desirable to improve on it; that one could substitute a more agreeable product. It followed that reality was, first, mutable and then expendable; its substance was abdicated for what could be revised and manipulated (Huxtable 2008, p. 424).

What Huxtable wrote about the distortion of reality in Williamsburg's repurposed buildings—"downgrading the evidence of the built world," as she put it—says something about the essence of reality itself. If "reality is not the only option," and can be "improved" with the self-deceiving intention of making life better or easier, it is inevitable that people will choose to make that change. What is surprising and frightening is that it happened in economics and finance, leading us into the Great Recession, and that it happened in psychiatry, inclining the profession and its patients toward false notions of what mental illness is and what needs to be done for those who are mentally ill. Here *reality itself* was supposed to be respected and preserved.

Denying reality amounts to short-circuiting the search for truth. Reviewing Michael P. Lynch's *The Internet of Us: Knowing More and Understanding Less in the Age of Big Data*, Jill Lepore argued that "The era of the fact is coming to an end: the place once held by 'facts' is being taken over by 'data.' This is making for more epistemological mayhem, not least because the collection and weighing of facts require investigation, discernment, and judgment [done correctly, we might add], while the collection and analysis of data are outsourced to machines" (Lepore 2016). Ultimately, in this process, the *phenomenon* under study is often relinquished. For some time now, psychiatry has been substituting biological and epidemiological data, much of it wrong (Ross & Pam 1995), for real facts and truth.

In her review, Lepore also quotes this important observation from an earlier book by Lynch, *In Praise of Reason: Why Rationality Matters for Democracy*: "Without a common background of standards against which we measure what counts as a reliable source of information, or a reliable method of inquiry, and what doesn't, we won't be able *to agree on the facts*, let alone values" (Lepore 2016; original italics). Could any one sentence more accurately describe the crippled paradox that the DSM is, or explain why this approach to classifying and diagnosing mental illness is neither valid nor reliable?

In July 2011, less than two years before the scheduled appearance of the DSM-5, David J. Kupfer, Chair of the DSM-5 Task Force, wrote a Commentary for the *American Journal of Psychiatry* on the role that neuroscience was expected to play in the revised classification and diagnostic system. "[O]ur recognition," one of his sentences reads, "of the significance of neuroscience and genetics in psychiatric diagnosis has supported DSM-5's novel integration of neurobiologic findings, such as inclusion within the text that accompanies diagnostic criteria sets the potential role of these factors in shaping risk and prognosis" (Kupfer and Regier 2011). Even repeated readings of this sentence do not clarify the mystery it creates about what neuroscience and genetics will contribute to the understanding and treatment of mental illness. Words slip and slide here, and do not cohere into the meaning that the sentence seems to promise.

This type of rhetoric is a style of speaking and writing that is intended to impress and tends toward the disingenuous. Kupfer avoids acknowledging, as far as possible, what is *not* known about the biological substrate of mental illnesses, while *implying* that what is not known *is* known, or will soon be known. It is as if the creators of the DSM-5 felt that, because so much data have been collected from the brains of the mentally ill that these data *should* explain mental illness, even though this is not the case.

Kupfer speaks here less as a physician or a clinical scientist than as a motivational speaker who is revving up the crowd to believe in an outcome that is nowhere as sure as he suggests. His words pass through smoke and bounce from mirrors. This is not reality, but the kind of rhetoric often heard and read now as neuroscience data are used in the attempt to explain human behavior—a rhetoric that derives more from faith (the feeling something is so based in part on wanting it to be so) than from knowledge (facts demonstrating that it is so).

In *physical science,* facts are determined, verified, collected and made into a (usually) valid story about a physical or chemical system. In *science fiction*, facts are extrapolated from the empirical discoveries of science, or simply made up. In *neuroscience fiction*, facts are also determined by the methods of science, collected and made into a story. But these stories, especially those concluding that a "broken brain part" is the cause of some mental illness, are not supported by the facts, and therefore do not constitute real science, but are instead speculative, and often self-serving and self-deceiving. The least convincing of these narratives are pure rhetoric, the language spoken by researchers and clinicians who are content to operate in a fictional universe that parallels the world occupied by those who live with and suffer from real mental illnesses.

Here is Jeffrey Lieberman, speaking at the opening session of the annual meeting of the American Psychiatric Association in San Francisco, in May, 2013, the year he was president of the APA. Again we hear the boundless optimism: "The scientific foundation of psychiatric medicine has grown by leaps and bounds in the last 50 years. The emergence of psychopharmacology, neuroimaging, molecular genetics and biology, and the disciplines of neuroscience and cognitive psychology have launched us into the mainstream of medicine and on a course for future growth and success" (Moran 2013). Lieberman's confidence in psychiatry's future persists in spite of some reality he allowed into the same address: "The pharmaceutical industry has all but abandoned the development of novel psychotropic agents. And *DSM-5* has become a lightning rod for self-styled critics and the antipsychiatry movement. Mental illness is alternately feared too much or not taken seriously enough, and psychiatry continues to be a punch line for jokes" (Moran 2013). None of this seems consistent with the glorious future that Lieberman sees for psychiatry, or even with the current status of the profession as he pictures it here.

In an article that appeared four months after the 2013 APA meeting, Lieberman's optimism seems undiminished, if baffling: "In the revisions that will follow the *DSM-5*, which was released in May, we anticipate that psychiatric diagnoses will move beyond phenomenologic criteria [mostly behavioral symptoms] to measures of pathophysiology and etiology and that they will involve laboratory tests to identify lesions and disturbances in specific anatomic structures, neural circuits, or chemical systems, as well as susceptibility genes—the kinds of tests that routinely inform the diagnosis of infection, cardiovascular disease, cancer, and most neurological disorders. The research that occasions these developments may not just enhance our ability to make diagnoses, but may fundamentally redefine the nosology of mental disorders" (Lieberman 2013).

This "redefinition" is precisely what Robert Spitzer had hoped would eventually happen when he issued the DSM-III—in 1980, 33 years earlier! The certainty that all mental illnesses are brain diseases and the expectation that identifying the biological cause of each mental illness would put psychiatry's diagnostic system on the same footing as other medical specialties were among the principal reasons why Spitzer felt that he could afford to be "agnostic" about the etiology of mental illness and the meaning of psychiatric symptoms. Having become disillusioned with the promises of Freudian psychoanalysis, he also wanted to rid the DSM-III of that influence, which was the theoretical foundation of the DSM-II. If the biological cause of a mental illness were found, there would be no *need* to define a psychological antecedent, or the meaning of symptoms.

More than any other factor, the medical model of mental illness—a materialist interpretation of both brain function and human experience—made the DSM-III and its later editions possible. Researchers who were guided by the biological theories of mental illness that came along during the 1960s and 1970s required a more concrete approach to diagnosis. The operational criteria of the DSM-III, consisting mostly of behavioral symptoms and syndromes, seemed to fill that need. If, as the medical model holds, every mental illness is a brain disease, there is no need to incorporate the meaning of a patient's experience into diagnosis or treatment.

The psychiatrist David Healy has written forcefully and persuasively about psychiatry's corruption by the medical model. In *Mania: A Short History of Bipolar Disorder*, he looked critically at the efforts to classify bipolar disorder and the studies aimed at establishing the effectiveness of the most familiar "mood stabilizing" drugs, noting the same distortion of psychiatric reality that we have been exploring here. "[B]y the mid-1990s, psychiatry was in a new world. No one listened to or looked at patients any more. If large randomized trials showed the drugs 'worked,' what was the point in talking to people? It was a new world also in which it was harder to be certain if any of the authors on these multiauthored papers could be regarded in any meaningful sense as discoverers of anything, and there was increasing doubt as to whether even the authorships were real" (Healy 2008, p. 176). Research based on the diagnosis of mental illnesses from symptoms of unspecified meaning would be *expected* to give results that are meaningless.

The full effect of psychiatry's manipulation of the facts and revision of reality has not yet been felt. The profession has not had a meltdown comparable to the Great Recession that was created by the economists' and bankers' denial of reality—these professions are, after all, subject to a bottom line in a way that psychiatry is not. But the air in psychiatry's bubble is escaping now from holes made by thousands of legal judgments against practitioners, hospitals and pharmaceutical companies brought by individuals and institutions. Psychiatry's comeuppance hangs only on the accretion of a critical mass of ethical and legal redress for the damage already done. Looking ahead, I think of how Albert Camus described his joy over the dissolution of the Vichy government in France, just before the end of World War II: "[A] prolonged hoax has collapsed" (Camus 1974, p. 270).

Reviewing *Shrinks: The Untold Story of Psychiatry*, a memoir by Jeffrey A. Lieberman, a staunch defender of the medical model of mental illness, Paul McHugh pulls no punches expressing his lack of enthusiasm for psychiatry's biological paradigm: "[Lieberman's book] demonstrates, perhaps unwittingly, how psychiatry is in crisis today—different from but just as crippling as the crisis of diagnosis and treatment that provoked Robert Spitzer to bring about *DSM-III*" (McHugh 2015).

Psychiatry Needs a New Paradigm

The transparent aim of *The Four Domains of Mental Illness*, to which this rather long essay is a prologue, is to change psychiatry's current paradigm. How does it happen that a set of ideas and rules which underlie and shape a discipline yield to another set of ideas and rules that change the fundamental nature and direction of the discipline?

Consider how the change in the culture of clerical sexual abuse occurred in the Roman Catholic Church (D'Antonio 2013). For several decades, there had been accusations, lawsuits and convictions against an increasing number of priest offenders. Then, in June 2002 during the U.S. Conference of Catholic Bishops, which was held in Dallas, an organized group of pedophilia survivors came forward and told their stories. What was left of the cover-up by the American hierarchy essentially ended in Dallas—not because the Church had found a conscience but because the Church's denial could no longer be sustained.

The bishops apologized for their enabling silence, asked forgiveness and promised reparations. During that same year, *The Boston Globe* aggressively covered the stories of five priests from the Boston archdiocese who had been charged with pedophilia. In short order, the crimes that had been attested to in Dallas and reported in Boston became a national issue. Priests in dioceses throughout the country were tried and convicted. Monetary reparations were made, forcing several dioceses into bankruptcy. The magisterium of the Church—the right it has historically claimed to be revered and obeyed—began a slow process of dissolution, fed by new credible allegations.

For a long time, clerical sexual abuse in the United States went largely unrecognized and unchallenged. The culture shifted gradually, until 2002, then suddenly. That is how cultures change and paradigms shift. The invalidity of psychiatry's current paradigm is being increasingly recognized now, and its magisterium is eroding. Some future event or events will, no doubt, tip the balance and make any further denial of the harmful consequences of this wrong way of conceptualizing, diagnosing and treating mental illness impossible. Until that happens, we need to be able to wrap our minds and hearts around the enormity of the lie that allowed this pseudoscience to dominate psychiatry for so long.

Left to its own devices, psychiatry is not likely to repair itself. The current paradigm has brought psychiatrists more prestige and more money than any previous paradigm. Upton Sinclair famously noted, "It is difficult to get a man to understand something, when his salary depends upon his not understanding it!" (Sinclair 1935, p. 109). And when he does understand, getting him to *do* anything about it is even harder. For many psychiatrists, challenging the falsity of psychiatry's current paradigm would amount to taking on what Al Gore, in drawing attention to another issue that most people are unwilling to deal with, identified as an "inconvenient truth." Acknowledging that most of the mental disorders currently considered brain diseases by the DSM-5 are actually maladaptive responses—Meyerian psychodynamic reactions—to life events would bring about a significant reduction in their professional status and income. And so, psychiatry's self-serving self-deception continues.

Chapter 3 An Approach to Diagnosing Mental Illness Based on the Psychobiology of Adolf Meyer

The approach to classifying and diagnosing mental illness that is introduced here is intended as nothing less than a reboot of psychiatry, which would ultimately lead to a paradigm shift. Unlike the DSM-III, DSM-IV and DSM-5, whose creators deliberately ignored all explanatory theories of psychic pathology, *The Four Domains of Mental Illness*—the FDMI—grew out of a philosophical anthropology, a point of view about the nature and essence of man, and about what it means to be mentally ill (Muller 2015b).

In creating the FDMI, the approach to understanding mental illness that was introduced by McHugh and Slavney in *The Perspectives of Psychiatry* (1998) was conserved, even as alterations and additions were made, reflecting the author's clinical experience and theoretical predilections. *The Perspectives of Psychiatry* and the FDMI are both based on the psychobiology of Adolf Meyer, *the psychological study of the person in the context of biology*. In *The Perspectives*, the presence of the psychiatrist and existential philosopher Karl Jaspers is also keenly felt.

Meyer believed that the human mind was a biological mind, and that the *psychobiological adaptation of consciousness* to all a person experiences—good, bad or indifferent—is the chief determining factor in a life. For Meyer, *maladaptations* to life's challenges were the reason for most mental illnesses, not brain lesions. Rejecting the dualistic idea that mind and brain exist and function in some kind of parallel way, Meyer intended *psychobiology* to signify what he called a "oneness with several aspects" (Meyer 1897).

Meyer's Rising Star

Adolf Meyer, the son of a Protestant minister, was born in 1866 in Niederweningen, Switzerland, near Zurich, and died in Baltimore in 1950 (Muller 2015a). He received his medical degree from the University of Zurich, where he showed little enthusiasm for psychiatry or working with psychiatric patients. After graduation, Meyer applied to the medical school for a position in neuropathology—his main interest at that time—but was turned down.

Expecting to find greater professional opportunities abroad, Meyer immigrated to the United States in 1892. He briefly practiced neurology in Chicago and after a year accepted a job as pathologist at the new Kankakee State Hospital in Illinois, where he continued his research in neuropathology. In 1896, after realizing that the essence of mental illness could not be found in cadaverous brains but only in living patients, Meyer left Illinois for Worcester State Hospital in Massachusetts to pursue his growing interest in clinical psychiatry. He brought a firm professional discipline to the program there, and was named clinical director. Under his leadership, Worcester became a prominent center for training psychiatrists.

In 1902, with his transition from neuropathology to psychiatry well underway, he moved to New York to become chief of the Pathological Institute of the New York State Hospital System. While in New York, he also served from 1904 to1909 as professor of psychiatry at Cornell University. In 1910 he was appointed chief of psychiatry at the Johns Hopkins University School of Medicine.

During the three decades that Meyer oversaw the department of psychiatry at Johns Hopkins (1910–1941), he became the most influential psychiatrist in North America, developing and promulgating a dynamic psychiatry that transformed the field. Theodore Lidz (1966), among others, has argued that only Sigmund Freud (1856–1939) had as much influence. Yet in spite of his renown, three decades after Meyer relinquished the chairmanship at Johns Hopkins, his impact on American psychiatry had been all but superseded—first by Freud's psychoanalysis, then by biological psychiatry.

Meyer's Faded Star

The main reason why Meyer's influence on psychiatry waned, one often hears, was that his approach was not systematized, and lacked a method, making it difficult to grasp and teach. Meyer concentrated on the unique experience of each patient and the meaning of the "facts"—his term—that he extracted from patients' stories. He pretty much avoided a general formulation of that experience, which would have been necessary to create a method. The nature and consequences of this limitation of Meyerian psychiatry are spelled out in Chapter 5.

Meyer wrote hundreds of articles that stolidly doled out some of the most profound insights into mental illness—and, just as significantly, mental health—ever recorded. But many of these articles are hard to stay with from start to finish. Meyer used terms that did not clearly signify what he was attempting to name and characterize: freedom became *spontaneity*; meaning became *sense*; and what we call here the self as active agent was rendered as *ergasia!* This is not the kind of vocabulary that takes a reader easily to the heart of the matter.

The way Meyer put down his thoughts in writing lacked the architectonics that would have allowed his vision to coalesce for the reader into an accessible whole. Extracting the gold from his often unfocused texts is a task that most psychiatrists have been unwilling to undertake. In both *The Perspectives* and the FDMI, the intention is to make explicit what Meyer, in many instances left implicit, and to formalize his inchoate legacy so its full potential can be realized. This author is convinced that, of all those who have put their minds to understanding mental illness and its remediation, including Freud, Adolf Meyer had the surest grasp of how these altered mental states were achieved—in spite of the limitations of his legacy, which we acknowledge.

When a youngster, Meyer's clerical father encouraged him to associate with children of other faiths. Possibly influenced by this paternal acceptance of different religious points of view, Meyer evolved into a conciliator, a fact that some of his critics hold against him (Double 2007). He was content to present his ideas about mental illness and its treatment without actively opposing other viewpoints, including the biological psychiatry of his time, and Freudian psychoanalysis, which swept through this country in the forties and fifties, eventually leaving psychobiology in its wake. Meyer may have felt overly confident that his heritage would endure in any case. Or, it is possible that he did not give much thought to what would become of psychobiology after he was gone.

Meyerian Psychobiology

A good deal of what Meyer stood for survives indirectly. The well-known biopsychosocial (BPS) model that integrates mind and body in medicine and psychiatry was created by George L. Engel (1977), who, as a medical student, studied with Meyer at Johns Hopkins. The BPS model draws from Meyer's psychobiology, though Engel's formulation by no means realizes the full potential of Meyer's vision (Davidson & Strauss 1995; Freedman 1995). This model is easy to apply clinically, but is not a method for classifying and diagnosing mental illness. Engel's legacy has been cited as being more eclectic than holistic, and criticized for its failure to acknowledge the recent contributions of behavioral genetics and cognitive neuroscience (Ghaemi 2010).

Meyer started with the "whole person" to a greater degree than Engel. "When I speak of 'person' instead of merely a mind," Meyer said, "I mean a biological entity, with a name and life history and inner continuity and actual record, an entity spread over a lifetime between conception and death and natural periods and phases and rhythms of action and rest, wakefulness and sleep, phases of maximal fitness and states of repair" (Meyer 1935). Meyer believed that most mental illness was due to maladaptive responses—*inauthentic adaptations*—people make to the demands put on them by the challenging and sometimes crushing circumstances of their lives. He named his approach to understanding and remediating mental illness *psychobiology*, a concept very different from the similarly-sounding biological psychiatry, which assigns the principal role in mental health and illness to brain function, and downplays the role of the self as active agent (Muller 2003).

The idea that freedom, even when limited, plays a significant role in how every life is lived runs through Meyer's clinical work, prolific writing and advocacy for those who had become mentally ill: "Whoever does not see and feel and respect that particular feature of a relative but actual 'spontaneity' [freedom] in nature and man has killed in himself a real part of human common sense" (Lief 1948, p. 578). Meyer took freedom to be the "natural upshot" of the integration of mind and brain and body that spells life itself, in such a way that each person becomes an "experiment in nature." To him, the fact that people are free—relatively free, anyway—should be obvious, a matter of common sense.

"Common sense" is a recurrent theme in Meyer's writing, and he insisted that his psychobiology is closer to the earth and easier to grasp than many people would suspect. Common sense implies a person's capacity to see others and the world without significant pathological distortion, even while that person is under pressure or facing disappointment and setbacks. Meyer believed that most people are capable of making, and in fact do make, the kind of common sense adaptive adjustments that are constantly required if one is to function authentically and productively.

People who are able to live in this way do so with what Meyer called "consensual common sense," which permits them to become participants in a social order and act as "agents" of that order. Those who act outside the consensus can learn from the negative responses of others to their overreaching and adapt themselves accordingly. But some people will not, or cannot adapt. A person who attempts to pay for something in a store with rocks instead of money is missing a basic element in this consensus, and probably other elements as well (Lamb 2014, p. 85). Meyer saw mental illness as the difference between this consensual common sense way of living and the way his patients lived.

Meyer's Healthy and Unhealthy Habits of Living

Under the somewhat limp heading of "mental hygiene," Meyer listed what he called the "habits" of a healthy, productive life as a starting point for understanding the nature of mental illness. These habits include an active life style, where action and accomplishment take precedence over a passive dreamy state that produces nothing of value; the capacity to get along with others and do a job well; the ability to resolve conflicts and overcome disappointments that are a part of daily life; and the willingness to accept what is beyond our control and influence, without being diminished by that acceptance. To live maturely is to learn to balance expectation against reality and to recover from the consequences when we fail to keep this balance, as everyone occasionally does. This is simple, common sense stuff, but also the foundation of a healthy life, a capability that crumbles when a person becomes mentally ill.

Unlike Freud, who is generally credited with being a pessimist about life—for him, a good therapeutic outcome was exchanging neurotic misery for the "normal" misery of everyday life—Meyer offered a more optimistic view of the world that largely put the individual in the driver's seat. Meyer believed it was possible to *prevent* mental illness by staying clear of the defenses that people often employ when facing stress, disappointment and loss. Stick with the good habits, he advised, and avoid bad habits. Meyer also promoted institutions that served vulnerable families and was instrumental in establishing the profession of psychiatric social work.

Bad habits can progress to maladaptive reactions, one evolving into the other. Existentially, developing a Meyerian good habit means authentically struggling with the demands that circumstances and our own choices force on us, rather than allowing ourselves to believe, through self-deception, that we are not capable of doing this, and acquiescing, under pressure, to one pathological option or another. Bad habits develop with repeated self-deception. Good mental hygiene amounts to suffering existentially, not pathologically.

Meyer could define what it meant for someone to be pathological in part because he understood what it meant to be normal. To Meyer, this meant living within the boundaries of consensual common sense. Before his first-year psychiatry students at Johns Hopkins began to study psychic pathology, he insisted that they limit themselves to observing what he called "the ordinary lives of others as well as our own," and devoted class time to this pursuit. He tried to convince his students that they could identify psychic pathology by gauging the difference between how their patients acted and the behavior of people who lived within the common sense consensus.

Meyer felt that as someone turns away from the habits of healthy living, often under the pressure of new challenges or negative experiences, the specific kind and degree of *maladaptive reaction* undergone and the *substitutive* activity adopted (in essence, chosen) will determine the kind and severity of the pathology that ensues. "The dynamic theory that I use," he said, "does not talk of symptoms; it talks of reactions that we want to understand and readjust in one way or another. . . . I like to pick out the abnormal reactions as I find them, with their setting and their content" (Malamud 1929). Meyer's experience taught him that ferreting out the facts of a patient's case and identifying the substitutive maladaptive reactions required a clinician to be a good detective.

In looking at what Meyer called the "setting" and "content" of normal and abnormal reactions, he was clearly concerned with the *meaning* of this behavior: "Practically all that psychobiology and psychology occupy themselves with in their present mood and mode of progress is the study of meanings and meaning factors and motivations . . . the basis of all collaboration and understanding between physician and patient, and the recognition of an active status also of the patient and person" (Meyer 1936). Reading these words, one can only wonder how the creators of the DSM-III, DSM-IV and DSM-5 could have deliberately dispensed with the meaning of the symptoms they designated for diagnosing psychiatric illness. Doing so has been an open invitation to wrong diagnosis, the proliferation of factitious mental disorders and invalid research (Muller 2008).

At the Phipps Clinic, Meyer and his staff had relatively long-term access to patients. After identifying the facts of their narratives—which Meyer took to be data, not just clinical impressions—the maladaptive reactions made by these patients to various stressors were identified. From this information, the meaning of the pathological habits (roughly, the DSM-5's symptoms) that ensued could usually be determined. Meyer believed that each of the facts disclosed in a patient's narrative had its place in the chain of cause and effect that ultimately became a maladaptive reaction, which he sometimes called a "substitute reaction." By tracking this chain of maladaptive thinking, feeling and acting, in its meaningful context, properly trained clinicians can identify the *psychodynamic cause* of a mental illness.

In the FDMI, following Meyer, mental illnesses are designated as pathological *reactions*. *Re-action* identifies the active response a person makes to some difficult life situation, and also names the psychobiological change that occurs because of the response. Meyer's pathological reaction implies a *defensive misuse of freedom under pressure*, which usually requires less courage and effort than an authentic adaptive response would have entailed. The DSM's less specific term, mental disorder, affirms only that something has gone wrong in a life, without regard to its provenance or meaning.

Most of these maladaptive reactions, including some that lead to psychosis, occur when people, in the context of a psychobiological deficit and/or certain previously learned bad habits, meet with resistance or rejection from a significant other, or become seriously impeded in a life project and lose courage in facing these challenges. Refusing to answer the invitation that the world continues to extend to them, even in disappointment and defeat, they retreat to a passive, defensive manner of feeling, thinking and acting. They do so in one or more of the pathological configurations of being that have come to be identified as mental illnesses.

These reconfigurations of self occur after certain bad habits acquire sufficient maladaptive power to disturb a person's psychobiological equilibrium, i.e., the balance between instinctive needs and social requirements. In time, the cognitive, emotional and behavioral manifestations of this imbalance can become automatic responses to future experience, leading to a distinctive *pattern* of maladaptive behavior. Meyer introduced the term *dissolution* to name an underlying process of structural collapse that occurs with some of these maladaptive reactions. When the mental function associated with consensual common sense weakens to the point of no longer promoting adaptive responses, primitive, instinctual responses may come into play (Lamb 2014, p. 215).

Meyer's notion of the maladaptive reaction owes something to the idea that we all have the capacity—indeed the inclination—to become our own worst enemy. For the clinician who is attempting to understand the essence and provenance of a mental illness, one or more of these defensive reactions is often the elephant in the room.

In Meyer's own words, "What is at first a remedy of difficult situations can become a miscarriage of the remedial work of life, just as fever, from being an agent of self-defense, may become a danger and more destructive than its source" (Meyer 1906). What Meyer meant by dissolution involves not only abandoning good habits and acquiring bad ones, but transforming a person's consensual common sense world of cause and effect in a way that fundamentally alters structures of thought, feeling and behavior.

Meyer recognized that once bad habits were sufficiently psychobiologically engrained, they became *automatic* and *habitual*, just as good habits are internalized. He used the word *unconscious* to describe these habits, but as an adjective, not as a noun as Freud had done to name a component of the psyche that held repressed desires, memories, etc. Though Meyer was a strong supporter of Freud at first, he later took issue with him on a number of points. It is important for Meyer's readers to understand that he did not subscribe to the Freudian "unconscious"—the noun—a pillar of psychoanalysis, a concept that is incompatible with Meyerian psychobiology (Lamb 2014, pp. 244–245). Freud's and Meyer's paradigms derive from very different notions of what it means to be a human being, whether sick or healthy.

The Essence of Meyer's Psychobiology

Meyer believed that, in trying to understand maladaptive reactions, the function of the mind that made behavior and, ultimately, personality possible could not be separated from the function of the brain that underlies these mental states. Meyer's maladaptive reactions encompass and surpass what the familiar reductive terms from psychology and biology used to parse the pathological alterations in mental life attempt to designate. In psychobiology, the entities that we so facilely call mind and brain (as if these were ever *real* entities) become one, coming together in the behavior and personality of the individual. To Meyer, a person is created in and through this integration. He is sharply at odds here with the notion of comorbidity, which is strongly favored in biological psychiatry and the DSM-III, DSM-IV and DSM-5, where multiple pathologies are diagnosed as distinct mental disorders rather than as multiple components of one integrated person's abnormal psychobiology.

Meyer was convinced that good habits could deteriorate into bad habits and that bad habits could be transformed into good ones. His core mission at the Henry Phipps Psychiatric Clinic at Johns Hopkins Hospital, which he founded in 1913 and directed until 1941, was to alter the bad habits that his patients had acquired that *were* their problem. The main strategy was to show patients how to build on strengths they already had—"habit-training"—which ultimately meant redirecting their misused freedom to achieve authentic goals.

Along with his pathological gaze, Meyer gave his patients a glimpse at a better life. He taught them techniques of survival based on healthy actions. His prescription: "*actual doing*, *actual practice*, a program of wholesome living [is] the *basis* of wholesome feeling and thinking" (Meyer 1922). This advice could be rephrased more colloquially and concretely as *Do better before you feel better*. In other words, don't use low mood as a rationalization for not doing what needs to be done *now*, and should have been done earlier; good advice for us all. This is Meyer, the closet existentialist, channeling Sartre's life-altering dictum that *existence precedes essence*, which is to say that what we *do* will determine the kind of habits we develop, and the kind of person we become. Sartre reversed the traditional philosophical stance that a person's essence is more fundamental and immutable than his existence (Sartre 2007, p. 22).

Independently of Sartre, Meyer came to the same conclusion, though he expressed his intuition in more pragmatic terms. The story of how Meyer put psychobiology into practice by working intensively with patients at the Phipps Clinic is told by Susan D. Lamb in *Pathologist of the Mind: Adolf Meyer and the Origins of American Psychiatry* (Lamb 2014).

In the failure to adapt authentically to the pressure of life events, good habits—such as confidence, courage and imagination—can deteriorate into the bad habits of psychobiological maladaptation. Meyer believed that all that we think, feel and say ultimately tends toward its expression as action. The blockade of authentic action—when, as Meyer put it, action becomes stuck in a "troubling fermentation of thought and fancy"—can lead to psychobiological imbalance. The anxiety that is concomitant with this imbalance, which is ultimately a disruption of the *harmony* between person and world, can provoke, among other cognitive reactions, phobias, paranoia and delusions, as well as disturbances of mood that include pathological anger, depression and mania (Lamb 2014, p. 172).

In grasping the malleability of habits, Meyer anticipated the modern notion of *brain plasticity*. He believed that the nervous system had two essential levels: the segmental level (consisting of the hardwired circuits of the brain that underlie motor response) and the suprasegmental layer (the neuronal extensions that arise later in response to a person's adaptation to environmental demands). These neuronal extensions become the substrate of the developing, plastic brain. Meyer used the following example to illustrate the two levels of the nervous system:

> We see the legs active in walking and dancing, but we also see the knee jerk when, in proper position, we strike the slightly stretched tendon. . . . Something similar can be shown in a psychoneurotic woman whose foot kicks out as soon as one comes near the knee with the hammer—evidently an anticipative response of the *person*, not a mere reflex, the operation resembling a delayed reflex, a reaction presupposing that she anticipated. What then is *she* (Meyer 1934, p. 431)?

The woman observed here is characterized as "psychoneurotic," a judgment consistent with her anticipatory fear of the approaching reflex hammer. Her reaction, "mistimed" as it is, is not a pure motor reflex, but *a function of the totality of her adaptive experience with the environment she has lived in and through since birth, in short of her personality—the kind of person she has become in her interactions with others.*

This illustration of neurotic behavior exemplifies what Meyer meant by psychobiology: the study of the person as an integrated psychological and biological whole, where neither mind nor brain can be considered or understood separately (Meyer 1915). Meyer did not originate the term psychobiology, which has been used by many clinicians and scientists to specify their approaches to both life sciences and social sciences. With Meyer's work in mind, Dewsbury (1991) described psychobiology as an attempt to "incorporate biological perspectives in the study of dynamic processes in whole, integrated, adapted, and organized organisms, not to reduce complex, dynamic relationships to physiological processes." In a lecture at Johns Hopkins that was part of the centenary celebration of the Phipps Clinic, which was founded and directed by Meyer, this notion was paraphrased somewhat more agreeably: *You can be interested in the biology of some mental function without believing that it is the whole story* (Smith 2013).

To Meyer, the brain was the "organ of personality," a formulation that made it impossible to believe in a material brain and an immaterial mind, or to accept the positivist reduction of the self to quantifiable data (Lamb 2006).

In his description of the neurotic woman's anticipatory response to the reflex hammer, Meyer was prefiguring the modern notion of epigenetics—the way the environment, one's lived experience in the world, alters genetic inheritance, principally through proteins that are made from DNA, through RNA (Mukherjee 2016). "Mind," he said, "like any other function, can demoralize and undermine itself and its organ, and the entire biological economy, and to study the laws of the miscarriage of its function and life is one of the conditions for any true advancement in psychic pathology" (Meyer 1906a). "Our patients are not sick merely in an abstract mind, but by actually living in ways which put their mind and the entire organism and its activity in jeopardy, and we are now free to see how this happens—since we study the biography and life history, the resources of adaptation and of shaping the life to success or to failure" (Meyer 1952, p. 4). Modern epigenetics is forcing us to rethink the notion of what is permanently "hardwired" in the brain at all levels of the brain (Francis 2011).

The French psychologist Maurice Merleau-Ponty (1908–1961) came early to the search for the location in the brain where the meaning of life events leaves its mark. His first major works, *The Structure of Behavior* (1967) and *Phenomenology of Perception* (1962), incorporate the neurophysiological perspective as well as the existential dimension of self-organization for which he is best known. Ellis, reviewing the work of contemporary psychologists, neuropsychologists and neuroscientists who are following Merleau-Ponty's integrative lead—and, in the process, attempting to correct what Damasio (1994) calls "Descartes' error"—concludes:

> We must develop a theory in which purposeful processes [like the woman's response to the reflex hammer in Meyer's example] are able to appropriate their needed substratum elements, rather than merely being passive epiphenomena of them or ontologically identical with them. . . . The Twentieth Century tried simply to turn its back on this problem. Purposeful [meaningful] activity was explained away as a purely mechanical process that only *appeared*, anthropomorphically, as if it were purposeful (Ellis 2006).

In spite of the original high expectations, and some current claims to the contrary, the data produced so far by neuroscience research into mental illness have not significantly contributed to the biological explanation of *any* mental illness. Many *correlations* between the productions of consciousness and neural function have been found, but, as McHugh and Slavney point out in *The Perspectives of Psychiatry* (p. 13) "correlation is not explanation," or usually helpful to our patients, either.

Researchers who continue to look for the biological "roots" of mental illness would do well to keep in mind this comment by the Meyerian psychiatrist Leon Eisenberg, who was affiliated with both the Johns Hopkins and Harvard psychiatry departments: "Psychiatry is all biological and all psychological. There is no mental function without brain and social context. To ask how much of mind is biological and how much social is as meaningless as to ask how much of the area of a rectangle is due to its width and how much to its height or how much of the phenotype is due to genes and how much to environment" (Eisenberg 1995). Meyer was not satisfied with the efforts of those who had attempted to classify mental illness, including Emil Kraepelin. He felt that Kraepelin's diagnostic categories, based mostly on biology, and often revised, were emphasized at the expense of patients' experiences and life stories. Meyer may as well have been talking about the neo-Kraepelian DSM-III, DSM-IV and DSM-5 which make the diagnosis of a mental illness a matter of matching symptoms of unspecified origin and meaning to symptom checklists that are said to define these mental illnesses, which are presumed to be *brain diseases* (Double 1990). "Very often the supposed disease behind [the mental illness] is a myth and merely a self-protective term for an insufficient knowledge of the conditions of [the psychobiological] reaction and inadequacy of our present remedial skill" (Meyer 1951, p. 585). Predictably, this approach has led to many wrong diagnoses (Muller 2008).

Before coming to America, Meyer was trained by, and worked with, some of the leading psychiatric researchers in Europe. The approach followed was based on the disease, or medical model of somatic illness, where patients' symptoms were matched to the findings of autopsies performed after their death. This same clinical-pathological model is the foundation of today's *biological psychiatry*, widely seen as a neo-Kraepelian derivative. Meyer's *psychobiology* is a radical departure from the medical model. Meyer believed that most mental illness was not caused by a somatic lesion, but came about through an alteration in mind *and* body due to maladaptive reactions to challenges that life invariably presents. These psychodynamic reactions have a *biological correlative*, which may account for the changes in brain structure and function that empirical investigators have observed in patients with some mental illnesses and interpret as the *biological cause* of the illness.

Perhaps adding the voice of another Meyer advocate would help the reader achieve a better overview of Meyerian psychobiology. We confidently conclude this section with a paragraph from an article written by Susan Lamb for *Medical History*, which summarizes the main points she made in *Pathologist of the Mind*:

> The fundamental premise of psychobiology was that an action of the body's nervous apparatus *and* its expression as mental activity constituted a single adaptive response of the human organism. Meyer called this adjustment a "psychobiological reaction" and made it a critical unit of analysis for psychiatrists. He described the brain as the "mechanism of sensory-motor plasticity," a responsive, not fixed, anatomical and physiological apparatus. Neural activity was expressed functionally as the mind, which he identified as the "mechanism of adaptation and behavior." According to Meyer, the result of this biological integration was the "person," an irreducible unit. A person adjusted constantly not only to his or her physical surroundings, but also to a complex environment of symbolic stimuli and tacit social codes—what he called "social adaptation." He reasoned that through an endless series of psychobiological reactions, a biological function called mentation integrated and regulated a complex suite of adaptive resources accumulated during human evolution, including physiological systems, instinctual urges, emotional responses, learning, memory, perception of reality, imagination, abstract reasoning, social co-operation, and altruism. Meyer's model of psychobiology framed mental disorders not as distinct diseases [an approach known today as the medical model], as did the majority of his peers in this era, but as types of maladjustment. He deemed a patient's psychobiological reactions to his or her environment—manifest in thoughts and behavior—to be observable natural phenomena, subject to scientific inquiry and a promising site of medical intervention (Lamb 2015).

What is identified here as Meyer's "observable natural phenomena" links psychobiology to the approach taken by the existential psychiatrists and philosophers, as will become apparent shortly.

Adolf Meyer, Our Contemporary

Reading Meyer now, one cannot help but think of him as a contemporary—he struggled with many of the same issues that still confound psychiatry. By 1911 psychobiology had sufficiently developed as a theory of mental illness so that Smith Ely Jelliffe, a contemporary of Meyer and a strong supporter of his thinking, could write, "our pathological findings may represent atrophies of unused association tracts which have resulted from the so to speak petrification of bad habits of mental adjustment" (Meyer, Jelliffe & Hoch 1911, p. 23).

Paul R. McHugh is fond of saying that if you think you have found something new in psychiatry, it's because you haven't read Adolf Meyer (McHugh 2017). As early as 1935, when Meyer's influence on American psychiatry was still at its peak, Meyer saw "two real difficulties to be overcome" to set psychiatry on a right—psychobiological—course: "In the first place, the scientifically trained person's fear that the common sense of everyday life has to be replaced, if one is to be on safe ground, by totally new methods, which then too often want to limit themselves to physics and chemistry and physiology and rigid statistics; and, on the other hand, there threaten oversystematizations in new endeavors in psychopathology, feeding on a similar disparagement of common sense with its propaganda of exclusive salvation by startling novelty of concepts and topics" (Kanner 1972, p. xvi).

This opaque, Victorian sentence needs to be read several times before its meaning can be discerned and its current relevance felt. But Meyer nails it: what he was fighting in 1935 is what psychiatry is still fighting in 2015—80 years later! The worm of Cartesian dualism, which is the ground of the positivistic, materialistic vision of human nature that Meyer was decrying, still twists in psychiatry's heart. Biological psychiatry fundamentally misrepresents who and what a human being *is*. Biological determinism is *not* the hand that nature dealt us, but a man-made distortion of that nature. Psychiatry's current paradigm is at cross-purposes with Being itself. Ontologically, this is not how it is.

Psychobiology had the potential to jump-start a paradigm shift out of Cartesian dualism, but Meyer did not reach that goal, and we are still stuck in the gap of the man-made disjunction of mind and brain. By situating the FDMI within Meyer's paradigm, we are trying to get beyond this counterproductive scission. Doing so requires working against the prevailing current of Western dualistic thought and custom that has plagued psychiatry from the beginning. To the list of reasons why Meyer's psychobiology did not outlast him we can add the seemingly inextinguishable affection of the Western psyche for certain dichotomies—distortions of psychological life that Meyer vigorously challenged.

Meyer's psychobiological approach was replaced, first in the 1940s by Freud's psychoanalysis, which ceded ultimate power in the human enterprise to the unconscious, and then, starting in the 1960s by biological psychiatry, which credited to the brain the principle role in making people well or mentally ill. Each paradigm, in its own way, shattered the notion of human autonomy and the self as active agent, which is the cornerstone of Meyer's theory of what it means to be a person. It is a tragedy that Meyer's concept of psychic pathology was abandoned before its full clinical potential could be realized. Reclaiming Meyer for psychiatry now amounts to looking back to find a way forward. (Considering the influence of psychoanalysis and biological psychiatry on individuals and culture, we could reasonably ask if people have a *need* to be ruled by one freedom-denying world view, or another.)

Meyer's Psychobiology and Existential Psychiatry

Psychobiology and existential psychiatry developed contemporaneously, though independently, along parallel tracks. Existential psychiatry was an outgrowth and adaptation of existentialism—the so-called philosophy of existence—that came about as a revolt against the limitations of analytical philosophy (Barrett 1962; Harper 1972; Muller 1987). Like existentialism, existential psychiatry began and flourished in Europe (May, Angel & Ellenberger 1958). Some of the standout figures include Karl Jaspers (1997), Viktor Frankl (1963), R. D. Laing (1965), Ludwig Binswanger (1963), Medard Boss (1963), Erwin Straus (1966) and J. H. van den Berg (1972).

Once it is acknowledged that the self as active agent is free to choose a life, it is just a small step to the notion that a pathological life can be chosen as well. Meyer's emphasis on discerning the essential facts of patients' narratives, indeed his entire philosophical anthropology, resembles the approach taken by the existential psychiatrists who see the development of mental illness as the result of a person turning away from the invitation that the world continues to offer even when things go badly, and then, often, from bad to worse. Feeling disempowered and demoralized, some people in these circumstances may inauthentically conclude that it is impossible to muster their free will to move forward and beyond their loss. Though it may not immediately seem so, a negative response of this kind *is* a choice, one that involves the *misuse of freedom* (Muller 2003). This classic statement of Sartre's on the nature of mental illness could just as well have come from Meyer: "I regard mental illness as the 'way out' that the free organism, in its total unity, invents in order to be able to live through an intolerable situation" (Laing & Cooper 1964, p. 6). Sartre's "way out" is Meyer's "maladaptation." Meyer and Sartre would have agreed that freedom is the way we respond to what others do to us and to everything else that fate throws our way.

In trying to understand how, by mishandling their freedom, his patients had become ill, Meyer came as close to dialectically joining person and world as anyone who ever attempted to discover the cause of mental illness. He rejected the notion that we can know only ourselves, and that other people remain essentially unknowable:

> I should quit being a physician and a teacher if I felt compelled to doubt the possibility of my studying and knowing your minds and those of my patients well enough to draw practical conclusions from such knowledge. If solipsistic philosophy, *i.e.*, the assumption that one can know only one's mind, were true,

> one might as well retire into absolute solitude. By making of mind something like the religious-philosophical concept of the soul, something opposed to the body instead of a function of the individual as a whole, traditional philosophy and psychology have rendered us a poor service (Meyer 1915).

This "poor service" was rendered by the positivist philosophers and psychologists who came to prominence in Europe during the last half of the 19th century (Giorgi 1970). These thinkers believed that human experience was too complicated to be understood intuitively, and was knowable only by reducing its complexity to data generated through the experimental methods of natural science. Meyer instinctively rejected this reduction of human experience, with its inevitable distortion of the human subject.

Truth stipulates that an entity is represented *as it is*, before preconception and bias transform it into something else. Understanding the essential nature of bias and its malignant influence on intellectual endeavor opens the way to accessing truth, not absolutely, but asymptotically. Ultimately, we need to think about the world in such a way that our "bias" tends toward a perspective that is valid.

One way to begin this process is by interrogating what the existential philosopher Edmund Husserl called the *Life-world*, the setting of our everyday experience, with its multiple horizons and multiple possibilities (Moran & Cohen 2012, pp. 189–193), employing Meyer's consensual common sense as we proceed. Why, we could ask, were two of the 20th century's best minds concerned with anything as seemingly mundane as common sense and the fact that our lives occur *in the world?* We need to recognize that Meyer and Husserl were thinking and writing in opposition to the logical positivists, whose paradigm grew out of the idea that philosophical inquiry had to be conducted *in the mind*, away from the contradictions and distractions of the everyday world—Husserl's Life-world.

To identify a phenomenon is to reveal the truth about some aspect of the Life-world by bringing it to light from its concealment in the everyday, pre-reflective stance that we take toward our experience most of the time (Heidegger 1962; Churchill 2014). Accurately intuiting aspects of a person's lived experience based on what is revealed to the observer's senses—which could be described as *objectively (validly) perceiving that person's subjectivity*—is what the existentialists and Meyer strove for. This was their implicitly shared telos.

William James (1842–1910) was an American philosopher and psychologist whose New-World existential thinking significantly influenced Meyer, uniting him in spirit with the European existentialists. He and Meyer shared their view that the truth about others could be intuitively known. James believed that "a form of being may exist uncontaminated by the touch of the fallacious knowing subject" (James 1920, pp. 5–6). Unlike James, Meyer was not a philosopher, and what he learned from James could best be described as existential psychology.

The Columbia historian Jacques Barzun identified the common ground treaded by James (1907) and the European existentialists in his biography *A Stroll with William James*. Barzun preferred James to the existentialists who, he felt, were "too opaque":

> After Kierkegaard, who *can* be read, Sartre, Heidegger, and their sources, Husserl, Simmel, and others show German academic discourse at its densest. It could be argued that the barbed-wire prose is due to the intricacy of the subject, but the base on which these doctrines rests is the Jamesian view that we make our universe out of experience by acts of thought and will; and this idea he managed to convey and elaborate without torturing his readers (Barzun 1983, p. 137).

To "make our universe out of experience by acts of thought and will" comes as close as a dozen words can come to describing what existentialism is about—and is surely a more concrete and accessible way of saying, as Sartre (2007) did, that "existence precedes essence." To his credit, Sartre, in addition to his often recondite ontological language could speak in a more common tongue as well. But Husserl's writing *is* "German academic discourse at its densest," and reading him *is* mostly "torture," even as we credit his seminal ideas and his influence on Sartre, Heidegger and others. (Readers who are game to approach Husserl second-hand are directed to the Appendix, "Edmund Husserl's Phenomenological Method, William James's Pragmatism and the Question of Validity for the FDMI and the DSM-5.")

The essential point here is that James, Meyer and the European existentialists saw the world in pretty much the same way, and that Meyer read James, and was strongly influenced by him. All opposed the logical positivists' reduction of human experience to empirical data, the founding error of the DSM-III, DSM-IV and DSM-5.

The Johns Hopkins Four Perspectives of Psychiatry

Though the second edition of *The Perspectives of Psychiatry*, which appeared in 1998, is a critical response to the DSM-III (1980) and DSM-IV (1994), McHugh and Slavney's way of understanding psychic pathology is in many ways consistent with the DSM-I (1952), which bore the mark of Meyer's psychobiology.

The DSM-I maintained the two categories of mental illness previously demarcated by Meyer: 1) illnesses due to a primary impairment of brain function (certain medical conditions, drug and alcohol intoxication, metabolic disturbances, brain trauma); and 2) those brought on by an individual's inability to "adjust" to life's struggles and letdowns, in which a consequent disturbance of the brain's biological substrate became a component of the psychiatric illness. Following Meyer, schizophrenia and manic-depression were not considered to be primary brain illnesses in the DSM-I.

Though the DSM-I owes a good deal to Meyer, there is little sense here of the integration of mind, brain and body that underlies Meyer's psychobiology. By no means is the FDMI a return to the DSM-I. This Meyer-inspired nosology, which also bore the marks of Freud's psychoanalysis that would underlie the DSM-II (1968), has many of the same limitations that are widely ascribed to Meyer's psychobiology. By incorporating the elaborations of Meyer's work made in *The Perspectives of Psychiatry*, and by introducing a number of complementary ideas from existential philosophy and existential psychiatry, many of these limitations have been surpassed in the FDMI.

In *The Perspectives*, McHugh and Slavney distinguished four types of mental illness based on how these illnesses are believed to originate, to the extent that this provenance can be gauged with our limited knowledge. This four-part division is a considerable refinement over the divisions made by Meyer (Lamb 2014, pp. 156–160) and in the DSM-I. In the FDMI, each of the four perspectives begets a corresponding pathological domain, a lived space created and inhabited by someone with a mental illness. In making a diagnosis, *domain*, which derives from the Latin *territory*, is a more embodied designation than *perspective* (a cognitive concept) because people live in domains, though not in perspectives.

Meyer, who was an existentialist in all but name, would have surely agreed that a psychiatric diagnosis should access and assess a patient's *lived experience*—colloquially, where the patient lives. The FDMI allows the clinician who is evaluating a patient for an abnormality in one domain to simultaneously assess deviances in other domains that may be contributing to the patient's altered mental life.

Dividing mental illness into four domains, which emerge from the four perspectives, allows a "first cut" to be made in parsing the varieties of psychopathological phenomena. Each domain in the FDMI derives from a psychobiological deviation from normalcy that can be distinguished from the other three—though, not infrequently, more than one type of deviation contributes to a person's illness. The essential nature of the four pathological domains characterized in the FDMI is adumbrated below:

First Domain: *Pathological Reactions Originating in Failures to Meet Life's Challenges and Recover from Setbacks*
Various manifestations of anxiety . . . anger . . . depression . . . dissociation . . . psychogenic psychosis

Second Domain: *Pathological Reactions Occurring in the Context of Aberrant Personality Development and Temperament*
Pathological personality styles . . . poor impulse control . . . psychosomatic illness

Third Domain: *Pathological Reactions Originating in Willed, Self-Gratifying and Ultimately Self-Destructive Behavior*
Alcoholism . . . drug abuse . . . insufficient or excessive control over food intake . . . pathological gambling . . . kleptomania . . . pyromania . . . trichotillomania . . . self-injury . . . excessive and misdirected sexual activity

Fourth Domain:

1. *Altered Mental States Due to Physiological Imbalance and Medical Disease*
Delirium caused by metabolic and electrolyte derangements . . . delirium caused by toxological poisoning and medical disease . . . autism . . . low IQ . . . learning disabilities (dyslexia) . . . physiologically induced anxiety and depression . . . neurodegenerative brain diseases with psychiatric symptoms

2. *Primary Mental Illnesses Emerging from a Putative Altered Brain Substrate*
   Some phenotypes of schizophrenia and manic-depression

Before developing the concept of the four domains further in Chapter 5, we will introduce the existential psychiatrist Karl Jaspers, already cited as an influence in McHugh and Slavney's *Perspectives of Psychiatry*, as well the existential philosophers Jean-Paul Sartre and Friedrich Nietzsche, whose philosophical anthropology, along with that of Jaspers's, parallels Meyer's (Martin Heidegger makes a brief appearance here, and comes back in force in the chapter that follows). And there will be more about William James, who may have been Meyer's primary influence.

In the meantime, a Map of the Four Domains, which appears at the beginning of Part II, offers an overview of the place that each of the most common mental illnesses, formulated as Meyerian maladaptive reaction types, finds in one of the four domains.

Chapter 4 To Understand, To Explain, To Know What Mental Illness Is

A logical first step into psychiatry's post-bubble world would be for the psychiatric community to come together to make a detailed list of what we do *not* know about psychic pathology. We would be in good company: both Socrates and Montaigne claimed that what they knew best was that they did not know anything much. Another list then needs to be made of what we do know, and where we have a realistic chance of learning more. Then we should ask ourselves what we mean when we say that we know something.

To *Understand*, to *Explain*

In his classic, often-revised treatise *General Psychopathology*, the German existential philosopher and psychiatrist Karl Jaspers distinguished two ways in which a subject under investigation can be known: *Verstehen*, which translates into English as *understanding*, and *Erklären*, which translates as *explanation* (Muller 2010). The German philosopher of history Wilhelm Dilthey (1833–1911) had already used these terms to name the different kinds of knowledge generated by the human sciences (qualitative psychology, history and literary criticism: *Verstehen*), and the natural sciences (quantitative psychology, chemistry and physics: *Ekläre*n).

With *understanding*, Jaspers designated the intuitive, psychological knowledge that one person can acquire about another person or some aspect of human behavior, what he called the "psychology of meaningful phenomena":

> Psychic events 'emerge' out of each other in a way which we understand. Attacked people become angry and spring to the defence [*sic*], cheated persons grow suspicious. . . . Thus we understand psychic reactions to experience, we understand the development of passion, the growth of an error, the content of delusion and dream; we understand the effects of suggestion, an abnormal personality in its own context or the inner necessities of someone's life (Jaspers 1997, pp. 202–203).

What Jaspers says here about *understanding* comes down to knowing a phenomenon subjectively by intuiting its essence. In contrast, *explanation* names a more objective way of knowing, based on empirical study, which discloses the *cause* of a phenomenon. In psychiatry, this cause is held to be the biological mechanism through which a symptom comes into being. To *understand* the meaning of a symptom is to know what part an abnormal thought, emotion or behavior plays in a patient's life narrative. To *explain* that symptom would be to know how the thought, emotion or act originates through a dialectical interplay of the patient's mind and brain with the world he lives in and through.

Jaspers's epistemological distinction between *understanding* and *explanation* allows us to realize that we can know the psychodynamic meaning of a symptom without knowing its biological cause. This insight should encourage clinicians not to eschew the understanding (meaning) of psychiatric symptoms just because the biological explanations of these symptoms elude them. It may eventually have to be conceded that some mental illnesses cannot be *explained* in the Jasperian sense, and that the fullest *understanding* that can be had is "explanation" enough. Ultimately, we aim to comprehend what William Faulkner, in his 1949 Nobel Prize acceptance speech called "the problems of the human heart in conflict with itself," not as writers of fiction, to whom Faulkner was directing this challenge, but as clinicians who can offer surcease to patients who come to us with conflicted hearts, minds and brains.

Jaspers's understanding-explanation dichotomy is an invention of epistemology, the philosopher's effort to discern the different ways we arrive at the truth about the world and its people. Meyer attempted to undercut this dichotomy in his psychobiological approach by first establishing the *facts* of a person's life then "reducing" these facts to the phenomenon or phenomena that constitute the patient's mental illness. At the same time, he acknowledged that a complementary altered brain substrate contributed to these phenomena, and that what we call the psychological and biological "components" of a mental illness are inseparable.

At present, with our limited knowledge, the full psychobiological understanding and explanation of a pathological phenomenon is not possible—but neither is it required to comprehend a patient's mental illness, or provide an adequate therapeutic challenge to it. David H. Brendel, in *Healing Psychiatry: Bridging the Science/Humanism Divide* (2006), proposes an active response to this stalemate. Bringing Jaspers's implied dialectic of humanism and science into the 21st-century, he recommends that both understanding and explanation be vigorously pursued for the patient's maximum therapeutic benefit. Brendel's "dialectical pluralism" is based on the pragmatic theories of Charles Sanders Peirce, William James and John Dewy. Curiously, Meyer, who was influenced by these philosophers, especially William James, is not mentioned here at all.

Brendel's pragmatic approach consists of what he calls the four *p*'s. He believes that the patient-therapist interaction should be: 1. *practical* (whatever tack the therapist takes, it must work for the patient and not be pursued just because it originates in some preferred theory); 2. *pluralistic* (both humanistic and scientific knowledge—Jaspers's understanding and explanation—should be brought to bear); 3. *participatory* (therapist and patient should work collegially, and those who know the patient should be consulted and, when possible, asked to take part in the patient's recovery); 4. *provisional* (no approach is to be considered the only way to work with the patient; the therapist needs to be willing to try other kinds of intervention, and stay open to suggestions made by the patient about how to proceed).

Along with healing wounded patients, Brendel sees psychiatric pragmatism as a way to heal a wounded psychiatry.

To Know

Whatever improved approach eventually replaces the DSM's wrongheaded and largely invalid way of doing psychiatric diagnosis needs to take into account the patient's subjectivity—which includes the meaning and context of symptoms—not by simply tacking on another DSM-like "axis," but by *making the articulation of this subjective experience the principle focus of the diagnostic process.*

After years of studying existential psychiatry, a tradition that is not well known in North America, and then later the psychobiology of Adolf Meyer, it became clear to me that the best way to diagnose and challenge psychic pathology is to begin, à la Jaspers, by *understanding what the patient is thinking, feeling and doing*. The ultimate goal is to get the patient *right*, so that the clinician's subjectivity intuits the patient's subjectivity. Achieving a valid and reliable classification and diagnostic method will require acknowledging that psychiatry is often less "medical" than is implied by the DSM, and that with some patients, psychiatry needs to be more art than science. A brain scan showing that a symptomatic patient has more, or less, blood flow in a specific brain area than normal subjects tells us little about the biological essence of the illness, or how to treat that illness.

Even if we were eventually able to offer a valid *explanation* for why people become mentally ill, we would still need to focus on *understanding* how and why each patient's life went wrong in its unique way. In this era of neuroscience, it is ironic that the greatest contributor to psychiatry in the last half-century may yet be seen as Aaron Beck, who gave us cognitive behavioral therapy (CBT). This approach associates negative thinking (which amounts to refusing the invitation of the world and its authentic possibilities following some disappointment, setback or trauma) with an increasing number of mental illnesses, and does so within the realm of Jaspers's *understanding* without looking to a biological *explanation* for these illnesses. Beck won the 2006 Albert Lasker Award for Clinical Medical Research. As of this writing, he is the only psychiatrist ever to receive that honor.

"Divorce your story and marry the truth." This advice, which was offered by the life coach and motivational speaker Anthony Robbins during a "TED Radio Talk" on National Public Radio (NPR) one Saturday afternoon (Feb. 28, 2015), coincidentally stated the basic premise of CBT. Reformulated in the language of the existentialists and Meyer, the prescription becomes: Drop the self-deceiving, limiting story that you have been telling yourself so you can embrace the possibilities that freedom permits once you sufficiently engage your will; exchange your maladaptive habits that got you into trouble for good habits that will permit a better life. Bradley Lewis has written a thoughtful book titled *Narrative Psychiatry* (2011) about the centrality of the stories people create in the process of living their lives, and how these stories, and clinicians' responses to them, shape the therapeutic relationship and its outcome.

Freedom: The Hallmark of Being Human, in Sickness and in Health

We hold that every human being, whether healthy or mentally ill, possesses a property of mind known as *consciousness*, which emerges from an interaction between the brain's neural substrate and its environment, making it possible for a person, over the course of a lifetime, to repeatedly choose one possibility over another. As pointed out by the existential philosopher Martin Heidegger, the world issues continuous, multiple invitations that we may respond to, or ignore. To make a free choice, we do not have to be *aware* at the time that we are doing so. A choice may be made with full awareness, total self-deceiving denial or a degree of awareness somewhere in between.

The capacity to make choices allows each of us to become a *self who is an active agent* and to live in a world with others who are active agents. This is the case even when freedom, the attribute that most uniquely defines humanness, is restricted by circumstance or by a compromised brain neural substrate.

Even though our freedom is limited, *we are absolutely free to choose and to act within the limits we face*, to select one limited possibility over another and to make the best of what comes of that choice. The familiar refrain "I had no choice," smacking of regret, does not mean that someone did not have a choice or make a choice, but that the choice was made between (or among) distasteful alternatives, and that the consequences were not entirely satisfactory. Being able to live with the not-so-transparent paradox that *limited freedom is still freedom* favors both productivity and mental health. Conversely, rejecting this paradox can lead to psychic pathology and paralysis. To a considerable degree, the choices we make, authentic or pathological, determine the person we become, while constitutional factors and circumstances, favorable or unfavorable, are always influences.

Jean-Paul Sartre: Freedom, Our Essence

The foregoing brief consideration of freedom owes much to the work of the existential philosopher Jean-Paul Sartre, who famously insisted that we are "condemned to be free" (Sartre 2007, p. 29). For Sartre, *freedom is our essence*, so we have no choice in the matter, which is the ultimate paradox of our "free" existence. It is clear from the totality of Sartre's writing that even he acknowledges that freedom means *relative* freedom.

Initially, Sartre's take on freedom seems to isolate the individual from others and from the social order. Many of his hard-edged aphorisms about what it means to be a human being—*Life begins on the other side of despair*; *Man is nothing more than he makes of himself*—can seem rigid and to lock the individual into isolation. On the contrary, Sartre sees us as united by the demands that our freedom makes on us, requiring that we respect the other person's freedom as we make our own choices, an idea he pursued in *Existentialism Is a Humanism*:

> I cannot set my freedom as a goal without also setting the freedom of others as a goal. Consequently, when, operating on the level of complete authenticity, I have acknowledged that existence precedes essence [we create our existence from the essence of our freedom], and that man is a free being who, under any

> circumstances, can only ever win his freedom, I have at the same time acknowledged that I must will the freedom of others (Sartre 2007, p. 49).

Intrinsically, inescapably, according to Sartre, we are responsible to others, and for others, who are caught up in the paradox of being "condemned to freedom," just as we are. We *are* our brother's keeper.

There is an apparent discrepancy between Sartre's concerns about our obligations to each other, as we pursue a shared freedom, and his declaration in *Being and Nothingness* (1956) that, because existence precedes essence, we are inclined to appropriate the freedom of others in the course of our own continuing self-creation. In *No Exit*, he famously concluded that "Hell is other people." In this well-known play, Sartre sharply delineated what he called the clash of alien freedoms that results when people try to use others for their own gratification and benefit, as, he makes clear, the contingent nature of our being inclines us to do.

Perhaps the key to resolving this incongruity is recognizing that when Sartre talks altruistically about sharing the burden and glory of freedom with others he is specifying that this mutuality can occur only under the conditions of what he considers "complete authenticity." At the same time, Sartre is on record as believing that people only rarely act authentically, and are, most of the time, self-deceived, inauthentically using others for their own purposes, as happens with the characters in *No Exit*. The altruism that Sartre describes can occur only by willing oneself into a state of near-secular perfection, which, it seems, he—an avowed atheist—at least at times, aspired to do. Most people do not seek Sartre's level of authenticity and do not value their own—and others'—freedom as much as Sartre did his, and theirs.

Atheist that he was, Sartre held himself to a higher moral standard than many who proclaim a belief in God and the afterlife: "Sartre's atheism is of course unpalatable to the believer, however much he may be sympathetic to Sartre the man. However, there are so many elements in his philosophy that can be combined with the Christian's faith. To take but one element: the word commitment. It certainly did not originate with Sartre though I never heard the word when I was in college or in the seminary many years ago." So wrote Alfred R. Desautels, S. J., in the pages of the Jesuit magazine *America*, adding this personal observation: "How many times did I see Sartre in Paris, already an old man, in cold weather, distributing political pamphlets for various groups who had made demands on him, knowing that he would agree and that the police would not touch him" (Desautels 1981). Sartre was well known for his generosity to others and for the time and money he gave to causes that served the disempowered. He was committed and engaged. If there were a designation of secular sainthood, Jean-Paul Sartre, the atheist, would be a strong contender. Skeptics might change their mind after reading his exposition of French antisemiticism, *Anti-Semite and Jew* (1948).

Limited Freedom and the Will to Power

While the world implicitly calls on us to respond as heroes—to reinvent ourselves in the face of disappointment, betrayal and catastrophe—we most often make less than heroic responses to the challenges life throws our way. Perhaps psychiatry's greatest failure—surpassing even the attribution of mental illness to an undemonstrated "broken brain part" or a "chemical imbalance"—is ignoring the consequences of our being "condemned to freedom," and downplaying our capacity to shape our lives, either within the bounds of what is considered normal, or outside those bounds, pathologically.

Struggling in and with the world, as we all are fated to do, some lose their nerve, or lose hope, and capitulate to one or more of the defensive psychodynamic modes that people employ when they are unable or unwilling to carry on the struggle. Those who have been betrayed and traumatized, in one way or another, to one degree or another, may accept that insult as the defining and insurmountable reality of their lives. They accept defeat because of some limiting life circumstance, or at the hands of another person. In effect, they broaden the harm done to them into a greater harm they do to themselves. They become their own worst enemy. Our first struggle is with the family we are born into. Many people remain caught up in unresolved family conflicts for their entire lives.

What Nietzsche called the "will to power"—and considered the "*Ur-fact* of all history"—can be thought of as a component of the will to live, the most basic human instinct. These three words, which sound ominous in a way the German philosopher never intended, simply mean that a person is free to overcome setbacks, even catastrophes, to become his best self, the "higher man." This act of self-perfection is not an isolated power play, since others are simultaneously engaging in the same project. We "conspire together" Nietzsche says, for power over ourselves and each other. Needless to say, this process does not always go smoothly (Ratner-Rosenhagen 2012).

The notion of "will to power" acquired a bad connotation in large part because Nietzsche's younger sister, hoping to ingratiate herself with the Nazis, approved their misreading of his work as a justification for Aryan superiority, eugenics and genocide. There is no question that the fulminant content and tone of Nietzsche's writing makes his work prone to this kind of distortion. But Nietzsche, who died in 1900, would have been horrified at the attempts made to paint him as a proto-Nazi.

It has been estimated that we use only a fraction of our cognitive power. It should be obvious that we also use only a fraction of our will to power—our *willpower*—as well. William James could have been channeling Nietzsche's intuition in his essay "The Energies of Men":

> Every one is familiar with the phenomenon of feeling more or less alive on different days. Every one knows on any given day that there are energies slumbering in him which the incitements of that day do not call forth, but which he might display if these [energies] were greater. Most of us feel as if a sort of cloud weighed upon us, keeping us below our highest notch of clearness in discernment, sureness in reasoning, or firmness in deciding. Compared with what we ought to be, we are only half awake. Our fires are damped, our drafts are checked. We are making use of only a small part of our possible mental and physical resources. In some persons this sense of being cut off from their rightful resources is extreme, and we then get the formidable neurasthenic and

> psychasthenic conditions, with life grown into one tissue of impossibilities, that so many medical books describe (James 1924, pp. 237–238).

When James spoke of the snubbed "incitements of that day," he was presaging what the existential philosopher Martin Heidegger would later describe as the *invitation of the world*—which is always there, and can be taken up or spurned—and is part of the self-world unit that is a prominent theme in both existential psychiatry and Meyerian psychobiology.

The increasing appreciation of the importance of the placebo effect in the efficacy of psychiatric medications, especially with drugs used to counter depression, can also be understood as a consequence of a person being offered a specifically targeted invitation—and accepting that invitation—to mobilize will into action against a depressing inertia (Lehrer 2010). If someone experiencing low mood is convinced that a glitch in brain chemistry is responsible, the expectation and hope that a drug can fix this malfunction may be a sufficient impetus to allow that person to marshal the will and energy to transcend the depression by dealing with what is really going on.

When faced with a negative experience or loss, many people slip into one mental illness or another as they react by telling themselves *I can't overcome this setback* when what they really mean is *I won't overcome this setback*. (This is what William James meant in the last sentence of the quote from "The Energies of Men.") Their often unrecognized choice—the refusal to will themselves beyond the loss, along with the inevitable anxiety and pain that accompany the loss—is based on self-deception, the lie we tell ourselves. It is ultimately this lie that is targeted in Aaron Beck's CBT.

We need to distinguish between mental illnesses that are rooted in this kind of refusal, which is the patient's own creation and usually subject to his attenuation or resolution (illnesses of the 1st, 2nd and 3rd domains), and an often graver condition that is more firmly rooted in biology, chemistry and neuroanatomy, and is driven, at least in part, by the structure and function of a compromised brain substrate (diseases of the 4th domain). While an illness of the first three domains may have been triggered by an inauthentic choice made in response to some negative experience, a patient may be so compromised by that response, both psychologically and biologically, that "talk therapy" will not engage him. Medication or electroconvulsive therapy (ECT), at least initially, may be necessary to get a therapeutic result. This is often the case with patients who have fallen into a state of melancholia, the most severe form of depression.

The fact is that most people do not know what they are capable of doing, either under the most favorable—or most trying—circumstances. This lacuna is part of the unexplored territory of the mind, considered in the broadest sense of that term, and cries out for systematic investigation. If psychiatry is to recover from the consequences of its wrong-headed insistence that the brain is calling the shots in what most people do, what we can think of as the terrain of human capability must be mapped and consciousness must be credited with the power to create what we are calling the self as active agent.

Once this capability is understood, we will be in a better position to say why so many people do not use the willpower at their disposal to overcome the setbacks that invariably come their way but react defensively instead and develop the symptoms of a mental illness. The final line in Samuel Beckett's novel *The Unnamable* could delineate a starting point for this investigation: "I can't go on, I'll go on." Someone who is caught in one of life's traps, with no inkling of how to reboot a formerly authentic life, might find in Beckett's words a precedent, a reason—and ultimately the will—to do so. Where there is a will, there is a way out, it seems. Sartre and Beckett recognize that freedom inheres in the very structure of human being.

In Caroline Kettlewell's memoir *Skin Game*, we are given a stunning example of how someone in the grip of a severe emotional crisis can sense the choice she has of either holding together at that level or sinking deeper into mental illness. By the time Caroline arrives at this especially low moment in her life, she has been cutting herself for more than ten years. She is 25 years old, a graduate of Williams College, married and working for an insurance company. These facts, pointing to normalcy and promise, belie the reality of Caroline's mental state: "I wanted to give up. Ten times a day I wanted to give up. I craved giving up. I would read, almost longingly, stories of nervous breakdowns and suicides and wonder, *How did they muster the nerve to default on their obligations?* Where would you begin such an abdication" (Kettlewell 1999, p. 156)?

It is uncommon for someone in Caroline's situation *not* to feel entitled to ratchet up her maladaptive response to the catastrophe that her life has become—by having a nervous breakdown or committing suicide. She is already anxious, depressed, anorexic and intermittently dissociated, and is periodically cutting herself. Yet Caroline feels "obligated" *not* to fall deeper into mental illness. She realizes that she has a choice about whether to default further on her obligations as a person, a daughter, the wife of a man she no longer wants to live with and the long-time holder of a dead-end job. Why? Because that is the kind of person she is: this far, but no farther. Recalling Beckett, Caroline can't go on, but she will go on. (In Chapter 11, Caroline Kettlewell is portrayed as an exemplar of the phenomenon of self-cutting.)

The Fallacy That the Brain Alone Creates the Products of Consciousness

After doing post-production work on "Particle Fever," a documentary about the Large Hadron Collider at CERN near Geneva, the veteran film editor Walter Murch was interviewed for *The New Yorker* about the possible theological significance of the Higgs boson, which has been tagged the "God particle." This sobriquet derives from the fact that the boson, which comes from smashing protons together at ultra-high speeds, gives matter its mass, without which the universe, including human beings, could not exist.

Murch began the interview by citing Muriel Rukeyser's belief that the universe is made of stories, not atoms and molecules, and then expanded on her insight:

> The tension is between finding ever more detail about atomic structure, and the story. It could be the equivalent of somebody looking at an old film, and realizing that the film came from a projector, and discovering that there is an image in the projector, and that it's made of molecules of grains of film—and

> then trying to find the mystery of the story by looking at ever more detailed molecules of film, thinking, If I finally get to the heart of that, will it tell me where my story comes from? While we know these are two separate universes (Mead 2013).

In this illustration, the ultimate understanding of the story told by the film is pursued through a stepwise reduction of the story to the apparatus that generates the moving picture viewed on the screen. The reductive sequence is: projector, image, celluloid (this is an *old* movie) and the molecular structure of the celluloid. The approach employs the techniques of natural science in the attempt to determine the meaning of human experience at the molecular level. This is the goal of a purely reductive biological psychiatry.

The futility of attempting to uncover the meaning of the film-story by explaining how the moving images on the screen are produced at the atomic level is obvious to Murch: "It may be that our story, whatever that is—existence—depends on the Higgs boson and atoms, but it depends on it the way the film depends on the molecular structure of the celluloid. That just happens to be the medium through which it is manifest, but the story predates the film and, in fact, actually created the film itself" (Mead 2013).

Murch's hermeneutic about the film and the projector parallels Meyer's psychobiological approach to understanding mental illness: the person's life-story—created by someone's (relatively) free will acting in and through an ever-changing environment—requires a functioning brain, but that brain is not the person's life-story and does not itself create this story, or the meanings that constitute the story. That task, with its joys and burdens, belongs to what we take to be the *self as active agent*, and not, in psychiatry's present paradigm, what would amount to an autonomous "molecular self" centered in the brain.

The ultimate fallacy of this notion is that because the brain is *necessary* to produce the products of consciousness, the brain is also *sufficient* to produce the products of consciousness. There can be no film-story without the film, and no life-story without the brain, but the film-story is not the film or its molecular constituents, and the life-story is not the brain or its anatomy and chemically mediated synapses.

The integration of the "two separate universes" that Murch alludes to—and from which Jaspers's epistemological distinction between *understanding* and *explanation* derives—is the Holy Grail to those who wish to go beyond a reductive approach in capturing the meaning of human existence, be it normal or pathological. The question now is, How far can this integration go? Some of the most frequently heard reasons offered to account for psychiatry's inability to find a "unified theory" of mental illness include the following:

Psychiatry has not reached its maturity. "Unlike other medical specialties," Paul R. McHugh is fond of saying, "psychiatry is a discipline that has yet to come of age." But, considering that psychiatry issues from a paradigm shaped by the DSM, the "broken brain part," the "chemical imbalance" and behavioral data manipulated by statistics, what kind of "maturity" could psychiatry realistically be expected to achieve?

Psychiatry does not yet have its periodic table. A "periodic table" is unlikely in psychiatry because there is nothing "periodic" about the defensive reactions or brain diseases that constitute mental illness that is analogous to the periodicity of adding electrons to unfilled orbitals of elements of increasing atomic mass as happens, going from left to right and top to bottom, in the periodic table. Perhaps the closest we could come to "periodicity" in psychiatric classification and diagnosis would be to establish a *hierarchy of defenses*—Meyerian maladaptive reactions—that reflect the nature and degree of the pathological transformation behind the phenomenon of each mental illness that is characterized in the FDMI. This would be a major advance.

Psychiatry has not yet found its William Osler. We believe that psychiatry *had* its William Osler in Adolf Meyer. Because psychiatry does not derive strictly from medicine, creating a valid paradigm for psychiatry is not, so to speak, as straightforward a mission as in other medical disciplines. Regrettably, Meyer did not leave us with a psychiatric equivalent of Osler's *The Principles and Practice of Medicine*, which could have been a cynosure that solidified psychobiology as psychiatry's ultimate paradigm.

Temporizations such as these are really leveraged *beliefs* that the integration of the "two separate universes" *will* occur. Such convictions persist in spite of the fact that the abundance of empirical evidence accumulated so far—both during the explosion of neuroscience and psychopharmacology that began in the 1960s and, at a slower pace, during the century before that—is not reassuring on this point. No one, it seems, has ever been able to put Humpty Dumpty, in any of his iterations, back together again.[1]

It is far from certain that knowing more about how the brain works would tell us significantly more about how *we* work, yet that supposition has become a major trope of our time. In an Op-ed article for *The New York Times*, the Baylor College of Medicine neuroscientist David Eagleman insisted that "Learning to better speak the language of the brain is our best hope for turning the chaos into order, for unmasking and addressing the hidden patterns behind disease" (Eagleman 2013). The message here is: the money spent so far for brain research on mental illness has been worth it, and we need to keep spending more. To many scientists and citizens, the thought that this scenario may not be right is unthinkable and unbearable.

The DSM-5 became the standard for diagnosing psychiatric illness during a time when neuroscience was producing data that were expected to *explain* psychiatric symptoms (in the Jasperian sense). But, contrary to that expectation, the DSM's checklists of mostly behavioral symptoms did not point the way to biological "explanations" that identified "broken brain parts" or "chemical imbalances." No unique pathophysiology has been identified for any mental illness. Neither the

1 Meyer's psychobiology does not attempt to amalgamate these polar-opposite ways of looking at the human organism. On the contrary, Meyer insists that the only way to achieve a Jasperian *understanding/explanation* of what we separate when we use the words *mind* and *brain* is to not create these disparate "universes" in the first place, but rather to study the person as one integrated biopsychosocial unit from the start.

original justification for, nor the goal of the DSM's atheoretical classification and diagnostic system based on symptoms of unspecified meaning has been realized.

The fact is that a clinician using the DSM-5 isn't required either to understand or explain (in the Jasperian sense) the symptoms that comprise a mental illness. But no *understanding* + no *explanation* = no validity! And that is where psychiatric diagnosis stands now.

Chapter 5 The Four Domains of Mental Illness

Hoping to open a path to a valid and reliable way of diagnosing mental illness—in part by breaking the hammerlock set by the DSM-III, DSM-IV and DSM-5 on meaningless symptoms and the syndromes comprised of these symptoms, a method that *implicitly denies human freedom*—a different way of classifying and diagnosing mental illness is proposed here. Designated as the *Four Domains of Mental Illness*, this approach derives from *The Perspectives of Psychiatry* by Paul R. McHugh and Phillip R. Slavney, which, in turn, is steeped in the psychobiology of Adolf Meyer and the existential phenomenology of Karl Jaspers. *The Perspectives*, which is a refutation of Freudian psychoanalysis, the medical model of mental illness and the DSM. It is descriptive, rather than prescriptive, and was never intended as a guide to classification and clinical diagnosis.

McHugh and Slavney distinguished four types of mental illness based on how these illnesses are believed to originate to the extent that this provenance can be gauged given our limited knowledge. In the FDMI, each of the four perspectives implies a corresponding pathological domain, a lived space created and inhabited by someone with a mental illness. We capture in these domains what is *seen* from each perspective, allowing a clinician to access and assess the patient's *lived experience* (Muller 2015a). J. H. van den Berg (1972) characterized the domain of someone with a mental illness as a "different existence." That difference is what a diagnosis—a word that has Greek roots and means to *know completely*—invites the clinician to understand and explain.

Identifying the Phenomenon of a Mental Illness

To be valid, a diagnosis must identify and characterize a real phenomenon, which is something that exists in itself, can be apprehended by our senses and is distinguishable from other phenomena. The existential philosopher Martin Heidegger defined a phenomenon as that which shows itself as itself. The word derives from the Greek *phainesthai*, which in Medard Boss's rendition is "to shine forth, to appear, unveil itself, come out of concealment or darkness" (Boss 1963, p. 28). That "clearing"—Heidegger's word—becomes, again quoting Boss, "the unconditional place for the appearance and emergence of everything that is" (Heidegger 2001, pp. xx–xxi).

The FDMI identifies and characterizes the *phenomena* behind the most common mental illnesses. Checklists of signs and symptoms are largely eschewed in favor of *descriptions of phenomena* that underlie what can be thought of as the deviant "style"—a component of van den Berg's "different existence"—manifested by someone with a particular illness.

Many characterizations of the mental illnesses parsed in the FDMI include an "exemplar" of the phenomenon of the illness. A phenomenological analysis (Appendix A) of these real life-stories, which embody elements constituting the phenomenon of the illness, and are common to all presentations of the illness, reveal the phenomenon's *general structure*: what makes it uniquely *that* illness. Exemplars are not the familiar "vignettes," derived from patients' stories, which are often used to illustrate a certain kind of pathology. The discussion that comes later in this chapter about what we are calling the "ontic-ontological divide" should help to clarify this point: vignettes are limited to the ontic, while exemplars elicit the ontological. The FDMI exemplars also go beyond the "prototypes" that were considered by the DSM-5 Task Force to replace syndromes of symptoms for diagnosing personality disorders (this tack was ultimately abandoned).

Symptoms are manifestations of pathological phenomena and are not unique to any mental illness. It is in determining the *meaning* of a symptom—by gathering the Meyerian "facts" of the patient's life-story and identifying the Meyerian "maladaptive reactions" to difficult life situations—that we begin to understand how this symptom, plus other symptoms of known or partially known meaning, comprise the phenomenon that is the patient's mental illness. Meyer thought of this process as "formulating" a diagnosis. (It is ironic that the DSM-III, DSM-IV and DSM-5, which are *anti*-phenomenological in this existential sense, repeatedly use the word phenomenology to signify *symptoms that have been shorn of their meaning*.)

We do not disparage using symptoms in psychiatric diagnosis per se. Lists of symptoms of a mental illness, like those found in the DSM-5, may be kept in mind as the process of getting a patient's unique story goes forward. But no symptom should be taken at face value, without understanding its meaning in the context of the story being told. Information from persons who know the patient, or details gleaned from the patient's psychiatric and medical history should also be scrutinized in this way and considered in making a diagnosis and deciding on a course of action.

The approach taken in the FDMI implies that psychiatry has already acquired more wisdom than many in the profession would care to acknowledge, particularly those who insist that the ultimate explanation for any mental illness depends on identifying some damaged component of the brain's neural substrate.

Some Different Terminology

In moving from an approach that relies almost solely on the evidence of symptoms for making a psychiatric diagnosis to the FDMI, which requires that a patient *embody the phenomenon of a mental illness*, some changes in terminology are in order.

- Jaspers's epistemological distinction between the two ways of knowing a mental illness—through *understanding* and *explanation*—is used in the FDMI to designate what can be learned from the human sciences and from the natural sciences about someone who is mentally ill. Keeping this distinction in mind helps us to grasp the uniqueness of Meyer's psychobiology.

- The term *mental disorder* has a strong association with the DSM and is used here only when referring to diagnoses already characterized in this way by the DSM-III, DSM-IV and DSM-5. It must be acknowledged that long before the DSM-III, Meyer embraced this term. Nonetheless, we prefer to speak of *mental illnesses*, at least when it comes to the psychic pathology of the first three domains.
- Bipolar disorder was first designated as such in the DSM-III (1980). In the FDMI, the older appellation, manic-depression, as used by Meyer and others, will be revived, signaling a break with the misconceptions about—and the numerous wrong diagnoses of—this condition spawned by the DSM checklist of behavioral criteria and an implied chemical imbalance/broken brain part.
- Illnesses of the 1st, 2nd and 3rd domains are considered to originate in *pathological maladaptive reactions*. This term was chosen, with a nod to Meyer's "reaction-type," because *reaction* signifies both a *response to a stimulus and the behavioral change that results from this pathological response*. Though this reaction is primarily a dynamic process, the brain neural substrate is necessarily involved: common sense tells us that the brain is involved in *any* act of consciousness. Some pathological choices may become psychobiological stressors of sufficient strength to alter the brain's structure and function. The distinction being attempted here between a *pathological maladaptive reaction* (1st, 2nd and 3rd domains) and a *mental disease* (4th domain) comes down to the relative psychological and biological contributions in the dialectical formulation of a mental illness or mental disease, to the extent that these distinctions can be validly made. Our knowledge about the causative role of biology in even the most common mental illnesses and diseases is limited, and we should not attempt to say more than we know.
- Fourth domain pathologies will be called *mental diseases* to signify that a compromised brain neural substrate *may* be the primary driving force behind these conditions. In mental diseases, consciousness is still operative, but freedom is restricted by biology so the range of choices open to the affected person is considerably narrowed relative to someone who does not have a mental disease, or even someone with an illness of the 1st, 2nd or 3rd domains. The existential psychologist Robert Romanyshyn (2012) has called this restricted freedom "bounded freedom."

Using the terms *pathological maladaptive reaction* and *mental disease* as defined here has the potential to attenuate, though by no means eliminate, the Cartesian divide between mind and brain, which has been a historic hindrance to understanding and treating all pathological alterations in mental life.

The Four Domains of Mental Illness

Dividing mental illness into four domains allows a "first cut" to be made in parsing the varieties of psychopathological phenomena. This differentiation is based on the presumed etiology of each illness, specifically on the relative contributions of what we so imprecisely yet so insistently distinguish as mind and brain.

Neuropsychiatrists have named the sequence believed to be involved in the production of a mental illness from abnormal brain function and structure *emergence*, distinguishable from *cause*, which implies a solo contribution of biology to the generation of a disease. The modern notion of emergence was prefigured in Meyer's psychobiology as a dialectical interaction of mind and body:

> We know, of course, that in these reactions which we know as mental, the brain forms the central link at work, although we know but little of the detailed working. . . . [A]s soon as we pass from the simple representative reactions such as sensations and thoughts, to the affective reactions, emotions, and actions, we get a distinct participation of the work of glands, of circulation, of respiration and muscular adjustments, so that organs serving *as such* . . . enter as intrinsic parts into emotions, appetites, instincts, and actions, so as to form the concrete *conduct and behavior*, which is the main thing deranged in our patients (Meyer 1908a).

Meyer's words go a long way toward convincing us that the mind-body distinction is essentially a false one, a legacy of the Cartesian dualism that marks and limits a good deal of Western thinking and behavior, and undermines psychiatry's efforts to understand and remediate mental illness. It seems as if, since Descartes, we have been struggling to put the "Humpty-Dumpty" of the lost mind-body-world unity achieved by the Greeks back together again, without much success. Meyer's psychobiology shares with the work of existential psychiatrists and philosophers introduced here the goal of recognizing and preserving the "oneness" of every person's experience. Scott D. Churchill, professor of psychology at the University of Dallas, has found simple words to show us what the often misunderstood phenomenological approach (explicit, to different degrees, in the existentialists; implicit in Meyer) is all about: "Unlike any analysis which seeks to divide the phenomenon into its presumably separate parts and then to reassemble the whole from these parts, the phenomenological method is an attempt to apprehend the parts from the point of view of the whole" (Churchill 2014). We can't put Humpty Dumpty back together again, but we can prevent him from falling off his wall in the first place.

By analogy with the gene and its genome, we hesitantly introduce here the tongue-resisting neologism *domainome*—more specifically the Meyerian Domainome—the four-branched array of maladaptive reactions, physiological derangements and brain diseases that comprise the world of mental illness as characterized in the FDMI.

Meyer insisted that most mental illnesses *emerge* out of lives dynamically rather than *impinge* on them biologically and were not brain diseases but psychogenic alterations in mental life, though always accompanied by some biological correlate. He uses *impinge* in much the same way that modern neuropsychiatrists use *emerge* to describe the production of psychiatric symptoms from a structurally and functionally altered brain substrate.

Here, in his own words, is Meyer's overarching view of the etiology of mental illness, which influences the approach taken in both *The Perspectives of Psychiatry* and the FDMI:

> As we study anomalies of mental activity and conduct we find some plainly due to extrapsychological events, for instance, happenings in the brain, such as vascular occlusions with consequent softenings or inflammatory processes, or simple senile atrophy, or intoxications; that is, conditions which in their etiology, evolution and outcome are clinched in terms of physiology and pathology of the nutrition and vascular apparatus of the brain. There are, however, other disorders in which the circulatory and nutritional facts are merely incidental, and which we find best expressed in terms of mental events or reactions and their consequences. As such I should mention the results of emotional shock or of emotional fretting, or of continued uncorrected and unchecked false reasoning. Since in these conditions certain infra-psychic biological reactions are frequently found to be at fault as well, through incidental loss of sleep, and malnutrition, etc., the physician is inclined to over-rate them in his psychophobia and, finally, to *assume* these sub-cerebral conditions as the noumenal or 'real' cause, even when he does not *find* them or has nothing whatever to work on (Meyer 1908b).

Meyer's division here is between 4th domain brain diseases and, essentially, all other mental illnesses. Meyer also distinguishes the *biological causes* of mental illnesses from the *biological correlates* of psychological illnesses. He understood the latter as the consequence of "infra-psychic biological reactions," the biological components of maladaptive psychological reactions.

The distinction between a mental disease and a mental illness was conserved in the DSM-I (1952), which was strongly influenced by Meyerian psychobiology, even as Freud's psychoanalysis was becoming psychiatry's new paradigm, and was slated to underlie the DSM-II (1968). In the current medical model of mental illness, all psychiatric illnesses are seen and treated as brain diseases, with the result that biological *correlates* are often wrongly taken to be biological *causes*. In some ways, little has changed since Meyer's time.

There is a direct evolutionary link between a) the distinction Meyer made between mental diseases that impinge on a person, from the outside, so to speak, and mental illnesses that emerge from a person's maladaptive reactions to difficult life circumstances and setbacks, what I like to think of as Meyer's two proto-perspectives (1908b); b) the extension and refinement of this division from two perspectives to four by McHugh and Slavney in *The Perspectives of Psychiatry*; and c) in the FDMI, the elaboration of these four *perspectives* into the more existentially tangible and phenomenologically explicit four *domains*.

A Significant Point of Divergence Between the FDMI and the Perspectives of Psychiatry

The four categories of mental illness that are differentiated in *The Perspectives of Psychiatry* are conserved in the FDMI. So is the designation of *disease* (1st perspective, 4th domain; in the FDMI, the *order* of the 1st and 4th perspectives/domains is interchanged so as to recognize the primacy of anxiety in the creation of most mental illnesses). However, we believe that parsing the 2nd, 3rd and 4th perspectives as *dimension*, *behavior* and *story*, as is done in *The Perspectives*, does not adequately differentiate or characterize the illnesses constituting these perspectives or their corresponding domains.

Consider: *all* that can be called human, whether normal or aberrant, is eventually manifested as behavior; *all* behavior is dimensional, which is to say that all behavior falls along a continuum from normal to aberrant; *all* behavior can be parsed as a series of stories that ultimately allow us to understand the shape of our lives, and also provide clinicians with a starting point for therapeutic intervention.

In the FDMI, what constitutes the *essence* of the dimension, behavior and story perspectives is recast as brief *descriptions* of three different, though sometimes interdependent, *types* of defensive psychobiological *reaction*—Meyer's term, signifying both the active participation of the person undergoing the reaction and the pathological change incurred.

Having myself been confounded (if only briefly) by the dimension-behavior-story way of distinguishing and elaborating the 2nd, 3rd and 4th perspectives (1st, 2nd and 3rd domains), I can only wonder if other clinicians have experienced similar difficulty. Perhaps this hurdle accounts, at least in part, for the reluctance of many mental health professionals to adopt the perspectives approach. In an evaluation of an article previewing the FDMI that I submitted to a psychiatric journal, a reviewer recalled this comment made by a colleague: "Well, the people at Hopkins may be smart enough to use these ideas, but I am not." I reject the notion that potential users of *The Perspectives* are not "smart enough" to understand its essential correctness. On the other hand, the FDMI's reimagining of the perspectives approach should make this later iteration of Meyerian psychiatry easier to grasp and use.

Meyerian Reaction-Types

The Meyerian reaction-types may be the closest we can get to, as Plato put it, "carving nature at its joints," by which he meant recognizing real distinctions that exist in nature, from which a good taxonomy can be made (Campbell, O'Rourke & Slater 2012). (In the parlance of phenomenology, this means identifying phenomena and distinguishing these phenomena from other phenomena and from epiphenomena.) Meyer's reaction-types are fundamentally different ways that people, through maladaptation to life's circumstances, come to deviate from consensual common sense in ways that lead to mental illness.

Each of the first three domains in the FDMI encompasses a different array of reaction-types, distinguished by what the self as active agent is reacting *to*, and *how*, it reacts.

The First Domain: Pathological Reactions Originating in Failures to Meet Life's Challenges and Recover From Setbacks

Because, for the FDMI, it seemed sensible (in the spirit of Meyer's trademark common sense) to consider the most prevalent mental illnesses first, the order of the domains that derive from the 1st and 4th perspectives were interchanged. This modification also permits the discussion of mental illness to begin with anxiety, rather than with brain diseases as is the case in *The Perspectives*—an advantageous strategy since maladaptive reactions to anxiety are generally seen as the root of all psychobiogenic illness. This switch was previously made by Chisolm and Lyketsos (2012) in their book *Systematic Psychiatric Evaluation: A Step-by-Step Guide to Applying "The Perspectives of Psychiatry."* Of course, clinicians must still rule out the more biologically based 4th domain causes of altered mental states before diagnosing pathological reactions of the 1st, 2nd and 3rd domains.

Reactions of the 1st domain are rooted in maladaptive responses to the anxiety that is inherent in stressful life events and negative experiences. These reactions include the multiple pathological manifestations of anxiety itself, phobias, agoraphobia, panic, post-traumatic stress and obsessive-compulsion, as well as depression, psychotic reactions and chronic anger. First domain illnesses can be thought of as maladaptive psychobiogenic responses made to life events by those who are unwilling or unable to make the kind of heroic response that Nietzsche outlined in *The Will to Power*—the necessity of overcoming the negative experiences, some small, others not, that we encounter as we live, love and work. Those who are more psychobiologically vulnerable because of a constitutional weakness of the 2nd domain are more likely to undergo 1st domain reactions in the face of psychological pressure.

To survive and prosper, it is sometimes necessary to rewrite one's life narrative and permit other arcs to enter and drive the story. The success of cognitive behavioral therapy (CBT) could be considered evidence that the negative thoughts, feelings and acts of those who have not accomplished this task evolve into the psychological deficits that must ultimately be overcome if mental health is to be regained.

The Second Domain: Pathological Reactions Occurring in the Context of Aberrant Personality Development and Temperament

We are not all born equally endowed with an intellect that favors a successful development and a fulfilling life. We do not all have the same advantages of parental and social support. We do not all achieve the developmental milestones that allow us to meet the next life challenge, and the ones that come after that. Most tellingly, not everyone develops the capacity to self-soothe in the face of negative experience so as to become resilient to the continuing blows and setbacks that are certain to follow.

Some conditions in our lives must be "good enough," in the Winnicott sense, for that to happen: we must have made a certain minimum number of positive responses to what was both good and deficient in our experience. William James, anticipating the 20th-century experts on development, caught the essence of what it means *not* to have the right resources at the right time: "the timely age goes by in a sort of starvation of objects [resources] and the individual grows up with gaps in his psychic constitution which future experiences can never fill" (Barzun 1983, p. 274). Some psychobiological deficits become lifetime companions.

People with these deficits who develop brittle selves may choose, or fall prey to, Meyerian maladaptive reactions in response to the anxiety that accompanies situations that chance and choice create. Some will be unable to control their impulses and may react explosively to events that most people learn to handle creatively. Some will lack the learned capacity to self-soothe and become hyperactive or easily distracted during everyday tasks that require focused attention. Others will develop pathological personality styles (personality disorders in the DSM-5), lasting patterns of thought, emotion and behavior that bring pain to them and those they interact with.

Meyer saw these individuals as "constitutionally undersupplied." He thought that a person's "constitutional make-up" depended on many influences, all interrelated, where, in some individuals, one or more factors could be identified as being predominantly contributory. Meyer believed that genetic heredity—what comes through from RNA to DNA to make the proteins that are the building blocks of our bodies—greatly influences the kind of person anyone becomes. But he also felt that most mental illnesses were not directly *caused* by this kind of genetic transmission, though some were. (Meyer would be appalled by the emphasis researchers in biological psychiatry put on heredity in the mental illnesses they are studying now.)

To Meyer, for most people, including those who become mentally ill, early childhood experience—the environment provided by parents or parent substitutes—was more important. What the infant, and then the growing child, receives by way of nurture—what might be thought of as psychobiological validation—and how he adapts (or maladapts) to this experience, whether forming good habits or bad habits, combined with what nature has provided in the genetic throw of the dice, are the most significant influences (Lamb 2014, p. 94).

Some who are constitutionally undersupplied will displace (perhaps polarize would be a better word) their psychological pain more to the biological side of the psychobiological unity. In this process, mental pain is attributed to a bodily defect and experienced as physical pain, leading to what has come to be known as somaticization or psychosomatic illness.

Many people with constitutional deficits develop temperaments that are not conducive to personal fulfillment or professional success, and consequently find themselves on the outside looking in. They possess too much or too little of one trait or another, or rely too much or too little on other people. This imbalance will prevent them from achieving what they aim for, often leading to frustration, anxiety and disturbed mood. Some, chronically caught in the throes of their frustration, will never find an emotional "center" to which they can retreat and regroup when the going gets rough. They find it difficult to control their impulses and thus develop (Meyerian) bad habits around their disinhibition. The result is often troubled relations with others, including violence, leading to what the DSM calls impulse-control disorders.

The Third Domain: Pathological Reactions Originating in Willed, Self-Gratifying, Self-Destructive Behavior

Those with illnesses of the 1st and 2nd domains are especially prone to developing 3rd domain conditions as well. Brittle selves are more likely to choose a self-destructive behavior, which, paradoxically, temporarily "soothes" anxiety and agitation. In this process, a life distortion occurs that portends misery that will far exceed the person's original distress.

Alcohol abuse, drug abuse, too much or too little control over eating, abnormal sexual behavior, self-cutting, uncontrolled gambling and kleptomania are some of the 3rd domain defenses that a brittle self may command while attempting to lessen its pain.

Freud wondered why patients choose one defense over another, and we are still asking that question today.

The Fourth Domain: *1st Stipulation*: Altered Mental States Due to a Known Physiological Imbalance or Medical Illness; *2nd Stipulation*: Primary Mental Diseases Emerging From a Putative Altered Brain Substrate

Altered brain physiology is known to cause delirium and to produce anxiety and depression, as well as the psychiatric symptoms of many neuropsychiatric diseases. The pathophysiology of some organic conditions (electrolyte imbalance) and diseases (tertiary syphilis) is well understood. The altered mental states that accompany delirium—with its myriad origins—give us a genuine sense of how known "chemical imbalances" can cause psychiatric symptoms.

Conditions owing to arrested psychobiological development of the brain—autism, mental retardation and learning disabilities—come under the 4th domain because of the likely primary role of biology and in some instances of heredity in creating these conditions. Physiologically induced anxiety and depression fall here as well.

Though empirical studies have uncovered functional and structural anomalies in the brains of those affected by many primary mental illnesses, no specific anomaly has yet been identified that satisfactorily explains any of these illnesses. Nonetheless schizophrenia and manic-depression are widely believed to be related to damaged components of the neural substrate that supports mental life, and are considered to be putative brain diseases in the FDMI.

While realizing that biology underlies all human activity, healthy or pathological, for some people who have been given what appears to be a solid diagnosis of schizophrenia, traumatic influences, especially those incurred during infancy and early childhood, can be seen as the psychobiogenic cause of the transformation that takes them from reality to psychosis. This is the case in the first, second and fourth detailed, and very different, clinical narratives that appear in Chapter 14 (in the third narrative, no information on Kim's early development was accessible to us). We simply do not know what the relative contributions of "mind" and "brain" are to any case of schizophrenia, to make heuristic use of an ultimately invalid distinction.

Manic-depression presents an even greater quandary for classification and diagnosis. The psychodynamics of the manic-depressive are not as well understood as the dynamic defenses of the schizophrenic. As in schizophrenia, there is as yet no biological explanation (in the Jasperian sense) that can stand as a cause in manic-depression.

The FDMI Is a Radical Departure From the DSM-5

Compared with the DSM-5, the FDMI is radical in two ways. First, our approach, which identifies the phenomenon underlying an observed aberration of thought, emotion or behavior goes to the root of the disturbance, to its essence, its origin (*radical* derives from the Latin *radicalis*, meaning root). Second, the FDMI is radical in the sense that it is "extreme," which is to say it goes all out to understand the *context* in which a pathological alteration in mental life has occurred. The approach taken in the FDMI represents a paradigm shift in diagnosing psychic pathology. This difference is demonstrated in Chapter 17 where I go through the steps of a Meyerian diagnosis for a patient I worked with for 21 months, comparing this result with the decidedly wrong diagnosis previously made by another clinician, who followed the DSM-IV and psychiatry's medical model.

The DSM-III, DSM-IV and DSM-5 were modeled on the idea of Emil Kraepelin (1856–1926) that mental illnesses were *categorical* disease entities, syndromes comprised of *symptoms* that demarcate one illness from another. (Hence the Venn diagrams that show the "overlap" of symptoms and the "comorbidity" for different illnesses.) The FDMI, in contrast, is based on a *dimensional* model of mental illness, which sees thought, emotion and behavior as falling along a continuum from normal to aberrant, where pathology is defined as a phenomenon that occurs beyond certain points in that continuum. Rather than speaking of comorbidity, the FDMI identifies *reactions from the first three domains and more biologically based conditions from the 4th domain* that could be contributing to what is ultimately *one* mental illness.

Just how different the FDMI is from the DSM can be appreciated when we recall that schizophrenia, alcoholism and PTSD were all considered Axis I disorders in the DSM-IV, while in the FDMI, schizophrenia falls in the 4th domain (2nd stipulation: putative altered brain substrate leading to a mental disease); alcoholism in the 3rd domain (willed choice of self-destructive behavior); and PTSD in the 1st domain (failure to meet life's challenges and recover from setbacks) (McHugh 2012). Though the DSM-5, which is similar in most respects to the DSM-IV, dispenses with multi-axial distinctions, schizophrenia, alcoholism and PTSD are all considered brain diseases in this 5th edition, which is not so in the FDMI.

It should be obvious that patients diagnosed using the FDMI approach would think differently about themselves and their problems than if they had been diagnosed using the behavioral criteria of the DSM-5. And, most likely, they would receive a different kind of treatment. Flesh is added to the bones of these assertions in Chapter 17, which features a detailed description and analysis of the author's therapeutic work with a man who was crippled by anxiety who had previously been misdiagnosed with bipolar II disorder in accordance with the DSM-IV criteria.

Employing a metaphor that is used in other disciplines as well, our approach is "bottom-up." We begin by trying to understand what a patient's life has been up to by uncovering the facts that comprise the clinical narrative. We then attempt to unveil the meaning of these facts and the maladaptive reactions behind them to establish a chain of causality. Only after the facts and reactions are in hand are we ready to think about how to name and "classify" the difference between this disordered life and one that is not psychologically problematic.

Adolf Meyer, the existential psychiatrists—Ludwig Binswanger, Medard Boss, J. H. van den Berg and R. D. Laing, to name just a few—and *The Perspectives of Psychiatry* authors Paul R. McHugh and Phillip R. Slavney all followed this "bottom-up" approach. In doing so, they also followed Edmund Husserl (1976), Heidegger's teacher, in characterizing phenomena by returning to what Husserl called "the things themselves" (Appendix A). This means starting with the Meyerian "facts" that need to be pulled out of a patient's life-story.

Our tack in the FDMI is 180 degrees from the "top-down" diagnostic path taken by Kraepelin, and in the neo-Kraepelian DSM-III, DSM-IV and DSM-5, where mostly behavioral symptoms of unspecified meaning and origin are "matched" to preconceived, "theoretical" notions of a mental *disease*. (This is the opposite of what Husserl meant by returning to "the things themselves.") In this approach, a "broken brain part" may be said to cause the patient's symptoms (as a spirochete bacterium is known to cause tertiary syphilis), resulting in claims that often devolve into neurobable. In the FDMI, the DSM's "top-down" diagnostic approach of "making criteria" is replaced by a "bottom-up" consideration of which phenomenon (or phenomena) from each of the four domains emerges from a Meyerian formulation of the patient's narrative.

The current tendency of clinicians to overdiagnose schizophrenia posed a particular challenge in creating the FDMI. Some psychotic symptoms may originate as 4th domain *diseases* (putative altered brain substrate leading to a disease). But other psychotic symptoms come from 1st domain *reactions* (failing to meet life's challenges and recover from setbacks) that emerge from aberrations in personality and mood. The DSM-IV, whose editors acknowledged in the introduction that they had "attempted to be neutral with respect to theories of etiology," did not offer clinicians sufficient direction to differentiate these two domains of psychosis. The DSM-5 followed suit.

It was neither helpful to clinicians nor fair to patients that both schizophrenia and brief psychotic disorder were taken to be Axis I disorders in the DSM-III and DSM-IV. Both disorders are still considered to be brain diseases in the DSM-5, which eliminated the inherently false distinction between Axis I and Axis II. Beyond insisting that *all* mental illnesses are brain diseases, the DSM-5 is still "neutral" with respect to the specific cause of any mental illness.

One year before the scheduled 2013 publication of the DSM-5, the Task Force editor in chief, David Kupfer, was asked to comment on a possible role for the Johns Hopkins four perspectives of psychiatry in the new edition. He responded that the perspectives represent:

> a theoretical ideal that, unfortunately, does not fit well with current constraints on psychiatric practice or methods of reimbursement. In the best of all possible worlds, all psychiatrists would have the time to approach patients from this vantage point. However, today's reality is that this can rarely happen, particularly in public systems of care. The well-trained psychiatrist working in such a system of care will draw on these perspectives while using the *DSM* to efficiently arrive at a reliable diagnosis that should lead to appropriate treatment (Edmunds & Small, 2012).

As when he attempted to estimate the role of neuroscience in the DSM-5, cited in Chapter 4 (Kupfer & Regier 2011), Kupfer's airy prose here slips and slides. He ignores the failures of the DSM-III and DSM-IV that were carried forward into the new edition, insisting that the time is not right to think more deeply and validly about the meanings of the symptoms patients present with. In other words, it is still acceptable *not* to distinguish a 1st domain psychotic reaction from a 4th domain psychotic disease because we cannot *afford* to do psychiatry right by validly determining a patient's subjective experience.

The Limits of Categorical Diagnosis

It is generally agreed that relieving a patient's suffering is the primary ethical goal of mental health intervention. This outcome will be more likely to occur if the clinician, during a therapeutic encounter, comes to terms with the pathological phenomenon underlying the patient's pain and dysfunction. In certain instances, however, it will not be possible to match a patient's presentation with a mental illness that has already been identified and characterized. It is better for the patient that we acknowledge this truth than mischaracterize the phenomenon and then proceed with a therapeutic course that follows a false perception of what is wrong.

Not every human experience, whether normal or pathological, is subject to the kind of sharp delineation that marks a discreet phenomenon. It is a corollary of the phenomenological approach to understanding the world that describing something well enough will often reveal its essence and render it intelligible. For some patients, the description of their "different existence" (van den Berg) may be the most accurate "diagnosis" possible, and all that is really necessary to understand what is wrong and decide what needs to be done. Meyer said of a patient whom he had examined: "We understand this case; we don't need any diagnosis" (Watson 1951, p. 22). He urged clinicians to learn as much as possible about a patient and pay attention to the *facts* revealed in the patient's narrative:

> An orderly presentation of the facts alone is a real diagnosis. Wherever facts or groups of facts occur often enough they naturally lead to the formulation of a terminology. With the public and often enough in the physician's mind the diagnostic terms tend, however, to assume an importance out of proportion with the actually correlated facts, and to represent a lofty vantage ground from which the facts are viewed condescendingly as a necessary inadequate illustration. In this way the actual and real foundation is surrendered in favor of frequently unsafe generalities (Meyer 1906b, p. 153).

"What we should act on," Meyer believed, "should be the facts. If the facts [derived from the patient's narrative] do not constitute a diagnosis we must nevertheless act on the facts. To jump from the facts at an arbitrary diagnosis and then to act on that abstract diagnosis is a procedure hardly ever needed in psychiatry, and bound to lead to self-deceit and confusion of the minds of all concerned" (Meyer 1906b, p. 168). Meyer believed that categorical diagnosis à la Kraepelin often amounted to following the line of least resistance, doing what was easy instead of coming to terms with a patient whose disordered life had become problematic:

> A diagnosis usually does justice only to one part of the facts and is merely a convenience of nomenclature. . . . Psychiatry has not reached, and probably never will reach, the stage where a small number of one-word diagnoses would be more than a formal index. It is, of course, convenient to have them, and there is a temptation to discuss the names and write papers about them; but as a rule that does not add much to our knowledge in psychiatry and only helps to undermine our standing beside other branches of medicine. . . (Meyer 1906a).

Ever the closet existentialist, Meyer knew that taking a categorical diagnosis as the last word about a patient's condition would allow the essence of the illness to take precedence over the existence (life) of the patient. (One of Sartre's key notions is that *existence precedes essence.*) In effect, Meyer implicitly urged using the *facts* of a case to identify the *phenomenon* (the essence of the illness) behind the patient's troubled life, then addressing the illness existentially, which is to say by engaging the patient in a therapeutic dialogue. He acknowledged the irresolvable conflict that runs through all Western dichotomized thought: the Cartesian distinction between the essential and the existential, a man-made division that exists only in thought and word, but which has the power, when wrongly reified, to undermine the way we think about anything and everything.

Meyer's *formulation*, as he called it, of a patient's case—establishing how the *bad habits* of living that comprise an illness were acquired—is the "bottom-up" approach to parsing psychic pathology. First, the *facts* are extracted from the patient's story and are then studied to determine their meaning and provenance. These meaningful facts are then used to determine the *reaction-type* that constitutes the patient's pathology (Lamb 2014, pp. 152–160). This is the approach taken in the FDMI, where psychic pathology is "typed" by first distinguishing four domains of mental illness—essentially by cause as far as cause can be understood—then identifying specific reaction-types within the domains.

The phenomena that Meyer's reaction-types point to are limned in the FDMI. For some illnesses, "exemplars," not of the illness but of the *phenomenon* of the illness, are provided. These exemplars are not simply vignettes, which are common in clinicians' writing, but life-stories that are described and analyzed so that the phenomenon of an illness is brought from the concealment of what Husserl called the natural attitude into the light of disclosure.

The formulation of Meyerian reaction-types encompasses an understanding of the choices that people make in the course of situations they create or have thrust upon them by others or by chance, as well as their inherent psychobiological (constitutional) capacity to deal with life's challenges and setbacks. In contrast, biological psychiatry, in league with the DSM-5, works from the "top-down" using checklists of symptoms to designate a mental disorder under the assumption that these symptoms of unknown provenance and meaning are caused by specific, if unidentified, glitches in brain structure and function.

"We should not treat our classifications with too much respect," William James wrote in *The Varieties of Religious Experience* (1902, p. 148). Like Meyer, James saw the danger of losing the reality of a unique person while identifying categories that describe the person's experience. Though he did not explicitly use the term phenomenon, James directed experiments conducted at his Harvard Medical School laboratory toward uncovering phenomena, while insisting that designating categories alone provides only the starting point for understanding anything or anyone. He recognized that no person, sick or healthy, could be grasped as what he called a standard unit.

Creating the FDMI, which identifies the phenomena behind designated mental illnesses and diseases, while insisting that the diagnosis not be the last word about what is going on in a patient's life can be, and has been, criticized as wanting to have one's cake and eat it, too. But in a Cartesian world, where dichotomies are inevitable—and inevitably distorting—having it both ways is often the only way to have it right (Appendix A).

When making a diagnosis, Meyer also asked that clinicians pay attention to the changes that occur as a patient moves from a healthy state to a pathological state, which, he felt, in many instances is more pathognomonic of the illness than any symptoms are. Meyer worried about clinicians "sacrificing [the patient] at the altar of vocabularies dealing with terminal states and with fixed fatalistic 'constitutions' and too dogmatically fixed 'disease entities'" (Meyer 1922).

How many clinicians, under the sway of the last three editions of the DSM and biological psychiatry, have done just that (Muller 2008)? And in spite of a caveat that appears in the introduction to the DSM-IV advising "there is no assumption [made here] that each category of mental disorder is a completely discrete entity with absolute boundaries dividing it from other mental disorders or from no mental disorder" (p. xxii). And yet the DSM-IV proceeded to classify and diagnose mental illness *as if* this were indeed the case. Clinicians followed these directions as if they were carving nature at its joints. The DSM-5 takes essentially the same approach to diagnosis as the two editions that preceded it.

Meyer's psychobiology was a reaction against Kraepelin's excessive biologism and categorization of mental illness, which eventually became the ground that spawned the DSM-III (1980), DSM-IV (1994) and DSM-5 (2013). The FDMI aims to change psychiatry's paradigm once again, this time back to Meyer's conception of what it means to be a human being, in sickness and in health. At heart, Meyer's approach was an American creation that took root in a freer intellectual soil than Meyer had known in Europe, and was influenced by the New World pragmatism of William James, George Herbert Mead and John Dewey (Menand 2001). Meyer thought of his approach to psychiatry as "common sense."

The psychology of William James greatly helped Meyer to develop his philosophical anthropology: the attempt to discover the essence, structure and meaning of the world we live in and through (Appendix A). The "common sense" that Meyer recognized in his psychobiology is of a piece with the concreteness of the existentialists that sharply contrasts with the reductive thinking of the analytical philosophers, who have been the dominant influence on psychiatry and psychology since the mid-19th century. Kierkegaard famously remarked that reading Hegel, the most prominent of the 19th-century analytical philosophers, was like reading from a cookbook to a starving man—which puts us in mind of how it often feels when we try to use the DSM to diagnose someone who presents with a problematic mental life. Though he was not an official member of the existential movement in European psychiatry, Adolf Meyer ultimately must be considered an existentialist.

The French psychoanalyst Marguerite Séchehaye, who was strongly influenced by the thinking of the European existential psychiatrists and by Sartre, captured the goal of the FDMI going forward when she succinctly described her approach to exploring the mind of her patients as "discovering the why of observed phenomena, the *function of the illness* and the purpose it serves the patient" (Séchehaye 1956, p. 107).

Realizing that the mind never operates independently from the brain, or from the rest of the body either, we hope to create with the FDMI an approach that is valid and reliable, with demarcations of mental illness that help us to accurately and reproducibly *see* the meaning, and intuit the origin of our patients' "different existence."

Clinicians who are willing to jump paradigms to use the FDMI will have a learning curve to contend with. Those trained in the way of the DSM and the "chemical imbalance" have a good deal to acquire from what psychiatry has already learned going back more than a century, a trove now largely declared irrelevant by the mental health profession (a good deal of this background is provided here). Furthermore, the burden for making a correct diagnosis will fall more squarely and heavily on the shoulders of practitioners who can no longer dodge that responsibility by appealing to checklists of symptoms and unspecified glitches in brain neurotransmission.

No approach to understanding human behavior, or system emerging from that approach, is perfect. Erik Erikson said of the eight stages of psychosocial development he characterized in *Childhood and Society* (1963) that this way of looking at epigenesis is for readers who can take it *and* leave it. Erikson understood that these stages do not constitute the whole story about human development. The same could be said of the four domains of mental illness: while we believe that this differentiation is valid, the approach taken in the FDMI will not always give us a satisfying picture of why someone is mentally ill. Meyer had misgivings about categorical diagnosis in psychiatry, and, even as we use this classification and diagnostic guide created from his psychobiology, we need to make his reservation our own.

The Range of Existential "Normalcy" and the Meyerian Pathological Reaction

"Every life is, more or less, a ruin among whose debris we have to discover what the person ought to have been." This deflating observation was offered by the

Spanish existential philosopher José Ortega y Gasset in *The Dehumanization of Art* (1956, pp. 132–133). Who among even the most "normal" of us would disagree with this assessment of our condition? It is impossible to write the word *normal* here without the quotation marks that signify the irony of what this word actually signifies.

To understand mental illness we must first try to come to terms with what *relative* normalcy is and then discover how a transformed pathological world spawns a life—a "different existence," as van den Berg called it—that diverges from the *relatively* free, *relatively* authentic life of someone who is not mentally ill. Making this distinction entails being able to distinguish existential suffering from pathological suffering. Recalling Ortega, we need to know what *kind* of ruin one has made of a life: whether or not pathological transformations have occurred in that process and, if so, the nature and extent of these transformations.

Karl Jaspers's "Ultimate Situations"

Jaspers has provided us with a detailed account of the basic struggle we engage in simply by living, and the limits of our human condition that make this struggle inevitable. At times, the situations that evolve because of these limits—what Jaspers calls *ultimate situations*—seem to mock our idea of being even relatively free and make us feel more like victims than players on the stage of life. As Jaspers wrote in *Way to Wisdom* (1954):

> We are always in situations. I myself can work to change the situation. But there are situations which remain essentially the same even if their momentary aspect changes and their shattering force is obscured: I must die, I must suffer, I must struggle, I am subject to chance, I involve myself inexorably in guilt. We call these fundamental situations of our existence ultimate situations. That is to say, they are situations which we cannot evade or change. . . . In our day-to-day lives we often [try to] evade them, by closing our eyes and living as if they did not exist. We forget that we must die, forget our guilt, and forget that we are at the mercy of chance. . . . [W]e react either by obfuscation or, if we really apprehend them, by despair and rebirth: we become ourselves by a change in our consciousness of being (pp. 19–20).

In an ultimate situation, we encounter an inescapable issue. We cannot eliminate it: we can only deal with the situation, or deny it. Of course, dealing with an ultimate situation requires us to accept its attendant *existential* anxiety and pain. But in refusing to take this risk, we set ourselves up for a more insidious *pathological* anxiety and pain by employing one defense or another against the situation.[1]

1 Defining and characterizing these ultimate situations was one of Jaspers's major contributions to existential philosophy and existential psychiatry. In some translations of his texts, ultimate situation is translated from the original German *Grenzsituation* as *boundary* situation (*Philosophy, Vol. 2*, 1970). This is a helpful but confusing metaphor, as boundary is widely used now to designate the emotional and physical distance that is to be maintained between therapist and patient.

When successfully worked through, the temporary "despair" that Jaspers sees as a potential consequence of experiencing the existential anxiety and pain of an authentic encounter with an ultimate situation may lead to a "rebirth" in which we "become ourselves" by coming to know our own life, the lives of others, and the reality of the world around us. This renaissance enlarges our existence and roots us more firmly in the ground of being. In this process, we become psychobiologically stronger and, therefore, less likely to employ pathological defenses in facing the challenges that follow.

No one has the strength or tenacity—or the time, for that matter—to continuously meet existence full-on in this way. A certain amount of denial is necessary to avoid being paralyzed by the often disturbing *truth* of our lives. The best we can do is to embrace our ultimate situations as they present themselves. In the absence of major contravening factors, this openness to what our life is about will allow a degree of psychobiological integration and development that is sufficient to support a relatively authentic life going forward. As with freedom, our realization of authenticity cannot be absolute and is necessarily relative.

It could be argued that all psychobiogenic pathology originates in inauthentic responses made to universal ultimate situations (loss, suffering, illness, mortality, death) and to ultimate situations unique to each person (for the most part, the consequences of an individual's choices and actions). Many of the 1st domain pathological reactions that we are about to survey emerge from Meyer's maladaptive reactions to Jaspers's ultimate situations.

Some of these reactions occur when a person's ultimate situation includes a significant change in meaning in that person's life. That the meanings attaching to all we encounter inevitably change over time does not diminish the fact that meaning influences everything we feel and drives everything we do. William James made it clear in *The Principles of Psychology* that the *mutability* of meaning is part of the ordinary flux of human experience:

> From one year to another we see things in new lights. What was unreal has grown real, and what was exciting is insipid. The friends we used to care the world for are shrunken to shadows; the women, once so divine, the stars, the woods, and the waters, how now so dull and common; the young girls that brought an aura of infinity, at present hardly distinguishable existences; the pictures so empty; and so for the books, what *was* there to find so mysteriously in Goethe or in John Mill so full of weight? (James 1904, p. 233).

Because, moment to moment, we are forced to use our freedom to create ourselves, it is not certain that we will respond adaptively (authentically) to the often anxiety-inducing changes in meaning that occur as we pursue this creation, often blindly. Alternatively, we may invoke one of Meyer's "faulty reactions." We still do not know why, under the influence of anxiety, people succumb to one defensive reaction or another, creating the pathology that clinicians eventually diagnose and treat. Freud also struggled with this question—calling it the "choice of neurosis"—changing his mind and his theory several times, never coming to a conclusion that satisfied him or anyone else (Sulloway 1983).

The Ontic, the Ontological and the Ontic-Ontological Divide

Adolf Meyer did not succeed in keeping psychobiology alive by passing it on to the next generation. The most commonly heard explanation for this failure is that he left no rigorous, systematic formulation of his approach to classifying, diagnosing and treating mental illness that could be taught and learned by those who came after him. McHugh and Slavney took a step toward that goal in *The Perspectives of Psychiatry*. A further step in this direction is being taken with *The Four Domains of Mental Illness*.

Meyer's voluminous writings mostly record individual and personal facets of his clinical cases. After eliciting from patients their life-stories and extracting the "facts" that constitute these narratives, he formulated (his term) what he cautiously called a diagnosis. Meyer's avoidance of developing the "general case"—a reduction of many similar patients' clinical stories to a diagnostic category—is seen by his detractors as a lack of rigor and structure and as a weakness.

The philosophical term *ontic* pretty much captures the scope and limit of Meyer's focus. Erik Craig describes the ontic dimension as "how we and all other particular beings show up in or lives, right here, right now." The ontic is personal, individual, specific. It is the story of how we ply our freedom, making the choices that weave the fabric of our lives. "Such everyday particular being is the human context wherein we all live and breathe and have our very own once and once only existence" (Craig 2015; Muller 2015b).

Philosophers use the conjugate term *ontological* to designate the universal characteristics that are common to all human beings, what might be thought of as the "general case." Ontology is the study of the structure of being itself—"being as being," as Heidegger said—as extrapolated from the ontic study of individual beings (people). To be considered ontological, according to Craig, a characteristic "must *obtain for every human being in every moment of every human being's existence.*" That we have the capacity to act freely is an ontological characteristic, or property, of human being. In the process of exercising that freedom, as we do when we make decisions and choices, we are acting ontically. While every person is a unique ontic creation, we all share the ontological condition of being human, with its possibilities and limitations.

Craig points to what Heidegger designated and characterized as the *existentials* of human being as the best foundation we have for grasping the ontological nature of any person (Heidegger 1962, p. 70). A partial list, as culled by Craig (2015), is rendered here in colloquial English, with Heidegger's less congenial designations appearing in italics:

> We are all alive, not dead, or never-born (*being-at-all, facticity*); we all have our being in this world (*being-in-the-world, being-there, Dasein*); we all have the capacity to understand something about our lives and the lives of others (*being-understanding-of-Being*); we all live our lives in time (*being-in-time*); we all live our lives in space (*being-in-space*); we are always in a mood, even if we don't realize it (*being-in-a-mood, attunement*); we all have bodies, which are our interface with others and the world (*being-embodied*); we all show

> some degree of care about ourselves and the world we live in and through, though the kind and degree of this caring varies greatly from person to person (*being-as-care, Sorge*); all our lives are co-constructed with others (*being-with-others, Mitsein*); our lives are finite (*being-finite*); our birth is the first step toward an inevitable death (*being-towards-death*).

To this list we should add our inclination to avoid becoming our authentic selves, capitulating instead to what Heidegger calls the influence of the "they"—what others expect us to be—a path that is often less arduous than taking a more self-determined, authentic tack (*being-alongside, falling, inauthenticity*). And we should not forget that we are, as Heidegger says, always "ahead of ourselves," which is to say on the way, never the same person from moment to moment, always in the process of *becoming* ourselves, rather than simply *being* ourselves (*being-ahead-of-itself*).

Heidegger clearly distinguished these *existentials*, or universal ontological characteristics, which identify our possibilities and limitations as human beings, from anything that could be considered *categories*, which serve to merely divide and group certain aspects of the world we live in and through. The *existentials* are the *properties* of human being that are common to everyone. Heidegger, who worked long and hard with the existential psychiatrist Medard Boss to integrate his ontology into psychiatric thinking, said that these properties are the "content" of psychiatry's investigation into mental illness (Heidegger 2001, p. 205). Jaspers's ultimate situations can be thought of as ontic encounters with ontological conditions.

We should not leave Heidegger before saying a few words about his concept of time, captured in the *existential* designations "being-in-time" and "being-ahead-of-itself." A mental illness that comes about through a denial or misuse of human freedom inevitably involves a simultaneous and inseparable mis-living of experiential time (as distinguished from clock time) as well. Healthy, authentic life unfolds in the present, which necessarily (ontologically speaking) pushes into the future. To Heidegger, that we are always "ahead of ourselves" in this way was simply the nature of things. While living a healthy life, operating with Meyer's "good habits," the past is at hand, but mainly as context and informant, not as the principal driver of thought, emotion and action, which is the case for many who are mentally ill. Identifying the different ways, or styles, of living time predominantly in the past, rather than the present, is essential to understanding the maladaptive Meyerian reactions that lead to mental illness.

Though Meyer, in writing about his work with patients, mostly limited himself to the ontic dimension, he did occasionally "jump the hyphen" and cross the ontic-ontological divide (this will become obvious as the FDMI unfolds). In insisting that biological changes occur in *all* maladaptive reactions, he implicitly pushed across the hyphen, into the "bio-ontological" dimension. We could say that Meyer "leaned toward" the ontological, both psychologically and biologically, but not far enough to leave us with a rigorous formulation of his luminous thinking about the nature of mental illness and its treatment.

In the FDMI, the yield of Meyer's mostly personal, *ontic* pragmatism will be combined with the *ontological structures*, whenever identifiable, of the maladaptive reactions parsed in each of the four domains. These structures, which derive from the work of existential philosophers and existential psychiatrists, go a long way toward supplying the rigor that is lacking in the psychobiological formulations Meyer left us.

Finally, we should point out that the ontic-ontological distinction—and the ontic-ontological divide that we identify here—is an invention of philosophers, which is absorbed in the actual living of a life (Heidegger 1962, pp. 32–35). These terms do not represent real entities, but are heuristic devices that help us to see what *is* real, and how our lives come to be what they are. "The question of existence," Heidegger said, "never gets straightened out except through existing itself" (Heidegger 1962, p. 33). Adolf Meyer, a pragmatist, would have agreed.

And he would also have agreed with what Karl Jaspers said in the introduction to his *General Psychopathology* to make clear that his approach to understanding and treating mental illness was not what is known now as biological psychiatry, or the medical model:

> [T]he principle of this book is to present a psychopathology which, in its concept-building, its methods of investigation and general outlook, is not enslaved to neurology and medicine on the dogmatic grounds that 'psychic disorder is cerebral disorder'. Our particular scientific contribution is not to imitate neurology and construct a system with constant cross-references to the brain—this always seems unreal and superficial—but to develop a standpoint from which to investigate the various problems, concepts and relationships within the framework of the psychopathological phenomena themselves (Jaspers 1997, pp. 4–5).

In these two sentences, Jaspers establishes the similarity of his own work, and that of other existential psychiatrists, to Meyer's psychobiology. Could there be a surer starting point for what we hope to achieve with the FDMI?

An Overview of Meyerian Diagnosis

As already noted, rather than "diagnosing" a patient's pathological condition using symptoms as criteria—as Kraepelin did and the DSM-5 now directs clinicians to do—Adolf Meyer preferred to, as he put it, "formulate" the patient's condition. Before going on to Part II, the reader would do well to consider this bullet point overview of his approach:

1. Get the patient's **story**. Listen to what is being said about how and why this life has become problematic. Consult others who are a part of the patient's present situation and past life to get their version of the story.
2. Identify the **facts** that constitute the story. What has changed for the worse in the patient's life? Who are the major players? What is the disappointment, setback or betrayal that could have brought on emotional pain and/or behavioral dysfunction?
3. Identify the chronic **bad habits** that are revealed in the patient's story and the accounts of others who know the patient. Meyer thought of these bad

habits as poor mental hygiene, which inclines a person to react inauthentically and adapt poorly to life experiences. Bad habits could be thought of as pre-pathological antecedents to maladaptive reactions.

4. Identify the **maladaptive reactions** that the patient has made in response to stressful and negative encounters with family members, significant others, friends, work, school, etc. These pathological choices involve a misuse of freedom and often emerge as elaborations of chronic bad habits.
5. Identify the **phenomenon** (or phenomena) underlying the pathological alteration observed in the patient's mental life.

In the chapters ahead, it is shown how, by following this five-step sequence, clinicians can identify and characterize the psychobiological phenomenon (or phenomena) that *is* the patient's mental illness:

Story → Facts → Bad Habits → Maladaptive Reactions → Pathological Phenomenon

Though Meyer did not use the word phenomenon, this concept overlaps implicitly with the endpoint in the Meyerian diagnostic formulation. "Phenomenon" comes from existential psychiatry, an approach to understanding and treating mental illness that is both similar to and complementary to Meyer's approach.

Part II

Classifying and Diagnosing Mental Illness

Map of the Four Domains

1st Domain	2nd Domain	3rd Domain	4th Domain*
Maladaptive Reactions of the 1st Domain Originate in Failures to Meet Life's Challenges and Recover from Setbacks. Biological Factors Contribute but Are Not Primary Causes. (**Stories** in *The Perspectives of Psychiatry*)	Maladaptive Reactions of the 2nd Domain Come About in the Context of Aberrant Personality Development and Temperament. Biological Factors Contribute but Are Not Primary Causes. (**Dimensions** in *The Perspectives of Psychiatry*)	Maladaptive Reactions of the 3rd Domain Are Willed, Self-Gratifying and Ultimately Self-Destructive Acts That Exceed the Limit of What Most People Consider Safe, Sensible and Authentic Behavior. Biological Factors Contribute but Are Not Primary Causes. (**Behaviors** in *The Perspectives of Psychiatry*)	Altered Mental States of the 4th Domain Are Due to 1) Physiological Imbalance, Medical Disease and 2) Primary Mental Diseases Associated With a Putative Altered Brain Substrate. (**Diseases** in *The Perspectives of Psychiatry*)
The Anxiety Spectrum Anxiety Reaction Pervasive Anxiety Reaction Separation Anxiety Reaction Pathological Stress Reaction Agoraphobic Reaction Phobic Reactions Panic Reaction/Panic Attack/ Panic Disorder Post-Traumatic Stress Reaction Obsessive-Compulsive Reaction **The Depression Spectrum** Depressive Reaction Adjustment Reaction Grief Reaction Dysthymic Reaction (Pathological Anger Reaction) **The Dissociation Spectrum** Dissociative Reaction Depersonalization Reaction Dissociative Amnesia Reaction Dissociative Fugue Reaction Dissociative Identity Reaction	**Pathological Personality Styles** Narcissistic Antisocial Borderline Schizoid Schizotypal Histrionic Paranoid Obsessive-compulsive Hypomanic (Hyperthymic) Avoidant **Psychosomatic Reaction** **Hoarding Reaction** **ADHD: A Non-phenomenon**	**Self-Destructive Choices** Alcohol Abuse Drug Abuse Anorexia Nervosa Bulimia Nervosa Abnormal Sexual Behavior Self-cutting Uncontrolled Gambling Kleptomania	1st Stipulation: **Delirium** *Metabolic Causes* Hypoglycemia and hyperglycemia Hyperthyroidism and hypothyroidism Vitamin deficiencies (D, B12, folate, nicotinic acid, thiamine) Excess of vitamin A and D Addison's disease and Cushing's syndrome *Electrolyte Causes* Dehydration Hyponatremic water intoxication Acidosis Alkalosis Deficiency or excess of ionic calcium, potassium, sodium and magnesium. *Toxological Causes* CO poisoning Lead and other heavy metal poisoning Organic solvents Insecticides Inhalants (ether, gasoline, glue) Plant and fungal poisons

The Psychosis Spectrum
Depressive Psychotic Reaction
Paranoid Psychotic Reaction
Other Dynamic Psychotic Reactions
Brief Psychotic Reaction

Medical Causes
Infectious disease
Neoplastic disease
Paraneoplastic syndrome
Intracranial space-occupying lesions
Head trauma
Traumatic brain injury (TBI)
Epilepsy
Vascular and blood disorders
Post-surgical complications
Vascular stroke
Heat stroke
Prescribed and prohibited drugs
Withdrawal from these drugs

Arrested Psychobiological Development of the Brain
Autism
Low IQ
Learning Disabilities (Dyslexia)

Neurodegenerative Brain Diseases With Psychiatric Symptoms
Alzheimer's and other dementing diseases, Pick's, Huntington's and Parkinson's
Tertiary syphilis
Tardive dyskinesia

Physiologically Induced Mood Disorders
Anxiety
Depression

2nd Stipulation:
Primary Mental Diseases Emerging From a Putative Altered Brain Substrate
Some Phenotypes of Schizophrenia
Some Phenotypes of Manic-Depression
Productive Hypomania

---

*The entries for delirium and neurodegenerative diseases in the 4th domain were adapted from Slavney, P. R. (1998). *Psychiatric Dimensions of Medical Practice*. Baltimore: Johns Hopkins University Press. An earlier version of the Map first appeared in Muller, R. J. (2015). The Four Domains of Mental Illness (FDMI): An Alternative to the DSM-5. In P. Zachar, D. St. Stoyanov, M. Aragona, A. Jablensky (eds.) *Alternative Perspectives on Psychiatric Validation: DSM, ICD, RDoC, and Beyond* (pp. 236–252). Oxford, UK: Oxford University Press.

The First Domain[1]

Maladaptive Reactions Originating in Failures to Meet Life's Challenges and Recover From Setbacks

1 As previously noted, the order of appearance of the 1st and 4th perspectives in *The Perspectives of Psychiatry* is interchanged in the FDMI, along with the corresponding domains.

Chapter 6 The Anxiety Spectrum

Awake, we are always in a mood, though we are not always aware of that mood. We most often recognize how we are feeling when we are anxious, angry, happy or sad because these moods are familiar to us and easy to identify. More complex moods require some introspection and analysis.

Anxiety

An inventory of human emotions would logically begin with anxiety, which can be counted as the *primordial mood* because this emotion is intrinsic to life itself. As human beings we are forced, from moment to moment, to create ourselves and find our place in the world with others. But whatever we mortals create—good, bad or indifferent—is subject to dissolution, because all human achievement is fleeting, a product of a life that is flux at its very core and not at all a solid thing. We are the only species who knows that we will die, and this knowledge is a paradoxical driving force in our effort to continuously create ourselves and establish an identity.

We cannot live without having some minimal notion of who we are. Anything that threatens to undermine our identity will cause us to feel painfully separated from what was formerly perceived as a supportive world. Anxiety is the name we give to this feeling of loss of presence and surety.

Anxiety is the ultimate dimensional emotion: some is required to motivate us to survive and prosper and warn us off dangerous exploits; too much forces us into what Vivian Gornick (2016) called "that frozen sea within," paralyzing us. Anxiety can be thought of as an interruption of the story we tell ourselves about who we are, causing our identity—"the thing you never stop becoming" (Friend 2014)—to be called into question (Fischer 1988). When our life narrative is compromised beyond a certain point, we may manifest one or more of anxiety's protean faces.

The commonest anxiety reactions are interrelated, but distinguishable, phenomena. A partial list that more or less follows the DSM-5 includes: pervasive anxiety reaction; separation anxiety reaction; agoraphobic reaction; phobic reactions; panic reaction/panic attack/panic disorder; and post-traumatic stress reaction.

Pervasive Anxiety Reaction

Pervasive anxiety describes a condition of anxiety that is similar in form to a personality disorder, which is broadly defined as a way of relating to others and the world that brings about persistent psychological pain and behavioral dysfunction. Pervasive anxiety, which includes the DSM-5's generalized anxiety disorder and social phobia, is a condition probably best described as *chronic anxiety that pervades everything a person feels, thinks and does*. This *anxiety* is said to be free-floating and may attach to anyone or anything. It promotes *fears* of what are perceived to be specific threats, as well as *worry*, which is an excessive rumination on the possibility that these threats could materialize. Jaspers saw this condition as "a primary psychic state, all-pervasive and dominating, analogous to vital anxiety and involving existence as a whole" (1997, p. 113).

The emotions and behavior associated with an all-inclusive anxious reaction are rooted in a fundamental dissonance between a person and the world he lives in and through. This pathology can be thought of as originating in the condition that Camus, in *The Myth of Sisyphus*, characterized as the absurd, which is an ontological condition, an attribute of being itself.

Absurd derives from the Latin *absurdus*, which has been translated as a gap, and also as out of tune and ridiculous. By the absurd, Camus meant the gap between our human tendency to seek meaning and value in the world—as part of the quest for creating an identity, a self—and the lack of *inherent* meaning and value one finds in that world, which often seems silent to, and even at odds with, this pursuit. Each person is consequently thrust into the project of subjectively creating his own meaning and value, a responsibility that induces existential anxiety, the anxiety that inheres in the act of existing. The English word *absurd* is an ironic rendering of Camus's ontological concept: ridiculous signifies that the task of living is trivial, an idea we reject, yet who can deny that many of our best efforts to live authentically are foiled by a world that is indifferent to these endeavors, often ridiculously so?

Pervasive anxiety can be thought of as a pathological amplification of this existential, "normal" anxiety. In the hierarchy of anxiety reactions—all stemming from the inability to handle existential anxiety in the process of self-creation, followed by a defensive response—the pervasive anxiety reaction is the entry-level condition. At the other end of the anxiety spectrum, the post-traumatic stress reaction (PTSR) and obsessive-compulsive reaction (OCR) lead to more complex and debilitating illnesses.

Those with pervasive anxiety are usually able to function socially and in the workplace, though in a compromised way. There are degrees of pervasive anxiety, just as pervasive anxiety differs in degree from the normal and healthy anxiety that prompts us to avoid danger, and, anticipating the fear of failure, to do what is necessary to succeed.

What most people do as a matter of course is difficult and even painful for those with this kind of global anxiety. They will worry about things others would never consider worrying about. Just showing up for work, for class or even for a social event can induce high anxiety. Any interaction with an individual or group can seem fraught with risk and danger. Pervasively anxious people will wonder, *Is it safe?* when the only real danger is the specter they are anxiously creating. High-functioning professional people, who face their work with doubt and fear, have been known to pass up social gatherings with co-workers, hoping to side-step what they identify as optional anxious pain.

Some people with this pathology are very good at masking their condition, and only those who know them well will discover their secret. They can live for years through a persona of competence and calm, all the while chafing under the mask they create to deal with this anxiety. While being cut off from the world by the interference of constant anxiety, important human needs go begging. Chronically anxious people are often unhappy and irritable.

The chronically anxious body is not a healthy body. Being constantly anxious to this degree alters normal physiology and stresses the entire organism, what Meyer thought of as the psychobiological unified self. Muscles are tense, and teeth grind at night as the body stays keyed up. It is difficult to fall asleep and stay asleep, and the sleep attained is often not restful. The relaxation that comes with sound sleep reduces the body's autonomic tone giving organs and systems a chance to recoup and regenerate from the day's encounters in a stressful world. This regeneration happens less efficiently in the chronically anxious person, increasing the damage of oxidative stress to the body.

J. D. Salinger's Holden Caulfield: An Exemplar of the Phenomenon of Pervasive Anxiety Style

I first read J. D. Salinger's novel *The Catcher in the Rye* as an undergraduate and was unimpressed. I could not understand why Holden Caulfield was at odds with a world that appears to have given him so much. Or why I should care about the problems he was having living his privileged life in New York City, where his parents made their home, and at Pencey Prep, the New England private school that he attended. Even so, I always intended to read the novel again, and, in 2014, four years after Salinger died, I did.

Rereading, I quickly came to see that Salinger's novel was the story of an adolescent who was living anxiously with what R. D. Laing characterized in *The Divided Self* as *ontological insecurity*. In this pathological condition, a person, for whatever reason, fails to achieve a state of psychobiological development sufficient to permit him to feel, as Laing says, "real, alive and continuous." *Ontological* signifies the properties and structures of all being on which turn our possibilities and limitations as human beings—the clay, so to speak, out of which we create our lives.

Holden Caulfield is a stranger in a strange land. To him, no one or nothing seems real. Everyone and everything seems *phony*, the word he uses at every turn to describe his reaction to everyone and everything.

Trying to explain the difficulty he has relating to his classmates and with the culture he finds so uncongenial at Pencey, Holden tells his friend Sally: "I don't hardly get anything out of anything. I'm in bad shape. I'm in *lousy* shape" (Salinger 2010, p. 142). Actually, he is in much worse shape than he thinks, or than a first-time reader of *The Catcher in the Rye* would surmise. As it turns out—and we discover this only at the end of the novel—Holden is writing his story from a mental institution where he has been hospitalized since having what, in the 1940s and 1950s, the time frame for Salinger's novel, was known as a nervous breakdown.

The upshots of Holden's ontological insecurity pierce every facet of his life. Walking up Fifth Avenue by himself is sufficiently intimidating to threaten his existence with extinction: "Then all of a sudden, something very spooky started happening. Every time I came to the end of a block and stepped off the goddam curb, I had this feeling that I'd never get to the other side of the street. I thought I'd just go down, down, down, and nobody'd ever see me again" (pp. 212–213).

Even in the instinctive act of walking, Holden is captive to his ontological insecurity: his existence is neither real, alive nor continuous (Laing 1965, Fig. 2). As a result, he cannot establish a foothold in the world and position himself so as to interact authentically with others. Holden has not been able to achieve what object relations theorists call *object constancy*, the capacity to identify and abide both positive and negative feelings toward the same person.

Nor is Holden's physical world constant. Stepping down six inches off a sidewalk curb feels to him like stepping off a cliff. Literally, the ground he walks on is not solid under his feet. We get a better idea of how tenuously and anxiously Holden clings to life from the incantation he directs to his dead brother during his walk up Fifth Avenue: "I'd say to him, 'Allie, don't let me disappear. Allie, don't let me disappear. Allie, don't let me disappear. Please, Allie.' And then when I'd reach the other side of the street without disappearing, I'd *thank* him. Then it would start all over again as soon as I got to the next corner" (p. 213). Holden's ontological insecurity has pulled him away from the rational world of cause and effect and consensual validation, and toward an inner sphere of schizoid deadness, a terrain that Laing demarcates graphically in *The Divided Self* (p. 81, Fig. 2). This condition has led to pervasive anxiety and depression (1st domain maladaptive reactions) and to a schizoid style of living through maladaptive reactions of the 2nd domain, described in Chapter 10.

Holden has no real identity, no idea who he is or any clear sense of who anyone else is either. Now we can understand his initially puzzling verdict that everyone is a phony. The fleeting identities he assumes in his desperate attempts to make his way through the situations he finds himself in—the masks he tries on, his personae, his false selves—leave *him* feeling like a phony. Simultaneously, he is alienated from the "phony" world he construes in accord with his anxiously distorted expectations of that world.

Ultimately, Holden is paralyzed by the challenge of *existing*, of creating himself from moment to moment, which is the imperative of being human. The one place he does feel at home and safe is at the Museum of Natural History. Arriving there, he fixates on an exhibit of deer drinking from water holes and birds "stuffed and hung up on wires." Holden envies the *deadness* of these objects:

> The best thing, though, in that museum was that everything always stayed right where it was. Nobody'd move. You could go there a hundred thousand times, and that Eskimo would still be just finished catching those two fish, the birds would still be on their way south, the deers would still be drinking out

> of that water hole, with their pretty antlers and their pretty, skinny legs, and that squaw with the naked bosom would still be weaving that same blanket. Nobody'd be different. The only thing that would be different would be *you* (p. 131).

Holden aspires to sameness and inertia, the essence of dead things, rather than to the authentic identity of being human, which entails the acceptance of ambiguity and change, and active engagement. In his passive, disengaged mode, he knows ahead of time how things will turn out: *everybody and everything* will be phony. Not much risk here. Ultimately, Holden's pathological anxiety comes down to his unwillingness to risk discovering the person he really is or could become.

Separation Anxiety Reaction

When development goes well enough and there are no supervening biological glitches or medical issues, a level of individuation may be achieved that is sufficient to secure a degree of selfhood appropriate to the person's age. To someone who has achieved this milestone, the forced separation from a significant other will be felt as a loss, and possibly experienced as painful, but not to the degree that it leads to major, long-term dysfunction.

If separation from a significant other occurs before this developmental goal is met, or after a serious loss or other negative experience, the consequences may be anxiety, depression and a significant disruption of the person's established routine. The somatic correlatives of separation anxiety include sleep disturbance, nightmares with the theme of separation, headaches and gastric disturbance.

Separation anxiety is usually associated with children but also occurs in adolescents and adults. Some developmental deficits persist beyond childhood, as is often the case with those who have personality disorders, especially those with narcissistic and borderline traits. When anxiety occurs after the withdrawal of a significant other, the clinician must determine if separation anxiety alone can account for this abnormal mood, or whether more complex psychic pathology is involved.

Pathological Stress Reaction

No life is without stress. Just getting out of bed every morning involves making the effort, against the pull of gravity, to exchange the passive horizontal position of repose for the active vertical stance of action—what anthropologists call the upright position—which is unique to humans. Only when upright can the self as active agent take a full stand in the world we live in and through. On rising, pulse and blood pressure also rise as the body prepares itself for new challenges and new tasks.

Stress is a word that designates the emotions and associated somatic responses that people experience as they engage in the challenges of everyday life, large and small. This existential stress is an element of all we attempt to do even within the "normal" range of human activity. Sartre coined the tag "coefficient of adversity" to designate the degree of difficulty that is inherent in any project we undertake.

Our struggle may be amplified by our own self-deception and resistance to engaging in the project, the obstruction of others and the society and culture that we inhabit at any given time.

Hans Selye dedicated his classic book *The Stress of Life* (1978) "to those who are not afraid to enjoy the stress of a full life, nor [are] so naïve as to think that they can do so without intellectual effort." Selye seems to be speaking here of existential stress, what he infelicitously called *eustress*, which implies the possibility of a good outcome and allows attention and effort to be focused on reaching that goal. He defines stress as the "nonspecific response of the body to any demand, whether it is caused by, or results in, pleasant or unpleasant conditions" (p. 74).

We are concerned here with what happens when existential stress exceeds certain limits and becomes toxic to both mind and body, through what we are calling a *pathological stress reaction*. We are characterizing this common condition as a phenomenon in its own right, hoping that those experiencing pathological stress alone will not be misdiagnosed with a more severe pathology, either mental or medical. On and off, those in the grip of a pathological stress reaction may feel anxious, angry and depressed, even though the psychobiological transformations that underlie the phenomena of anxiety, depression and anger have not been fully invoked. Diagnostic overreaction leads clinicians and patients to seek solutions that are often excessive and self-defeating.

Selye called the pathological stress reaction *distress*, his take on the state of mind and body that ensues when someone is overpowered by the demands of life. There is ample evidence that the wear and tear of severe distress can alter body chemistry. Selye, an endocrinologist, was the first to identify the hypothalamic-pituitary-adrenal (HPA) axis as the body's modulator of stress. He identified the link between pathological stress and diabetes, obesity, hypertension, autoimmune disease, gastrointestinal disorders, cardiovascular disease, cancer and other medical conditions.

Selye saw mind and body as a single entity, as Meyer did in his integrative psychobiology. It is no surprise that even a partially inauthentic choice made in response to an overwhelming life issue—a Meyerian defensive reaction—should be a strong-enough psychological stressor to cause medical pathology.

Diagnosing a self-limited distress reaction puts the clinician in a position to show a patient how to reduce the damage this condition does to mind and body (Ratey 2008). Proven methods of stress reduction include techniques that promote self-soothing, especially when a somatic correlative of stress—such as pulse rate or blood pressure—can be monitored (biofeedback); regular exercise; good nutrition, which among other benefits reduces oxidative stress in cells; and the habit of restorative sleep that allows the body to repair and refresh itself, a hard-sell in a culture where many people view sleep as a luxury they cannot afford. When Nietzsche said, "That which doesn't kill me, makes me stronger," he was not taking into consideration the effect that prolonged, unrelieved distress can have on the human body. The adage "Stress Kills" better describes what can, and often does, happen in these situations.

We list the pathological stress reaction in the 1st rather than the 4th domain because distress originates in a dissonance between person and world and not in an autonomous malfunction of the body as occurs in a primary brain disease.

Agoraphobic Reaction

When anxiety is focused on a particular object or situation it is said to become a *fear* of that object or situation. Fear of something that most people cannot imagine fearing is a *phobia*, which is an irrational and pathological fear that those unaffected often find ludicrous. It has been suggested that a phobia, in any of its multiple forms, can be understood as an exaggerated anticipatory fear of encountering something or someone, in other words, *fear of the fear* associated with such an encounter. Put another way, this is a fear of being afraid.

To live is to stratify risk. Usually without being conscious of doing so, we assess the downside—including the danger—of most of what we undertake. There is an unspoken consensus about the risks associated with much of what we do: *Sure that could happen with X, but what are the chances?* The person who becomes phobic about X, on the other hand—the outlier from the consensus—feels that the chance of something going catastrophically wrong is indeed high, in fact that catastrophe is imminent, and X is fearfully, phobically avoided.

Agoraphobia would seem to be a good place to start any discussion of phobic reactions since what is feared here—open spaces—is about as basic and nonthreatening an encounter as most people can imagine. Agoraphobia must be understood as a particular kind of fear of the world itself, not just the market place, which the Greek-derived word specifies.

This phobia makes one think of the anxiety that is felt by those who go through psychotic reactions, including schizophrenia, and retreat from reality to escape the worst of their anxiety. Unlike schizophrenics, agoraphobics stay with reality, but retreat from the world that extends beyond their room, house or hospital ward. They inhabit a walled-off, attenuated world, feeling only a relative, defensive safety there. Crippled by this phobia, they usually remain cognitively intact, but their isolation greatly restricts what they can undertake. Eventually, even an intact cognition will be diminished if the invitation of the world from outside an agoraphobic's walls is sufficiently spurned.

In *General Psychopathology*, Jaspers cites Carl Westphal (1833–1890) on what Jaspers designates the phenomenon of agoraphobia: "Patients suffer an enormous anxiety, real fear of death together with terror, when they want to cross an open space, find themselves in empty streets, or stand outside tall houses or in other similar circumstances. They feel oppression in the chest, palpitations, a sense of freezing, of being hot in the head, of perspiring, of being clamped to the ground, and a paralyzing weakness in the extremities and a fear of falling" (1997, pp. 136–37). Like all faulty reactions, this particular kind of reactive phobia perturbs the psychobiological unity of the self to produce an array of biological alterations.

Phobic Reactions

Jaspers sees those who have specific phobic reactions as being "beset by an irresistible and terrifying fear of perfectly natural situations and performances" (Jaspers 1997, p. 136). By replacing performances with actions here (to compensate for vagaries in the translation from the German), Jaspers's brief description becomes a good definition of a phobia.

What do people develop phobias to? Just about everything, it turns out. Any list of phobias would necessarily be a partial list: animals (of all kinds and sizes); the natural world (wind, water, lightning, fire, germs); natural conditions (heights, enclosed spaces, darkness, cold); entities and objects (blood, needles, electricity, weapons); driving in cars, driving through tunnels, crossing bridges, riding in elevators and trains, flying in airplanes; becoming somatically ill (hypochondria).

Those who have phobic reactions either avoid the object of their fear or become extremely anxious when that object is encountered. Since phobia is a specific type of anxiety, the differential between a phobia and pervasive anxiety reaction, separation anxiety reaction, agoraphobic reaction, panic reaction, post-traumatic stress reaction and obsessive-compulsive reaction must be carefully considered.

Panic Reaction/Panic Attack/Panic Disorder

A panic attack is the body's biological response to a strong anxiety reaction. The severest attacks can seem like an assault on the body. Panic deals a psychobiological blow far more devastating than the hit taken, say, in pervasive anxiety reaction and differs from that more or less constant state by striking episodically. The clinical literature identifies these episodic attacks as unexpected, unprovoked and lacking a trigger, which suggests to some an endogenous cause, especially in patients where panic attacks can be induced by an infusion of lactic acid (Maddock, 2001).

While panic attacks have been observed to run in families, no definitive data confirm a genetic, or any other biological, cause. Nonetheless, it is likely that patients whose anxiety produces panic symptoms have a physiological vulnerability absent in those with severe anxiety alone. In this model, a panic reaction can be understood as a psychobiological amplification of anxiety that involves the body more radically.

A psychological trauma of sufficient strength to make someone feel that the world, formerly experienced as a relatively safe place, is, in fact, not safe has been identified in many patients as the psychological fault line that predisposes them to later panic attacks. Such traumas include a brush with death and the death of another, highly valued person especially when this death occurs suddenly and unexpectedly.

"Everything changed," a 32-year-old patient of mine told me after her 43-year-old sister died in her sleep of a heart attack. My patient did not know that this kind of thing could happen. After her sister died, the world was no longer the same place she had previously *believed* it was; safety, stability and permanence were no longer guaranteed. Her first panic attack—the herald attack—occurred several weeks later while she was driving home from work with her husband, who had just told her that a neighbor died earlier that day of a heart attack while shopping at a supermarket. In the year before I evaluated her, this young woman had 25 panic attacks and went to an ER 25 times. Each time, she was discharged after her symptoms had subsided (Muller 2003, pp. 11–14).

The DSM-5 criteria for panic attack include feelings of unreality (derealization); feelings of being detached from oneself (depersonalization); fear of losing control or going crazy; and fear of dying.

This terror is manifested in the body of the psychobiologically unified self as somatic symptoms—*the body announcing its terror*—which the DSM-5 lists as: palpitations, pounding heart or accelerated heart rate; sweating; trembling or shaking; sensations of shortness of breath or smothering; feeling of choking; chest pain or discomfort; nausea or abdominal distress; feeling dizzy, unsteady, lightheaded or faint; paresthesia (numbness or tingling sensations); chills or hot flashes.

Considering this wide array of somatic symptoms, one could ask why a panic attack is considered a 1st domain reaction, rather than a 4th domain brain disease. We chose to put panic in the 1st domain because we understand anxiety—even the anxiety that induces severe somatic symptoms—first and foremost as a dis-relationship between person and world, which can lead to a significant loss of identity. We might think of panic as a vulnerable psyche interacting with a world that has come to be perceived as inhospitable and dangerous so that its vulnerable body loses its healthy stance and produces somatic symptoms.

A panic attack is believed to begin with anxiety that is severe enough to cause the release of more adrenaline than the body can adequately handle. Heart rates and breathing rates increase considerably, expelling carbon dioxide from the lungs so that the blood level of this gas is lowered below the normal range. The resulting hypocapnia causes respiratory alkalosis, with an increase in blood pH above the normal range, and consequent vasoconstriction. Many of the somatic symptoms of a panic attack can be explained by these anxiety-driven physiological changes.

Benzodiazepines, which bind to GABA receptors in the brain and in peripheral systems, potentiate the GABA inhibitory tracts, dampening the effects of the adrenaline surge. Deep breathing causes less carbon dioxide to be expelled and has a similar calming effect (breathing into a paper bag also increases the amount of carbon dioxide retained). Selective serotonin uptake inhibitors (SSRIs) have been successfully used to control the symptoms of all anxiety reactions, and paroxetine has been especially effective for panic.

While the salutary effects of medication last only as long as a drug is taken, cognitive behavioral therapy (CBT) has been found to cure patients of their panic reactions—no surprise since the anxiety thought to underlie panic is known to be responsive to this type of psychotherapy.

A number of medical conditions can increase susceptibility to panic attacks. A partial list includes: hypoglycemia; hyperthyroidism; Wilson's disease; mitral valve prolapse; pheochromcytoma; stimulants such as amphetamines, cocaine and caffeine; and withdrawal from prescribed and proscribed drugs. Panic attacks vary in frequency and severity.

Another diagnosis—panic disorder—is used to designate serial panic attacks, like those experienced by the patient described earlier, who had one attack a month for a year before I evaluated her in the ER. The DSM-5 criteria for panic disorder include recurrent and unexpected panic attacks (number not specified), persistent concern about having additional attacks and worry about the consequences of the attacks as well as significant behavioral changes. This repeated pattern of episode and response signifies a condition different from a single episode, or a series of more widely spaced episodes and poses a greater threat to the patient along with a greater challenge to the clinician.

Post-Traumatic Stress Reaction (PTSR)

Post-traumatic stress disorder (PTSD) first appeared as a diagnosis in the DSM-III in 1980, spurred in part by the large number of casualties racked up in the Vietnam War, and was carried through to the DSM-5 in 2013. The ever-increasing number of diagnoses of this illness triggered a chorus of criticism that the problems designated as the syndrome of PTSD were in many cases symptoms of other disorders including anxiety, phobia, depression and substance abuse (McHugh & Triesman 2007). Reading through the lengthy DSM-5 symptom list for PTSD, it becomes evident that all of the criteria except B(3)—reliving an original life-threatening trauma, sometimes with hallucinations and dissociative flashbacks, especially having that trauma triggered as a repeat, real-time experience by some auditory or visual cue—appear in the checklists of other DSM disorders.

It has been pointed out that many of the questions asked of patients in the diagnostic interview for PTSD rely on their memory of the traumatic event, and that these memories, as reported, often do not correspond to the event itself. Seeking a PTSD diagnosis, some patients are looking for validation and sympathy, others for disability benefits. And some who are said to "make criteria" for PTSD never experienced a significant trauma, much less a life-threatening one.

But even critics of the DSM-5 PTSD diagnosis acknowledge that PTSD is a real phenomenon, and that some of those diagnosed with the disorder had been correctly diagnosed. In addition to war trauma, the PTSD diagnose has been made in those injured by physical and sexual assault, accident and natural disaster.

John M. Kane, professor of psychiatry at the Hofstra North Shore-LIJ School of Medicine, gives this succinct account of what differentiates those who succumb to the power of a traumatic event and go on to develop PTSD, from those who are able to get beyond the trauma and lead normal lives:

> The person's response [to a traumatic event] is dependent upon her personality, her genome, her experiences, and her own level of development of successful and beneficial adaptive responses to stress. But like the immune system, which can be responsible for a range of responses that span the entire spectrum from insufficient to beneficial to excessive to harmful, the individual's response to a stressful and catastrophic event can be insufficient, appropriate, or excessive. With a healthy or adaptive response, the memory of the event recedes with time. It is tempered, and, while not forgotten, it is moved back to a safe distance from day-to-day activities and life. Thinking about the event elicits an appropriate level of sadness or sorrow that does not interfere with the individual's ability to live and to function.
>
> If the person has an insufficient adaptive response, then the memory does not recede. Minor events . . . trigger an active replay of the [traumatic event]. A vivid memory occupies center stage, a reenactment of the entire scene, over and over, in a paralyzing manner that is incompatible with normal life. These

individuals are at risk for post-traumatic stress disorder (Tracey 2006, pp. 125–126).

Moving from the DSM's syndromal formulation of PTSD, based as it is on a checklist of symptoms and signs, to a Meyerian psychobiological concept of a post-traumatic stress *reaction* (PTSR) we begin with criterion B(3) from the DSM-5: "Dissociative reactions (e.g., flashbacks) in which the individual feels or acts as if the traumatic event(s) were recurring. (Such reactions may occur on a continuum, with the most extreme expression being a complete loss of awareness of present surroundings.)" (p. 271). This deviant state seems to qualify as a phenomenon in its own right. A diagnosis of PTSR would then distinguish patients who *relived dissociative flashback episodes* from those who do not but who have other features of PTSD that include significant related alterations of emotion, cognition and behavior; social and occupational dysfunction; avoidance of situations that threaten to revive the experience of the original trauma; sleep disturbance; irritability; anger; hypervigilance and exaggerated startle response. These patients would seem to be better served by the appellation *chronic traumatic stress reaction*, which is a lesser pathology.

With this distinction, the PTSR would become a rare condition and most patients with symptoms of post-traumatic stress would be diagnosed with *chronic traumatic stress reaction*. Under this rubric, many of those with current PTSD diagnoses would be considered misdiagnosed (Dobbs 2009).

Conceived as a post-traumatic stress *reaction*, the original trauma in PTSR becomes one with the psychobiology of the person who experienced the trauma, which may lie dormant or partially dormant for some time but is subject to reactivation by internal or external cues. The reconstituted trauma can feel as if it is occurring in the moment, and is accompanied by amplified autonomic activity: increased heart rate, breathing rate and blood pressure.

Defined in this way, what ultimately characterizes the PTSR phenomenon is *an involuntary transposition of past and present*. In this process the past does not stay in the past as it should, but instead impinges on the present. Time's fractured tense is a pathological variant of being-ahead-of-itself, one of Heidegger's existentials (Chapter 5). This is the healthy norm, where the past is under control, while the present stays open, allowing the possibilities of an authentic future to be pursued. For someone in the grip of a PTSR, the past bursts its normal bounds and comes to destructively haunt the present and future. One's being is altered in a way that impedes an authentic overcoming of a past trauma. With apologies to Heidegger, we could think of the PTSR as a consequence of being-*behind*-itself, which is to say being more open to the past than to the future.

As with any loss or trauma, at any level, the response—and the recovery or lack of recovery—will depend on the individual: on what is broadly called his constitution, or psychobiological strength, as well as temperament and personality, which in turn depend on genetics and epigenetics. Trauma specialists have empirical evidence that the belief one could have died as a consequence of a trauma usually causes a more profound psychobiological wound, which takes longer to heal.

The social context in which post-traumatic stress is processed is also a key factor. After finishing military service, many Vietnam veterans returned home to discover that the Veterans Administration (VA) was not honoring its promise of medical and psychiatric support and that family members, friends and employers were ambivalent about the value, and even the legitimacy, of what they had done in country (Allen 2014).

Just as panic reaction is a significant step up in psychobiological perturbation from pervasive anxiety reaction, post-traumatic stress reaction (PTSR) stands a level higher than panic. In its classic form, anyway, each of these three reactions is a discreet phenomenon. Since the treatment of, and prognosis for, each of these psychobiological reactions to trauma is different, clinicians should make every effort to distinguish these phenomena, and reserve a PTSR diagnosis for the relatively small number of patients who *relive their original trauma in real time*.

In evaluating a patient for PTSR, clinicians would do well to eschew the "top-down" checklist of DSM's nonspecific symptoms and pursue a Meyerian "bottom-up" approach beginning with a psychological history that includes a detailed social history; an exploration of the patient's cognition and temperament; current and past medical conditions; and drug and alcohol use before and after the traumatic event. A similar, though less detailed history should be taken of family members, going back as many generations as possible. These family members, along with spouses, significant others, friends, employers and co-workers should be questioned to confirm (or rebut) the information provided by the patient.

It is the conclusion of several studies that trauma treatment programs which hospitalize patients for long periods of time and encourage patients to keep their trauma alive—ostensibly so it can be "dealt with," rather than "covered up"—can actually be detrimental to recovery. Such an approach underplays the tendency of a traumatic injury's effect to fade naturally with time, especially when others encourage and support a return to something like a normal routine and normal life, different as this will undoubtedly be from what the patient knew before the trauma.

In an article for *The New Yorker*, Dexter Filkins (2012) told the story of Lance Corporal Lu Lobello, who fought in Iraq and did benefit from dealing with his trauma, though in a somewhat unique way and without any help from the mental health profession. On April 8, 2003, while on patrol in Baghdad, Lobello and the men under his command saw a blue Mercedes sedan coming toward them, as Iraqi insurgents kept up their heavy fire. Civilians in that war often could not be distinguished from combatants, and fearing that the occupants of the car posed a threat—many American soldiers had already been killed by seemingly friendly natives—Lobello and his men opened fire on the Mercedes. When the car came to a stop, James Kachadoorian and his two young sons were dead. His wife, Margaret, stepped out of the bullet-ridden car with her daughter, Nora, whose shoulder had been badly injured in the attack. When they came under fire, the Kachdoorians were returning from an outing and were just blocks from their home.

This firefight was the most intense combat Lobello and his men had seen in their 17 months of deployment. A month later, their tour was over and they returned to the United States. Lobello was assigned to a Marine base in Nevada. He had managed to hold himself together in Iraq, but away from the war and the men he commanded there he began to come apart. Testing positive for marijuana, Lobello was demoted. He was angry and bitter over the demotion and quarreled with his superiors. After testing positive for painkillers in 2006, he lost command of his squad. "I completely broke down," was how he described his reaction.

Lobello married in 2009, but the marriage did not slow his downward spiral. "He loses it pretty bad," his wife told Dexter Filkins. "He punches walls, breaks things." As soon as Lobello set foot back in the United States, he had a good deal of trouble sleeping. His nightmares replayed the Kachadoorian killings. And he became paranoid.

"One time," Filkins reports in the article, "Lobello ran into the parking lot of his apartment building in his underwear, clutching his AR-15, preparing to shoot a man he believed had been following him. A few months later, he was detained by the police outside a veterans' clinic: he'd lain down on the floor and refused to leave until a doctor examined him. He was diagnosed with severe post-traumatic stress disorder. The Marines gave him a disability payment of a thousand dollars a month, and he started receiving treatment, mostly in the form of antidepressants." No longer an active Marine, Lobello was separated from the culture that had provided a positive meaning for his combat service, including exculpation for killing the Kachadoorians. In a civilian culture, he felt "excommunicated," not only from the fraternity of the Marine Corps, but from the absolution of the combat kills that came with it. Feeling himself to be in a different moral universe, Lobello was faced with the need to find a new meaning for what he had done in Iraq.

Jonathan Shay, a psychiatrist who has written two books on war-induced PTSD, sees this need as being rooted in a "moral injury," which occurs, he told Filkins, "when you've done something in the moment that you were told by your superiors that you had to do, and believed, truthfully and honorably, that you had to do, but which nonetheless violated your own ethical commitments. It's bad moral luck. Unfortunately, war is filled with that." Lobello began to come to terms with his moral injury by trying to find the surviving Kachadoorians. As it turned out, Margaret and her daughter, Nora, who though seriously injured in the attack made a remarkable recovery, had immigrated to the United States and settled in Glendale, California, which had a large Armenian community. Lobello's first contact was through a Facebook message to Nora: "I need to talk to you, if you let me. I have so much to say to you. I have so much to say." Margaret and Nora agreed to a meeting—this was almost 10 years after the attack—and Lobello drove from La Jolla, where he had been living, to see them. "Finding the Kachadoorians wasn't simply about physically finding them," he told Filkins. "It allowed me to give meaning to this experience that all of us had shared and none of us understood."

Lobello was looking to reclaim the identity—the self—he had lost somewhere between the trauma he had both inflicted and endured in Baghdad and the downhill course he took after returning home that led to his discharge from the Marines, "less than honorably," as he described his exit. Filkins felt that "what he was really looking for was absolution."

Lobello's meeting with Margaret and Nora, who by this time had two boys of her own, identified themselves as Christians. It was clear from their words and their affect that these women were still suffering terribly because of their loss.

But, influenced by what they read in the Bible about forgiving those who had done wrong, they seemed inclined to forgive Lobello and the other Marines who participated in the attack.

At the meeting in Glendale, Lobello recalled how he and his fellow Marines felt as soon as they realized what they had done to the Kachadoorians. "We thought that any vehicle, you know, was going to try to hurt us. I don't know if it was your vehicle or one before that almost ran over one of our guys. So, once that happened, we just figured—it was just what we ended up doing." The ambiguity of the situation the marines encountered and reacted to—inevitable in the kind of war they were fighting—was inseparable from the moral ambiguity that became even more intense after Lobello was forcibly separated from the Marines. "We just had no idea that there were families out there," he told the Kachadoorians. "What we thought at first was, Why are they driving here? We didn't understand."

By the rules of war, the Marines had done their duty. As men, they felt culpable. By going to Glenwood to meet with Margaret and Nora, Lobello took the first step toward moving beyond the psychobiological stalemate that *was* his post-traumatic stress: he was stating the ambiguity, in front of the surviving victims of his act of war, as clearly as he could, trying to understand what had happened, what had gone wrong, and why. In doing this, he was solidly in the instrumental mode of cause and effect that Meyer and Sartre saw as the basis for a healthy life. He was challenging his initial defensive reactions in the aftermath of the overwhelming tragedy where he was simultaneously instigator and victim.

"But we want you not to hurt," Margaret said. "It's not your fault. I am right? . . . . You have done as best you can to come here and say I did it. I appreciate this." A few days later, after returning to La Jolla, Lobello received a Facebook message from Nora: "when you came I feel so happy & I feel doing grate on my life & with my family, I really changed . . . & the same time I feel I get a third brother & the third son to my mom . . . thanks to you for everything." Neither Lu Lobello nor Margaret and Nora Kachadoorian will ever be the same as before the attack—what they lost is irretrievable. But because of a mutual acceptance of the reality of what had happened and because the Kachadoorians were willing to forgive Lobello once they understood the ambiguity of the situation he faced before ordering the attack, they have a good chance of avoiding a life hamstrung by post-traumatic stress.

Writing in *The New Yorker* about the yearly ceremonies that commemorate the 1994 Rwanda genocide killings, Philip Gourevitch (2014) came to this conclusion about memory and trauma: "So there is memory that we manage, and there is memory that manages us." For the severely traumatized, this dichotomy names the balancing act that is a part of the unavoidable processing, in one way or another, of what cannot be forgotten, only given meanings that tip the balance toward managing a hurtful experience rather than being managed by it.

Obsessive-Compulsive Reaction (OCR)

The obsessive-compulsive reaction (OCR)—similar to what the DSM-5 calls obsessive-compulsive disorder (OCD)—is one of the many ways those who experience overwhelming anxiety attempt to spare themselves from these feelings, instead of authentically confronting the real cause of their anxiety. This defensive ploy has a certain internal logic: as long as an unbearably anxious world can be held at bay by obsessively focusing on some idea or belief, then acting compulsively on it, a person is somewhat protected from that inhospitable world and spared the worst of its pain. But, like an addictive drug, the OCR defense works only as long as it is actively used and must be continuously reemployed.

The OCR phenomenon consists of experiencing *obsessions*—bizarre, intrusive, unwanted, sometimes horrifying ideas that won't go away—and *compulsions*—repetitive and persistent acts carried out in the attempt to lessen the anxiety bound up with these obsessions. The most common obsessions are 1) startling, recurring thoughts (fear of contamination, pathological doubt); 2) violent thoughts and images (portending injury or death to self and others); 3) violent urges (to harm or kill oneself or someone else); 4) an excessive need for order and symmetry.

In an OCR, obsessions are paired with their corresponding compulsions: 1) fears of contamination are fought off by avoiding even harmless "contaminants," and over-the-top efforts are made to neutralize these agents by excessive hand washing and the indiscriminate use of antimicrobial agents; pathological doubt is countered with repeated checking (where checking once would be sufficient to convince someone without this problem), and what has been dubbed "doing-undoing," where the doubt is dealt with by, in effect, retracting the thought, emotion or act that obsessively comes into question; 2) violent thoughts and images are often countered by an unnatural and disadvantageous avoidance of persons, places and things that threaten to bring on these unwanted thoughts and images; 3) violent urges to harm self or others may be wrapped in shame and painfully ignored, or held at bay with deliberate distractions or brief prayers; 4) the excessive need for order and symmetry is pursued by imposing on objects at hand an unnatural arrangement that would not be of interest or use to anyone who does not have this excessive need.

One of my patients became obsessed with the idea that as he was driving his car, pedestrians to the left and right of him were being struck and sometimes killed. Stopping the car and verifying that this horrific event had not occurred did nothing to neutralize this unsettling notion. As the obsession increased in intensity and frequency, he felt compelled to give up driving altogether.

Most basically, an OCR begins with the fear and belief—to the point of obsession—that an element in someone's world is a serious threat, often to his life, or, as happened with my patient, to the life of someone else. This *anxious feeling*, which is experienced as intolerable, is countered by some "magical" (i.e., irrational) act that a person feels compelled to perform. OCD patients show a range of insight into their condition. Some are convinced that their repetitive compulsive act will prevent the evil they are obsessed with from finding them. Others, taking into account the considerable evidence to the contrary, do not believe that their action will ultimately be effective but continue to act compulsively anyway.

In rounding out his description of the phenomenon of compulsion, Karl Jaspers sketches the boundaries of compulsion with three other phenomena: the delusion, the over-valued idea and ordinary (not pathological, obsessional) doubt.

Jaspers's prose is compressed here, and slow-moving, as it is all through *General Psychopathology*, but his words are ultimately revealing and probative:

> In the case of *delusion* a judgment is made which is held on to with full conviction, not only with a consciousness of validity but with a sense of absolute certainty. In compulsive belief, there is no question of absolute certainty. With *over-valued ideas* belief is strong, the topic itself is the only thing that matters and the psychic life is normal and unchanged so far as the individual himself is concerned, whereas in compulsive belief he considers his belief to be morbid. In the case of *ordinary doubt* a judicious weighing of the pros and cons leads to an indecision, experienced as a psychologically unified judgment on the situation. In the case of compulsive belief, however, conviction is held simultaneously with a knowledge of the very opposite (Jaspers 1997, p. 135).

The lack of a "psychologically unified judgment" experienced while acting on a compulsive belief is a hallmark of the OCR. The degree of self-deception implicit here—self-deception figures heavily in all Meyerian reactions, indeed in all psychodynamic defenses—is substantial. *Knowing* that an action taken against an obsession "works" only as long as that action is being performed, then *repeating* this action in response to the inevitable resurgence of the original provoking anxiety that occurs once the action is discontinued seems like an endeavor of pure desperation.

Sherwin Nuland: An Exemplar of the Phenomenon of Obsessive-Compulsive Reaction

Sherwin Nuland (1930–2014) was a clinical professor of surgery at Yale Medical School, and wrote a number of books about doctors and how they practice medicine (Gellene 2014). In *How We Die: Reflections on Life's Final Chapter*, the author unveiled the physiological mechanism behind many of the major causes of death in the Western world and showed why death is rarely the "good" death that we all hope for. *How We Die* won the National Book Award for nonfiction in 1994.

"We die," Nuland wrote, reflecting on what he seems to take as the ultimate meaning of death, "so that the world may continue to live. We have been given the miracle of life because trillions upon trillions of living things have prepared the way for us and then have died—in a sense for us. We die, in turn, so that others may live. The tragedy of a single individual becomes, in the balance of natural things, the triumph of ongoing life" (Nuland 1994, p. 267).

The man who so eruditely gave us this insight also wrote the following account of the lowest point in his own life in his autobiography *Lost in America: A Journey With My Father*.

> From my late thirties until my early forties, I underwent a period of depression that gradually deepened into an intensity so absolute that I finally required admission to a mental hospital, where I stayed for more than a year. Neither medication, psychotherapy, the determined efforts of friends nor the devotion

> of the few people whose love never deserted me had even the most minimal beneficial effect on my worsening state of mind. Finally, faced with my resistance to all forms of treatment till then attempted, the senior psychiatrists at the institution in which I was confined recommended the draconian measure of lobotomy. Their justification for such a drastic course was that disrupting the brain's neural pathways might bring an immediate end to the complex of obsessional thinking and behavior to which I had succumbed.
>
> I was, in fact, completely disabled by pathological preoccupations and fears. Obsession with coincidences; fixations on recurrent numbers; feelings of worthlessness and physical or sexual inadequacy; religious anxieties of guilt and concerns about God's will; ritualistic thinking and behavior—they crowded in on one another so forcefully as to occupy every lacuna in my mind. I cowered before them, not only emotionally but physically, too—my hunched-over posture reflected my decline into helplessness. Rational thinking was driven out by a ferocity of fear that consumed all energy and pride. I came not to have a moment's peace from the din and deluge of that rampaging stampede of obsessional ideations. So profound was my depression and so tyrannical the jumble of unbidden thoughts and compulsive actions that they ruled the hours of my days and the days of my years. I feared the obsessions, I feared the threatening loss of control, and I feared the fear—all at once. Mostly, I feared for my sanity (Nuland 2003, pp. 4–5).

This part of the story comes at the beginning of the book. The remaining 205 pages spell out how, and to some degree why, Sherwin Nuland fell so far. The subtitle, *A Journey with My Father*, adumbrates the plot line.

Nuland's parents immigrated to the United States and settled in a small apartment in New York City's South Bronx, along with other relatives from Eastern Europe, including a grandmother and an aunt. The Nudelmans—Sherwin, who was born in New York, changed his name—held on to the old ways, not the least of which was the Yiddish language they had spoken in Russia.

Nuland was raised on the dark side of the American Dream. This nightmare was created by the Nudelman family's default on the possibilities that came with living in the New World, and was led by Nuland's overbearing father, who never learned to speak English, acquiring instead some bizarre hybrid of Yiddish and English. Nuland's "journey" with his father was a love-hate affair, which created deep emotional scars that, in spite of his considerable professional success, led to the near-fatal coming apart in his early forties that he describes so hauntingly.

The Nudelmans brought with them from Russia a family history of sorrow that only deepened in New York. Serious illnesses and the deaths of adults and children in their extended family cast a pall that spawned several episodes of serious depression for Nuland, beginning in high school and culminating in the hospitalization he describes in his book. Nuland recalls the walks he took with his parents as a child along the major Bronx thoroughfares:

> There was always trouble to talk about, and never any solutions. If there were stories of triumph to be told during those walks, or of difficulties overcome, I

> never heard about them—or at least I don't remember them. Worry, pessimism, regret, discontent, anger—that was the agenda, and my parents seemed rarely to agree about any of it (p. 48).

The Nudelmans' saturnine world—"the family's characteristic pessimism" (p. 51) —sharply contrasted with Nuland's academic success. He always did well in school, while suffering a cultural and emotional disconnect between what he experienced at home where nothing was guaranteed and no one was safe, and the optimistic America that was unfolding for him beyond the Nudelman's apartment. He graduated from NYU, was admitted to Yale Medical School, and, later, to a residency program there and was chosen to be the chief surgical resident.

But what was right in Nuland's life did not heal what was wrong. "As the years passed," he acknowledged, "being lost in America would give way to being lost in life" (p. 101).

One can think of Nuland as eventually *needing* to undergo the various pathological reactions he describes after his familiar, transformed world of depression could no longer function as a sufficient refuge from his anxiety and the self-disintegration that hounded him. Stronger Meyerian reactions, and greater pathological transformations, were required. These transformations were mostly various and fierce obsessive and compulsive reactions, in the context of agitated depression, which were marked by self-doubt, guilt and masochism, and led to crippling rituals. In the process of disintegrating, Nuland was acting out all the doom-and-gloom negativity that his family had imposed on him from his earliest days, which he had kept in check by a successful career and a degree of social accommodation.

While hospitalized, Nuland's life was totally overtaken by his 1st domain pathology, which was most likely rooted in his aberrant 2nd domain personality development. We see Nuland in the throes of a major breakdown of mind and body. We can only guess what features of the various pathological personality styles of the 2nd domain he may have exhibited prior to his hospitalization. At the depths of his illness, these traits would have been snowed under by the more dominant 1st domain pathology.

Eventually, Nuland was saved by electro-convulsive therapy (ECT), which made it possible for him to leave the hospital—after just barely escaping a lobotomy—and resume his life and surgical career. He received twenty ECT treatments. Gradually, the depression lifted and the obsessions and compulsions became less dominant:

> It crossed my mind that it was no longer necessary to give in to them each time one or another would flash into consciousness. Why not figuratively turn away and refuse to succumb? Why not respond to their pernicious urgings with some dismissive formula, like "Ah, fuck it"? As recently as a month earlier, I could not have entertained such a notion, so tightly was I being held in the grip of those iron chains of agitated depression. Until then, rejecting an obsessional thought had only stoked anxiety, but on that morning [in January 1974], release seemed for the very first time achievable. I felt like a child who has matured just enough so that he no longer has to avoid stepping on the sidewalk cracks.

> Then and there, I resolved to abandon my pathological limitations in a single determined stroke. It was as though the electro-shock had burned away a tightly coiled network intertwined in my brain, constricting free will. . . . And so, I recovered. I recovered so well, in fact, that in the four remaining months of hospitalization, I lost all but the dimmest memory of the obsessions and saw my depression disappear entirely (pp. 7–8).

As Nuland credited ECT with "unsticking" his brain, he also recognized that it was ultimately the *return of his freedom*, long ceded to the defenses that constituted his illness, which allowed him to resume the life he had lived before becoming ill.

Obsessive-Compulsive Reaction vs. Obsessive-Compulsive Style

The FDMI's 1st domain obsessive-compulsive *reaction* is a phenomenon that is different from the 2nd domain's obsessive-compulsive *style* (Chapter 10), what the DSM-5 calls obsessive-compulsive personality disorder (OCPD). The OCR is rooted in an overall distortion of the world that is constructed and elaborated by the patient. This alteration in mental life often includes the patient's capacity to recognize the inherent unreasonableness and ineffectiveness of these obsessions and compulsions. In the most serious OCR cases, loss of insight about the non-effectiveness of obsessions and compulsions, along with a general withdrawal from the external world, can lead to psychosis, as happened with Nuland during his long hospitalization.

Generally, 2nd domain pathological personality styles—the DSM-5's OCPD—are relatively stable configurations of self that do not lead to the kind of breakdown that Nuland experienced. The obsessive-compulsive style describes those who are preoccupied with order, seek perfection beyond its own rewards, pursue work at the expense of leisure and socialization, and are inflexible about rules and values sometimes to the point of scrupulosity. Mental health professionals, consumers of mental health services, the public and the media often do not distinguish the 1st domain OCR from the 2nd domain obsessive-compulsive style, citing all obsessive-compulsive behavior as OCD. In the FDMI, these two distinct phenomena appear in two different domains, which should make it easier for everyone to observe this distinction.

Chapter 7 The Depression Spectrum

Adolf Meyer said that psychiatry became real to him only after he grasped that his patients' issues and problems paralleled his own experience in life. When Meyer left Switzerland, where he was born and raised, to work permanently in the United States, his mother, whom he had always regarded as a pillar of stability, developed a depression that lasted three years and required hospitalization. Meyer came to see that his absence had triggered her illness and realized that her refusal to accept this change in her life was a maladaptation to the situation that led to what he called a depressive reaction. This woman, who developed a serious mental illness in spite of her apparent previous mental stability, eventually recovered, reclaiming the good habits which she had temporarily exchanged for bad ones.

Depressive Reaction[1]

"A normal depression," Meyer felt, "is a state evolved to protect ourselves; as we are depressed, we want to be let alone more or less in order to get a chance to build up our fences again and strengthen ourselves instead of proceeding headlong in unfit action" (Lief 1948, p. 305). In this formulation, depression is a strategic retreat from the normal world, which shares a similarity of form with the more drastic strategic withdrawal that occurs in various kinds of psychosis, including schizophrenia.

Meyer saw the brain as the "organ of personality," which had the power to "undermine" itself and every other organ in the body. (No wonder, as pharmaceutical company ads constantly remind us, that *depression hurts.*) We can only speculate about what Meyer would have made of the brain scans of depressed patients that show decreased glucose metabolism in the limbic system, without providing any explanation (in the Jasperian sense) for the etiology of the illness. Most likely, he would maintain that this change was a psychobiological consequence and correlate of the depressive reaction, and not its cause: "And it has become my conviction that the developments in some mental cases are rather the results of peculiar mental tangles than the result of any coarsely appreciable and

1 Before diagnosing a 1st domain depressive reaction, 4th domain depression caused by medical conditions, prescribed medications and proscribed drugs must be ruled out.

demonstrable brain lesion or poisoning—the natural further development of inefficient reaction-types" (Meyer 1908), by which Meyer meant bad habits rooted in immature and neurotic defenses. He saw the ground for a depressive reaction as "a faulty hanging-together of the mental reactions or adjustments, shown by and promoted by previous maladjustments" (Meyer 1908).

Meyer did not see depression as a brain disease (a 4th domain condition), but as a maladaptive response to a situation that others who were developmentally and constitutionally stronger might well have handled without becoming depressed (making depression a 1st domain illness). Nor was Meyer convinced that, because some people could process adversity instrumentally and others became depressed by more or less the same life challenge, molecular genetics played a significant part in a depressive reaction. He realized that, then as now, "we are always promising ourselves lesions." To Meyer it was the *entire psychobiological organism* that responded with a depressive reaction, and there was no way for him at that time to parse the genetic contribution, whatever it might be.

Meyer's psychobiological formulation of depression is very different from the current take on this illness by biological psychiatry: depression *originates* in some malfunction of brain structure or function; the life change called major depression is the *result* of this malfunction; and the first line of attack against this disease is antidepressant medication.

Sartre's Depressive Transformation

Meyer would almost certainly have agreed with Jean-Paul Sartre about the world transformation that Sartre saw as underlying depression (Muller 2003). As an ontologist, Sartre was concerned with the structure of being and the changes that occur in that structure when a person becomes mentally ill. In a slim volume titled *The Emotions: Outline of a Theory* (1948), he spelled out his idea of the phenomenon of depression, the psychogenic etiology of this emotion and the meaning of its symptoms.

Sartre begins by describing the instrumental world of cause and effect—what Meyer called the world of consensual common sense—where people implicitly understand that their actions largely determine the kind of life they will have. Ontically, this is the world of normalcy. (Ontic designates what is unique in the structure of an individual's being, while ontological specifies the structure of being itself, the way things are for everyone.) Because the normal, instrumental world is experienced as a *differentiated* world—some of what it offers appeals to us, some does not—we selectively respond to its multiple possibilities: choices are made; projects are undertaken; goals are set; risks are taken; a certain amount of frustration and pain is tolerated; and, when necessary, gratification is deferred. Using our freedom in this way, we are ultimately responding to what Heidegger called the *invitation of the world*, the *differentiated* world.

According to Sartre, in the depression that follows what Meyer called a maladaptive reaction to a loss or negative experience, what was once differentiated is *dedifferentiated*—Meyer called this process *dissolution*, a corollary of many maladaptive reactions. A passive stance replaces the former active stance. In that passivity, the notion of cause and effect is weakened. The depressed person withdraws from people and from work and loses interest in much of what was previously appealing. The terrain of the dedifferentiated world is flattened relative to its differentiated state, homogenized, stripped of its former color and experienced as black and white.

The acuity of the instrumental, differentiated world, a prerequisite for normal mood, is blunted and its invitation spurned. Sartre believed that a "trick" of self-deception—the lie we tell ourselves—is at the heart of this transformed experience. The unacknowledged refusal to respond to the instrumental world of cause and effect—*I won't do it*—becomes *I can't do it.*

The depressed person's "attitude of excuse," as Sartre called it, seems less inevitable when viewed in the light of the concluding words of Samuel Beckett's novel *The Unnamable*: "I can't go on, I'll go on" (Beckett 1955, p. 414). How do we really know what we are capable of doing when the chips are down? Psychiatry has little to say about the inherent capacity of people—either those whose behavior is within the normal range or those who have been diagnosed with a mental illness—to use their free will to shape their experience. Psychoanalysts believe that depression entails a decathexis—a withdrawal of involvement—from the world, a notion that is compatible with Sartre's dedifferentiation and Meyer's dissolution.

Sartre's dedifferentiating transformation—the ontic change implicit in Meyer's *depressive reaction*—is the essence of 1st domain depression. This change alters the very nature of a person's being and relation to the world. Depression is rooted in the power of a biologically sustained consciousness—*the capacity of the self as active agent to choose one option over another*—to replace rational instrumentality with magical thinking. Depression can be thought of as a regression in the service of the ego (Freud)—a retreat from the world of cause and effect, with its constant expectations and demands. Dedifferentiation reduces the call of the world, and its burdens, as a rheostat diminishes the strength of light and sound.

Sartre was not the only existentialist to take on the concept of differentiation as this ontic variable relates to mental health. To Karl Jaspers, a psychiatrist turned philosopher, differentiation meant "the breaking up of vague experiences into several well-defined ones, thus giving richness and depth to the total experience. Low-level individual phenomena differentiate into higher ones; the vague instinctive life gains in content. Increased differentiation brings increased clarity and awareness. Undefined intuitions and feelings give place to clear, definite ideas" (Jaspers 1997, p. 14). To Socrates, the unexamined life wasn't worth living. To Jaspers, the undifferentiated life was a diminished, often pathological life. (The notion of *hyperdifferentiation* is introduced in Chapter 16 as a way to understand the ontic transformation that occurs with mania and mixed states in manic-depression.)

For Mrs. Meyer, living in her dedifferentiated world—rejecting most of what was still available to her in spite of her son's "abandonment"—*was* her depression. The tacit, self-deceiving rationalization involved in such a regressive transformation goes something like this: *How can the world expect me to continue as before considering what I have lost and what I have been through? Surely this is too difficult.*

Depression is a refusal to accept the fact that the world is often gratuitously unfair. To the depressed person, what Albert Camus in *The Myth of Sisyphus*

(1955) recognized as the *silence* of the universe—its unresponsiveness to our ultimate needs—can be deafening. For Camus, the task of the self as active agent is to *create* meaning in a world that has, and offers, no inherent meaning, and to impose order where disorder—entropy—is frequently the default state.

In a silent universe that is often deaf to our needs, we all experience frustration, and many people go on from there to develop full-blown depression. Depression is the *demand* of the person who has lost someone or something important that events *should* have and *could have* been otherwise—that ontologically, the world should *not* be silent, entropic and meaningless. This *insistence* triggers the ontic transformation that changes the contours, surfaces and textures of an instrumental world into the dedifferentiated, pathologically flattened landscape of depression.

These are the "shoulds" and the "coulds" that are challenged in cognitive behavioral therapy (CBT), a therapeutic approach that has been especially successful in remediating depression. It is the therapeutically-assisted relinquishment of these demands that permits the undoing of the defensive reaction, allowing a formerly depressed person to reclaim the differentiated world of normal mood. The clinical prescription, Do Better Before You Feel Better, appeals directly to the capacity of the self as active agent, mired in pathological inertia, to choose existence over essence, and reinvent itself. (Generally, for us all, depressed or not depressed, if we do better, we *will* feel better.)

Sartre's sense that, to a great extent, we manufacture our own life catastrophes, including depression—from circumstances in our lives that we find wanting or vexing—is captured incisively, if glibly, by Tallulah Bankhead's character in Matthew Lombardo's play *Looped*: "There is always going to be pain in life. But suffering? That one is optional" (Smith 2013). Bad stuff finds us all. Then *we* get to choose how much the bad stuff dings us.

Those who are depressed may become acclimated to the flattened landscape of their magically transformed world—in spite of the pain they suffer there—and may, in their own way, revel in that attenuated, less demanding world. Some will be reluctant to relinquish the relative safety of this haven as those in the grip of a psychosis are reluctant to leave their more drastically transformed orb, sequestered as it is from the demands of reality. Some will need a *reason* to relinquish their depression, such as the encouragement of a clinician, or the placebo or the stimulant effect of an antidepressant drug.

In 1935 when F. Scott Fitzgerald was living in Los Angeles and writing fiction had become almost impossible for him, he was asked by *Esquire* editor Arnold Gingrich to submit more of the short stories that had contributed so much to his literary reputation, and his bank account. Fitzgerald replied that he did not feel up to the task, and made no promises. Gingrich came back with a suggestion: write about what it's like to be a blocked writer and how you came to be in this situation. Fitzgerald took the assignment, producing three articles that appeared in *Esquire*. Later, these essays, along with other texts by and about the author, were collected and brought out as *The Crack-Up* (Fitzgerald 1945), edited by his friend and fellow Princetonian Edmund Wilson. The result was a description of Fitzgerald's mental state at that time (the three articles take up only 16 pages of the 347-page book).

Fitzgerald was seriously depressed, and with good reason. His wife, Zelda, who had been previously hospitalized at the Phipps Clinic and Sheppard Pratt Hospital in Baltimore was sinking further into schizophrenia, and slipping farther away from him. Fitzgerald struggled to pay the bills, as the income from his novels and short stories, high in the 1920s, fell dramatically during the decade that followed. His fiction was about the good times that followed America's recovery from World War I, the period known as the Jazz Age, and meant little to readers who were being crushed by the Great Depression. By 1935 the author who had made a spectacular debut and a good deal of money with his first novel, *This Side of Paradise*, published in 1921, was all but forgotten.

Fitzgerald drank heavily and would fit anyone's idea of an alcoholic. As alcohol blunted the edge of his pain, it contributed biologically to his depression and took a significant toll on his body. He died of a heart attack in 1940 at the age of 44.

As Meyer would have said, Fitzgerald was attempting to escape the predicament of no longer being successful and famous (Muller 1996). It is clear from what he wrote in *The Crack-Up* that his life had undergone a process of dedifferentiation, a transformation that was partially numbing the pain he felt but also increasing his suffering in other ways. Fitzgerald had turned his back on a world that, he believed, had turned its back on him.

He found some solace in the company of Sheilah Graham, a nationally syndicated Hollywood reporter and a celebrity in her own right. She tried to convince him that *he* was the ultimate author of his "cracked" state and could recover. But Fitzgerald believed that he lacked the "vitality" to reignite his formerly active and productive life. He was convinced that you either had vitality, the spirit that moved you, or you didn't:

> I might have asked some [vitality] from [Sheilah], neatly wrapped and ready for home cooking and digestion, but I could never have got it—not if I had waited around for a thousand hours with the tin cup of self-pity. I could walk from her door, holding myself very carefully like cracked crockery, and go away into the world of bitterness, where I was making a home with such materials as are found there—and quote to myself [from Matthew 5:13] after I left her door: *'Ye are the salt of the earth. But if the salt hath lost its savour, wherewith shall it be salted?'* (1945, p. 74).

At this point, Fitzgerald would not permit anyone or anything to "salt" his dedifferentiated, alcohol-laden life, which he was wallowing in. We get a clearer idea of how much of the world Fitzgerald had rejected, and how vigorously he had rejected it, from this stark acknowledgment:

> I do not any longer like the postman, nor the grocer, nor the editor, nor the cousin's husband, and he in turn will come to dislike me, so that life will never be very pleasant again, and the sign *Cave Canem* [Beware of the dog] is hung permanently just above my door. I will try to become a correct animal though, and if you throw me a bone with enough meat on it I may even lick your hand (p. 84).

In this bitter and nasty *cri de coeur*, Fitzgerald shows us how far his maladaptive reaction—the dedifferentiating transformation which, along with its biological correlatives *was* his depression—had taken him from the instrumental world of cause and effect, and from being fully human. The choice of the flattened, dead terrain that he was sluggishly moving in and through came, inescapably, with the low mood of the proverbial "dog's life."

Meyer's Depressive Reaction, Sartre's Depressive Transformation and the DSM-5's Criteria for Depression

Sartre's characterization of the transformed world of the depressed person allows us to *understand* (in the Jasperian sense) the psychogenic etiology of Meyer's depressive reaction. His theory also permits us to see the meaning of the nine symptoms comprising the syndrome of major depression, parsed in criterion A of the DSM-5 (pp. 160–161) by relating these changes in thought, emotion and behavior to the altered ontic landscape of the depressed state:

1) *Depressed Mood:* The word depression carries its own hint about what this emotion does to mind and body. Someone who is in a sustained depressed mood experiences the feeling of being pushed down—*de-pressed*—by a world that has for the most part been renounced because of a negative experience or loss. It is expected that sadness would be the dominant emotion because losing someone or something formerly valued—or even losing the possibility of acquiring someone or something highly valued—is cause to feel an emptiness, a hole in our life where that person or entity once resided, or could have occupied had things turned out better. Sadness, and its ache in the heart, informs us that we are no longer living in a world that is as satisfactory to us. Joy, the emotional opposite of sadness, is the feeling that comes as someone or something of great significance *enters* a life.

2) *Diminished Interest:* When one's world has been ontically transformed by the depressive reaction, interest in people and activities decreases because the former link to the larger world has been significantly weakened in the effort to ease the pain of loss. The depressed person perceives acting as *too difficult*, and so does not act, or at least not as avidly as previously.

3) *Weight Loss or Gain:* Some depressed persons will try to fill the void in their lives created by a loss with food. Most of those who do this will gain weight. Others will relate to food in a diametrically opposite way, neglecting it as part of their rejection of the larger world. They will invariably lose weight.

4) *Insomnia or Hypersomnia:* If the depressed person feels anxious and agitated, there is often a tendency to sleep less than formerly. Going from the waking state to somnolence, and from there to sleep requires an implied trust between person and world. The absence of that trust may make it impossible to "let go" and accept the ambiguity implied in sleep, with its various demons. Some who are depressed ruminate incessantly, which makes it hard to relinquish day for night. Anxiety and agitation also increase the autonomic tone of the central nervous system, making it biologically more difficult for someone

to "shut down" the apparatus of consciousness. In contrast, those who's sleep is excessive may be so de-pressed by their depressive transformation and so uneager to face the world, even minimally, that they reject the human upright stance and remain in bed, staying passively horizontal.

5) *Psychomotor Agitation or Retardation:* Some who are depressed will have more energy than before their illness, others will have less. Again this change depends on the nature of the person's depressive reaction. Those with psychomotor agitation deal with their pain by revving their mental and physical motors, in the (failed) attempt to run away from their pain. Like those depressed patients who eat too much, they think and act too fast. On the other hand, patients with psychomotor retardation acquiesce to the downward push of de-pression, slowing their mental and physical motors in a strategic retreat from the normal pace of the instrumental world, which they find too fast to maintain.

6) *Fatigue or Loss of Energy:* It is no surprise that many patients who have dealt with their loss through a depressive reaction have a chronic lack of energy and report fatigue. Some are exhausted by their continuous rumination on their state of loss. Others are drained by the demands of the instrumental world, which, though rejected, continues to make itself felt.

7) *Feelings of Worthlessness or Guilt:* A significant loss will lead most people to question their own worthiness. For some who capitulate to a loss through a depressive reaction, this feeling will be exaggerated and made worse because the dedifferentiated world they inhabit is not a ground for working through these kinds of feelings. Once the seed of guilt takes hold in the dedifferentiated world of the depressive reaction, it can grow freely there. It can also grow into paranoia and delusion as will become evident shortly.

8) *Diminished Cognition and Indecisiveness:* It would be hard to imagine that the ontic transformation involved in the depressive reaction would facilitate thinking, concentration or decisiveness, which belong to the instrumental world of cause and effect. Intuitively, dedifferentiation is inimical to these efforts.

9) *Suicidal Ideation:* The dedifferentiation attained in a depressive reaction is a withdrawal from life and, in some instances, a step toward death. It is not hard to imagine a depressed person, who is dealing with the unique features of this reaction and its associated pathological pain, to continue to dedifferentiate a life to the point where the prospect of living loses all appeal, and the invitation of the world ceases altogether. Some people in this situation will make the decision to end their lives.

To diagnose a major depressive episode, the DSM-5 requires that, just to meet criterion A, five or more of these symptoms must be present during the same two-week period (after ruling out a medical condition as a cause of the depression, as well as mood-incongruent delusions or hallucinations). At least one of the symptoms must be 1) depressed mood or 2) loss of interest or pleasure. The number of combinations of these symptoms that could satisfy this requirement has been estimated, and it is a very large number indeed.

Diagnosing the Phenomenon of Depression

What emerges from this consideration of the psychobiological etiology of depression and the meaning of its symptoms are descriptions of the altered world of someone who has undergone a depressive reaction in response to a negative experience or loss. This analysis allows us to see something of the *structure* of the condition we identify as depression, to intuit its *essence* and to designate this condition as a *phenomenon*.

Though each person's depressive reaction (as characterized by Meyer) and dedifferentiating ontic transformation (as characterized by Sartre) is unique, the essence and structure of an individual's experience can be extracted, analyzed and compared with that of other depressed people. In this way, we can come to know what depression *is*. We can characterize the *phenomenon* of depression and use that knowledge to identity similar pathology in others.

We believe that the notion of comorbidity, as applied to mental illness by the DSM-5, is not a useful way to designate the simultaneous appearance of separately defined clinical entities. Those with depression who are also anxious and dependent on alcohol or drugs do not have several separate illnesses but one illness—originating in multiple domains as defined in the FDMI—that involves all these distortions of the normal world. Each distortion contributes to the depressive reaction and the simultaneous deformation of the contours, textures and surfaces of an ontically transformed world.

It seems reasonable that the *severity* of the depression someone falls into after making a pathological response to a loss is related to how much the depressed person's view narrows down to what has been lost and excludes what continues to be possible in spite of the loss. This contraction of life *is* the dedifferentiation wrought in the strategic transformation of the depressive reaction. Those experiencing the greatest ontic perturbation would have the most intractable illness and probably benefit most from antidepressant medication. These drugs, as well as ECT and TMS, most likely function as stimulants to "jump start" the brains of severely depressed patients at the somatic pole of their psychobiological unity, and not by remediating a "chemical imbalance" in limbic neurotransmission as biological psychiatrists claim. We believe that the difference between what we are calling depression here and what Freud and others called melancholia is the degree of the depressive transformation and accompanying dedifferentiation.

Many people diagnosed with a variety of mental illnesses who depend on—and swear by—their psychotropic medications have, in effect, *refused* to relinquish the defensive reactions that figure prominently in the way they construct their lives and interact with others. They rely instead on a drug that ultimately functions either as a stimulant or a tranquilizer, or as a placebo, to partly offset the psychobiological perturbation that is a consequence of their defensive reaction, lessening the symptoms that emerge from this perturbation. In such cases, clinicians may passively conspire with patients to deny and cover up the self-deceiving choice of the pathological reaction from which a mental illness has emerged.

Depression and Suicide

Suicide is an uncommon phenomenon. When you consider what people suffer because of medical illness, physical injury, the deprivations of old age, mental illness, personal failure and the betrayal of others, one wonders why more people don't choose to end their lives.

Many are deterred from suicide by religious dictates, the social stigma associated with giving up in the face of hardship and the reluctance to abandon others by making this kind of exit. Even without these proscriptions, and under the most trying circumstances, life is often obstinately embraced until the very end. People just don't want to die.

At times we have all thought about the possibility of taking our lives. Who has not wondered what would happen if the steering wheel were turned just slightly to the left as an oncoming car approaches? Or considered the consequences of jumping out of a window eight stories up? Most of us quickly reject the projected outcome of these actions. We don't want our lives to end in this way.

But some people do commit suicide, most of them during the course of a severe depression. This mental state is not just the feeling of loss or sadness that is familiar to all of us or even the condition described as major depressive disorder in the DSM-5.

How do we understand the state of mind of a depressed person who is at serious risk for suicide? Meyer believed that depression is an inadequate, "maladaptive" psychological response to a loss or other negative experience—an unwillingness or constitutional disinclination to move beyond the incident—which has biological correlates. In what Meyer called a depressive reaction, Sartre saw a "dedifferentiation"—an emotional, affective and cognitive flattening and emptying, a change in essence—of a person's formerly instrumental world of cause and effect. In this transformation, a good deal of what was once perceived and lived by the depressed person as interesting and important is now re-construed as empty and unappealing.

The invitation of the world to respond to its possibilities, formerly accepted, is rebuffed. The severely depressed person turns tail on the world of cause and effect, retreating to a lower state of being. In some instances, this regression may evolve into a strategy for regrouping, and returning to a normal mood.

The structural transformation of a person's world that depression *is* occurs to different degrees, which is why depression varies in severity. This transformation can also be reversed, which is ultimately what it means to recover from depression.

In the kind of depression that becomes the ground for suicide, people find themselves isolated, alone and in despair. Guilt, shame, anger and other negative emotions dominate. Prior accomplishments and honors become remote, empty memories. Most suicides occur when a severely depressed person loses both hope and the capacity to imagine a future.

For someone in this extreme emotional state, religious and social constraints against suicide may be dedifferentiated along with everything else, losing their prohibiting power and culminating in disinhibition. And the normally inhibiting realization that others would be badly hurt by ending one's life may be swallowed whole by overpowering negative emotions and an all-encompassing hopelessness. Alcohol and mind-altering drugs can greatly contribute to depressive dedifferentiation, separating the depressed person further from the instrumental world of cause and effect that is the ground for an active and healthy life. These substances can be 4th domain primary biological causes of depression.

Some who devolve into a state of despair and then commit suicide appear to have had "everything." Those familiar with Robin Williams's work and the essential facts of his life—but not the contents of his heart and mind—would say that Williams was one of these fortunate people. Sometimes, having "everything" is not enough.

Carl Jung, R. D. Laing and others made the distinction between the real self and the persona, the mask a person presents to the world. All we ever saw of Robin Williams—from his stand-up routines, his appearances on late-night TV, his movies, his performances for charity—appeared as creations of his persona, the *act* that he so successfully put on for us.

While the persona is faring well, the real self "underneath" the mask may be out of touch, cut off, dying. No matter how successful our "act" is, we are stuck with this "real" part of ourselves—unless, of course, we choose to end our lives. For some who make this choice, like Robin Williams, the creations of their persona live on (Itzkoff 2014).

Adjustment Reaction

An adjustment reaction is defined as a response to some stressor or negative experience that is milder than the depressive or anxiety reactions characterized so far, with less severe symptoms and less overall disruption of life and work. Lesser world transformations of the kind previously described for depression and anxiety no doubt underlie these pathological reactions. Adjustment reactions are different from the boundary situations that were considered earlier because, in these situations, pathological defenses are not necessarily invoked, and the suffering involved is existential rather than pathological.

Grief Reaction

Losing someone one deeply cares about, whether a family member, friend or sexually significant other can feel like having a part of one's existence ripped out, leaving one in freefall. This is the existential condition of grief, the emotional fallout that often comes with the death of some valued person. Grief, sometimes called bereavement, is a more or less authentic response made to a reduced world. The grief response largely preserves the instrumental world of cause and effect, restricting the pain suffered there mostly to existential pain, the pain caused by the loss itself, without significantly invoking immature, neurotic or Meyerian maladaptive defenses. A grief reaction is a lesser response than, say, an adjustment reaction, which though relatively mild, is still in the pathological spectrum.

Grief implies a certain degree of coping and dealing with a world diminished by loss, of eschewing the self-deceiving conceit "I can't do it" in favor of an explicit (or implicit) "I will get through this." To grieve is to acknowledge feelings of loss while not dedifferentiating and deconstructing the instrumental world of cause and effect. In grief, the pain is worked through existentially, without the kind of depressive world transformation that at first seems to make things easier, but then devolves into a pathological condition that is ultimately more devastating and harder to work through. Those experiencing grief would do well to be aware of this beckoning transformation so as to be in a better position to avoid it. Their clinicians should assist them in this effort.

In his treatise on psychotherapy, *Persuasion and Healing* (1991), the Meyerian psychiatrist, and professor of psychiatry at Johns Hopkins, Jerome D. Frank coined the term *demoralization* to signify a number of mental states that include discouragement, disappointment, frustration, worry and grief. These emotions derive from a loss of power over one's environment in the wake of negative experience or loss but are distinguishable from major depression, even as the potential for a depressive reaction looms. Again it seems that what distinguishes the demoralizing reactions that Frank describes from depression is the absence of defenses that transform the instrumental world into the dedifferentiated world that spawns a pathological mood. (Jerome Frank began his work on depression while Freudian psychoanalysis still held sway in psychiatry. He was one of the first clinicians to insist that depression could be understood as a reaction to some negative event occurring at any time in one's life and was not a production of the unconscious caused by early sexual trauma.)

Freud made a distinction between mourning and melancholia, both triggered by loss, but a loss processed—reacted to, in Meyer's parlance—in very different ways. Mourning is a process that leads to a death being ultimately accepted as final, so that the person is felt to be irretrievably gone. This is the work of grief. In melancholia, the lost object (person) is magically and inauthentically kept alive as an internalized image that serves as a proxy for the dead person. To lose someone to death authentically is to allow that person to die twice: first, when clinical death is pronounced; then with the realization that the person will no longer be present in any accessible way. When this reality is not acknowledged, a pathological melancholia can take hold that sets some on a path to serious depression.

Much has been made in psychiatry—especially by the DSM-5 Task Force—of the differential between grief and major depression. The stickiest part of this question seems to be distinguishing if and when a grief reaction becomes a depressive reaction and deciding whether patients should be medicated for their grief/depression. Perhaps this is not the best way to pose the question. Rather we might inquire into the *nature of the reaction* undergone by the person who has suffered the loss, with the idea of determining if instrumentality has been largely preserved, or whether a depressive reaction, with a dedifferentiating transformation, has occurred and altered the structure of the person's being, and relationship to the world.

While the DSM-5 essentially counts symptoms and measures the time since the loss occurred to make a determination of grief vs. depression, the method developed for the FDMI looks to the *phenomenon* of what is being experienced by the person working through a loss. Questioning and observing the patient, talking to others who know the patient's situation, preferably before and after the loss, and matching these facts (Meyer's "facts" extracted from the patient's narrative) to what has been said here about both the instrumental world of cause and effect and the dedifferentiated world should allow a clinician to gage where the patient is in the grief-depression spectrum. Clearly this call will be more difficult to make with some patients than with others.

Grief is sometimes complicated by what has been called survivor guilt. This is the feeling that, while the gift of life continues for one person, it was taken, perhaps prematurely and unjustly, from the deceased. The anniversary reaction is another complication of the grief process. A birthday can enhance a memory or trigger an augmented response to a death through a regression that partially undermines the healing achieved in the grief process. We measure our lives in various units of time, and a year is an especially strong cultural prompt.

Dysthymic Reaction

As some people are chronically anxious, others are chronically sad or unhappy. For those with a dysthymic temperament, it does not take a specific negative experience or loss to bring on feelings of sadness or unhappiness: this is their emotional ground state, an orientation to the world that is more or less fixed. The dysthymic reaction is distinguished from depression by the fact that, if a dedifferentiating transformation does occur, it is not as encompassing as with depression and from grief by the fact that dysthymia is not pegged to the loss of a valued other.

In the life of the dysthymic person, brief periods of joy may supervene but these experiences quickly fade to the default mode of sadness. In dysthymia, it is as if the world is encountered through a filter that removes the "highs" from the spectrum of normal emotional response. This transformation most likely originates in maladaptive reactions to difficult life experiences that were not as traumatic, or strongly reacted to, as incidences that underlie neurotic, borderline or psychotic pathology. Those with dysthymic temperaments have some of the same somatic complaints as people with depression, only to a lesser degree.

Pathological Anger Reaction[2]

Anger is an emotion that is familiar to everyone. An episode of anger may dissipate quickly and harmlessly or evolve into a murderous rage. Between the benign and malignant endpoints in the spectrum of this dimensional emotion, a seething, chronic anger may come to dominate a person's thinking, feeling and behavior. This is pathological anger.

In spite of the universality of anger, psychiatry has not addressed this emotion as a phenomenon in its own right. Anger is mentioned in the DSM-5 only as a symptom, primarily in personality disorders and drug withdrawal syndromes. In fact, there is not even an entry for anger in the DSM-5's Index, or Glossary of Technical Terms. (Academic and business institutions are way ahead of the DSM

2 Pathological anger appears with depression in the 1st domain because, though a different phenomenon, this serious and chronic loss of emotional control derives from a world transformation that is similar in some ways to a depressive reaction.

on anger. Most people in the workplace who regularly display angry behavior will sooner or later be required to take classes in anger management.)

It is clear that what angers some people leaves others unaffected. Anger does not arise so much from situations that are inherently anger-provoking as from the meaning a person gives to these situations. Shakespeare's Hamlet recognized that "[T]here's nothing either good or bad, but thinking makes it so" (Act 2, Scene 2). Anger lasts only as long as someone continues to construct a particular situation angrily. Or, put another way, as long as one refuses to *stop* being angry, and continues to indulge in this emotional regression, which is often perversely satisfying.

Sartre saw anger as an attempt to reduce the tension inherent in a difficult situation by redefining the situation so a less demanding solution could be found. In *The Emotions*, he turned the spotlight on himself:

> It is easy to understand the fit of anger which seized me when I could no longer reply to someone with whom I had been bantering. . . . It was a matter of carrying on the discussion at another plane: I was unable to be witty; I made myself formidable and intimidating. I wanted to inspire fear. At the same time I used derived (ersätz) means to conquer my opponent: abuse and threats which were *equivalents for* the witticism I could not find, and, by the abrupt transformation which I imposed upon myself, I became less exacting in my choice of means (pp. 38–39).

As happened with Sartre in this recollected event, anger changes the nature—and the *structure*—of the moment. Going from the instrumental world of normal mood to the transformed world of anger involves what he called the "breaking of one form and the reconstitution of another." Only consciousness, Sartre believed, "by its synthetic activity, can break and reconstitute forms ceaselessly" (1948, p. 40). The self as active agent, powered by the brain, calls the shots here (Muller 2009).

Corrosive, debilitating and destructive anger is a particularly appealing defense for those who live in what the existential psychiatrist Viktor Frankl (1963) called an "existential vacuum," or "inner void," where life is meaningless and empty. Angry words and destructive acts are often used in a defensive attempt to fill that void. Becoming an angry person can create what Erik Erikson called a negative identity—if you can't be good, you can at least be bad—by someone who decides, for whatever reason, that it is *too difficult* to remain in a rational, instrumental, discursive mode.

Anger is a fall from a higher to a lower state of being, a transformation that leads to a degradation of self and the abuse of others. Angry people implicitly acknowledge as much when they admit, "I lost my temper," or simply, "I lost it."

The pathologically angry person occupies a world that differs structurally from someone who only occasionally becomes angry, then quickly returns to a ground state of normal emotion. His is a "different existence," a pathological state. Anger is often a component of more complex and serious mental illnesses. When clinicians fail to recognize pathological anger in its own right, this phenomenon is often mistaken for, and diagnosed as, one of these illnesses. Chronic anger can be misread as irritability, which can then be counted as one of the cardinal symptoms of bipolar disorder. Like depression, chronic anger can compromise, and even paralyze cognition and volition, leading to an incorrect diagnosis of dementia. And this kind of angry transformation is often a component of the lethal mix of emotion, cognition and volition present in those who commit murder and mass murder (Appendix D).

Depressed persons are often angry, and Freud believed that depression is "anger turned inward." Lacking an adequate outlet for expression, anger might well be "turned around" to drive the structural dedifferentiation of a depressive reaction. Conversely, it is imaginable that a demoralized, hopeless person, inhabiting an undifferentiated, structurally flattened, de-pressed (pressed down) world might make a further structural transformation (as Sartre describes in his own angry reaction) and lash out angrily in pain, enviously retaliating against someone who still lives in the differentiated, rational and more rewarding world of cause and effect.

Chapter 8 The Dissociation Spectrum

Dissociation is generally considered to be experienced along a continuum that begins with a nonpathological detachment from one's immediate surroundings, such as walking on a beach or driving on a highway. The specifics of self and environment are "tuned out" in favor of a state of reverie that a neutral environment may favor. These common experiences are more coping mechanism than defense mechanism and are often employed to offset boredom or reduce stress. Daydreaming is another example of this kind of "tuning out."

So is compartmentalization, where certain noisome elements of one's life are held at bay, for a time anyway. President Bill Clinton made great use of this strategy as he fought the Articles of Impeachment brought against him in 1998 by the House of Representatives. Of course Clinton was greatly supported in this ploy by a long-running booming economy and the fact that his ratings with the American people were higher *after* impeachment had been voted by the House. In compartmentalization, psychic integration is maintained as attention is directed away from some unpleasant, and potentially damaging situation in a process that could be thought of as "walling off." Sometimes, what is walled off resolves as a matter of course, sometimes not.

Dissociative Reaction

Depending on the degree of disruption of the formerly integrated functions of consciousness, memory, identity and perception, what begins as a coping mechanism may evolve into a defensive reaction to psychological, physical or sexual trauma. These maladaptive reactions may come into play gradually or suddenly and may be transient or chronic.

The DSM-5 dissociative disorders are renamed dissociative *reactions* here, and the order in which these reactions are grouped has been changed to reflect what appears to be an increasing degree of pathological severity: depersonalization reaction, dissociative amnesia reaction, dissociative fugue reaction and dissociative identity reaction.

Depersonalization Reaction

The main feature of a depersonalization reaction is a *detachment* from what we have been calling the self as active agent. Sometimes this reaction of a formerly integrated self occurs to the point where a person becomes an observer of the body formerly experienced as his own. During these episodes, even though a person's fundamental sense of reality is preserved, there can be an impairment of social and professional function. The dissociative reaction is distinguished from a psychotic reaction by the fact that, in dissociation, a person becomes *detached* from reality, attempting to be spared from the pain of past trauma or the possibility that a new stressor could deepen the original traumatic wound. With psychosis, this quest involves a more severe psychobiological transformation through which the experience of reality is *lost*.

All his life, the screenwriter and film director Ingmar Bergman struggled with the trauma of having had a mother who did not want the baby she gave birth to. Caught in a loveless and fraught marriage, which having this infant prevented her from leaving, Mrs. Bergman periodically abandoned her son, forcing others to provide the care that she was too self-absorbed and broken to provide herself. Bergman grew to maturity simultaneously needing the love and support of women and angrily rejecting the women he became involved with. The painful deficits incurred in his early development had rendered him incapable of forming an enduring bond with them.

Bergman described in his autobiography, *The Magic Lantern* (1989), his first sexual encounter, at age 15, with his school friend Anna. The conflict that would color every relationship he had with women was evident during that first encounter. The sex was rough: he hit Anna, bruising her lip. It was as if Bergman was repeating the physical abuse he had witnessed between his mother and one of her man friends, who had also physically attacked the young boy, splitting off a sliver of a front tooth. Bergman's parents did not get along and were sometimes violent toward each other. The father, a Lutheran pastor, was a religious tyrant and regularly dosed his son with anxiety and guilt.

Bergman makes it clear that he was not wholly and integrally himself in that first sexual encounter:

> To me, all this was interesting but unreal. What was happening around me was like bits of film loosely put together, partly incomprehensible, sometimes simply sad. I found to my surprise that my senses did indeed register the external reality, but the impulses never reached as far as my emotions. They inhabited a closed room and were produced on command, but never rashly. My reality was so profoundly divided that it had lost consciousness (Bergman 1989, p. 117).

Many of the hallmarks of a dissociative reaction are clearly present in this recollection, most tellingly the acknowledgement that the experience seemed "unreal." The simile "like bits of film loosely put together" signifies how fragmented Bergman must have felt during the sexual act. "Partly incomprehensible" can only mean that he was not fully processing what was happening between him and Anna. As happens in a dissociative reaction, external reality was preserved, though "profoundly divided," since *he* was dissociated from *it* to the point where he "lost consciousness" of *it*.

While rehearsing a play on January 26, 1976, Bergman was taken into custody by the Swedish police and accused of tax fraud. Confined to a cell after being suddenly separated from the creative process that was so important in his efforts to sustain a tenuous identity, his precarious psychological integration did not hold. In another dissociative reaction, Bergman became detached from his own body. In *The Magic Lantern*, he described his state at the time as being "deep down in a motionless vacuum, painless and free of emotions":

> I closed my eyes . . . then sensed there was someone in the room and opened my eyes. In the sharp light, a few metres away, I saw myself as standing and looking at myself. . . . I was standing on the yellow rug looking at myself sitting in the chair. I was sitting in the chair looking at myself sitting in the chair. . . . So far, I who was sitting in the chair was the one in charge of reactions. This was the end, there was no return. I could hear myself wailing (Bergman 1989, pp. 90–93).

Bergman's dissociative reaction was not a strong enough defensive maneuver to save him from further decompensation and his breakdown that followed. He experienced what he called "a deep depression, the first real depression of my life, because I couldn't create." He was hospitalized and heavily medicated—after experiencing a more pathological depressive reaction, with its strategic regression, which he apparently required to deal with this crisis. The act of artistic creation that had kept Bergman integrated in the world of work and people had been forcibly taken from him—unjustly, as it turned out, because the tax fraud accusation was bogus, concocted by the Swedish government as jealous payback for the worldwide acclaim that he had received as a screenwriter and film director. After a brief incarceration and subsequent hospitalization, Bergman resumed working through his psychobiological deficit by making films. He achieved a degree of integration sufficient to do well in a fifth marriage that lasted until he died at the age of 89.

Barbara Young, in *The Persona of Ingmar Bergman: Conquering Demons through Film* (2015), reconstructs Bergman's traumatic infancy and childhood. She identifies the damage done to him by his dysfunctional family, the pain he suffered and, finally, his attempts to heal himself by creating characters in his plays and films who were proxies for him and those who had played significant roles in his life. In working through his pain by experiencing the conflicts of his stand-in characters—and putting this experience front and center for everyone to see—the artist acted as his own therapist. Through this artistic creation, Bergman recreated himself.

Dissociative Amnesia Reaction

Anyone who has experienced anxiety or stress—and who has not?—knows that these states can interfere with cognitive performance. Feeling anxious or stressed after a sudden scare or overload, who has not forgotten to remove a house key from a door lock on the way out? Or not shown up for an appointment? If the stressor is mild, the anxiety state quickly clears and memory returns to normal. If the stressor is a major trauma, cognition may be impaired for intermediate or long periods of time. This more serious amnesia is not ordinary forgetfulness, but a psychobiological aberration that leaves apparent gaps in the capacity to recall events and information.

Some people who experience significant trauma dissociate themselves from the pain and the memory associated with it. Only later—sometimes after a "trigger" event—does the memory present itself. This recall can occur gradually or suddenly, wholly or in parts. Such forgetfulness can be understood as the mind and the brain initially refusing to allow a painful experience into conscious awareness, which would be necessary for the "memory" to be accessible.

This kind of amnesia is a defensive reaction that involves self-deception—essentially a lie one tells oneself, in this case to deny and shut out an experience that is judged too difficult to bear, though probably without realizing that such a judgment has been made. A dissociative amnesia reaction (formerly psychogenic amnesia) can be understood as a *selective dissociation of one aspect of a person's life-story*. It takes a highly traumatic event and a strong censoring response (reaction) to force the memory of a significant event out of conscious awareness. True cases of dissociative amnesia are rare.

Dissociative amnesia reactions have been reported following psychological, physical and sexual trauma. Those experiencing post-traumatic stress reaction (PTSR) sometimes have temporary or long-term amnesia for a traumatic event and the circumstances associated with the event. Along with the real phenomenon that a dissociative amnesia reaction can be, there are a number of reported cases of what has become known as false memory syndrome (FMS), where the so-called recovered memory was of an event that never occurred.

Paul R. McHugh, in *Try to Remember* (2008), presents cases of (mostly) women who, sometimes years or decades after the alleged event, accused men, most often their fathers, of sexual abuse. In many instances, these women were encouraged—induced may be a better word—to believe that a current dysfunctional state originated in this abuse. The title of McHugh's book echoes the prompting of therapists, with many different kinds of credentials, who encouraged patients to "try to remember" the event that "ruined" their lives. It takes self-deception to suppress the memory of a traumatic event that actually occurred. It takes a differently motivated kind of self-deception to craft a memory of an event that never happened.

Dissociative Fugue Reaction

Dissociative fugue reaction (formerly psychogenic fugue) occurs even more rarely than the rare dissociative amnesia reaction—few clinicians ever encounter it—and represents a significantly higher level of pathology. The word *fugue* comes from the Latin *fugere*, which means *flight*. In a dissociative fugue, a person suddenly leaves the scene of a chronically traumatic environment or acute event and travels, sometimes long distances, taking on a new, or partially new, identity. The entire memory associated with the former identity may be lost, unlike a dissociative amnesia reaction where only some memories are lost. As the person pursues a life with a different or mixed identity, new—anterograde—memories are encoded.

As would be expected, the "new life" a person begins in this way is not free from psychological pain or functional impairment. Still, someone may fly under the radar at least until caught out as the new identity, under pressure from new challenges, begins to fray. When the fugue state ends—this condition usually lasts from hours to months, but may be more refractory—memory from the person's original life and identity returns. The memory created *during* the fugue sometimes disappears.

Dissociative fugue reaction can be thought of as psychic pathology with legs. Not only are traumatic memories hidden from consciousness as in the dissociative amnesia reaction, but the physical environment in which these memories were created is abandoned, and precipitously. People, places and events associated with the trauma are left behind. Those using this defense literally get the hell out of Dodge!

Before diagnosing a dissociative fugue reaction, dissociative identity reaction (DIR)—the most severe pathology emanating from a primary dissociation defense, as well as other primary psychiatric reactions that are known to suppress memory and effect behavior in this way—must be ruled out. So must physiological and medical conditions that can produce these alterations.

Dissociative Identity Reaction (DIR)

Approaching the dissociation of an individual into multiple identities as a *reaction* to a traumatic experience rather than as a set of symptoms characterized by the DSM-5 as dissociative identity disorder (DID) permits a fundamental question to be asked immediately and directly: Is the often dramatic deviation from normal behavior captured in this designation a real phenomenon?

Of all the DSM-5 categorical diagnoses, DID may be the most controversial, as well as the most elusive. The seemingly confident stance implied in the DSM definition betrays no sense of this uncertainty: "Dissociative Identity Disorder [formerly Multiple Personality Disorder] is characterized by a) the presence of two or more distinct personality states or an experience of possession and b) recurrent episodes of amnesia" (DSM-5 2013, p. 291).

The conditions to be ruled out before making the DID diagnosis include the imaginative play of children; religious dissociative reveries that were prevalent in the Middle Ages and continue into the 21st century, in some cultures more than in others; psychotic reactions; and medical conditions such as substance abuse, epilepsy, brain infections, brain tumors and other brain lesions.

True to its commitment to being atheoretical about etiology, the DSM-5 omits any serious consideration of the psychodynamic meaning of DID. (A move was made in that direction in the DSM-IV when the DSM-III appellation multiple personality disorder (MPD) was dropped in favor of DID, which implies something about the mechanism behind this phenomenon.) True to our approach in the FDMI, we wish to know what motivates the deviation from the norm that occurs when a person employs more than one center of identity around which to organize and live a life. What psychological needs are met? What is being gained, and at what cost?

In the 1st domain reactions that have been characterized so far, the self as active agent reacts pathologically to anxiety and pain produced in certain life encounters with a compromised—though *singular*—consciousness. In this process, which often involves the structural (ontic) transformation of a person's world, a single identity is pathologically modified so as to live through what cannot, or will not, be authentically encountered.

In the FDMI's dissociative identity reaction (DIR), the self as active agent takes its defensive strategy a step further by distributing to *multiple centers of identity* the pain that usually originates in a physical, psychological or sexual trauma. This dispersion is followed by a coalescing of elements separated from a formerly (if tenuously) unified self around one or more of these additional identity centers. The so-called "personalities" that emerge from this dispersion can differ from each other in name, style, character, age and, in some cases, even race and sex. It is as if the dissociating person were saying, I can't/won't deal with what the world has done to me: let X handle the pain, where X is another identity created for that purpose. In many instances, psychobiological deficiencies of the 2nd domain—originating in intrinsic limitations of intellect, temperament and personality development—predispose a person to react in this way.

The person who dissociates—whether reacting defensively to severe trauma, or capitulating to a therapist's support of a fabricated one, as McHugh describes in *Try to Remember*—forfeits the self's structural integrity. Simultaneously, that person's authenticity is compromised through the artifice of making another "personality" or "alter" responsible for some of the thoughts, feelings and behavior which it deems unacceptable. In this process, the original, tenuously unified self becomes a partly *inactive* agent by surrendering some of its freedom to what could be imagined as a dissociated fragment of the original self, created for that purpose. The DSM-IV maintained that behind this "switch" there are ". . . distinct identities or personality states that recurrently take control of the individual's behavior . . ." (1994, p. 477). This account seems to shift the responsibility for dissociative pathology to the illness itself, relieving the patient of that liability.

While trying to persuade us that "alter personalities" are not real people, Colin A. Ross, in his book *Multiple Personality Disorder* (1989) addresses the issue of what kind of phenomenon MPD actually is:

> The most important thing to understand is that alter personalities are not people . . . [but] highly stylized enactments of inner conflicts, drives, memories, and feelings. At the same time they are dissociated packets of behavior developed for transaction with the outside world. They are fragmented parts of one person: There is only one person. The patient's conviction that there is more than one person in her is a dissociative delusion and should not be compounded by a *folie à deux* on the part of the therapist . . . MPD is an elaborate pretending. The patient *pretends* that she is more than one person, in a very convincing manner. She actually believes it herself (p. 109).

We can imagine a psychobiologically vulnerable individual, particularly someone with 2nd domain pathology, who is facing an overwhelming trauma that causes her (women account for most dissociative reactions) significant anxiety and emotional pain choosing the dissociative route *around* the pain by assigning it to another personality fragment created for that purpose rather than attempting to face and work through the pain authentically. Clearly, this is an act of self-deception.

But why would someone employ *this* defensive reaction (DIR) over some other, less pathological 1st domain reaction? In the hierarchy of reality-denying pathological reactions, psychosis is the ultimate, the most drastic reaction; the DIR seems to be next down that list. In characterizing the creation of an additional personality as a "dissociative delusion," Ross blurs the boundary between what at first appears to be two different pathological reactions and phenomena: dissociation and psychosis. That conflation may be just what is required to correctly characterize the phenomenon of the DIR. The specter of self-deception—the lie we tell ourselves—can be felt hovering over the person who is coming to believe that *another person* who has appeared within her is responsible for some of what *she* is feeling and doing.

Ross believes that a clinician who holds to this view of the DIR would do well to begin by refusing to acknowledge the reality of more than one person. Nonetheless, it may be necessary to "talk to alters" to begin the integration of a fragmented personality. The emphasis could then be quickly shifted to issues that the originally integrated person put up the dissociative defense to avoid:

> The alters, put another way, are *devices*. Like any theater, the personality system is based on certain conventions and structural rules. Part of the therapy is mapping and dismantling these, replacing them with normal, happier, and more functional rules and structure. The patient is acting *as if* she is more than one person, but she isn't. This is different from Hollywood acting because the patient is so absorbed in the different roles that she believes in their reality (pp. 109–110).

Just because a person instigates a dissociative identity reaction does not mean that the ensuing pathology is not a real phenomenon, as is sometimes claimed. An exception would be instances of malingering where "alter personalities" are deliberately feigned.

Like all 1st domain reactions, dissociative reactions are dimensional. Depending on the trauma sustained and the extent of the psychobiological transformation made in response to it, the subsequent pathology may fall anywhere along a spectrum that includes "simple" dissociation, depersonalization, dissociated amnesia, dissociated fugue and dissociated identity. Because we believe that every mental illness can exist in dimensions of severity, the FDMI does not follow *The Perspectives of Psychiatry* in seeing dimensionality as the defining property of 2nd perspective, or 2nd domain, illnesses.

Chapter 9 The Psychosis Spectrum

Many clinicians believe that all psychotic symptoms have an organic cause, which would make psychotic depression a disease of the 4th domain. The fact is that some patients with severe depression go on to develop psychotic symptoms (mostly delusions and hallucinations) from their already psychologically weakened depressive states, with themes—guilt, low self-esteem, self-reproach—that are related to the depressive content of these states. A depressive psychotic reaction is considered here a condition of the 1st domain. (Phenomena of 4th domain psychotic conditions are characterized in Chapters 12–16.)

Depressive Psychotic Reaction

It is not difficult to see how, in those with certain psychobiological vulnerabilities, the dedifferentiating transformation that leads to severe depression can progress to psychotic depression. If a strategic depressive retreat is not sufficient to spare the patient from what he cannot, or will not deal with, psychosis can lead to a world so different from the one known as reality as to be only marginally related to it (Lief 1948, p. 305). This psychotic world has its own unique ontic structure, meaning and language. The designation depressive psychotic reaction, which lacks the modifying word dynamic, is not meant to ignore the dynamic forces that are clearly in play in this pathology. Though depression can prepare the ground for, and coexist with, psychosis, psychotic depression is a single phenomenon.

Paranoid Psychotic Reaction

Paranoid psychotic reactions are elaborations of character pathology in the absence of depression sufficient to drive the psychosis. Like depressive paranoid reactions, these are 1st domain conditions and often have a 2nd domain diathesis.

Paranoia is a feeling that is familiar to everyone. This phenomenon is anxiety expressed as an exaggerated fear of an external threat and exists along a continuum. Like anxiety, some paranoia is good, but too much can be paralyzing.

Being paranoid, a person implicitly denies chance occurrences, insisting that events which most people consider random are malignantly interconnected, and maliciously motivated by others. Paranoia involves making connections that should not be made. This condition is a learned incapacity—a Meyerian bad habit that ultimately involves various modes and degrees of self-deception—of not being able to accept coincidence as a normal occurrence in life. The psychologist Philip G. Zimbardo sees the thought process of the paranoid person as reasoning "correctly from a false premise" (Herbert 1989). *If* the threat were real, the response *would* be appropriate.

The word *paranoia* is used to designate both normal and pathological states along the continuum of this phenomenon. Delmore Schwartz must have understood how thin the dividing line between these states can be when he famously said, "Even paranoids have real enemies" (Herbert 1989).

Why would someone want to break the bounds of reality by creating a false external threat? One explanation is that a person with a tentative identity chooses to create enemies so as *to become the persecuted one*, instead of no one, and as a ploy for relating to others, if perversely. No person can live without some sense of who he is and of his place in the world. As Erik Erikson pointed out, people prefer a negative identity—an existence at odds with the directives of the norm—to no identity at all. The identity-creating power of paranoia is probably what makes this maladaptive reaction the most stable of the psychotic defenses, allowing patients to remain compensated in their delusions for long periods of time. Also, there is no shortage of people or situations for those who need and choose to be paranoid to appropriate for this purpose. Those so inclined have access to an infinitely renewable source of experience to be paranoid about.

As early as 1860, Bénédict Morel, a French physician, realized that "In many instances, psychosis is nothing more than an exaggeration of the usual character" (Séchehaye 1956, p. 80). Later, Meyer expressed the same idea, using virtually the same words (Lief 1948, pp. 247–259). If the nature of the psychosis produced depends on the person's 2nd domain character pathology, as Morel and Meyer implicitly believed, each person will become psychotic for their own reasons and in their own way.

This seems to have been the case with Mrs. K, who found her way to exceed the boundaries of authentic, decent behavior by accusing her grandchildren of acts of petty theft that cast them, and their mother whom she treated hatefully, as failures. For some reason, Mrs. K *needed* to see her daughter and grandchildren in this compromised way. Mrs. K had some of the risk factors for paranoia, including advancing age, relative social isolation and problems hearing and seeing, though she still ambulated well and her health was good for a nonagenarian.

At 95 years of age, Mrs. K lives alone in a ranch-style house on half an acre of land in a rural suburb. On most days during the spring, summer and fall when the weather is good, she works outdoors in the garden. During the fall of her 95th year, she raked 40 bags of leaves. During the winter, when the snow is six inches or less, Mrs. K shovels the driveway out to the road; after heavier accumulations, she calls in someone with a plow. She never complains about having to cope with the long, cold winters.

Mrs. K pays her own bills and never overdraws her checking account. She prefers to spend most of her time alone and encourages only occasional, short visits from family members. She has no friends and wants none, even though neighbors occasionally make overtures to her. She keeps up with the outside world by watching the news on cable TV. In 1986 Mrs. K's husband died suddenly from heart failure. She has never shown any sign of mourning and, in fact, seemed rejuvenated by her husband's death. Though Mrs. K values life in her advancing years and takes good care of herself, she has made it clear that she is not afraid to die.

Mrs. K has a good quality of life and can still do many of the things that were always important to her. Her sense of the world is largely intact. She appears thin and frail, but for a nonagenarian, her health is good. Her close vision has deteriorated because of macular degeneration, and she can no longer sew, but beyond 6 feet she sees well. She takes 81 mg of aspirin every other day, and receives monthly subcutaneous injections of vitamin B12 and folic acid. Mrs. K has had occasional chest pains since her mid-80s, which her doctor attributes to angina. Sometime after that she was found to have atrial fibrillation. Her only prescription medications are Cardizem and Plavix.

Mrs. K has a son and a daughter, both in their 60s. The daughter and her four grown children live nearby; the son lives in a distant city. The daughter, who is divorced, does Mrs. K's grocery shopping and drives her to doctors appointments.

Mrs. K's mental life is intact, except for this one glitch: She claims to believe that her grandchildren come in the middle of the night, or when she is away during the day, to steal her possessions and that her daughter knows and approves of this. The "stolen" items include sheets, towels, pots and pans, milk and orange juice. According to Mrs. K, her sterling silver and antiques are being sold and replaced with cheaper items by her grandchildren so they can pocket the difference. These accusations have been made time and again, over a period of many years. Mrs. K also claims that her phone is being tapped. She puts all the blame for this intrusion on her grandchildren and does not feel that either the phone company or the government is involved. According to Mrs. K, the grandchildren listen in on her phone calls because they want to know when she is going to sell her house and when they will get their inheritance.

Mrs. K alleges that her grandchildren steal from her and covet her money because things are not going well for them. Being reminded that three of the grandchildren have good jobs and that the fourth has a husband who makes a respectable living does not sway Mrs. K from this belief. She has been able to convince herself that her grandchildren need the money they steal from her to survive, and that she is their savior. Mrs. K's apparent hatred for her family, manifested in many ways over many years, appears to be transformed through this self-deception into an act of *their* betrayal. The ultimate reason for this woman's hatred is opaque, but there has always been something about her family being successful and happy that has threatened her and tweaked her envy.

The roots to Mrs. K's ambivalence about her family go back decades. After bestowing some favor on her son or daughter, she would frequently ask, "Why am I doing this for you?" as if the answer were not apparent to her. She seemed to give with one hand only to take back with the other. On her daughter's wedding day, as the bride walked from the church toward the limousine that was taking the couple to the reception, Mrs. K was heard to say, "I'm sorry I ever let that girl get married." The ceremony had gone well and no one could have known at the time that the groom, a lawyer who was on his way to a successful career, was also on his way to a confrontation with alcohol that would eventually end that career as well as contribute to the dissolution of his marriage. When Mrs. K's son was in grammar school she told him, "Nothing you do will ever make any difference to me." On several occasions at that time she also said, "One day you will come home and find me dead on the floor, with the gas on." By any standard, this is nasty, cruel stuff.

Mrs. K clearly meets criteria for what the DSM-5 designates as delusional disorder, persecutory type. Though she has often directed outbursts of anger tinged with paranoia at family members, she has never shown any indication of being clinically depressed or even of having had a sustained period of low mood. No case can be made for psychotic depression, or for schizophrenia. Mrs. K has never been manic or hypomanic. Neither she nor any of her blood relatives have ever been diagnosed with or treated for a mental illness.

Shortly after her 97th birthday, Mrs. K suffered a right-sided parietal-occipital hemorrhagic stroke. Already impaired by macular degeneration, her sight was further compromised by the occipital component of the stroke, leaving her legally blind. Her speech was not affected, and she still had the use of her arms and legs and could walk with assistance. Mrs. K understood what had happened to her and was cooperative with the hospital staff, though she continued to verbally abuse her daughter during visits, once calling her a "devil."

Mrs. K was given the choice of returning home with a caretaker or going to a nursing home. Her daughter, who had been the object of her derision for so long, declined to oversee her care at home and Mrs. K was transferred to a nursing home. She settled in quickly, never complained about having to be there, never asked about returning home and eventually became one of the staff's favorite patients. "They think she's a nice old lady," the daughter said, unable to hide her surprise. The paranoia that Mrs. K had exhibited at home seems to have died out in the nursing home. She never made an accusation against anyone there.

Mrs. K's Plavix was continued and a low dose of Seroquel was started and continued for several months, not because she was agitated or psychotic but because that was the institution's policy (she was as psychologically stable off the drug as on it). At first, her daughter visited regularly, but these visits upset Mrs. K. She did not complain when her daughter visited less frequently.

While at the nursing home, Mrs. K had no significant medical complications and did not develop bed sores or infections. Eighteen months after being admitted, she took a downward turn, stopped eating and drinking and died peacefully two weeks later. She was 98 years old.

How do we understand the drastic change in Mrs. K's behavior following her stroke? The disappearance of her paranoia after she entered the nursing home (on Seroquel, and off) does not support the idea that her psychotic symptoms emerged from a brain disease that was mollified by an atypical antipsychotic drug. While it could be argued that brain changes brought on by the stroke itself quashed the psychotic emanations of a diseased brain, it seems more likely that the sequestration of Mrs. K from her daughter and grandchildren imposed by the stroke—the daughter visited the nursing home rarely, the grandchildren not at all—attenuated the ambiguous, highly charged feelings she experienced while regularly interacting with them.

It is probable that, prior to her stroke, Mrs. K had not been able to contain these negative feelings, which likely caused anxiety sufficient to produce a paranoid psychotic reaction. The reason *why* she felt so threatened by and hateful toward these blameless people is ultimately a mystery, and most likely rooted in some 2nd domain pathology.

It is clear from the narrative that Mrs. K's ambivalent behavior toward her son was already evident when the boy was in grammar school and grew more pronounced as he became older; the ambivalence toward the daughter started later. This pattern fits Morel's belief that psychosis is an "exaggeration of the usual character." Mrs. K, though hateful toward her family through much of her adult life, became psychotic only in her 80s, after her husband died. The need *not* to be close to family members—emotional intimacy apparently being intolerable to her—probably increased as she aged, lived alone and then lost some of her vision and hearing (Muller 2006). In this model, the delusions and hallucinations generated in her paranoid reaction were "exaggerated" responses to increased anxiety originating in a perceived threat from her adult children and grandchildren.

Other Dynamic Psychotic Reactions

What Morel saw, in effect, as exaggerated reactions to pathology of the 2nd domain are by no means limited to paranoia. All character pathologies, or personality disorders, weaken the ontic ground in which a person is rooted, sometimes sufficiently to incline that person toward a psychotic reaction. These dynamic reactions can occur when histrionic, narcissistic, borderline, schizoid and obsessive-compulsive defenses can no longer "protect" someone from destructive internal or external threats.

Brief Psychotic Reaction

Brief psychotic reaction names essentially the same pathology that is specified in the DSM-5 as brief psychotic disorder. This decompensation occurs as a sudden onset of psychotic symptoms in the absence of a medical condition (including delirium), the effects of drugs or alcohol or a mood disorder (depression or mania), with or without significant identifiable stressors. As in the more chronic psychotic reactions, these brief reactions, which can last from minutes to months, are often elaborations of 2nd domain pathology.

No psychotic illness—not Mrs. K's 1st domain paranoid reaction, and not the more serious 4th domain psychotic reactions that will be characterized later on—can be validly diagnosed by counting symptoms of a syndromic construct, as the DSM-5 prescribes. To make a valid diagnosis, the essence of the patient's pathological experience must first be ascertained from the narrative, then compared with the phenomena in the FDMI's spectrum of psychotic reactions. If a satisfactory match is not found, the patient's illness should be described in as much detail as possible so this "different existence," as van den Berg named it, can stand out and, in effect, announce itself as itself.

The Second Domain

Maladaptive Reactions Occurring in the Context of Aberrant Personality Development and Temperament

Chapter 10 Aberrant Personality Styles

Anyone hoping to understand and characterize the deformation of existence that has come to be known as mental illness would do well to first come to terms with what life is like for those who do *not* have a mental illness—in other words, what it means to be "normal," to make the best of one's life, in what Voltaire in *Candide* called "the best of all possible worlds." (The emphasis in this aphorism falls on *possible*, not *best*.)

The fact is that all of us—those with and without a mental illness—construct our existence *from moment to moment*. We maintain that existence within a flux which only *appears* to be static and solid. One does not have to recognize or acknowledge this fact for it to be so. Whatever we do, or don't do, inevitably involves a response, or a non-response. A response that ignores the environment we find ourselves in is still a response.

It is impossible *not* to be in an environment. Even if one is imprisoned and held in solitary confinement, this attenuated venue is still our environment. We are all inescapably related to our surroundings, which is to say that *we and everyone and everything else in our domain are not separate but dialectically interrelated*. (In a dialectical interaction, A and B do not exist separately as A and B, but inextricably as A-B.) Mental illness is a distortion of the dialectical interaction between the self as active agent and the world, and a deformation of that self, leading to what J. H. van den Berg (1972) characterized as a "different existence."

Second Domain Deformations of Personality

Illnesses of the 2nd domain, which originate in anomalies in the development of personality and temperament, often produce a more entrenched and enduring pathology than 1st domain reactions. Those who develop 2nd domain illnesses have a variety of psychobiological deficits—constitutional factors, "fault lines" in the structural self—that put them at a disadvantage compared with those without these deficits, whose lives play out on a more level field. They live with what we are calling in the FDMI *pathological personality styles* (Shapiro 1965), what the DSM calls *personality disorders* and what other clinicians, including Otto F. Kernberg (1970a), designate as *character pathology*. Their behavior can be thought of as Meyerian maladaptive reactions that have hardened into chronic Meyerian bad habits. Joel Paris has observed that "Personality disorder can be conceptualized as personality traits that do not work" (Paris 2012, p. 57).

The luck of the draw in one's parents and the throw of the genetic dice do not favor everyone equally. (The philosopher Sören Kierkegaard, who had a hunched back, famously groused that he had not been "consulted" about being born and took umbrage that this decision had been made for him!) Not everyone receives the minimum parental and social affirmation required to develop a degree of selfhood that is necessary to withstand the challenges of life and to succeed as a person. In a very real sense, our earliest years last forever. Those with genetically inherited or developmentally acquired 2nd domain psychobiological deficits may play on a field that is anything but level, causing even their daily routine to be an uphill slog. A 2nd domain deficit, whatever the origin, means that a person will have a lesser *capacity* to deal with the challenges that life inevitably imposes.

When psychobiological development does not reach some minimally satisfactory level—proceeding in a "good enough" way, as Winnicott would have put it—a person may not achieve an adequate identity, or sense of self, and will be less likely to act as a free and purposeful self and with adequate reflection and good judgment. Such a person will be more likely to "jump" at this or that possibility—impulsively—without properly sizing up the likely outcomes and consequences of these actions. Lack of impulse control is a common feature of 2nd domain pathological personality styles.

Meyerians and existentialists implicitly believe that being free is the essence of being human. But they also acknowledge the paradox that inheres as freedom is exercised—or not—by someone with a significant psychobiological deficit. The degree to which freedom can be exercised is always relative to a person's psychobiological constitution as well as the micro and macro environments in which the person is participating at any given time.

We will attempt to characterize the most common pathological personality styles by, ultimately, identifying the *phenomenon* that constitutes each style. In many instances, a person will display one or more of the *traits* that comprise a particular style but not the phenomenon itself. Clinicians should keep this distinction in mind and not take the trait for the phenomenon.

As clinicians and thinkers about mental illness, we identify traits and characterize phenomena so as to better understand the *person* who is mentally ill. This thinking is purposefully "circular," allowing us to come full circle in a venture that otherwise would be unproductively open-ended. The concepts of trait and phenomenon are not entities, but different, if ultimately inseparable, ways of "grabbing" at, and trying to "solidify" the unsubstantial self. Without the insights that exploiting these concepts make possible, a patient's problematic life experience would remain inaccessible and unthematized.

Narcissistic Personality Style

The concept of narcissism—useful because it helps to codify and explain a significant slice of human behavior—derives from the Greek myth of Narcissus (Zweig 1968) as retold by Ovid in the *Metamorphoses* (Ovid 1960, pp. 67–73). Narcissus, a physically attractive 16-year-old boy, had rebuffed everyone who requested his friendship or love, with, according to Ovid, a "pride so fierce no boy, no girl, could touch him." After being rejected, a young suitor offered this prayer: "May Narcissus love one day, so, himself, and not win over the creature whom he loves!" Sympathizing with the rejected boy, Nemesis, Goddess of Vengeance, arranged for Narcissus to find a pool of water with a shining, silver surface in an isolated part of the forest. As Narcissus bent down to drink from the pool, he became infatuated with the image reflected back to him.

Eventually, Narcissus came to understand the kind of trap Nemesis had sprung on him. "I burn with love of my own self. . . . When my lips go down to kiss the pool, his rise, he reaches toward me. You would think that I could touch him—almost nothing keeps us apart." Nothing, that is, but the sameness of the self and its love object. To love himself, without the hope of being loved in return, was Narcissus's punishment from the gods for breaking the basic rules of sociality: categorically rejecting others, turning inward and relying totally on himself.

Narcissus was caught in an irresolvable dilemma: he could not possess the image he pined for, but he could not bring himself to leave the pool and pursue his life elsewhere, either, as that would have meant abandoning the unattainable image! "What love, whose love," he asks, "has ever been more cruel?" Narcissus came to realize what his dilemma would ultimately cost him. "I know I have not long to live, I shall die early, and death is not so terrible since it takes my trouble from me; I am sorry only the boy I love [Narcissus's image in the water] must die: we die together." After his death, Narcissus was transformed into the flower that bears his name, which was the final cruel act of the avenging gods on this prideful son.

Identifying the Phenomenon of Narcissistic Style

Out of the Narcissus myth was born the modern notion of narcissism (Muller 2014a). After reading Ovid's version of the story, Freud described what he called the *narcissistic type*: a person with minimal tension between ego and superego, whose main interest is self-preservation and who is eager to actively engage the world as its leader. Essentially, the narcissistic type identifies with an idealized self-image and a set of entitlements derived from that image.

As with any behavior that has the potential to develop into a full-blown mental illness, narcissism can be parsed into discrete modes: *good* for those whose identification with an ideal self-image is strong but less than total; *bad* for those who lose themselves in various ways to that self-image, usually by overidentifying with it, as Narcissus did; and *really bad* for those who totally fuse with the ideal self-image and proceed to act destructively, even criminally, against others who refuse to affirm and perpetuate that image. We are all narcissists, and necessarily so. It is to our advantage to know what kind of narcissist we are and how this affects us and those around us. Elizabeth Lunbeck, in *The Americanization of Narcissism* (2014), makes the case that the phenomenon of narcissism has two, distinctly opposite, faces.

Healthy Narcissism

We are born into a social network, having been conceived by others and delivered into the world by others. From birth on, we need and seek the approval of those around us. Heinz Kohut (1977), who founded the self-psychology school of psychoanalysis, based his theory of self-development on the notion of *narcissistic mirroring*. In this process, the infant's sense of self-worth is reinforced by empathic adults—primarily the mother—who, through their demeanor, reflect back to the infant the sense that he is present, important and cared about (and also, as R. D. Laing put it, what reality is). This mirroring allows him to develop an identity. Later, others assume the mirroring role, affirming and validating him through the stages of his life.

Having a concept of how things should be for ourselves, others and the world is a crucial element in living a good and productive life. Healthy narcissism implies a reasonably well developed narcissistic mirror that permits an adaptive acceptance and love of self. This capacity frees us to relate to others with mutuality, without demanding that they see us only in flattering ways (Vaillant 2000). People with this kind of narcissistic mirror will be able to survive their own shortcomings and failures as well as the criticism and betrayal of others.

Historically, being called a narcissist has not been a compliment, though a hint of glamour attaches to the label. In *Narcissistic Leaders: Who Succeeds and Who Fails*, Michael Maccoby (2007), a psychoanalyst trained by Erich Fromm, explains why some narcissists achieve the pinnacle of success while others crash and burn. He distinguished what he called the *productive narcissist* from those who ultimately succumb to the negative side of the narcissistic style and whose pathology does them in.

Maccoby sees the following traits as the strengths of productive narcissists: the desire to change the world and create meaning; independent thinking/risk taking; passion; charisma; voracious learning; perseverance; alertness to threats; and a sense of humor. The pantheon of Maccoby's productive narcissists includes Jack Welch, Bill Gates, J. Craig Venter and Oprah Winfrey—household names who changed the world they found themselves in. "The narcissistic personality, as I am defining it here," Maccoby says, "rejects how things *are* for how things *should be*. Narcissists do not react to the external world so much as they try to create it." Never mind, Maccoby insists, that these people are self-absorbed, bend others to their will and put the bottom line ahead of other people's feelings: they get things done and they are worth their salt. We could easily admit the late Steve Jobs and Bill Clinton to this pantheon.

Productive narcissists live under their own power in a way that is fundamentally different from anyone who could be considered independent and self-directed but lacks this personality trait.

Pathological Narcissism

Maccoby names other narcissists who turned out to be worth less than their salt, such as Monsanto's Robert Shapiro and Vivendi's Jean-Marie Messier. Ultimately, these business titans succumbed to the faults that inhere in the narcissistic style of living and threaten to destroy all productive narcissists: not listening to colleagues and employees; oversensitivity to criticism; paranoia; anger; overcompetitiveness; overcontrol; isolation; exaggeration and lying; lack of self-knowledge; and grandiosity. (We feel reverberations of Richard Nixon's self-destruction and Donald Trump's grandiloquence here.) In the business world, some of this over-the-top behavior is necessary and productive (witness Steve Jobs) but too much brings the company down. Maccoby's way of distinguishing the productive narcissist from the failed narcissist—the line between them is often thin and wavering—is a classic example of the dimensionality of human behavior, which means that a trait may be lived in a way that is good, bad or really bad. In Maccoby's failed narcissists, we can see the extreme self-absorption of Narcissus and the capitulation of the superego to the ego that Freud identified in the narcissistic type.

In contrast to the varieties of healthy narcissism, *pathological narcissism* is generally understood as an ongoing defense against a major emotional trauma that is usually experienced early in life. Kohut saw the narcissistic injury as originating in a failure of those most responsible for the care of the infant to affirm and validate him. Later, in a compensatory effort to overcome feelings of inferiority and establish an identity, a person traumatized in this way creates an idealized self-image, which requires that others affirm and validate that image to an unrealistic—"ideal"—degree. George Vaillant has suggested that rather than attributing the self-centered behavior so characteristic of pathological narcissists to their "vanity, grandiosity and entitlement," these reactions should be understood as responses to their untranscended trauma: "An effective way of surmounting the pejorative connotations of the term 'narcissism' is to translate that multisyllabic epithet into the simpler and more empathic phrase 'in pain'" (Vaillant 1992).

If love is taken to imply the capacity for mutuality and giving, pathological narcissists do not, as is often said, love themselves too much but too little. This is why they demand that others "love" them totally, and that the world affirm them absolutely. Pathological narcissism is a compensatory partial fusion of self with others and the world that goes beyond the identification necessary for healthy affirmation and validation. This pathology can be thought of as a perturbation of the dialectic that rules in the normal engagement of self and others, where mutuality, rather than exploitation, is the standard, even though this standard is not consistently met. Narcissus did not love himself at all, since he could only love his *image*. He lived in the ultimate closed system—the casting of self as its own love object—and he could not even partially connect with others.

Exemplars of the Phenomenon of Narcissistic Personality Style

Some of Maccoby's productive narcissists, and all of his failed narcissists, would meet the criteria for *narcissistic personality disorder* specified by the American Psychiatric Association's *Diagnostic and Statistical Manual of Mental Disorders* (DSM-5). The main features of this pathology are grandiosity, the need for admiration and a lack of empathy that persist over time and to a degree that causes significant emotional and behavioral dysfunction. Those with a narcissistic personality act to get their needs met without regard for the cost to others—one reason why they are said to be "self-absorbed"—while often simultaneously demanding the full approval of these same others. When affirmation and validation are withheld or withdrawn, narcissists may lash out at the withholder or crash and burn emotionally. Their grandiosity is a compensatory cover for a weak self and a weak identity, the result of developmental stifling by an early psychic injury.

Christopher Lasch argued in *The Culture of Narcissism* (1978) that our culture is narcissistic to the core, and he was not talking about healthy narcissism. It is no accident that our celebrities are exaggerations of ourselves. The life of the late Diana, Princess of Wales, is now understood as an iconic tale of a narcissistic personality. Tina Brown in *The Diana Chronicles* identifies Diana's original narcissistic injury (though she does not call it that) as an emotional abandonment by her father following her parents' separation when Diana was five. The father withdrew and sulked and seemed to be involved with his children only while he was taking home movies and photographs of them. This, Brown says, is where Diana got the idea that love comes from being captured by a camera lens.

Twenty years later, when her marriage to Prince Charles was unraveling, the original narcissistic injury was very likely reactivated. Once again, Diana looked to the camera for salvation, this time from the tabloid press. And for a while, that strategy worked, up to a point:

> The sunshine of publicity in which Diana would at first be happy to bask, posing and smiling for the cameras, grew steadily hotter and harsher. As the superheated imperatives of an invasive press bumped up increasingly against the milder human necessity of privacy, scattered rains gave way to drenching gales and then to spectacular and finally lethal hurricanes. . . . Diana herself had accelerated the climate change that ended up making her life literally impossible (Weber 2007).

Brown's extended meteorological metaphor (admittedly made of purple prose) is meant to capture the nature of the defensive trap that Diana set for herself when she played the publicity game, attempting to get from the press and its readers the affirmation and validation denied to her by Prince Charles. Predictably, the response by Charles and the Royal Family to Diana's narcissistic ploy was scorn, which no doubt deepened her original narcissistic wound.

The Narcissism of Small Differences

Freud's thinking about narcissism evolved over his long career, and he called one of his elaborations the *narcissism of small differences* (Freud 1910). This variety of pathological narcissism demands that everyone see the world as the narcissist sees it, often down to the smallest details. Paradoxically, narcissists who demand this total mirroring will be more in conflict with those whose world view is closest to their own—where the differences are small—than with others who see the world in a very different way. Presumably, these very different people can be discounted by the small-difference narcissist from the beginning because they do not contribute at all to his idealized self-image and consequently are no threat to it.

Any endeavor where passions run deep and enthusiasms run high, where people are brought together in the heat and light of the same narcissistic mirror, harbors the seeds of its own entropic destruction. Think of how Freud and his closest disciples fought and split ranks as the theory of psychoanalysis diverged from shared ideas. The same thing happened with the major players in the existential movement. Existentialism was, at heart, a revolution in Western philosophical thought. Once the key figures in the movement began to see certain things differently—even though they agreed on much more than they were fighting over—alliances and friendships fractured. Sartre and Camus had an especially bitter falling out (Aronson 2004).

Malignant Narcissism

Pathological narcissists are often attractive and sociable and have the kind of magnetic personalities that draw others to them. They form alliances easily and then find it incomprehensible that someone who was once so committed to them would ultimately refuse to continue in a relationship where there was no mutuality and where emotional and physical abuse was a frequent consequence of frustrating the narcissist's demand for unqualified admiration and subservience.

To pathological narcissists who are abandoned in this way, loss can be experienced as a virtual death. Some are able to imagine restarting their lives only by killing the person who "killed" them (Muller 2011). They find themselves in a situation analogous to Narcissus's when he realized that he would never possess his self-image in the pool—only they kill the other (real) person, instead of accepting their fate as Narcissus did. For these *malignant narcissists*, who can live only in their narcissistic mirror and personify a more virulent phenotype than the narcissistic personality style, the killing is rationalized as an act of self-defense. This is why so many killers can steadfastly and convincingly maintain their innocence, in court and in media interviews, in spite of solid evidence pointing to their guilt (think O. J. Simpson). Malignant narcissists who resort to murder for "self-preservation" are often sociopaths, and sometimes psychopaths, and act in ways described under the rubric of antisocial personality. When wounded pride is the primary narcissistic injury, murder can take the form of an honor killing.

The behavior of the world's worst dictators—history's monsters—can be understood as originating in defenses attributed to malignant narcissists (Goode 2003). A dictator will often fuse an idealized, grandiose self-image with some divinity, in the process justifying his manipulation of everyone and everything toward an end of his own choosing, without regard for any external limits. Studying the life of Adolf Hitler, Timothy W. Ryback (2003) concluded that, for Hitler, "the mortal and the divine were one and the same: that the God he was seeking was in fact himself." This is the ultimate narcissistic fusion, which, in Hitler's case, fueled the ultimate narcissistic malignancy.

The identification of malignant narcissism is generally credited to Erich Fromm (1964), but Otto Kernberg made this concept a part of the psychiatric and psychoanalytic discussion, though neither the DSM-5 nor earlier editions of the DSM mention it. Besides narcissistic qualities, Kernberg saw the malignant narcissist as having paranoid and antisocial traits, as well as aggressive and sadistic tendencies unbridled by conscience (1970b). Many serial killers and mass murderers are malignant narcissists.

Some Kill Those They Love

Loving and being loved are widely held to be among the highest human achievements. Yet it must be acknowledged that what starts out well in the name of love often ends badly and sometimes tragically. Stories of lives that have come to ruin through foundering love are common. Newspapers, films and TV offer example after example of failed love in its natural state, which is to say before clinicians get to weigh in with a diagnosis.

The ultimate pathological fracture of a love relationship occurs when one person dies at the hand of the other. That is what happened May 3, 2010, to Yeardley Love, a senior and varsity lacrosse player at the University of Virginia who was murdered by her ex-boyfriend George Huguely. This story immediately became a national media event (Muller 2011).

Several hours before Love's body was discovered by her roommate, bystanders witnessed an angry verbal exchange between Love and Huguely, who was also a senior and a varsity lacrosse player at UVA. In the weeks before the murder, Huguely had called and texted Love incessantly, telling friends that he hoped to revive their relationship, which she had ended.

Huguely admitted to police that he had broken into Love's off-campus apartment in Charlottesville and shaken her repeatedly as her head struck a wall. The 6-foot-2-inch, 209-pound defense player was arrested and charged with first-degree murder. He acknowledged causing Love's death, which his attorney claimed was "an accident with a tragic outcome" (Timanus & Brady 2010).

Just about everyone experiences the end of a romantic or sexual relationship, with subsequent emotions that can range anywhere from mild disappointment to despair. How people react in these situations depends on multiple factors related to the kind of life they have had up to that point and especially on how they handle loss. Ultimately, the outcome of this kind of trauma turns on whether the bereft person can foresee a viable future after the loss of the love object.

Most people will find a way to fold this kind of painful experience into the ongoing flow of their lives and will eventually outgrow their need for the person who disappointed or rejected them. But for a few, the "ongoing flow" stops and life essentially comes to a halt. These people, in effect, blame the "ending" of their lives on the lost lover. Some in this situation will wallow in a living death, others will commit suicide and a very small number will kill the person who has "killed" them, in a vain attempt to get back their life.

What kind of person "needs" to kill someone in order to continue living? We all owe a part of our identity—how we see and think of ourselves—to an image we have of who we are, which depends in part on how others see us. When that self-image is reasonable and the values supporting it are good, we call this aspect of development healthy narcissism, which can become a compass for an ethical and productive life. But in some people, this component of their being is constructed pathologically, usually as a defense against an early psychological injury. The compensating behavior of pathological narcissism includes an exaggerated sense of entitlement and an angry, often violent response to anyone who challenges that entitlement.

The more important another person's approval is to one's identity, the more damage will be done if that affirmation and validation are withdrawn. For some pathological narcissists, their self-image *is* their entire self: shatter it and there is no more person. For those with the most extreme form of this character trait, at some point the choice can seem to be between killing the person who shattered that self-image and took their life away, or remaining "dead" themselves.

This may have been how George Huguely saw things the night he allegedly murdered Yeardley Love. Similar stories are told weekly on *Dateline* and *48 Hours Mystery* of husbands murdering their wives and, less often, of wives murdering their husbands. On camera, these murderers often brazenly and convincingly assert their innocence in spite of the evidence against them. And they do have a point: to them, the murder *was* self-defense. In the mind of such a killer, the moment the trigger is squeezed, the knife plunged, the body shaken and slammed, their version of justice is realized. The person who took their life has been neutralized. This annihilation creates a chance for them to reboot their shattered self-image with new narcissistic defenses. Even after being caught and punished, they feel that what they did was justified and worth the price paid.

It is possible to propose this type of motive for murder and still hold the person morally and legally responsible. After all, killing another person involves a choice, even if the act is rooted in a dynamic defense that is related to an earlier failure to authentically rebound from a narcissistic injury. The paradox here is sobering but hardly exculpatory.

And Some Die of Marriage

The toxic love spawned by failing narcissistic defenses does not usually end in murder, as happened with Yeardley Love. More often these failing defenses kill slowly and indirectly as happens in Sam Mendes's 2008 film *Revolutionary Road* (Mendes 2008), which was based on Richard Yates's novel of the same name (Yates 1961; Muller 2011).

April Wheeler (played by Kate Winslet) and Frank Wheeler (played by Leonardo DiCaprio) buy a house in a Connecticut suburb and settle in for the 1950s version of the American Dream. Frank commutes to Manhattan for his job as sales manager of a company that makes business machines. April stays home, looks after their two children and acts in local theater. Offstage, she continues her act as Frank's wife. Frank has his own act going as husband and company man.

The emptiness of their marriage is more painful to April than to Frank. In an effort to shake some life into their deadened relationship, she suggests that they sell the house and move to Paris. Against all evidence, April believes that Frank has a talent he has not yet had the opportunity to cultivate. She expects that with leisure time he will "find himself," while she works to support the family—an unjustified, impressionist leap that is as histrionic as it is narcissistic. At first Frank demurs, but then, with his pride tweaked, he agrees to make the move, with no idea of what he might want to accomplish in Paris. April sees the move as the key to the marriage she fantasizes about.

This planned Paris excursion is just one example of how April and Frank play off each other like reflections in a room of mirrors. Committed to their marital "vital lie"—the lie people tell themselves about who they are because they can't face who they really are or what it would take to act authentically—they fumble around in the wreckage they have created, becoming more and more exasperated with their situation and angrier at each other.

April and Frank are pathological narcissists. They identify with a self-fabricated image of who they *think* they are and how things *should* go for them that does not correspond to anything real. Self-absorbed in this fantasy, they become isolated from the larger world and, ironically, from each other. Their lives are a shell game made from the outside in, mostly show and little substance. Both recognize the other's lie but not their own.

Something has to give here, and eventually it does. April gets pregnant and wants to end the pregnancy because she sees children as part of the trap of married life that she is trying to escape. (She is eerily indifferent to the two children she already has, which is no surprise considering the kind of narcissist she is). Frank vigorously opposes the abortion but April proceeds anyway, making use of a rubber device designed to evacuate the fetus. Hemorrhaging, she calls for help but dies at the hospital.

April could no longer maintain the ideal image of her marriage, but she could not relinquish or authentically transcend that image either. As her narcissistic defenses failed and her vital lie imploded, she approached the brink of psychic death. Her life was as good as over before she induced the abortion.

It has been said that every marriage is a struggle over who gets to be the crazy one—or, in marriages like this, the crazier one (April wins here). Marriage is also a struggle over who gets to die last. By default, that one goes to Frank.

No one wants to reduce a work of art to a sound bite. Still, I'll bet Richard Yates would have wanted us to see that we can die from the lies we tell ourselves and each other—particularly when those who are telling the lies are also holding each other to the expectations of their marriage vows, which include the promise of forever.

Antisocial Personality Style

Antisocial implies pathology that strikes at the heart of the social order, its customs and its laws. To be antisocial in this way is to be in conflict with society itself, sometimes to the point of abrogating the social contract. No other mental illness is associated with behavior that is so pointedly evil or universally censured. Narcissists harm others, and malignant narcissists sometimes kill, but their bad acts are usually limited to specific individuals and situations.

The challenge of understanding the antisocial style is compounded by the terms *sociopath* and *psychopath*, which are generally not clearly defined in the literature and are often used interchangeably. The DSM-5 makes no effort to distinguish between the antisocial person, the sociopath and the psychopath (pp. 659–663). This inexplicable oversight permits the confusion arising from the conflation of these diagnostic terms to persist.

The DSM-5 allows the diagnosis of antisocial personality disorder to be made when only *three* of the seven symptoms of Criterion A are met (Criteria B, C and D are obvious rule-outs). Since these seven criteria, which derive from symptoms of unspecified meaning and etiology, also apply to other psychiatric disorders, and because only three of the seven criteria are required to make the antisocial personality diagnosis, the DSM's diagnostic specificity is poor. These criteria neither constitute nor define a phenomenon and set an alarmingly low threshold for diagnosing a mental illness that comes with a serious social stigma

Some thought was given here to reducing the confusion that prevails in the literature because of the synonymous use of antisocial personality disorder, sociopathy and psychopathy. It was decided that *sociopath* should be used as a synonym for the antisocial style, and *psychopath* (which *sounds* worse than *sociopath*) should be reserved for the worst of the worst offenders.

Antisocial personality style is generally construed as a type of antisocial thinking and behavior that colors and dominates a life. In some instances, symptoms of this pathology, including harming animals and setting fires, begin as early as childhood or adolescence. Far more men than women are diagnosed as sociopaths.

An underdeveloped moral sensibility, or weak conscience, scorn for the feelings, well-being and rights of others, a tendency toward dishonesty and a disregard for the law are some of the key components of this phenomenon. But by no means do these elements compose a *unique phenomenon*, which is required to designate a mental illness. To accomplish this task, some flesh needs to be put on these bones by seeing how this phenomenon plays out in the real world. We have previously defined a phenomenon as an entity that exists in itself, that can be apprehended by our senses and is distinguishable from other phenomena.

An Exemplar of the Phenomenon of Antisocial Personality Style

The character of Amy Dunn in Gillian Flynn's novel *Gone Girl* (2012) exemplifies the phenomenon of the pathological narcissist who is also a sociopath. We first see Amy as the perfect wife: beautiful, sexually proficient and available, smart, well-educated, from an upper-middle-class WASP family, with money of her own. She seems perfectly matched to her husband. From the outside, their life together appears ideal.

Then, during the Great Recession, Nick and Amy lose their jobs. Amy is nonplussed and feels they can live off her money. Nick is stung by his professional set-back and does not know how to rebound. He is depressed, drinks too much and hangs out with his unemployed friends instead of looking for work. He also neglects Amy.

Hoping for a new start, Amy and Nick move from their brownstone in Brooklyn, New York to Carthage, Missouri, Nick's hometown. But Nick has been badly singed by his layoff and pulls further away from Amy. Things go from bad to worse for this once apparently perfect couple. Nick begins an affair with a much younger woman, one of his students at a local college where he teaches a writing course.

The story takes an astonishing turn once Amy finds out about the affair. Amy doesn't want Nick out of her life, but she doesn't want to forgive him, either. What she really wants is to stay married on her terms, and ultimately to destroy him. Nick's betrayal has triggered a response—a Meyerian reaction—that leads her into a domain of serious and striking pathology. We learn from Amy what it means to be a pathological narcissist and a sociopath.

Amy hatches a diabolical plan. She vanishes from their home—on their fifth wedding anniversary—leaving evidence of a bloody struggle. Amy's disappearance quickly becomes national news, and Nick becomes the number-one suspect. Amy has secretly bought an old car and hit the road with the plan to kill herself and leave evidence pointing to Nick as her killer.

On the run for several days, Amy rents a motel room in a broken-down town. The natives are friendly and she parties with them, only to have what is left of the $10,000 she escaped with stolen by two of the people who befriended her. With neither friends nor money, she drives to St. Louis and contacts Desi, a high school classmate and former boyfriend. Desi wants to help Amy as a way of helping himself to her. He installs her in the palatial, walled-off second home he uses to get away from his mother and the pressures of the life that has brought him considerable financial success.

Desi controls every aspect of Amy's life, showering her with attention and every material thing she could possibly want as she cunningly fights off his sexual advances. Desi will not let Amy contact anyone or allow her off the property. She lives as a prisoner in the lap of luxury. Amy temporizes in this captivity until she can't take it any longer, then hatches a plan that gives her the next move in her wicked scheme. She lures an overeager and unsuspecting Desi into her bed, has sex with him and spikes his wine with a sedative. While he is out cold, she cuts his throat, steals his Mercedes and heads back to Carthage and to Nick.

Living under the same roof with Nick again, Amy has to reinvent her plan to punish and vanquish him. Her initial scheme to pin her "murder" on Nick has been foiled by fate. Now she tries to manipulate him into taking responsibility for the clues she left to implicate him in this "murder." She also blames her "abduction" on Desi and uses that lie to justify his cold-blooded murder as self-defense.

Nick, on the spot and in the media spotlight, suspected by the police of trying to kill his wife, tries to clear his name. Like any good detective, he looks into Amy's past. He questions Tommy, whom Amy has accused of raping her, and Hilary, whom she has accused of stalking her and throwing her down a long stairway.

Seven years earlier, Amy and Tommy, a self-described nerd, had met at a party. To Tommy's surprise, Amy encouraged him and they dated for about three months. Tommy felt from the start that there was a "catch" here and after three months he recognized what it was: Amy didn't really care for him but was putting on an act for some unknown, self-serving reason. Tommy called her less often and started seeing another woman. Amy found out, came over one night and initiated their one and only sexual encounter.

A short time later, two cops appeared at Tommy's door: Amy had accused him of rape. A rape kit revealed wounds that were "consistent with forcible rape." Searching Tommy's apartment, the cops found two ties on the posts of his headboard that were "consistent with the ligature marks" found on Amy's wrists.

Amy had staged the rape, creating her own "wounds," lacerating her wrists and planting the wrist ties.

Things were looking bad for Tommy, but then, without a word, Amy dropped the charges. Shortly after that he received this unsigned note from her: *Maybe next time you'll think twice*. Tommy tells Nick: "Amy likes to play God when she's not happy. Old Testament God. She doles out punishment. Hard."

And not only to the men in her life. When Amy was 15, she befriended Hilary at the exclusive boarding school they attended. Not a member of the in-crowd, Hilary, the self-described "kid from Memphis," was surprised when Amy went out of her way to include her in the inner circle of mostly East Coast girls. Hilary became Amy's second fiddle, gladly accepting the role, along with the prestige that came with it. Things went well until a boy from a neighboring school, whom both girls had met at a dance, called *Hilary*, probably because he was too intimidated by Amy's attractiveness and apparent self-possession to call her. A few days later, the midterm grades came out and Hilary's average was slightly better than Amy's. Then Hilary, but not Amy, was invited to a girl's home for Thanksgiving.

Then things got weird. Amy began asking Hilary to do "dumb things": color her hair to match Amy's; buy the kind of clothes that Amy would buy; prank call Amy's parents in New York; even stand outside Amy's house and tell her mother that she was going to take Amy's place. Hilary was sufficiently in thrall to Amy not to realize that she was being set up.

And then things got weirder. Hilary: "Girls at school start looking funny at me. I'm shut out of the cool circle. Fine. But then one day I'm called in to see the headmistress. Amy has had a horrible accident—twisted ankle, fractured arm, cracked ribs. Amy has fallen down this long set of stairs, and she says it was *me* who pushed her" (p. 291).

Amy put out the story that Hilary was obsessed with her and was stalking her. As "proof," she cited the "dumb things" she had put Hilary up to, which included staking out Amy's house and talking to her mother. Amy's parents took out a restraining order against Hilary, and the school expelled her. Amy had created Hilary to suit her purposes. When Hilary no longer filled that role, Amy tried to destroy her.

Hearing Hilary's story, Nick now realizes that Amy is a "psycho bitch," a liar of "dazzling caliber," an "insatiable sociopath." Amy gleefully confides to Nick that she slit Desi's throat without provocation: "You just have to decide to do it and then do it. Discipline. Follow through. Like anything. You never understood that" (p. 388). Killing Desi, for Amy, was no big deal, just what she had to do at the time. Amy knows that, in not having a conscience, she is different from Nick and, reflecting her narcissistic omnipotence, implies that she is the better person. At the end of the novel, Tanner Bolt, Nick's lawyer, tells him: "Amy's basically exploiting the sociopath's most reliable maxim. . . The bigger the lie, the more they believe it" (p. 390).

Amy's final manipulation of Nick was to get pregnant by inseminating herself with Nick's sperm. (They had been to a fertility clinic several years earlier, and she preserved one of the samples in their refrigerator.) She will harm the unborn baby, a boy, she says, if Nick leaves her. Amy still needs Nick to take the blame for the "clues" she left that were intended to implicate him in her murder.

But Nick has one more trick up his sleeve. His lawyer and one of the cops from the original investigation still believe that Amy killed Desi and are trying to prove it. "I will stay close to her," Nick says, "until I can bring her down."

Amy's narcissistic wound was so deep that, at age 15, she was willing to risk her own life to stage the "accident" that she blamed on Hilary, and, later, to commit suicide to punish Nick for his infidelity—narcissists sometimes kill themselves immediately after killing the person they believe betrayed them. Amy has no sorrow for what she has put her parents through, no regret for causing the agony they felt while she was still "gone" and feared dead. She tells us why, revealing in the process how well she understands the meaning of her illness:

> I know I should feel sorry for them, but I don't. I've never been more to them than a symbol anyway, the walking ideal. Amazing Amy in the flesh. Don't screw up, you are Amazing Amy. Our only one. There is an unfair responsibility that comes with being an only child—you grow up knowing you aren't allowed to disappoint, you're not even allowed to die. There isn't a replacement toddling around; you're it. It makes you desperate to be flawless, and it also makes you drunk with the power. In such ways are despots made (p. 259).

"Amazing Amy" is not just an epithet that Amy picks to designate the specialness of her singular childhood. *Amazing Amy* is the title of a series of books her parents wrote, based on Amy's early life, which made them rich and famous, and also put a good deal of pressure on Amy to be the perfect daughter and the perfect person. Amy's primary narcissistic trauma, in the guise of a blessing, originates in her parents' traumatic insistence that she play the role of being perfect. Amy feels she was used by them and had been denied her childhood.

The anxiety that came with her single-child status, along with the expectation that was forced on her to live up to the Amazing Amy character in her parents' books, was most likely what she *reacted to* and *defended against*, and ultimately led her to adopt a narcissistic and antisocial personality style. It was no accident that, as a child, not being allowed to "disappoint" or even "to die," was what she later did, or threatened to do, to get revenge on her parents, her husband and her friends! It was as if Amy had decided: Not only will I not be perfect, I will be *awful*. Thus was *her* "despot" made.

We see in the behavior of Amy Dunn the phenomenon of the narcissistic sociopath—also known as the malignant narcissist—embodied in fictional flesh and blood. "Fiction," Adam Gopnik (2014) points out, "departs from the truth to intensify it."

Michael Corleone and Tony Soprano: Sociopaths of a Different Type

In Frank Coppola's film *The Godfather*, the Corleone family exemplifies another type of antisocial style. They make their money by purposely breaking the law. In fact, disregard for the law *is* their business.

In the scrimmage of legitimate business, there are often sharp elbows and bruised ribs as well as vicious betrayals. But there are limits to these excesses of behavior imposed by the dictates of conscience and the fear of being punished for breaking the law. To the Corleones, however, these constraints do not apply. Internally, no voice says "No" as they carry out their violent and unlawful acts. "It was just business," is the explanation and justification they offer for killing someone who happened to get in their way.

While acting as criminals, the Corleones also function as successful capitalists. Between murders, they spend time with their families and attend church. We can think of the Corleones as being selectively amoral. Within their organization, they create their own code of morality—loyalty to the "family," which includes omerta, the imperative of silence. They have their own "judicial system" for those who break that code. Who can forget the scene at the end of *The Godfather* where the action shifts back and forth between a baptism and a multiple mob hit? Reassuring Latin words, which initiate a crime boss's child into the Christian life, alternate with machine-gun fire that terminates the lives of several "family" members who have broken the rules.

The TV series *The Sopranos* tells another story about what it means to balance the exactions of organized crime with the demands of what we think of as ordinary life. For all his success in the mob, Tony Soprano has crippling panic attacks. Desperate for a surcease of this misery, he puts down his gun and spills his guts to a psychiatrist. This criminal sheds tears before an agent of the society he lives to undermine.

A good deal of the literature on what we are calling the antisocial style presumes that this pathology is a lifetime malady, an idea associated with the belief that the sociopath has a brain disease, another unproven notion. Before taking on the question of the sociopath's chronicity clinically, we would do well to recall how, in *The Godfather III*, Michael Corleone (Al Pacino) comes to feel the full burden of his life of crime and tries to legitimize the "business" that he now heads. Anguished over the absence of his estranged wife (Diane Keaton), who left him because she couldn't take being married to a gangster any longer, and the resistance he faces from those within the organization who do not want their operation to change, he says, with a hint of despair: "Just when I thought I was out, they bring me back in." It is not easy to turn around a life of crime, but Michael Corleone convinces us that he has the desire and the will required.

Psychodynamics of the Sociopath

How does someone come to disregard the law as a matter of course? Breaking laws, and harming people in the process, can be seen as upshots of what some clinicians, including George Vaillant (1975), consider a defensive, "antisocial" reaction. To Meyerian and existential clinicians, antisocial behavior, like all defenses, is a choice. This is so whether the instigator recognizes these acts as having been *deliberately* chosen or not.

In most instances, this kind of bad behavior is not the direct consequence of a brain that is genetically "hardwired" to produce evil, though some brain injuries are known to induce antisocial behavior in previously solid citizens. Consistent with Meyer's belief that the brain is the "organ of personality," it is no surprise that the antisocial brain "lights up" differently than a "normal" brain does in functional magnetic resonance imaging (fMRI).

Vaillant believes that sociopaths are "neither born that way nor incapable of change." He titles an article that is based on his work with three incarcerated narcotic addicts who had long criminal records "Sociopathy as a Human Process" (Vaillant 1975). He tries to discern here the etiology and meaning of the sociopath's behavior, in contrast to the "agnostic" approach taken in the DSM-5. He challenges the common notion—as articulated in Hervey Cleckley's *Mask of Sanity* (1941)—that sociopaths are incomprehensible and inhuman and incapable of experiencing emotion.

"Over a period of time," Vaillant realized, "seemingly organic and immutable deficits emerge as [i.e., turn out to be] dynamic and understandable defense mechanisms." Like all defenses, the sociopath's arise in the course of an inauthentic attempt to deal with extreme anxiety. Sociopaths, according to Vaillant, do not readily disclose the origin of their trauma and consequent anxiety—what was done to them by commission or omission, sometimes as children, sometimes later—in contrast to borderlines who often wear their trauma on their sleeves.

Like borderlines, sociopaths do not have the kind of early experience with parents or caregivers that lets them develop an even relative self and object constancy. They do not acquire the trust that allows them to feel both positively *and* negatively about the people and situations they encounter, without becoming extremely anxious and reacting defensively to that anxiety. The result, as Vaillant says, is that "the interpersonal relationships of sociopaths remain perpetually murky and entangled."

Some who find themselves in this situation—not knowing who they are; unable to depend on the responses of others to the degree that "normal" people can; not being oriented to the world in a way that sustains them—will, in defense, align themselves *against the society they experience as alien*. This stance is infertile ground for growing a conscience. The sense of what is right and wrong, permissible and forbidden, which most non-sociopaths acquire early, is not an element in their development. Because of this deficit, the sociopath's course in life shrinks to pursuing the immediate, concrete needs of survival at any cost.

In this process, the world, for the sociopath, does not acquire the broader meanings that "normal" people take for granted. And so the sociopath develops what David Shapiro called the "fluent insincerity" that characterizes so much of antisocial behavior: "[E]gocentric interest in the immediate, concrete circumstances of communication often overrides, in his awareness, any detached interest in its objective content. He is, in other words, not so much interested in *what* is said to him as in the possibilities the situation offers. He is, and consciously so, not so much interested in what he says as in how well it works" (Shapiro 1965, p. 168). The sociopath's "fluent insincerity" is a direct consequence of his orientation to an unforthcoming world and an underdeveloped self.

Out of kilter with the world at large, the sociopath's anxiety prevails to the degree that he imagines that *everyone feels this kind of anxiety* and lives in his kind of world. Immature defenses—Meyerian reactions—come into play, especially acting out defenses. The most common types of acting out, according to

Vaillant (1992), include: "tantrums, apparently motiveless assaults, child abuse, and pleasureless promiscuity."

Vaillant offers this summary of what he learned working with the three incarcerated sociopathic patients: "All had lacked a benevolent, sustained relationship with the same-sexed parent. All were afraid of intimacy and of assuming responsibility for it. None could believe that others could tolerate their [own] anxiety, and all devoutly feared responsibility for achieving success by open competition. They could neither identify with authority nor accept its criticism" (Vaillant 1975). Anxious about an open, dialectical interaction with others that involves more or less fair competition, the sociopath loads the deck in his favor by playing outside the rules of consensual common sense and the law. He uses whatever illegal and immoral means it takes to *win*. It is in the act of making these choices, that he *becomes* a sociopath. In this process, Nietzsche's authentic "will to power" turns into an inauthentic defensive will to subvert the social contract.

The sociopath feels that because he will not win if he follows the rules, he must break the rules. Ultimately, he trades the *anxiety* about this failure—which he cannot or will not face and transcend—for the *fear* associated with living outside the law: the threat of being apprehended, convicted, imprisoned or killed, as well as the contempt of the society whose rules he spurns.

This sociopathic transformation is at the heart of the phenomenon of the antisocial style. No other pathology targets the social order so directly and to this degree. The sociopath's choice of reaction *strikes out at society itself*, as if *it* were the cause of his trauma and consequent debilitating anxiety. "David Helbros," whose story is told in the section on borderline personality style, displayed a number of sociopathic traits, along with borderline traits (Muller 1994). David's motive was clear: he blamed "the country" and his parents for not validating his sexual desire for men. By acting out, he struck back at the society which, he felt, had marginalized him.

Believing that sociopaths are made and not born, Vaillant offers a way to replace the immature defenses that comprise this style of living with less destructive defenses:

> Successful treatment demands that the therapist try to help the patient develop a *substitute* for each defense. For example, addicts give up addiction bit by bit; their abstinence is achieved by a process analogous to mourning. Countless criminals have replaced acting out with reaction formation [behaving in a way that is opposite to one's true feelings, as implied in the clinician's direction to patients: *do better before you feel better*] and projection with altruism [deriving pleasure from giving to others, rather than attributing to them one's own aggressive tendencies] (Vaillant 1975).

To accomplish this goal, the anxiety that was originally processed as unbearable, and then reacted to (in the Meyerian sense) with a defensive acting out must be faced for what it is:

> The only way that the therapist can show the sociopath that anxiety is bearable is by bearing it *with* him and by *not* trying to alleviate it. The therapist must

> recognize that his wish to control the sociopath's anxiety (whether by psychotropic drugs or by solitary confinement), is countertransferrence. In fact, the therapist's own anxiety can be openly acknowledged to the sociopathic patient. Brought up to believe that anxiety is too dreadful to be borne and too awful to confess, the sociopath is reassured that someone can be anxious and yet in control (Vaillant 1975).

Becoming a sociopath is a patently inauthentic act. To be "cured" or "rehabilitated," the sociopath, at some point, has to face the *truth* about where he has gone wrong and how he has harmed others. Thomas Malthus (1766–1834), who is most remembered for his efforts to convince his fellow Englishmen to keep the population in line with the farmers' capacity to produce food, believed in the value of the truth for its own sake. What he says in this rumination applies to everyone everywhere and to no one more than the sociopath: "The most baleful mischiefs may be expected from the unmanly conduct of not daring to face truth because it is unpleasing" (Malthus 1986, p. 364).

Like all those who deal with their anxiety by employing immature psychodynamic defenses and undergoing Meyerian maladaptive reactions, the sociopath rejects alternative authentic responses, searching for a "safer" way around the anxious situation. This self-deception, which has been characterized by Heidegger, Sartre, Laing and others originates in a universal ontological weakness, a "soft-spot" in the structure of human being. Among other ways, the ontological inclination toward self-deception is ontically expressed in the myriad defenses and reactions that, collectively, have come to be known as psychic pathology.

Finally, according to Vaillant, the sociopath, who has divorced himself from society, must find a way to *rejoin* that society. One-to-one therapeutic relationships, while a good way to begin this process, are alone not enough to catalyze this integration:

> Sociopaths know only too well that they have harmed others; they can meaningfully identity only with people who feel as guilty as themselves. They can abandon their defenses against grief only in the presence of people equally bereaved. Only acceptance by peers can circumvent the sociopath's profound fear that he may be pitied. Only acceptance by "recovered" peers can restore his defective self-esteem. Finally, the psychopath needs to absorb more of other people than one person, no matter how loving, can ever provide. Sociopaths need to find groups to which they can belong with pride (Vaillant 1975).

This is a hopeful bet on the capacity of those whom we call sociopaths, who have succumbed to a lower path, to find a higher one through their will to power and the support of the society they have wantonly trashed (Krog 2015).

The Psychopath

And then there are those for whom, for whatever reason, there *is* no higher road, no way back from the person they have become defensively. We will call these individuals *psychopaths*. They are the worst of the worst, people who cannot live in society without doing further damage to it. They are the terrorists we often hear about in the media; the serial killers we see in the TV series *Criminal Minds*, who have occult, and sometimes psychotic reasons for the crimes they commit; the mass murderers who shoot up schools and malls, and bring down airliners; and history's political and military monsters (Hitler, Pol Pot, Idi Amin). They are the non-contrite. They need to be held accountable for their crimes and separated from society rather repatriated to it.

One can think of psychopaths as starting out with an even more unbearable anxiety than sociopaths. Perhaps they underwent an even greater psychobiological trauma; received less psychological support in their earliest years; or have a weaker constitutional ability to deal with their difficult experience authentically. One could imagine sociopaths and psychopaths as existing in a continuum where, after a certain point, the latter can be distinguished from the former. Amy Dunn was bad, but Hannibal Lector (*The Silence of the Lambs*) was incomparably worse.

One can think of psychopaths as malignant narcissists (described in the preceding section on narcissistic personality style) who are also criminals. The Corleones, in *The Godfather*, break any law that stands in their way and kill people when they deem it necessary. Their lives are tainted by a criminal mind set, but they struggle to keep a semblance of family and friendship. Those whom we are calling psychopaths do not have this capacity. They live further inside themselves, and lack the empathy and ability to connect with others that is required to be part of a "crime family" like the Corleones. They have even less of a conscience than sociopaths, and their crimes are more idiosyncratic and horrific, which is to say oriented toward fulfilling more primitive and instinctual needs.

The murders that drive the stories on *Dateline* and *48 Hours Mystery* are primarily the acts of sociopaths. The stories told on *Criminal Minds*, on the other hand, are mostly about psychopaths. Some are psychotic, acting on delusions and hallucinations as the bodies pile up.

Huck, a major player in the award-winning TV drama *Scandal*, is a textbook psychopath. If he must kill someone as a team member of the "gladiators"—a consortium of high-powered Washington "fixers" headed by Olivia Pope—he does so without remorse. But then Huck cannot resist using his knives, saws and hatchets to cut the bodies he creates into pieces. At his killing scenes, arms, legs, feet, fingers, teeth and the occasional surgically severed head lie strewn across the floor. Huck makes no effort to keep the ectopic blood he liberates from his victims off *his* arms, legs, face and clothes. Seeing this carnage, one cannot help but wonder what happened to just killing people. A mere sociopath would stop there.

In one episode, Huck forcibly extracts two teeth (without anesthesia, of course) from his fellow gladiator and sometime girlfriend, Quinn, to get information. After Quinn gives Huck what he wants, they are quickly colleagues and lovers again, engaging in coitus in Huck's office. In another episode, after extruding the promise from a minor character not to reveal facts that could put Huck and his family in mortal danger—yes, he has a wife and a young son, though they are periodically estranged—he quickly produces a knife and slits her throat, because he cannot be sure she would keep her word. The moral ambiguity that is the beating heart of *Scandal*'s zigzag, explosive storylines easily accommodates Huck's psychopathy.

Working with patients, it will not always be possible to tell the sociopath from the psychopath (in most of the psychiatric literature, this step is not attempted). When the distinction cannot be satisfactorily made, we should fall back on identifying the facts that constitute our patients' stories and, from there, try to discern the psychodynamic etiology and meaning of the pathology behind their deviant lives.

Borderline Personality Style

The identification of the mental illness that has come to be known as borderline personality disorder (BPD) emerged from the observations of clinicians that some of their patients did not respond well to the kind of therapeutic efforts that benefit most patients. The American psychoanalyst Adolph Stern is generally credited as the first to use the borderline appellation: "Repeated failure in the past taught me that the knowledge we possess was not adequate to treat these people" (Stern 1938). Helene Deutsch, a psychoanalyst who worked with Freud and later practiced in Boston noted that, while some of her patients appeared to function normally, they "force on the observer the inescapable impression that the individual's whole relationship to life has something about it which is lacking in genuineness and yet outwardly runs along 'as if' it were complete" (Deutsch 1942).

Deutsch captures here the underlying *brittleness* of self that characterizes people with the borderline style, while simultaneously pointing out that they can appear to others and function "as if" their lives were not in thrall to a serious mental illness. Overall, "as if" persons, as Deutsch calls them, are good at deceiving themselves about the meaning of their actions. They seem blind to the ways they blight their own lives and, inevitably, the lives of others.

John Gunderson, a professor of psychiatry at Harvard Medical School and an authority on personality disorders, met his first borderline patients while he was still a resident: "These were patients everyone was complaining to their supervisors about, and nobody knew what to do for them. I published some descriptive comments about them because I wanted to place some control on the situation, which seemed scary to me. After that, colleagues started sending me patients with not just borderline, but with narcissistic personality disorder or with antisocial personality, because they thought I knew how to treat them. But I didn't!" (Arehart-Treichel 2014). The borderline diagnosis generally designates patients who are distinguishable from those who are seen as neurotic or psychotic. In kind and severity, their pathological dysfunction usually falls somewhere between neurosis and psychosis. The borderline tag wrongly infers that people having this style live on the edge of psychosis and tend to cross that line to become psychotic. In fact, the borderline state is a relatively stable condition of instability. Borderline patients rarely become psychotic, though some are prone to "micropsychotic events," which usually resolve quickly.

In the DSM's 3rd, 4th and 5th editions, the diagnostic criteria for BPD derive primarily from clinical and theoretical reports of psychoanalysts—minus, of course, their psychoanalytic explanatory theories. These criteria consist mostly of behavioral symptoms, with meaning and etiology purposely ignored.

Meyerian and Existential Elaborations on the Meaning and Etiology of the DSM-5's Behavioral BPD Symptoms

The DSM-5 (2013, pp. 663–666) constructs its diagnostic criteria for BPD around three basic properties of the borderline person's brittle self: instability of interpersonal relations, instability of self-image and instability of affect. Mostly behavioral criteria are provided for making the diagnosis. This approach ultimately fails by not showing the clinician how to recognize the unique phenomenon that we are calling borderline personality style. Consequently, many patients who "meet criteria" specified by the DSM-5 are diagnosed with BPD even though they do not evince this phenomenon.

In the FDMI, the DSM-5's three basic properties of borderline pathology are reduced to two—why try to separate affect from self-image and affect from interpersonal relations when these properties of the self are inseparable in the lives of those who we are trying to understand? The underlying nature of the borderline self will be considered first, then the borderline's interpersonal relations, since this sequence seems closer to the natural order of things.

Instability of the Borderline's Self and Self-Image, and the Associated Unstable Affect

The myriad manifestations of borderline personality style emerge from a brittle self, an ontic deficit that usually originates in 2nd domain aberrant personality development and temperament.

A major and not surprising consequence of the borderline person's brittle self and ill-begotten identity is a universal, painful and sometimes unlivable *ambivalence*—toward self, others and everything that comprises his environment. Ambivalence here means having opposite, conflicting views that prevent the person from developing a minimally cohesive and consistent notion of self, others and the world. This conflict ultimately leads to what psychoanalysts call a *lack of self and object constancy* (make that relative self and object constancy, since no person is indefinitely constant for anyone). To borderlines, nothing or no one, including themselves, seems even relatively reliable, and thus knowable. Needless to say, many defenses—Meyerian reactions—are employed in the course of living in this compromised way.

Arguably, the borderline's ur-defense is *splitting* (Muller 1992). Unable to tolerate the inevitable anxiety that inheres in a universal, identity-killing ambiguity—which consists of irresolvable opposite and conflicting ways of thinking, feeling and acting—the borderline may choose to assess everything as *alternately* all-good *or* all-bad: first with one polar valuation, then switching to the opposite pole once it becomes clear that this first way of polarizing experience is untenable (in fact, *both* of these split "poles" are unlivable). The borderline exchanges the "gray" of authentic life for the inauthentic, alternating "black-*or*-white" defensive "solution" served up by the splitting defense (Grotstein 1997).

Through this black-or-white thinking and feeling, a stronger, if temporary and pathological identity is created to replace the weaker, or non-existent identity that comes with the unsplit, undefended ambiguity previously experienced. In splitting, the borderline becomes the person who *temporarily* encounters (someone, something, everything) *distinctly this way or that way, with some confidence.* Like all defenses, the splitting defense "works" only as long as the "defender" can keep it going.

And, like all defenses, splitting does not play out well with those who live by what Meyer called the rules of consensual common sense, and, by implication, consensual behavior. These people have more or less learned how to accept the ambiguity—the good and the bad, the "gray"—in what they encounter as they make their way through the world with others. As the borderline's intrapsychic conflict temporarily lessens through splitting, the interpsychic conflict with others often increases. Trying to "save" himself from an ambiguity that he cannot accept involves a regression in service to the self. The borderline's thinking, emotions and behavior eventually come to be perceived by "normal" people as crazy. He fares poorly in a world that does not sanction the different way he has come to live in it.

The 2nd domain borderline style, begotten in an aberrant development of personality and temperament, often begets willed, self-gratifying and self-destructive acts of the 3rd domain. Splitting is hardly a permanent solution to the demons that plague the borderline, which makes him a prime candidate for these inauthentic compensations. Drug and alcohol abuse, loss of control and over-control of food intake, excessive gambling, self-injury and threats or attempts to end his life are just some of the 3rd domain escapes a borderline may choose.

For someone with a borderline style, Meyerian reactions of the first domain are common as well, especially depression, which can be severe and unrelenting, particularly after a setback or significant loss. To deal authentically with any loss, the meaning and value of what has been lost must first be acknowledged. A borderline may be unable or unwilling to recognize the "unsplit," authentic meaning of what was once his but is his no longer (Muller 1992). Imagine someone trying to work through the loss of a significant other while still feeling ambivalent about what that person had originally meant to him.

It should come as no surprise that the emotions and affects of borderlines, who lack even relative self and object constancy, are all over the place. Or that borderlines often feel empty, paranoid and suicidal, and make dramatic threats to end their lives. In the throes of pursuing a borderline life, a brittle, loosely held self cannot put down roots and receive adequate sustenance from the world, much less perceive that world accurately.

Instability of the Borderline's Interpersonal Relations and the Associated Unstable Affect

Those with borderline style are often outgoing and affiliative. They seek out others for fun and profit, but always with a brittle, underdeveloped self. Their search is of a different kind than that of someone free of this pathology. All relationships are based on need—the lone, isolated self is usually a pathological state—but borderlines, with their particular brand of van den Berg's "different existence" (1972), have a different kind of need.

This need, really an overall neediness, is best described as desperation, which often inclines borderlines to select unsuitable people to fill a variety of rolls. When these relationships run into trouble, or, worse, come to an end, the borderline often reacts excessively, and sometimes violently. The borderline self, in its brittleness, instability and insecurity is in a weak position to take on the challenges of a significant relationship. With little autonomy to begin with, the give and take, and the ups and downs of any serious interaction with others are often not competently negotiated.

This deficit of self shows up most strikingly in the borderline's inability to find the right *emotional distance* with another person. What those without borderline pathology would consider a desirable closeness in a relationship, the borderline often experiences as too close. The brittle self is threatened and overwhelmed and cannot tolerate the wholeheartedness and commitment that intimacy demands.

In these instances, the borderline tends to withdraw. His pulling back strains and often destroys a relationship. Being alone now, the borderline feels abandoned and betrayed. He simultaneously desires and cannot tolerate intimacy. Anger and depression, reactions of the 1st domain, are common as the borderline "feeds" on others whom he desperately needs but does not know how to satisfy or keep in his life.

Non-borderline partners often do not comprehend what is happening during this withdrawal or grasp the reason for the abuse that is heaped on them by the borderline as he pulls back. The borderline's love interest, friend or co-worker, who was once idealized, may now be devalued and trashed as a consequence of his black-or-white thoughts and emotions jumping to the opposite pole.

Borderline personality style is a template for tempestuous and failed relationships: in love, in friendship and at work. Borderlines tend to burn through many lovers, many friends, many employers and many colleagues. They often alternately embrace and trash the mental health professionals who try to help them. Joel Paris has noted this paradox: "BPD patients are highly help-seeking, even if they can be difficult to help" (Paris 2012, p. 57).

Some Further Thoughts on Borderline Splitting

Why do some people respond ambiguously to everything they encounter, then deal with the anxiety that accompanies this response by constructing their experience alternately as all-good or all-bad? Most clinicians who have tried to explain the origin of the splitting defense pretty much agree that trauma—emotional, physical, sexual—can induce the sense that, to one degree or another, the world is an unsafe place. Erik Erikson saw this feeling, and the insecurity it provokes, as one reason why people fail to acquire "basic trust" in the world (Erikson 1963).

It is crucial to understand that the kind of trauma that leads to borderline pathology need not be a singular traumatic event, though it can be. Even subtle pressure applied by parents or other authorities and influences can cause the kind of trauma that establishes the ground for splitting and other defensive reactions—if this "interference" stifles a key facet of a vulnerable person's essential life project.

Karen Horney's "Resigned Person": An Exemplar of the Phenomenon of Borderline Personality Style

In the early 1980s, while reading Karen Horney's *Neurosis and Human Growth* (1950), it became clear to me that what she called the "resignation solution" to the problem of basic anxiety was the same phenomenon that is *implied* by the constellation of mostly behavioral symptoms used to designate and diagnose BPD in the DSM (at that time the DSM-III-R, whose BPD criteria are essentially the same as those in the DSM-5) (Muller 1993).

Horney identified and characterized three major neurotic personality types, chosen (her word) early in life, to the problem of basic anxiety, which she defines as "the feeling of being isolated and helpless in a world conceived as potentially hostile." These defensive overreactions seem similar in form to Meyer's maladaptive reactions to challenges or negative experiences made later in life, which derive from a misuse of freedom. We will consider only Horney's "resignation" solution, which is the exclusive move "away from" the world and its perceived dangers. The exclusive moves "toward" this world (the "self-effacing" solution) and "against" it (the "expansive" solution) lead to very different pathologies.

Karen Horney (1885–1952), a psychiatrist and psychoanalyst, was born in Germany and trained in Europe. Later she practiced in New York. Though initially influenced by Freud, she rejected his ideas about instinct and drive and came to see neurosis as a failure of interpersonal relations, "a disturbance in one's relations to self and others."

In Horney's theories about what she calls "neurotic transformation," the notions of freedom and choice are everywhere evident. Horney was phenomenological to the degree that she *described* in great detail what she saw as the three fundamental neurotic types (Horney 1950; Muller 1993). She gave vivid descriptions of the resigned person's/borderline person's pathological self-other-world interactions, in the process transcending her analytic perspective.

Hoping to do justice to Horney's skill as an observer, as well as to her psychological insight, I have excerpted sections of her description of the resignation phenomenon verbatim from *Neurosis and Human Growth*. This overview is fashioned around eight cardinal points:

> 1) In analysis [the resigned person] may comply with the obvious rules, such as being on time or saying what is on his mind, but assimilate so little of what is discussed that the work is rendered futile. His expectations from therapy are limited and negative. Analysis should rid him of disturbing symptoms. Whatever he hopes for should come easily, without pain or strain. The analyst should do the work. He is willing to wait patiently for the analyst to present the clue that will solve everything. He may not mind observing things in himself. What he always minds is the effort of changing. The resigned person may have had a long experience with the analyst's patience and understanding and yet, under duress, may feel that the analyst would drop him at a moment's notice.
>
> 2) Expansive trends may show in his having rather grandiose fantasies about the great things he could do in his imagination, or about his general attributes. Furthermore, he often feels consciously superior to others, and may show this

in his behavior by an exaggerated dignity. On the other hand, if self-effacing trends are in the foreground, resigned people tend to have a low estimate of themselves. They may be timid and feel that they do not amount to much.

3) The resigned person does not set goals or make long-range plans. What does he actually want to do with his life? The question has never occurred to him and is easily discarded, as if it were none of his concern. He restricts his wishes. He believes that it is *better* not to wish or to expect anything. Sometimes this goes with a conscious pessimistic outlook on life, a sense of its being futile anyhow and of nothing being sufficiently desirable to make an effort for it.

4) The resigned person may have numerous sexual relations, breaking out of them sooner or later. They should not, as it were, degenerate into love.

5) In or around adolescence he often does things that show remarkable energies and gifts. He may be resourceful, surmount economic handicaps, and make a place for himself. He may be ambitious in school, first in his class, excel in debating or some political progressive political movement. At least there often is a period in which he is comparatively alive and interested in many things, in which he rebels against the tradition in which he has grown up and thinks of accomplishing something in the future.

Subsequently there is often a period of distress: of anxiety, of depression, of despair about some failure or about some unfortunate life situation in which he has been involved through his very rebellious streak. After that the curve of his life seems to flatten out. People say he has gotten "adjusted" and settled down, that he seems to have lost his zest for living.

6) If he has no financial means, the resigned person may take occasional jobs or else sink down into a parasitic existence. If moderate means are available, he may restrict his needs to the utmost in order to feel free to do as he pleases. The things he does, however, often have the character of hobbies. Or he may succumb to a more or less complete inertia. This inertia bears within it the danger of deterioration. The inertia in thinking can be well observed in analysis and often is a great hindrance to work. Simple mental operations become difficult. Whatever is discussed during one hour may then be forgotten—not because of any specific "resistance" but because the patient lets the content lie in his brain like a foreign body.

7) The resigned person is a subdued rebel. Whether his rebelliousness remains passive or becomes active depends on the relative strength of expansive and self-effacing trends and on the degree of inner aliveness he has managed to salvage.

8) Another characteristic of the resigned person is his *hypersensitivity to influence, pressure, coercion* or *ties* of any kind. This is a relative factor too in his detachment. Even before he enters into a personal relationship or a group activity the fear of a lasting tie may be aroused. And the question as to how he can extricate himself may be present from the very beginning. Before marriage, this fear may grow into a panic. The sensitivity to coercion constitutes a real difficulty in analysis—the more difficult the more the patient is not only negative but negativistic. He may harbor an everlasting suspicion that the analyst

> wants to influence and mold him into a preconceived pattern (Horney 1950, pp. 259–290 passim).

Overall, Horney's resigned persons take a passive stance in pursuing relationships with others and in work, and feel detached from the ongoing flow of their lives. They do not have a constant self-image or concept of anyone or anything else, either. This poorly defined sense of themselves and their environment often leads to turbulent shifts in mood, affect and behavior.

In many instances, resigned persons appear normal until adolescence when the pressures of a looming adulthood trigger a meltdown of what Helene Deutsch called their "as if" lives. A resigned stance leads to the demise of resigned persons'/borderline persons' inner lives and can eventually paralyze their behavior. Though Horney does not use the term "splitting" in *Neurosis and Human Growth*, most of the attributes of the resigned person she describes are consistent with this defense.

Merely citing anger and aggression does not begin to capture the acuity or destructiveness of the situations that borderlines may create as they cycle through their changes of perception and mood. If hell has no fury like a scorned woman, neither has hell anything on the fire and brimstone borderlines are capable of generating when "abandoned"—which usually occurs when they are paying the price for their pathological behavior that plays out with others who occupy a very different world of consensual common sense.

Borderlines are often chronically angry and luxuriate in this emotion as it supplies their weak self-image with an inauthentic substitute identity (Muller 2009). The most fulminant symptoms of borderline pathology usually lessen in intensity over time, and, in some instances, eventually "burn out" (Stone 1990; Vaillant 1992).

"David Helbros"

One of my borderline patients, "David Helbros," was at the peak of his acting out during the 15 months we worked together. It is tempting to say that his borderline symptoms were classic, and they were, but, more significantly, David embodied the phenomenon implied in the DSM-5's BPD, and which is explicitly formulated as borderline personality style in the FDMI. David also personified what Otto Kernberg (1975) so incisively named *borderline personality organization*, and what Karen Horney labeled the resigned person. From head to toe, David was the kind of pathological person whom the controversial diagnosis of BPD (Vaillant 1992) was created to identity.

David came from a socially prominent, upper-middle-class family, with parents who had a solid marriage. By his own tally, they gave him everything that money could buy. And, like Horney's resigned person, David showed early promise as an adolescent, though this was a turbulent time for him. He began to decompensate in his early 20s. His marriage fell apart, messily and traumatically, and he dropped out of college, though he did finish later on.

David's borderline diagnosis presented me with a quandary: in spite of his classic borderline behavior, I could not identify the trauma that had surely influenced this life that I had come to know so well. I looked hard and long from every angle and came up dry. David was the consummate "splitter." He split himself, me, his parents and everyone and everything else that was part of the highly conflicted, highly charged scene in which his therapy played out.

This splitting defense, clearly a Meyerian reaction, was so evident in everything David brought to our therapeutic encounter that it occurred to me that such a clear-cut, defensive psychodynamic strategy probably had a brain correlative as well (Muller 1992). His case was so compelling and encompassing that I published a book, *Anatomy of a Splitting Borderline* (Muller 1994), which presents David's story and its analysis from three different interpretative viewpoints.

But I still had no idea *what* trauma had triggered David's splitting and the rest of his borderline pathology. Then, 20 years after the book came out, I awoke one morning with the answer. About halfway through the 15 months we worked together, it became clear to me that David—an inveterate and unabashed womanizer since early adolescence—also had strong sexual feelings for men. At that time, these feelings would undoubtedly have been unacceptable to him, and surely unacceptable—even shocking—to his parents and most of his friends.

David was living a double life. He had had numerous girlfriends, an early wife, a divorce and then many more sexual encounters with women. But all this time he also had a sexual desire for men that he could not openly admit or pursue. I became convinced that the prohibition against following through on these feelings, which he saw as "forced" on him by his parents, his social circle and by American society, was sufficiently traumatic to cause him to "split," to "resign" from the world, to "organize" as a borderline, call it what you will. The almost constant anger he displayed toward his parents and his seething contempt for the politics and social constraints of what he repeatedly and acerbically called "the country" (the United States) were undoubtedly reactions to what he was experiencing as an invalidating rejection of his closeted sexual feelings for men. He was rebellious in the same way that Karen Horney's resigned person is rebellious.

David's homoerotic feelings were so deeply hidden and ego dystonic that when I confronted him about what had hung in the air for so long, he sprang out of his chair, put a gash in my forehead with his fist and broke the smallest finger on my left hand (which still has the crook he imparted to it).

Theories that purport to explain borderline splitting, including those of Karen Horney (1950), Heinz Kohut (1971), Margaret S. Mahler (1975), Otto F. Kernberg (1975), James F. Masterson (1976), Daniel N. Stern (1985) and others, postulate trauma occurring during infancy or early childhood. To justify my interpretation of the etiology of David's splitting and subsequent borderline pathology, the window of vulnerability—the age span over which someone is psychobiologically susceptible to the kinds of trauma associated with borderline personality style—would have to be extended (Muller 1992).

My search of the borderline literature did not reveal any citations supporting an extension of this window of vulnerability. (If I have overlooked anything, my apologies to the authors.) I did, however, take heart when George E. Vaillant, who is an expert on personality disorders, expressed his belief at a grand rounds presentation at the University of Maryland School of Medicine (March 12, 1990) that borderline pathology could be induced by trauma occurring at any time up to age 30!

The proposal that psychological splitting—a psychodynamic reaction to trauma experienced by someone who is constitutionally vulnerable—can be biologically imprinted on the human brain is in line with Meyer's psychobiological concept of how most mental illness originates in maladaptive responses to life's challenges and negative experiences.

I believe that David's long-suppressed homoerotic feelings, which most likely began in early adolescence, triggered a need—brought on by the trauma he suffered knowing that his family and friends would almost certainly condemn the expression of these feelings—to split everyone and everything he encountered. Inexplicably, it took 20 years for me to figure this out! Perhaps other clinicians have been equally slow to grasp the impact of adolescent and early adult trauma on their borderline patients.

I considered using David as the exemplar of borderline personality style but chose not to revisit the "guts" of his case (my book tells his story in all its gory detail). The overall therapeutic strategy was to show him how he was using the splitting defense to avoid an authentic life. In spite of considerable intelligence and a good grasp of philosophy and literature, he could not, or would not, process emotionally much of what he grasped cognitively.

David repeatedly demonstrated a clear understanding of what he had done to himself and his family—during our sessions, anyway, while he felt secure enough to briefly drop his splitting defense. But he rarely *acted* on this insight to change his behavior. As Karen Horney realized, the resigned person (David) readily accepts the clinician's interpretations but does so as if this insight had nothing to do with him or required anything of him. I did everything I could to engage David on the level of emotion, and he did improve, but there were complications as there often are when working with borderline patients.

How Validly Has the Borderline Concept Been Used?

Both David Helbros and Karen Horney's resigned person embody the phenomenon of what has come to be known as the "borderline" personality. But all five editions of the DSM offer criteria for this "disorder" that are so broad and non-specific that many, if not most patients who get the diagnosis do *not* represent the borderline phenomenon that is identified and characterized in the FDMI. According to Vaillant (1992), "personality-disordered patients are often called 'borderline'—if they tend to deploy a wide variety of immature defenses."

BPD has been called a "wastebasket diagnosis," and there is good reason for adopting this epithet. Adolescents and young adults who are dysfunctional, who act up and act out, and who generally annoy and disappoint everyone they encounter often reflexively receive this diagnosis. To repeat a theme that often appears in this text, that is the price we pay for a diagnostic system which relies on symptoms of unspecified meaning and unknown etiology.

In 1992 Vaillant published an article with the challenging title "The Beginning of Wisdom is Never Calling a Patient a Borderline." The subtitle was less provocative:

"The Clinical Management of Immature Defenses in the Treatment of Individuals with Personality Disorders" (Vaillant 1992). Though the term "wastebasket diagnosis" does not appear in the article, this notion is implied in his account of how easily and incorrectly a patient may come to be tagged as a borderline. "One resident's borderline," Vaillant observed elsewhere, "is another resident's spouse" (Muller 2008, p. 76).

A psychoanalytically oriented psychiatrist, Vaillant asks clinicians to focus on addressing the psychodynamic defenses—the "immature" (image-distorting) defenses—that account for most of the pathology manifested by those with personality disorders. This is a major step up from the DSM, and a down-to-earth, empathic approach to working with these difficult patients.

There is wide agreement among clinicians who see borderline patients that the most significant advance in therapeutic technique for challenging this mental illness has been Marsha M. Linehan's dialectical behavior therapy (DBT). DBT is a more angular and targeted iteration of cognitive behavioral therapy (CBT) and fosters a dialectical integration of the patient's pathological past with a progressively less pathological present and future (Linehan 2015).

Linehan's dialectic reminds us of Sartre's dialectic of being and nothingness: "Thus the self which I am depends on the self which I am not yet to the exact extent that the self which I am not yet does not depend on the self which I am" (Sartre 1956, p. 32).

Schizoid Personality Style

Because so much of the preceding discussion of borderline personality style has dealt with the borderline's tendency to use the splitting defense, it seemed like a good idea to begin the consideration of schizoid personality style by characterizing the very different type of splitting employed by the schizoid in the attempt to preserve a self under siege.

A clinician entering the territory inhabited by a schizoid senses a very different kind of lived space than that occupied by a borderline. Borderlines, attempting to diminish the severe anxiety and insecurity they feel because of their brittle selves, may "split" their experience and "resign" from the world, as Karen Horney saw it. But their black-or-white defensive tactics play out in a way that preserves a good deal of the real world in which they live so uneasily. Schizoids go a step further than borderlines. They "split" their experience between consensual reality and an "inner," imagined, idiosyncratic world of their own making. This defensive scission is aimed not just at escaping the demands of the real world, as borderlines do, but at creating another, safer interior space. Here, schizoids can, to a degree, craft their own world, which is heavily influenced by imagination and fantasy.

In *The Divided Self*, R. D. Laing, who was strongly influenced by Sartre and Heidegger, shows how freedom is misused by the schizoid person to create an alternative, pathological life. Laing maps the territory inhabited by the schizoid using two line drawings reproduced in Chapter 13 as Figures 13.1a and 13.1b to show how the schizoid person withdraws from what he feels are unlivable demands made on him by the world that is created through consensual validation. (These drawings appear in Chapter 13, and not here, because the sections on schizophrenia were written before the descriptions of pathological personality styles.)

It is only through our bodies—the interface between our inner and outer worlds—that we can know ourselves and show ourselves to others. Figure 13.1a pictures the embodied person as related to the "other": life is vital, perception is real, action is meaningful. "The embodied person," according to Laing, "has a sense of being flesh and blood and bones, of being biologically alive and real; he knows himself to be substantial. . . . He is implicated in bodily desire, and the gratifications and frustrations of the body. The individual thus has as his starting-point an experience of his body as a base from which he can be a person with other human beings" (Laing 1965, p. 67). Laing's embodied self is an element of what we take to be psychobiological "normalcy." In a schizoid (Meyerian) reaction (Figure 13.1b), someone keeps a "part" of himself in the real world (his interaction is illustrated by the broken-line ellipse). But, at the same time, he also creates what Laing calls the "inner self" (illustrated by the broken-line circle), so as to minimize direct contact with the instrumental world of cause and effect, which he experiences as terrifying and unlivable.

In this world, the "false self" that is shown to others is a mask, a persona. The schizoid's life lacks vitality, and his perception is unreal, which is to say different from what Meyer called the world of consensual validation. Laing calls the schizoid's action futile, but for most schizoid persons, "less effective" would suffice. With schizotypal and schizophrenic persons, who split themselves off from the world of consensual validation to greater degrees than the schizoid, action often does become futile, leading to different, distinguishable and more pathological phenomena as will be seen further on.

In what seems an irony in Laing's terminology, the split-off, withdrawn, pathological "inner self" becomes the schizoid's "real self!" Perhaps this is because the world of imagination and fantasy—contrasted with the instrumental, consensually validated world of cause and effect—is *the most "real" life the schizoid experiences*. This is his *refuge* from the *terror* of a world he chooses to no longer fully participate in. The purpose of the schizoid defense is to protect what remains of that person's tenuous self from being annihilated by reality (Muller 1987, pp. 103–132).

But, according to Laing, the schizoid's strategy ultimately fails: "No one feels more 'vulnerable', more liable to being exposed by the look of another person than the schizoid individual. . . . Either he turns the other person into a thing, and depersonalizes and objectifies his own feelings towards this thing, or affects indifference" (Laing 1965, p. 76). Depersonalization and objectification of others account for many elements of the schizoid's style.

The essential feature of what the DSM-5 calls schizoid personality disorder is "a pervasive pattern of detachment from social relationships and a restricted range of expression of emotions in interpersonal settings" (DSM-5 2013, p. 653). To "make criteria" for this disorder, four or more of the following seven symptoms must be present: 1. Avoidance of close relationships, including family; 2. Choice of solitary activities; 3. Low sexual interest; 4. Few activities bring pleasure; 5. No close friends or confidants; 6. Indifferent to praise or criticism; 7. Emotionally cold and detached, with flattened affect.

The diagnosis of schizoid personality style using these criteria is made more challenging because people may display four or more of these "symptoms," to one degree or another, and *not* be pathological, just different from the norm (there are, it seems, very few real schizoids). This brings us back to the fundamental point that making a psychiatric diagnosis based on symptoms of unknown meaning and origin can be neither reliable nor accurate. To say the least, the DSM-5 greatly oversimplifies what this kind of pathology is about, missing the schizoid phenomenon by a wide margin.

It is never satisfactory to take symptoms at "face value," and the danger of doing so is particularly evident when working with a patient who may be schizoid. It is not people per se whom schizoids shun, as the DSM-5 implies, but the terror they experience when they become emotionally involved with another person. Both positive and negative emotions, intimacy and self-disclosure, which are generally tolerated (if problematically) by people without major mental illness, are more than the schizoid can handle even under the best of circumstances (Manfield 1992, p. 207). Donald Winnicott put it this way: schizoids "prefer to make relationships on their own terms and not in terms of the impulses of other people" (Winnicott 1965, p. 73). If this is not possible, they choose to be by themselves.

Ralph Klein, who was a colleague and collaborator of James F. Masterson, understood that because the schizoid's withdrawal from the world of consensual validation did not derive from social interaction itself but from a *terror-filled emotional reaction* that occurred in the course of this interaction, the schizoid may show two different faces—and opposite affects—to the consensually constructed world he is forced to live in (Masterson & Klein 1995, pp. 25–27).

Klein's identification of two schizoid types—the "classic schizoid" and the "secret schizoid"—based in part on the earlier work of W. R. D. Fairbairn, presupposes the distinction between *emotion* (what a person is feeling) and *affect* (the body's outer manifestation of that feeling). This dichotomy is not explicitly recognized in the DSM-5, which identifies only the classic schizoid. Classic schizoids manifest the restricted affect and isolation identified by the DSM-5 (criterion number 7), which are related to criteria 1, 2 and 3.

In contrast, "secret schizoids" are socially available because they are capable of at least the *form* of sociality. But they are emotionally shut down and emotionally unavailable, keeping their real feelings and personalities under wrap, risking little or nothing of their inner selves as they deal with the world through a persona. Their scission from the world of consensual validation is less than with classic schizoids. In Laing's Figure 13.1b, the "inner selves" (broken-line circle) of secret schizoids would be depicted as being less separated from the larger, solid-line oval that represents the authentic, embodied self.

We have chosen a secret schizoid for our exemplar of the schizoid personality style. While maintaining a highly successful outer life, inwardly this person is ruled by the same psychodynamics as the classic schizoid.

The Fifty Shades of Christian Grey: An Exemplar of the Phenomenon of Schizoid Personality Style

Fifty Shades of Grey, the film, which evolved from the novel of the same name by E. L. James, achieved its blockbuster status as a story of dominant-submissive love between a 27-year-old billionaire alpha male and a young woman who has just graduated from college with a degree in English and a 4.0 GPA. On one level, the film is a graphic portrayal of this 3rd domain paraphilia and is worthy of study from that perspective. Less obviously perhaps to the general moviegoer, *Fifty Shades of Grey* is also a dead-on portrayal of what Ralph Klein called the "secret schizoid."

Christian Grey is a classic sexual dominant. As he tries to convince Ana Steele to be his 18th submissive partner—she will be the first "girlfriend" he introduces to his parents—he tells her that he has never had what would pass for a normal connection with a woman: he does not do relationships; his women do not spend the night. In his luxe Seattle apartment, where he keeps a grand piano and plays Chopin (the "sad" Chopin, Ana points out), he also has a locked Red Room that splendidly displays the paraphernalia he requires to indulge his sexual proclivities.

Christian has prismatic insight into his sexual pathology. "I'm fifty shades of fucked-up," he tells Ana. He tries to pursue this pathology as authentically and considerately as he can. In attempting to recruit Ana to his world of dominance and submission, he wants her to know what she would be in for. He insists that she read and sign a contract, with her as "the Submissive," citing specific sexual acts she would and would not be willing to engage in with him.

Christian functions splendidly in his outer world of cause and effect—he is, after all, a billionaire at 27. He is well bred and charming and, on the surface, operates efficiently, even generously. He has no friends, just loyal associates to whom he is loyal as well. He has had no girlfriends, but there have been many prior submissives, as he acknowledges to Ana. He is formal and polite with his parents, but there doesn't appear to be any emotional tie there either. Unlike those who have other pathological personality styles, Christian does not seem to be much affected by how the people in his life see him, or react to him. Except, that is, for Ana.

This is Christian's "false self." It is the persona with which he takes on everyone and everything that constitutes the warp and woof of his life. There is success here, but also a certain deadness, which Laing identifies as a component of the schizoid's false self (Figure 13.1b).

Christian seems detached from his persona and eerily in touch with another, hidden, "inner" world. He appears to *act* in the outer world but to *live* somewhere else, inside himself (Jamie Dornan brilliantly captures this scission and the pain it causes Christian). Christian has all the characteristics that the DSM-5 sets out for schizoid personality disorder except for symptom number 3: he has an intense interest in sex, but this is "otherworldly" sex, which fills the need of his inner, "real" self, as Laing paradoxically calls it.

Normal sex is generally understood as mutual, which implies a give and take. Christian gives and takes, but only what he chooses to give and take. While in some ways being considerate of Ana's feelings, his sexual play is limited to dominating her, even as he pleases her. Much to her amazement and disappointment, he will not allow her to touch him. He gives her his body, while remaining emotionally closed off to her.

Christian's dominant-submissive choice for sexual gratification most likely derives from the trauma that led to his schizoid scission: the submissive sexual stance he was enticed into, as a teenager, by a woman who was his mother's friend and is still his friend, only platonically now. This is the trauma that he could not work through and surmount in the exterior world of cause and effect. Thus was born Christian's "inner," schizoid self.

Ana is first drawn into Christian's schizoid world because she is sexually attracted to him. Even when things between them become really difficult, she continues because she has fallen in love. His world is foreign territory for her—she is clearly not schizoid and has no need to be dominated. She resides in the instrumental world of cause and effect, even as she makes repeated forays into Christian's disordered world by submitting to him sexually. While he tries to dominate her, she tries to normalize him. The tension between these ultimately incompatible ways of living and loving becomes increasingly strong as they attempt to find common ground, fail, move apart, and then find each other again, if only temporarily.

Harry Guntrip has described this facet of the schizoid phenomenon as the "'in' and 'out' situation": the schizoid alternates between tenuously moving emotionally toward another person only to retreat when the anxiety attending this contact becomes too much (Guntrip 1969, p. 49).

The end for this couple comes when Christian faces a business crisis and his persona begins to crumble under the pressure. As he is pulled into an unnamed emergency, he withdraws from Ana even further, but then asks her for sex, explaining that he would like her to see the worst he could do to her. This, it turns out, is delivering six heavy lashes to her bare buttocks, with a belt. She submits, but later tells him "I can't do this." She returns the keys to the expensive car he bought for her and takes the elevator from his apartment, with its splendid view of Seattle, back to the real world. As the elevator door closes, each says the other's name.

All through the film, I looked for signs that Ana would draw Christian out of his inner schizoid world. There were some heartening moments, but he was too far into that inner space to relinquish its safety. Ana's psychological strength was at least as strong as Christian's schizoid illness. Their parting was a stand-off. There is talk of a sequel to this film. Stay tuned.

In the meantime, by characterizing and comparing the worlds inhabited by Ana and Christian and observing their ultimately unsuccessful efforts to find a common ground to pursue her understanding of mutual love and his need for paraphilic sexual gratification, we see the differences between them—her relative normalcy, his pathology—in a way that permits us to recognize the phenomenon of the schizoid style. (In Chapter 11, in the section on Abnormal Sexual Behavior, Christian Grey is briefly looked at as a sexual sadist.)

Schizotypal Personality Style

Dimensionally, schizotypy can be thought of as a pre-psychotic state. This condition can also be seen as a retreat from a terrifying and unlivable world that is intermediate in degree and endpoint from what is manifested in schizoid personality style and schizophrenia. The schizoid, the schizotype and the schizophrenic all "split" from the world (*schiz* is the Greek prefix for split or divide) to create "inner" states of being that offer varying degrees of surcease from the terror experienced in a no-longer-hospitable world of cause and effect and consensual validation.

Figure 13.1b is a graphic portrayal of this scission of self where the outcomes of schizoid personality style, schizotypal personality style or schizophrenia depend on how far the defensively created "inner self" is situated from the partly abandoned world of cause and effect.

In *The Divided Self*, Laing describes a classic schizotype, David:

> David was eighteen when I saw him. He was an only child whose mother had died when he was ten. Since then he had lived with his father. From grammar school he had gone to university to study philosophy. His father could not see the point of his son consulting a psychiatrist as there was nothing, in his view, for him to see a psychiatrist about. His tutor, however, was worried about the boy because he seemed to be hallucinated and acted in various somewhat odd ways. For instance, he attended lectures in a cloak, which he wore over his shoulders and arms; he carried a cane; his whole manner was entirely artificial; his speech was made up largely of quotations (Laing 1965, p. 70).

Clearly, David's pathology falls a notch to the right of schizoid personality style in the dimensional spectrum of the split self (if there are few schizoids, there are undoubtedly fewer schizotypes). Laing thinks of him as "borderline," which is to say borderline psychotic. David's oddness puts him more in league with someone who has largely escaped from reality than, say, Christian Grey whose lesser retreat permitted him to at least *appear* normal and function in a way that does not immediately arouse suspicion that he is seriously mentally ill.

Laing's description suggests that David created himself from the outside in. Put another way, his actions are all persona, or false self. There is no indication that David is interacting with the world in a way that follows authentic feelings, desires or plans of his own.

Laing came to believe that David's act (persona, false self) derived from his efforts, beginning as a small child, to please his mother. Mother and son seemed to function as opposite faces of the same coin. After his mother died, David took over many of the household tasks she had performed, never complaining or outwardly showing any sign that he had been shortchanged by her death. He became, outwardly anyway, the person she wanted him to be. He didn't seem to realize that it could have happened any other way:

> He had grown up taking entirely for granted that what he called his "self" and his "personality" [persona] were two quite separate things. He had never seriously imagined any other possibility and he took it equally for granted that everyone else was constructed along similar lines. His view of human nature

> in general, based on his own experience of himself, was that everyone was an actor (p. 71).

David was convinced that every person participated in the world in the same way he did. Living in this self-referential, closed-off manner, he did not have the opportunity to reality-test his thoughts and actions with others in the world of consensual validation. David's real self was split off from the world he play-acted in, and this real self never became evident to him or to others through his actions. David's life typified what Laing called "schizoid organization" (p. 73). He was a classic schizotype.

That David was able to hold his life together as long as he did surprised Laing. But such a metastable situation—"not being himself," as Laing put it—could not be indefinitely sustained. By the time David saw Laing, he had begun to decompensate.

For many years, David had dressed in his mother's clothes and playacted parts from women's dramas before a mirror. He felt safe doing this because it was part of his false self. But then he began to feel as if he *were* a woman, with a woman's feelings that seemed real to him. These feelings were overtaking him and seemed a part of his real self. This terrified David. He responded by changing his persona, making himself look like a caricature of a man. "The boy," Laing said, "was a most fantastic-looking character—an adolescent Kierkegaard played by Danny Kaye. The hair was too long, the collar too large, the trousers too short, the shoes too big, and withal, his second-hand theatre and cane!" (p. 70).

Rhetorically, Laing asks why would anyone want to do this? The answer he offers is that David felt compelled to alter and augment the performance of his false self in an effort to save his increasingly threatened real self: "[H]e found that he was driven to dress up and act in his present manner as the only way to arrest the womanish part that threatened to engulf not only his actions but even his 'own' self as well, and to rob him of his much cherished control and mastery of his being" (pp. 72–73). With David's worsening condition in mind, Laing offers this insight into the schizotype: "The individual is developing a microcosmos within himself; but, of course, this autistic, private, intra-individual 'world' is not a feasible substitute for the only world there really is, the shared world. If this were a feasible project then there would be no need for psychosis" (pp. 74–75).

Having taken the first steps toward entering an "inner" world of his own defensive making, the schizotype flirts with psychosis by further removing himself from the shared world of consensual validation. Writing the words "need for psychosis," Laing speaks for everyone who embraces the tenets of existential and Meyerian dynamic psychiatry, and sees that at least some of those who become schizophrenic do so because of a Meyerian *reaction* against what they experience as a terrifying and unlivable world.

Histrionic Personality Style

Arthur Miller's play *The Crucible* is based on an incident that occurred in Salem, Massachusetts in 1692: Nineteen men and women were hanged after religious and community leaders convinced themselves and others that these citizens had practiced witchcraft and were in league with Satan.

Miller understood that the story he was telling—which was driven by a collective histrionic reaction devoid of reason and decency—typifies a phenomenon that can show its face anytime, anywhere, in any guise. *The Crucible* opened in New York in 1953, at the time Senator Joseph McCarthy was falsely accusing hundreds of Americans of being communists or communist sympathizers. In his introduction to the Penguin edition of the play, Christopher Bigsby noted that

> Beyond the question of witchcraft lies the more fundamental question of human nature, for which betrayal seems an ever-present possibility. *The Crucible* reminds us how fragile is our grasp on those shared values that are the foundation of any society . . . not only do accused witches still die, in more than one country in the world, but groundless accusations are still granted credence, hysteria still claims its victims, persecution still masquerades as virtue and prejudice as piety (Miller 2003, pp. xvi, xxv).

The apparent ordinariness of histrionic behavior can mask an evil that passes for righteousness. Pathological narcissists do far more harm than histrionic people—at work, at home and everywhere else—but their behavior is usually easier to spot as deviant (Maccoby 2007). Those whose life and work are touched by the histrionic style can hide in plain sight for long periods of time before the damage they do is recognized.

Identifying the Phenomenon of the Histrionic Style

To paraphrase Shakespeare, everyone wants to be on stage, to leave the ground state that more or less limits us to rationality and fair play, and rise to where emotion has a greater role so that plain worldly stuff can be transformed into *drama*. Some take this inclination too far and change a world nominally governed by reason, fact and balance into a parallel universe ruled by emotion. In Thornton Wilder's play *The Matchmaker*, one character says of Ermengarde, a histrionic person if there ever was one, that there is nothing to tell her that the chaos that goes on inside her head isn't the way of the world outside her.

The DSM-5 characterizes histrionic personality disorder as "A pervasive pattern of excessive emotionality and attention seeking, beginning by early adulthood and present in a variety of contexts . . ." (DSM-5 2013, p. 667). To qualify for the histrionic diagnosis, someone must exhibit at least five of eight behavioral traits, which include: the need to be the center of attention; the inclination to be provocative and seductive; shallow and rapidly shifting emotions; excessive concern about physical appearance; impressionistic speech that is lacking in detail; excessive expression of emotion, and self-dramatization; the tendency to be excessively influenced by others and by circumstances; and an assessment of self, others and situations, including relationships, that is shallow and often overvalued.

Rather than attempt a categorical diagnosis by subscribing to a checklist of symptoms, I prefer to describe the thought, emotion and behavior that I believe constitute the phenomenon of the histrionic style. The naturalistic approach taken here, which incorporates my experience with a number of histrionic managers whom I encountered at work (Muller 2014b), yielded the following *partial structure* of the phenomenon (Churchill & Wertz, 2014), which is elaborated in the discussion that follows:

- Histrionic persons lose their sense of proportion. What is primary under the rule of reason becomes secondary as emotion overflows its boundaries to produce magical thinking, emotion and behavior that often take the form of *exaggeration*. Unable to distinguish between phenomenon and epiphenomenon—between signal and noise, sense and nonsense—those with a histrionic style warp the *context* of a situation and, in doing so, change its meaning. Put another way, they do not see to the heart of things. It is as if they had deliberately chosen to ignore Matthew Arnold's advice to "see life steadily and see it whole." When it comes to making judgments, those with a histrionic style, succumbing to exaggeration and overreaction, often get it wrong. The ultimate casualty here is the *truth*, which they eschew in favor of a more emotionally gratifying transformation of their experience. To the histrionic person, the "truth" of a situation becomes the interpretation of the facts that carries the most self-validating emotional charge.
- After achieving an emotional high, those with a histrionic style are loath to let this feeling go. It is their comfort zone (to the extent they can be said to have one), their preferred "ground state," which often becomes the foundation of their identity.

The approach taken to find this partial structure of the histrionic manager parallels the tack Sartre followed in *The Emotions* (1948), where he parsed the structures of anger and depression (1st domain reactions considered in Chapter 7).[1] In a histrionic reaction to anxiety that leads to a *histrionic transformation*, the ground of one's being changes from "instrumental" to "magical," terms Sartre used in his description of anger and depression. "Magical" here means that rationality is superseded by an overly emotional construction of the world and its meanings.

The histrionic person's world is *dedifferentiated*—another term from Sartre's *The Emotions*—which is to say the link between cause and effect is loosened, allowing the differences between rational and emotional constructions of experience to be blurred. This smoothing over of differences and distinctions effectively extends the histrionic person's boundary of "normalcy." Thoughts, feelings and behavior are allowed that would be unacceptable to someone who is not in thrall to a world impregnated with emotion.

1 The phenomenon of the histrionic manager characterized here using intuitive phenomenology is, in some ways, in line with the "hysterical style" described by David Shapiro in *Neurotic Styles* (1965), his study of neurosis that is rooted in psychoanalytic ego psychology. Though Shapiro and I begin our investigations from very different starting points and adhere to different philosophical anthropologies, we ultimately overflow our perspectives and reach somewhat comparable conclusions about what it means to be histrionic.

The histrionic reaction, which is a psychobiological transformation of self and environment, can produce an intoxication that is undoubtedly hormonally modulated. Those who react to their environment in this way experience a delight that is absent in their ground state. This pleasure reinforces the idea that the histrionic style is the *correct* way for them to feel, think and act. A good deal of the consensual common sense truth about everything we call life can become distorted under the spell of this intoxicating transformation.

Those who carry a high emotional charge tend to have highly charged interactions with others. For the histrionic person, the stated point in a contentious encounter is often not the real point but the pretext for a histrionically transformed goal. In other words, it's not about *X*—it's about *Y*, the *emotional gratification* that *X* makes possible. Friends, spouses and co-workers who are touched by the histrionic person's need to live an emotionally heightened life can suffer significantly after being drawn into this pathological orb.

Always ready to exaggerate, people with a histrionic style have a tendency to see the venial flaws of others as mortal flaws, at times savagely punishing those with good character and estimable achievements because of some peccadillo that others would ignore or forgive. Because they have lost their sense of proportion and context, they are especially prone to snatching defeat from the jaws of victory.

Histrionic persons have trigger points which, when tweaked by others or by events, set them off, sometimes angrily and aggressively. Their constant alertness to potential danger—a hyper suspiciousness, really—is a hallmark of histrionic pathology. Certain types of people threaten the histrionic person's parallel universe more than others. The emotionally solid and consistently rational person may appear especially dangerous.

An Exemplar of the Phenomenon of Histrionic Personality Style

In 1994 I began a 10-year stint evaluating psychiatric patients in the emergency room, eventually seeing about 3,000 patients (Muller 2003). The ER is the ultimate ensemble act. There is a hierarchy, of course, but collegiality rules most of the time. The ER attendings were, almost to a person, a delight to work with. So were most of the nurses, though some could be difficult in ways that I have never known a physician to be difficult. Those of us who did this work agreed that the hardest part of the job was dealing with the psychiatric service managers, mostly nurses and social workers, who assigned and supervised the shifts.

One day, I received a memo from the psychiatric services manager listing several complaints about me that had been communicated to her by the ER head nurse. The accusations were vague and gratuitous, and I cannot recall a single one. Nonetheless, this manager appeared upset and threatened by what she had heard and tossed some ambiguous threats of her own my way. I continued to do my job.

I do not remember how long this unpleasantness went on, but at some point I was informed that one of the nurses had told the ER head nurse that either I would have to leave the ER or *she* would. Now this was a real surprise because the nurse who issued the ultimatum was not one of the emotionally labile nurses who could be counted on to flare up from time to time but a rather quiet woman in her thirties who was considered a good clinician. I knew her only slightly and there had never been an open conflict between us.

The psychiatric services manager continued her threats, and I continued to do my job. Then the threats stopped. I received a copy of a To-Whom-It-May-Concern letter from the emergency department director, who was an excellent physician and the best boss anyone could hope for. In his brief text, which was complimentary and supportive, he seemed to be refuting specific points, most likely those made against me by the ER nurse manager in her memo, written several months earlier to the psychiatric services manager (which I never saw).

My best guess is that the emergency department director found out what was going on and told the nurses involved to knock it off. And, of course, they did. The nurse who wanted *me* gone left the ER and took another job at the hospital. I never saw her again. The me-or-her ultimatum was drama, pure and simple. Reason won out, and histrionics—the inauthentic victory of emotion over reason—were shown the door.

A year later, the psychiatric services manager had found other targets for her hysterical aggression and was picking fights with many of the people she was ostensibly supervising. At least one person quit because of her harassment. When her superiors finally saw what she was doing and realized that she could not be redirected, they unceremoniously fired her.

As this story demonstrates, histrionic thinking and behavior derive more from emotion than reason, creating a condition that causes problems for both those who display this emotional style and those they interact with. When histrionic people "manage" others in the workplace, a destructive dynamic often supervenes as employee and manager pursue the goals of work, frequently at cross purposes (Muller 2014b).

Paranoid Personality Style

The appearance of Mrs. K as an exemplar of the 1st domain paranoid psychotic reaction (Chapter 9) introduced the notion of paranoia. Mrs. K's paranoid reaction comes at the psychotic end of the paranoid dimensional spectrum. At the neurotic end of this spectrum, a lesser paranoid response belonging to the 2nd domain, adopted early by some and maintained throughout a lifetime, is parsed in the FDMI as the paranoid personality style.

How do we understand this defensive style and the Meyerian maladaptive reactions that constitute this particular expression of what van den Berg called a "different existence?" Mrs. K resorted to paranoid delusions about her grandchildren to justify her strong negative and aggressive feelings toward them. Her accusations—that they stole from her and listened in on her phone conversations—involved significant and purposeful distortions of the verifiable truth. Her paranoia was limited to her immediate family.

"Paranoia," according to Meyer, "is a mental perversion of slow and gradual development, a chronic constitutional transformation of the personality" (Lief 1948, p. 93). Meyer cites Kraepelin's belief that the mental constitution of those who eventually express the paranoid style was, as Meyer put it, "different from the start" (Lief 1948, p. 108). This notion is in line with the proposal that 2nd domain illnesses originate in the context of aberrant personality development and temperament, where biology contributes but is not the primary cause.

Paranoia, as it manifests in all its dimensions, from, say, mild suspicion to paranoid schizophrenia, is a distortion of the meaning and intention of another's thoughts, feelings and actions. Meyer identified what he called the "paranoid type" as someone who is ready to infer suspicious and persecutory motives where these motives do not exist, and where only a paranoid person would think they do. According to Meyer, "These persons are continually concerned with what other people may think; they further attribute intentions to indifferent actions of others, more and more without judgment or attempt at verification of their suspicions" (Lief 1948, p. 115). Those with a paranoid style do not require a "reason" for their suspicions. They expect the worst from others and from events, and readily conflate the possible and the probable.

As with all mental illnesses, being paranoid is a way of misusing freedom in an effort to exceed the boundaries of what most people see as authentic and fair, boundaries they implicitly agree to live within. How unfair is it for the paranoid person to falsely accuse another person of motives and acts that are being inferred without justification? It is no surprise that, as Meyer recognized, paranoia inclines a person toward isolation: the gratuitous constitution of others as suspicious and dangerous is inherently a socially destructive stance.

Because there is an endless supply of potential new enemies, paranoia is one of the most sustainable of the dynamic defenses. For someone who is experiencing persistent and severe anxiety—and consequently not establishing an identity or a foothold in the world—paranoia can function as a temporary fix. As far as identity is concerned, to be the one who is plotted against is preferable to being no one at all. (Erik Erikson convinced us that some people will take on what he called a "negative identity" rather than continue to struggle with having no identity.) This compromise with the facts, and thus with reality, serves a purpose and has a meaning, difficult as this may be to grasp for someone who is unfamiliar with defensive psychodynamics.

Identifying the Phenomenon of the Paranoid Style

The "different existence" of the paranoid person entails a pathologically transformed world, but one that preserves what Sartre and Jaspers called differentiation: the ability to identify, assign meaning to and respond to what the world has to offer. This capacity to differentiate is lost in serious depression (Chapter 7) and, in a different way and to a greater degree in psychosis (Chapter 9 and Chapters 13–15). According to Jaspers, the paranoid person

> shows a high degree of differentiation, sharp powers of criticism and an ability to think, but none of this interferes with his belief in the content of his delusional ideas [delusional here does not mean psychotic]. He has had certain experiences and for him they carry as much, if not more, weight than anyone else's. He integrates these experiences with others and he builds up

> his delusional system quite seriously and with deep involvement and holds unshakably to it. Contrary ideas do occur to him, but he brushes them aside disparagingly. He does not lack power to differentiate the discrete sources of knowledge but he insists on his own source, whether supernatural or material (Jaspers 1997, pp. 197–198).

What Jaspers says here about paranoia and differentiation is a part of the paranoid personality style (2nd domain) but not psychotic paranoia (1st and 4th domains). Jaspers saw paranoia as consisting of "delusion-like ideas." The content of these ideas, he said, "have 'meaning' in terms of the patients' life experiences, wishes and hopes, fears and anxieties" (Jaspers 1997, p. 409).

One way to understand paranoia is as the need to make connections where no authentic connections are to be made. To accept coincidence and fortuity as a part of normal life requires a degree of sureness about oneself as well as trust in the world. The German existential psychiatrist Viktor von Gebsattel (1883–1976) noted that those who are paranoid "see meanings everywhere in meaningless occurrences. No accident can be treated any more as mere chance" (Jaspers 1997, p. 286).

Those who are chronically and habitually suspicious live with the expectation that they will be lied to, tricked, manipulated and taken advantage of. Attempts to convince them otherwise rarely succeed and are often interpreted as further efforts to undermine them. The paranoid style, or mode, embodies a certain rigidity and resistance to any influence that threatens to mitigate this notion. An implied mantra might be: Don't confuse me with (new, relevant) facts because my mind is already made up. The paranoid person "tunes out" information that most people would process and allow to influence their thinking and behavior—but not before expending considerable effort in deciding, once again in this instance, that the information is not to be trusted.

Put another way, the paranoid person chronically and habitually fails to test large sectors of what we call reality accurately and fairly. Shapiro tells this story about a paranoid patient: "after some time in psychotherapy, a suspicious patient conceded, perhaps overstating the point, that he never actually listened to what the therapist said; he listened, rather, for signs *in* what was said of what the therapist 'really thought'" (Shapiro 1965, p. 64). "Signs" here mean "clues" to the mystery of what the psychotherapist was *really* up to.

A good deal of what those who are paranoid imagine about the motives of others is a *projection* of their own anxious, angry and aggressive thoughts and feelings. Mrs. K created hateful delusions about the motives and behavior of her grandchildren. Some deep-seeded anxiety that her family's gain would mean her loss—that she would lose them if things went too well for them—was probably one component of this projective drive. She had always been ambivalent about their success, first praising them, then, unaccountably, verbally undermining their achievements. Often, she acted in an openly destructive way, ripping into whoever may have scored a victory. At other times, the aggression that she could not directly acknowledge either to herself or to them was acted out indirectly through projection.

Mrs. K's pathology was, of course, a 1st domain psychotic reaction. The 2nd domain paranoid personality style also has roots in this projective defense. Both pathologies allow their adherents to stay mostly connected to the external world, with a clear sensorium, as they forge their own unique compromise with reality. In 4th domain paranoid schizophrenia, the connection with the external world, and with reality, is largely broken (Chapter 14).

Richard Nixon: An Exemplar of the Phenomenon of Paranoid Personality Style

By any standard, Richard Nixon came from a modest background. Born in Yorba Linda, California, in 1913 in a house his father built, he grew up in a family that was short on money and long on conflict. His parents had very different personalities: his mother was quiet, self-effacing and always encouraged the young boy; his father was impatient, strong-willed and difficult to please.

Trying to satisfy both parents most likely took a toll on the boy's development, especially his ability to integrate thoughts and feelings of opposite emotional polarity. The conflicts he faced at home undoubtedly set the stage for his life-long pessimism and crisis-haunted view of the world. He came to feel that the world was not a safe place or a particularly good place, either, and learned to be suspicious of everyone and everything. Later, that suspicion ignited his paranoia.

Richard Reeves gave this crystalline account of the meaning of Nixon's epic paranoia, which became a major factor in his downfall after the Watergate break-in: "His view of the world was a bad mirror image of himself, of his own darkness. He did not like people because, more often than not, he distorted their motivations to match his own" (Reeves 2001, p. 65).

Nixon projected his suspicious and hateful feelings onto everyone and everything around him. He undoubtedly created this deliberately distorted image of others in a defensive attempt to reduce the painful "charge" of his own negative feelings. This tactic, however, interfered with the formation of a stable identity, which further increased his anxiety, promoting more suspicion, projection and paranoia. Nixon's life exemplified the paranoid style, as well as the inauthenticity that is at the root of this world- transforming distortion (Muller 1987, pp. 187–201).

Nixon won the 1972 presidential election by a comfortable margin. But he inherited the Vietnam War, which had divided the country for many years. During the campaign, Nixon repeatedly said that he had a plan to end the war, but he never revealed it. Once elected, he could not admit defeat in Vietnam, though it was obvious that's where we were headed. He had to save face—needing to preserve his tenuous, paranoid identity—and he did this by *creating more enemies*. The infamous "Enemies List" bore the names of hundreds of people who had "crossed" Nixon by opposing the war and disagreeing with him on other issues. Some of these "enemies" were denied access to the Nixon White House, others were targeted for reprisals, or fired.

Nixon's suspiciousness and paranoia were the direct cause of the Watergate break-in on June 17, 1972, and the cover-up that followed. Insecure in the White House in spite of his electoral mandate, Nixon dispatched, through his minions, five men to break into the offices of the Democratic National Committee at the Watergate building. He wanted to know what the opposition party was planning to do about a number of issues. The burglars were caught, Nixon vehemently denied any involvement with the break-in and the Watergate scandal materialized. He resigned on August 9, 1974, under the threat of impeachment and removal from office.

Having to deal with the Vietnam War and Watergate, the two years that preceded Nixon's resignation was a time of unimaginable stress for him. As would be expected, his paranoia reached new levels. We have a record of these times—in Nixon's own words and voice—from the White House tapes that preserve what was actually said, day to day, by Nixon and those who were doing his bidding at that time.

In this excerpt from a transcript of a conversation in the Oval Office with his national security advisers Henry Kissinger and Alexander Haig on December 14, 1972, we can see how close to the edge Nixon came: "Never forget the press is the enemy, the press is the enemy. The establishment is the enemy, the professors are the enemy, the professors are the enemy. Write that on the blackboard 100 times" (Glaister 2008). This irrational political hatred, obsessively stated, is comparable to the equally irrational ravings of Senator Joseph McCarthy during the 1950s.

Though Nixon was contemptuous of most of the people he encountered as an adult, he especially despised intellectuals and graduates of Ivy League schools—the latter group probably, in part, because he was offered a scholarship to Harvard but had to turn it down because his brother was ill and Nixon was needed to work in the family grocery store. (He attended Whittier College in Whittier, California, his home town at that time.)

Consider these words from Nixon's White House tapes, recorded in June and July, 1971, a year before the Watergate break-in (Hughes 2007):

> The guys from the best families are most likely to develop that arrogance that puts them above the law.
>
> If they're from any Eastern school or Berkeley, those are particularly the potential bad ones.

Once Nixon became aware that workers in some White House offices had photographs of John F. Kennedy, he directed images of all former presidents to be removed. How threatened Nixon must have felt by Kennedy, then dead for almost a decade. As an intellectual and a Harvard man from a good family, Kennedy was everything Nixon despised.

Richard Hofstadter, a professor of history at Columbia University, noted in his classic text *The Paranoid Style in American Politics* that "A fundamental paradox of the paranoid style is the imitation of the enemy" (Hofstadter 2008, p. 32). The *imagined* enemy, that is. Whatever arrogance and inclination to act "above the law" that can be fairly credited to journalists, college professors and Ivy Leaguers—many of whom were virulently against Nixon and what he had done with his Presidency—Nixon raised that ante by an order of magnitude. Not long before he resigned, he stated that if the President does something, then it can't be wrong. In the end, Richard Nixon fused with the idea that, as President, he could do *nothing* wrong, a delusional idea to be sure. Simply put, the law did not apply to him.

In pursuing the theme of paranoia in American politics, Hofstadter makes the point that those who govern with a paranoid style can have, in spite of this pathology, a core of productive selfhood: "[T]he idea of the paranoid style as a force in politics would have little contemporary relevance or historical value if it were applied only to men with profoundly disturbed minds. It is the use of paranoid modes of expression by more or less normal people that makes the phenomenon significant" (Hofstadter 1964). No one would deny that Nixon was a talented politician who, in spite of his paranoia, had a keen grasp of international affairs. He did, after all, open China to the West, a move that was culturally and economically good for the United States. This was the same man who hated journalists, college professors and Ivy Leaguers, and retaliated against some of them. Nixon was both crazy and not crazy. Perhaps, as so many are, he was as crazy as he needed to be.

Possibly without realizing it, in characterizing the paranoid style, Hofstadter saw to the heart of what psychiatry had long designated as a personality disorder. He grasped that "a mentality disposed to see the world in this way may be a persistent psychic phenomenon, more or less constantly affecting a modest minority of the population" (Hofstadter 1964). Richard Nixon was one of the "walking wounded" who embodied this pathological phenomenon. Had he not gotten caught in the act for instigating and covering up Watergate, he would have finished his Presidency, and been seen by the people who agreed with him as a success! Those with a paranoid style walk among us.

Hofstadter saw the paranoid person as a "double sufferer." In so doing, he identified an important component of the phenomenon of the paranoid style: "We are all sufferers from history, but the paranoid is a double sufferer, since he is afflicted not only by the real world, with the rest of us, but by his fantasies as well" (Hofstadter 1964). Make that the *consequences* of his fantasies. This could be Richard Nixon's epitaph, and that of many others who lived the paranoid style. (Richard Hofstadter never got to see the full expression of Nixon's paranoia. He died in 1970 of leukemia at the age of 54.)

Obsessive-Compulsive Personality Style

The obsessive-compulsive style—the DSM-5's obsessive compulsive personality disorder—is not the same phenomenon as the obsessive-compulsive reaction (OCR) that was characterized as a 1st domain illness in Chapter 6. In most instances, obsessive-compulsive style is a lesser pathology, and does not involve obsessions and compulsions as such. The pathological transformation of self, other and world that *is* this style is less drastic and of a different kind than what occurs in the OCR.

Some elements of the obsessive-compulsive style are adaptive, helping people to see their life projects through and produce work of high quality. "Good" obsessive-compulsive traits serve a purpose and are under the control of their owner. (Polishing a written text or reading page proofs, I deliberately put myself in this mode. When the task is finished, this temporary "trait," which is goal-directed and time limited, disappears.) Those having an obsessive-compulsive style, on the other hand, lose control over these traits, which then become limiting and even crippling.

The DSM-5 offers a detailed description of the obsessive-compulsive personality style, which they call obsessive-compulsive personality disorder. According to the DSM-5, the essential feature of this mental illness is

> a preoccupation with orderliness, perfectionism, and mental and interpersonal control, at the expense of flexibility, openness, and efficiency . . . [those affected] attempt to maintain a sense of control through painstaking attention to rules, trivial details, procedures, lists, schedules, or form to the extent that the major point of the activity is lost. They are excessively careful and prone to repetition, paying extraordinary attention to detail and repeatedly checking for possible mistakes. They are oblivious to the fact that other people tend to become very annoyed at the delays and inconveniences that result from this behavior (p. 679).

Someone with an obsessive-compulsive style compulsively follows rules of his own pathological construction. These defenses—maladaptive Meyerian reactions—usually impose on this person a degree of rigidity. Rituals created by obsessive-compulsives are formulaic behaviors that are defenses against severe, often incapacitating anxiety. If someone is convinced that not stepping on the sidewalk's sectional dividing lines is the "right" thing to do, he can hope to be spared the worst of his anxiety while this avoidance ritual is in play.

The emotional rigidity acquired by those with an obsessive-compulsive style often extends to moral and ethical issues. Scrupulosity—the anguish felt about not adhering sufficiently to rules and laws, secular or religious—is the price that many with this personality style pay.

It should come as no surprise that obsessive-compulsives tend to defer gratification while pursuing the high goals they set for themselves. They are excessively self-critical and hard on themselves, and often chose to live below their means as a way of maintaining control over their lives—more specifically, as a way of not *losing* control. They put leisure and friendship second to work and achievement, essentially undermining their efforts to find fulfillment with others. When their high expectations of others are not met, which is often the case, the result can be resentment and anger.

I had a patient who angrily lived in the 2nd domain, with an obsessive-compulsive style. A hot-reactor, he took vacations, but these were short vacations. Always close with a dollar, he would not allow himself the expense of more than a day or two away, even though he had the means to go anywhere he wanted and stay as long as he wanted. No obligations kept him from leaving home, or beckoned him to return there. As with everything he did, he kept himself on a short leash during these brief and modest forays. Try as he did, he found it impossible to relax. His psychological rigidity extended to his body; he has been on antihypertensive medication for 25 years.

Identifying the Phenomenon of Obsessive-Compulsive Style

Someone who is in the process of developing an obsessive-compulsive style is too anxious and psychically fragile to directly take on the ambiguity and complexity of an authentic, "normal" life. Despairing of ever achieving order and stability in the "normal" way, this person may instead attempt to order and stabilize often extraneous elements in his exterior world—in the process, reconstructing both himself and his environment. In creating excessive and non-productive symmetry and perfection, one gives up on achieving a realistic approximation of symmetry and perfection in an authentic dialectic between himself and a "normally" constructed environment. This is a common element of the obsessive-compulsive style.

Wilhelm Reich is often cited as having described obsessive-compulsive people as "living machines" (Reich 1949, p. 199). The anxious person who "opts" for the obsessive-compulsive style adopts a defensive stance of machine-like rigidity in a temporary and only partially successful effort to hold off an amorphous and terrifying chaos. According to Shapiro,

> These people feel and function like driven, hardworking, automatons pressing themselves to fulfill unending duties, "responsibilities," and tasks that are, in their view, not chosen, but simply there. One compulsive patient likened his whole life to a train that was running efficiently, fast, pulling a substantial load, but on a track laid out for it. In other words, they do not feel like free men (Shapiro 1965, p. 40).

One sees here the consequences to the obsessive-compulsive person of the "shoulds" and "oughts" that cognitive behavioral therapists help patients to identify and relinquish by reclaiming the freedom they surrendered in embracing these defenses.

For obsessive-compulsives, even fun and relaxation are pursued rigidly and systematically. These normally spontaneous activities are as taxing and draining as their work. Everything becomes the project of a *driven self* that is answering the call of the "shoulds" and "oughts" which dominate their thinking. In this process, what Martin Heidegger characterized as the authentic "invitation of the world" to accept its offerings takes a back seat. A paradox inheres in the "shoulds" and "oughts" that compel obsessive-compulsives: they are driven by internal needs to meet *imagined* external expectations. Proceeding as if the world were "inviting" them to make some particular compulsive response, it is *they*, through the projection of their needs onto the world, who have created these pathological desiderata.

Wilhelm Reich's characterization of those who live obsessionally and compulsively as "living machines"—whether in the 1st domain with an OCR or in the 2nd domain with an obsessive-compulsive style—understood how freedom is relinquished by those who take refuge in these defenses. A machine, after all, is a thing that is made to do someone else's bidding. It is used to fill a need, according to someone else's plan. This is not the authentic role for a human being, whose essence it is to be free, within, of course, the constraints of the situation he finds himself in.

Those who are attempting to transcend their obsessive-compulsive style could learn a good deal from reading Milan Kundera's novel *The Unbearable Lightness of Being* (1984). Freedom is portrayed here as the euphoric feeling that Kundera's protagonist, Tomas, a surgeon who was practicing in Prague in 1968 during the Russian invasion of Czechoslovakia, achieves once he realizes that everything he formerly believed he *had* to do was a product of his own choosing. After leaving Prague, he eventually came to see that there was *nothing* he really had to do, and that, while he had never been obsessive-compulsive—his "shoulds" and "oughts" were never that severe—he *had* been his own existential jailor.

Adrian Monk: An Exemplar of the Phenomenon of Obsessive–Compulsive Style

Adrian Monk, star of the TV series *Monk*, which aired 125 episodes from 2002 to 2009, is an exemplar of the phenomenon of obsessive-compulsive style. Monk, played by Tony Shalhoub, also demonstrates that in spite of his obsessions and compulsions, he can solve crimes that stump healthier minds.

Monk's work bringing criminals to justice has a tragic back story. While he was a stand-out detective for the San Francisco Police Department, his wife, Trudy, died in a car bomb explosion. Monk initially believed that the bomb was intended for him but later realized that Trudy, a journalist, was the target all along—she had been investigating some high-end illegal activity.

Monk was prostrated by his loss. He could not work for three and a half years and became housebound during that time. He lost his job with the SFPD. Monk had obsessive-compulsive tendencies since childhood, but Trudy's death shifted these defenses to a higher gear, leaving him a recluse and a crippled man. Gradually, with the help of a nurse-companion, Monk recovered to the point where he could practice as a private detective and serve as a consultant to the SFPD homicide department.

Monk is obsessed with order and symmetry. At a crime scene, disorder and asymmetry can send him into a tailspin, diverting him from his task. In one episode, as he interrogates two colleagues of a woman who has just been murdered, Monk looks behind him and sees two glass coffee pots on a hotplate. The pot on the left holds slightly more coffee than the one to the right. It is immediately obvious that Monk has noticed this and is perturbed. He ceases his questioning and pours some coffee from the pot on the left side into the adjacent pot. The left pot still has more coffee. The man he was questioning points out that one pot is for regular and the other for decaf. Monk does not care. That is not his concern and not his problem. He transfers more coffee from the first pot, but the amounts are still unequal. Another objection from the man has no effect on Monk. A third transfer leaves both pots with the same amount of coffee. Monk, having satisfied his need for symmetry, is ready to go back to work.

In an episode where Monk and his nurse are at a restaurant in Mexico, Monk, who is aware that they should not drink the native water, turns down his waiter's recommendation of four or five high-end bottled waters—including Pellegrino and Perrier—because they are not *his* brand. In strictly rational terms, this makes no sense. You could say that Monk is being rigid for the sake of being rigid and that is precisely what he is doing. As long as he drinks *his* brand of bottled water, he will know who he is. To drink another brand is to veer off the rigid course that keeps him in line and helps him to conserve his identity.

Besides his obsessions and compulsions, numerous phobias threaten to throw Monk off his course. According to *Wikipedia* (2014), "Monk has 312 fears, some of which are milk, ladybugs, harmonicas, heights, imperfection, claustrophobia, driving, food touching on his plates, messes and risk."

Monk's work solving crimes and bringing criminals to justice is a triumph of his will—Nietzsche's "will to power"—over an illness that could otherwise have kept him a recluse. A capacity to focus intensely on a task is common in obsessive-compulsives, and he makes extraordinary use of this trait. While solving crimes for the SFPD, Monk continues to be obsessed with Trudy's death and with his search for her killer. His success bringing other criminals to justice is a partial compensation for his failure to solve this crime (until he does in the last episode of the series).

Through a special gift—for spotting discrepancies, finding patterns and making connections that others miss—Monk creates an identity which transcends his illness: he becomes the person who does brilliant detective work, in spite of, and to some degree because of, that illness.

Objections could be raised about using a fictional character as an exemplar to flesh out the phenomenon of a mental illness. It has been said that those who write fiction "lie to tell the truth," and with Adrian Monk this appears to be the case. Watching Monk live as a three-dimensional character in this TV series, we realize that the writers really have captured the phenomenon of obsessive-compulsive style.

Hypomanic (Hyperthymic) Personality Style

Hypomania did not find its way into the DSM until 1994 with the 4th edition. In the DSM-5, this mood state is defined as "A distinct period of abnormally and persistently elevated, expansive, or irritable mood and abnormally and persistently increased activity or energy, lasting at least 4 consecutive days and present most of the day, nearly every day" (Criterion A, p. 124). Clinically, hypomania is manifested principally as a mood state intermediate between depression and mania in persons having bipolar I disorder (a 4th domain condition described in Chapter 16).

We are concerned here with a different type of hypomania—a different phenomenon—one that is not a mood *state* like the DSM's hypomania, but an aggregate of mood *traits*, a *personality style*.

John D. Gartner, a psychologist and clinical associate professor of psychiatry at Johns Hopkins University School of Medicine, has characterized this phenomenon in *The Hypomanic Edge*. His colorful subtitle, *The Link Between (a Little) Craziness and (a Lot of) Success in America*, is undoubtedly a concession to a commercial publisher—this is a trade book, after all. Though a tilt toward a popular audience can be felt in many parts of the book, Gartner's efforts to demonstrate that this kind of hypomania is a real phenomenon are not compromised.

Because Gartner's "hypomanic edge" is a different phenomenon than the hypomania experienced by those with bipolar I and bipolar II disorders, a less confounding way to designate this phenomenon might be *hyperthymia*, or, better, *hyperthymic personality style*. Though, in the past, attempts have been made to formally characterize the hyperthymic personality, none of these efforts has had much of an impact on clinical practice.

Wikipedia defines the hyperthymic temperament as an "excessively positive disposition similar to, but more stable than, the hypomania of bipolar disorder" (both bipolar I and bipolar II, presumably). *Hyperthymia* derives from Greek roots (highly active + spirit) and has also been described as excessive activity verging on hypomania. "Verging" is a key word here because those who manifest Gartner's "hypomanic edge" do not experience the incapacitating depression and mania that come with bipolar I. Gartner acknowledges that his hypomanics "live on the edge, between normal and abnormal" (Gartner 2005, p. 2), with just "a little craziness."

Gartner claims that the hypomanic style is "hereditary." Following Meyer, I prefer to think of this condition as a *psychobiological adaptation* that some people make to the totality of their life experience, which includes a contribution from heredity. This defense is mostly a productive one, which after repeated reinforcement solidifies into a series of Meyerian *habits*, mostly good, some bad. Through the consolidation of these habits, hypomania *emerges* (Meyer's term) as a *personality style*, with its advantages and pitfalls. Those with a hypomanic edge find their place in the FDMI's 2nd domain.

The hypomanic's movement in and through the everyday world is more like skating on ice than walking on grass, the default surface trod by most of us. This attenuation of friction permits a less earth-bound and constrained life: more energy, more connections with others, faster cognition and greater achievements. Sometimes these benefits come at the expense of reduced traction in the world of cause and effect. When the phenomenon of hypomania is approached in this way, the reason why hypomanics tend to exceed boundaries and get in trouble becomes more transparent.

In *The Hypomanic Edge*, Gartner characterizes the *domain* of the hypomanic person, and then elicits the *phenomenon* of the hypomanic style. He tells the life stories of several well-known people who, in different ways, changed the world, not only through their talent but because of their hypomanic edge—how they lived their lives and did their work, in a faster lane. The list includes Christopher Columbus, John Winthrop, Roger Williams, William Penn, Alexander Hamilton, Andrew Carnegie, the Hollywood Selznicks and Mayers, and Craig Venter. Gartner also acknowledges that *he* lives on the hypomanic edge.

Gartner began his study of the hypomanic temperament by culling a list of hypomanic traits from reports in the psychiatric literature and from the DSM-5 (pp. 124–125). Speaking by phone with ten Internet CEOs, he asked:

- Are you filled with energy?
- Are you flooded with ideas?
- Are you driven, restless, and unable to keep still?
- Do you channel your energy into the achievement of wildly grand ambitions?
- Do you often work on little sleep?
- Do you feel brilliant, special, chosen, perhaps even destined to change the world?

- Do you ever feel euphoric?
- Do you become easily irritated by minor obstacles?
- Are you a risk taker?
- Do you overspend in both your business and personal life?
- Do you act out sexually?
- Do you sometimes act impulsively, with poor judgment, in ways that can have painful consequences?
- Do you sometimes talk fast?
- Are you witty and gregarious?
- Does your confidence make you charismatic and persuasive?
- Are you also prone to making enemies and feel you are persecuted by those who do not accept your vision and mission? (Adapted from Gartner 2005, pp. 4–5).

All the CEOs agreed that these traits—with the exception of paranoia and sexual acting out, which are obviously self-incriminatory—figured prominently in their daily lives.

Gartner's list of hypomanic traits has a good deal in common with every list of narcissistic symptoms ever compiled (no surprise here). It is probably not too much of a stretch to say that *hypomania (hyperthymia) is the emotional ground state for many narcissists*. Gartner believes that "*All* hypomanics are narcissists" (2005, p. 266).

Describing his own hypomanic edge, Gartner reveals that, while preparing to write his book, he spent $12,000 on other peoples' books! "Why not take them out of the Hopkins library? Because I want them now! Because I can't waste time going out to get them! Because I'm impatient! I'm captaining the SS Hypomanic Edge here! I need to move! I need to move fast and keep moving!" (Duffy 2005). Several of the hypomanic traits on his list come into play in this one act.

A main theme in Gartner's book is that many of those who make it big in America owe their success to their hypomanic edge. "I'm American, and I kind of like Americans. I'm hypomanic and I kind of like hypomanics. I think that overall, this is an advantageous trait to have as a country. When you take the pluses and the minuses—and there are a lot of minuses—but when you add them up, I'm saying you get a positive number" (Duffy 2005). One of the minuses that Gartner recognizes is that hypomanics tend to ignore the boundaries that most people observe implicitly, and consequently they "don't play well with others."

This section on hypomanic personality style was written in October 2015 (out of sequence) when Donald Trump was leading in the polls as he pursued the Republican nomination for the 2016 presidential election (Leibovich 2015). It is no exaggeration to say that while Trump actively sought the nomination, he put on a clinic of narcissistic and hyperthymic traits, displaying an enduring personality style (Muller 2016) which embodies many of the pluses and minuses that Gartner draws our attention to in *The Hypomanic Edge*. The noticeably high-energy Donald Trump often noisily accused his competitors Jeb Bush and Ben Carson of having "low energy."

Trump is the American success story. His plusses are obvious. His minuses are transparent to most people, though, by all appearances not to him—in true narcissistic fashion. Trump could easily serve as an exemplar of the phenomenon of narcissistic style *and* hypomanic style.

But for the distinction of exemplar of the hypomanic style, we nominate Craig Venter, whom Gartner profiled in *The Hypomanic Edge*. This talented and acclaimed molecular biologist, who was the first to sequence the human genome—*his* genome, of course—has reaped the benefits and paid the price for his hypomanic edge. The reader is referred to Gartner's gripping account of this remarkable life (2005, pp. 239–292). It should come as no surprise that Venter wrote his own version of this journey, or that he titled his story *A Life Decoded: My Genome: My Life* (Venter 2007).

Avoidant Personality Style

Avoidant personality style is considered in Chapter 17, and the author's patient, Peter, is designated as an exemplar of the phenomenon of this 2nd domain pathology. Peter's story, elicited during a 21-month course of psychotherapy, illustrates how the FDMI is used to diagnose patients with multi-domain pathologies.

Psychosomatic Reaction

For someone who subscribes to the idea that mind and body are dialectically inseparable, it is a short step to seeing that, under certain circumstances, mental conflict and its coupled anguish could paralyze a body part, be expressed in the dysfunction of an organ, or be experienced as physical pain. No mind exists separately from a body, no body exists separately from a mind.

"Depression hurts," media ads for some antidepressants inform us. To feel de-pressed—literally, pressed down by the weight of a pathologically transformed life—is to experience both mental and physical pain. "*The whole body,*" Jaspers believed, "*may be conceived as an organ of the psyche*" (Jaspers 1997, p. 236).

We can begin to understand what happens in a psychosomatic reaction—which, in its varied manifestations, has been called somatiform disorder in the DSM and conversion by psychoanalysts—by postulating a unique type of disequilibrium that can occur within our psychobiological oneness. In this process, what is psychologically maladaptive becomes somatically maladaptive as well.

How, in the course of expressing some need, does the psyche, through a psychosomatic reaction, find its way into the body? If, as Freud believed, there is a choice of neurosis, and, as Meyer believed, a choice of maladaptive reaction-type, there may also be, at least in some instances, an organ or physiological process that becomes vulnerable to psychic infiltration, through a constitutional weak spot, so to speak. This is the main reason why the psychosomatic reaction is seen as belonging to the 2nd domain.

Karl Jaspers, in his *General Psychopathology* (1997, pp. 236–246), goes a long way toward disclosing the mysterious phenomenon of the psychosomatic reaction.

"It is very difficult," he says, "to separate what is determined physically and what is determined psychically. The psyche looks for certain prepared channels in the body to produce its pathological effects. If, for instance, pains in the joints have existed due to a past arthritis these pains can be psychically continued after recovery or they can be reinvoked" (p. 239). Under conditions of relative psychic and somatic health, a kind of homeostasis prevails between mind and body. But in certain maladaptive reactions, the psyche may dynamically exceed its normal bounds and the homeostatic state may become compromised, allowing a psychosomatic illness to take hold: "Organs and physical predispositions have to meet the psyche halfway. It looks as if the psyche chooses the organs in which to manifest itself by dysfunction, or as if it chooses the functions into which its own disturbance can enter, like an interloper, as it were" (p. 241). Jaspers goes so far as to say that "organic illness accompanied by anatomical changes can *have a psychogenic source*" (original emphasis, p. 239). He singles out diabetes and colitis, which, he says, "can start after some psychic commotion, and may be worsened through it" (p. 239).

For some people who are in mental anguish, medical problems, which often include somatic pain that is often less stigmatizing and easier to bear, can become a welcome diversion. A psychosomatic reaction may provide a partial surcease of psychological pain, while initiating a more profound biological maladaptation, centered in the body.

Alterations in psychic and somatic homeostasis can profoundly influence a person's thought, emotion and behavior: "Disturbance of function can develop and fixate in areas that by chance happen to be active during an affect. An upsetting message comes over the telephone, the hand holding the receiver feels as if paralyzed, 'writer's cramp' sets in and so on" (p. 242). The writer's psychic reaction to the bad news he receives has *found a way into his body*, producing a somatic correlate of the psychic injury.

Perhaps the writer's project was fraught to begin with. Without acknowledging this conflict, and perhaps even deceiving himself about it, he may welcome a reason to disengage from writing, just for a time, or, maybe, indefinitely. The arm holding the phone that brought the bad news may then accommodate his unexpressed wish to be rid of his writing project by responding with "writer's cramp."

Paralysis is a classic Freudian conversion symptom, where psychic energy is allegedly "converted" (a term borrowed from physics) into a somatic symptom. Jaspers, an existential psychiatrist, and Meyer, a "closet existentialist," distanced themselves from the "energetic" theories of Freudian psychoanalysis. In Jaspers's formulation of the writer's paralyzed arm, nothing is "converted." Rather, a meaningful *reaction* occurs—in Meyer's terms, a maladaptive reaction—that allows the writer to, in effect, use his psychic trauma as a *reason* for not continuing his writing. Like all defenses, this one is a retreat made in the face of a major challenge, aided and abetted by the lubricant of self-deception.

Z: An Exemplar of the Phenomenon of Psychosomatic Reaction

It goes without saying that clinicians can and must learn from their patients. It seems no less evident that they can also learn from those they encounter socially who display aberrant styles of living. Observing these people during the course of their everyday lives often permits a closer look at the phenomena that develop following Meyer's maladaptive reactions than is usually possible in a clinical setting.

An opportunity of this kind came my way during the late 1990s. I gradually made the acquaintance of a woman in her early 80s—let's call her Z—who moved into the apartment building where I had lived for some time. At the time, Z's second husband was struggling with colon cancer that was seen as terminal when diagnosed. He died in 2000, leaving her well provided for.

Z had been through a good deal, and I admired her courage in the face of adversity. She befriended me, no doubt seeing me as a lifeline. I was busy professionally at the time but called her every evening. The calls lasted about 20 minutes. She did most of the talking, updating me on the events of her day and discussing articles she had read in the local newspaper and stories that caught her attention on the TV news.

Gradually, over a period of three years, her end of the dialogue turned dour. The accusations against others became stronger, her tone angrier. At first, I was spared from her wrath. Eventually, I too, was targeted for transgressions that, later, I realized amounted to my refusal to affirm her narcissistic needs. I came to see the shape of her pathological response to everyone and everything she encountered. In time, her anger, and then her threats, made it impossible for me to continue talking to her, and we, too, became estranged.

Z turned out to be very different from the person she pretended to be. She presented herself as the personification of kindness and selflessness. In fact, she was the center not only of her own world but of *the* world. To her core, Z believed that everything she felt, thought and did was normal, in fact, that her life should define the norm. Anyone who challenged this notion was soon discarded. Over a period of several years, it became clear to me that, in her long life, this woman had wrecked every relationship she ever had.

Z lived her life as a pathological narcissist. As the years wore on, the resources available to affirm and validate her became scarcer. The emotional pain she suffered in the absence of this needed affirmation found its way into an increasing number of somatic weak spots that accepted and amplified her psychic trauma. To get some idea of how susceptible Z's body was to psychic stress, consider this. On hearing from her internist, by phone, that the result of a recent blood test showed a glucose level of between 150 and 160 mg/dl, she immediately developed diarrhea!

All day and all night long, at one site or another, Z's body announced that something was wrong with the way she was living her life: shortness of breath, chest pain, back pain, leg pain, eye pain, stomach pain, headache. Blocked emotions tweaked vulnerable places in her aging body, urging psychic anguish into somatic pain. As each ache appeared, it was puzzled over and meticulously described to others. Meanwhile, the related psychic issues ground on, unacknowledged and unaddressed. Z became a champion somaticizer, and a walking pharmacy. She dramatized her medical problems—to herself, to others and to her doctors (she saw her cardiologist every six weeks). When the psychic and somatic pain became too much for her to handle alone, she would check herself into the hospital, staying as long as her insurance would allow her to stay. Here she found a new stage for her drama.

Z's medical conditions and medications included:

Cardiac arrhythmia: Digitalis, atenolol, aspirin (81 mg every 3 days)

Z's first arrhythmic episode occurred in her early 80s. "It came out of nowhere," she told me, "while I was talking on the phone to a girlfriend." Z claimed to have chest pain only during runs of tachycardia that occurred when she woke from nightmares, which usually included something bad happening to a dead family member.

Hypertension: Atacand.

Esophageal Reflux: Tums.

Z often had severe chest pain, which her doctors thought might be due to angina. But each time she came to the ER with chest pain, shortness of breath and tachycardia she doggedly refused an angiogram. Her internist and cardiologist both pushed her to have this procedure, but she refused, citing the risks. She told me, "I sign the form, I die, and they collect the money. No one can do anything about it."

Z's cardiac symptoms are also typical of panic attacks, a possibility she would not even entertain, reasoning that panic is a psychiatric disorder, and she is not the kind of person to have a psychiatric problem. Z mentioned a woman she knew who had been diagnosed with panic attacks who tore her kitchen apart during one episode. "I'm nothing like that," she insisted. During her worst attacks, Z told me, she felt like she was going to die.

Z took her pain to be self-validating. In not dealing with what was going on in her life, she would focus instead on some dysfunction of her body. Her somatic pain became manifest at an increasing number of sites. Z's passionate, ongoing discussion of this distress became a substitute text for an authentic dialogue about her past and present life, which she avoided.

Hypertension and esophageal reflux were likely somatic correlatives of Z's personality style: anxious, angry, fractious, controlling. Her panic attacks were probably also rooted in this disturbed dialectic of mind and body. She would have been shocked to hear this, vigorously denied it, and lashed out at whoever pointed it out.

Cataracts: Mydriacyl.

Glaucoma: Xalatan, Trusopt

Z did not want to have surgery for her cataracts and glaucoma. "They will have to tie me down," she told me. "I'm afraid of anything invasive." Z's vision had become progressively worse. Telling me about an upcoming appointment with an eye surgeon, she said, "If he doesn't do something to help me, I may just make a scene." And that is what she did after the surgeon told her, "I'm going to be blunt: 99% of your optic nerve is gone." He recommended an operation that would remove the cataracts and reduce the ocular pressure from glaucoma (measured that day in the low 20s), which had been diagnosed 30 years earlier. Because of her outburst, he insisted that she "get another surgeon."

Z pretended not to understand the surgeon's pique, and was miffed. Clearly, she had not related his abandonment to her lawyer's suggestion, made more than once, that she find herself another lawyer. Nor did she seem to recall that, after making a nasty and harassing call to a woman at the bank that had handled her husband's estate, she received a letter from one of the bank's lawyers saying that, if she called again, they would go to court to get rid of her as a client. How many times must her internist and cardiologist have resisted the impulse to pass her on to other clinicians? And how many times, over the decades, was she told by friends to, in effect, get herself another friend?

Z held tenaciously to the point that she had not misbehaved in front of the surgeon who pronounced the dire verdict. Clearly, she was terrified at the prospect of needing surgery, and being told there was no guarantee that the operation would save her sight. Z insisted that her fear about the surgery was not "her"—which amounts to an inauthentic disowning of the situation—but something separate that she did not choose, and could not control. "I'm hurting and suffering in a way no one else understands," she told me. To Z, her response was normal: "I'm not a psychiatric patient. If I were, I would not be living this well-ordered life."

Several times, she spoke of doing something to remove herself from all this. "I want to give up," she said, mentioning an overdose of pills, but then quickly backtracked saying again that this was not *her* talking. The biggest concession Z would make to having any psychiatric issue was taking 0.5 mg of Ativan before bed, for sleep. She did this timidly and reluctantly, taking the lowest possible dose, by cutting a 1 mg tablet in half.

Z also had arthritis in her hands, neck and back; sciatica, which caused severe back and leg pain, for which she had been hospitalized several times; and osteoporosis, which left her with a pronounced Dowager's Hump. She had also been treated for a one-sided kidney stone.

"I'm a completely different person now compared to 20 years ago, when I was not taking any medicine," Z wanted me to know. She had a hard time starting the day, but usually improved as the afternoon wore on. Some days were better than others. On bad days, she described herself as feeling "dopy" and overcome by "drunkenness"—this from a woman who had never touched alcohol.

"I just want to put my head down," she would tell me. And often she did just that, trying to make up for poor sleep the night before. Usually, she went to bed between 10 and 11 p.m., staying awake until 3 or 4 a.m. What was ruining Z's sleep? Was she punishing herself for the kind of mother and wife she had been? Both her daughter and her first husband died young—the daughter of breast cancer at 36, the husband of alcoholism, in his 50s.

Z did not wish to change, saw no reason to change and refused to change her fundamental take on the world. She was too invested in her anger, resentment and bitterness to alter this stance, around which she had constructed her later-life identity. She hinted at, but did not specify, other abuses in her life—trauma worse than that experienced nursing her mother, daughter and second husband to their deaths; worse than what the bank put her through in settling the second husband's estate. Compounding these ordeals, her daughter's three children all died young, and her son-in-law was killed in a robbery.

Z continued to be the guest of honor at her day-in-day-out pity party, the center of attention, the subject and object of mental anguish (anxiety, masked depression) and physical pain (chest, back, legs, etc.). She ran from doctor to doctor, including a podiatrist, after she discovered a discoloration in one toe nail. But there was never a word about seeing a gynecologist, even though her daughter had died of early breast cancer. This seemed like modesty to the extreme. Z spoke of her first husband, rarely and coldly, as "Mr. R." Her second marriage, to a younger man, was celibate.

Z refused to acknowledge that her chronic anger, which often surfaced in flashes, and her masked depression were anything but inevitable, attributing these troubling emotions to the perpetrators and circumstances of her situation. She acknowledged no other possible response to the hand that had been dealt her. She continued to ascribe her difficulty sleeping and her almost constant fatigue to the side effects of the medications she was taking. She did not acknowledge that her anger might be depleting her energy and sapping her will and strength to do much more than get through each day and each night. On the other hand, she would admit, "I'm just making it," acknowledging her low emotional reserves.

The pain in her right leg became worse. "There's something else wrong with me that the doctors are missing," was a complaint she made several times. She asked if I knew of a "total diagnostic program" that would go over her from head to foot, looking at all systems. "I feel like someone is beating me on the back with a whip. I ache all over." Indeed, she seemed to be beating herself up with the losses and betrayals that have marked her life. Several times, she wondered out loud if she had cancer, citing people she knew who had leg pain and went on to die of the disease.

The nightmares, which she described as "awful," continued. "I really need to talk to someone about this," she confided but then let the matter drop. Most likely, she was struggling with unresolved conflicts involving two dead husbands, a dead daughter, the daughter's three dead children and a murdered son-in-law. When I gently suggested this possibility, she brushed off the idea saying there was nothing in her past that she needed to consider further.

Z described her dreams as "bad" and "dirty," featuring filthy bathrooms and the smell of feces. (Her husband's surgery for cancer included the attachment of a colostomy bag, which she maintained for him.) "There's a big difference between my conscious life and my unconscious life," she told me, which was the first indication I had from her that she suspected anything was amiss in her mental life. I took her use of "unconscious" here to mean that she was acknowledging, then immediately denying, some kind of psychological cover-up. "Consciously," Z blamed her dreams on the medication she was taking.

It became progressively more difficult for me to play a part in Z's soap opera. It seemed that her numerous expansive fantasies—in which she imagined herself as a good, generous, intelligent woman—were defensively challenging her lived sense of being small, insignificant and empty. Always in battle mode, she would say, "This little 5'3", 110-pound woman has to go up against..." Undoubtedly, her sense of being small and weak, and having been treated poorly in the past, fed her feelings of emptiness and drove her need for narcissistic "perfect mirroring." When I said something that contradicted her position on a subject, she would invariably come back with, "You are taking what I say out of context." What she really meant was that, in disagreeing with her, I was taking away her *narcissistic* context.

As told here, Z's story focuses on her propensity to create psychosomatic illness, which, as a 2nd domain reaction, is believed to come about through an aberrant development of personality and temperament. Z revealed nothing of her childhood or adolescence, and never mentioned her parents, though she provided vivid details of the other phases of her life. We are left with no way of understanding how she came to be the person she was. We can only surmise that her early years were not the ground for an optimal development.

After the inevitable rupture of each of her many friendships, Z would lick her wounds and rededicate herself to the course she had set. But at the end, there were no more friends. She burned through them all. She had been estranged from her two brothers for many years, and there were no other close relatives. All that was good about this woman and all the good she did were eventually swallowed up by the behavioral expressions of her complex 2nd domain pathology.

Z died of pneumonia in her commodious apartment, alone. She had been discharged from the hospital several days earlier, following an episode of the cardiac condition that had plagued her for so long. There was no funeral. And there was no obituary, or even a death notice in the principal newspaper of the city where she was born and had lived for 92 years.

Hoarding

Hoarding seems best considered as an element of the obsessive-compulsive *style*, which would make it a 2nd domain reaction, though an argument for placing this illness in the first domain (less convincing, I believe) could also be made.

Hoarders fight ferociously to hold on to some entity that most of us would not have accumulated to that degree in the first place. The overfull refrigerator does not *symbolize* the emptiness of a wounded psyche but is the *acting out* of that emptiness. The excess food, way beyond what would be necessary for sustenance, is an attempt to displace and compensate for what the hoarder lacks psychically (Frost and Steketee 2010). So is anything else that has been collected too much and held too tightly (Acocella 2014). Some of the objects most commonly acquired to excess are furniture, books, newspapers and magazines, correspondence and old records, and, less commonly, though more poignantly, animals.

Like all mental illnesses, hoarding is dimensional: most hoarders use the defense neurotically, but some hoarders psychotically transform and reconstruct their world around the articles they amass to excess.

ADHD: A Non-Phenomenon

If ADHD (attention deficit hyperactivity disorder) were a real phenomenon and a real diagnostic entity, the illness would belong to the 2nd domain. It appears to be neither, but instead a way of arbitrarily categorizing a number of different alterations in mental life originating in diverse etiologies, having different meanings and requiring different treatment approaches (Nigg 2006). By taking attention deficit and hyperactivity symptoms at face value, as the DSM-5 does, without regard to etiology and meaning, the real phenomenon is masked.

In construing ADHD mainly as a biological disorder, the approach taken by the DSM-5, the freedom of the patient is mostly denied. So is the patient's pathological misuse of freedom that is itself often the problem. This extreme biologism also minimizes the unwitting and unacknowledged contribution of parents and others to the patient's aberrant state. Faced with someone who is hyperactive and distracted, the clinician's best course of action is to look to the person's life-story, elicit the Meyerian facts that constitute the story, and, from there, attempt to unmask the phenomenon or phenomena behind the "ADHD" symptoms.

Daniel Goleman (2014) has suggested that those who are cognitively "scattered" because of their "ADHD" may be so because of what Adolf Meyer called *bad habits* that were developed early in life, or perhaps later on. As with many mental illnesses, the evidence is increasing that medication controls ADHD symptoms only in the short term, rather than addressing a fundamental cause of these symptoms. Cognitive behavioral therapy has been successful with numerous patients who have, for whatever reason, not learned to focus their attention and efforts. We can imagine this kind of behavioral retraining as having a long-term corrective effect on the hyperactive person's correlatively activated biological substrate.

The Third Domain

Maladaptive Reactions Originating in Willed, Self-Gratifying, Self-Destructive Behavior

Chapter 11 Ceding Control Over Alcohol, Drugs, Food, Sex, the Body's Integument, Gambling and the Itch to Steal

Any deliberation about etiology in addiction invariably turns on the polarities of disease and character failure. In the clinical thinking informed by the DSM-5 and the medical model of mental illness, the idea that the abuse of any substance is due to a weakness of character is dismissed, often indignantly. In the current disease model of addiction, the role of freedom, and the misuse of freedom, has been all but banished.

Alcohol Abuse

No one's freedom is ever absolute in the sense that we can do anything we want. Whatever we attempt is contingent on our current circumstances and on restrictions that our prior choices have put on what we can subsequently do. Clearly, addicts have fewer choices open to them—less freedom—than before addiction overtook their lives.

Creating Chemically Induced Elevated States, Repeatedly

I have learned a good deal about addiction from patients I have worked with in various clinical settings. My single most informative learning experience occurred while I was attending a departmental seminar in 1981 or 1982 at Western Psychiatric Institute at the University of Pittsburgh. The psychiatrist giving the talk, an addictions specialist, opined that the cocaine "high" was equivalent to the gratification achieved in a sexual orgasm. After the talk, there were questions from the audience. Identifying himself as a patient at Western Psychiatric Hospital, a young man who was sitting in the back of the auditorium stood up and said, as far as I can reconstruct his words, "Doc, you have this all wrong. Cocaine is a hundred times better than any orgasm."

From someone who is in a position to know, we are told that cocaine can provide an experience that trumps sex, what many see as the ultimate high. Most people have to work hard for the "natural" highs they get from their interactions with others, professional achievements and athletic victories. Others choose to bypass this struggle and go directly to a heightened state by putting substances into their body that act directly on the pleasure centers of the brain.

Some people who use and abuse drugs and alcohol have had success that derives from well-earned and well-rewarded efforts. Others are unable to feel any genuine satisfaction, much less anything like a naturally heightened state, in spite of what they accomplish. These people are at higher risk for abusing and becoming dependent on the potentially addictive substances that they "experiment" with.

People who get their highs naturally do so by engaging in a dialectical interaction with an environment that supports, if inconsistently and unevenly, their creative efforts. Those who use drugs and alcohol to artificially achieve their highs do so in a way that not only separates them from this (relatively) creative dialectic, but is antithetical to it, curtailing freedom—available choices—once the original free choice has been made to use a mind-altering, addictive substance.

The residual freedom of those who use addicting drugs includes the freedom to continue to harm and ultimately destroy their minds and bodies. The novelist Michael Chabon has said of the alcoholic that "his death is one of the most carefully planned and prepared for events in the world" (Chabon 1988, p. 78). I have had patients—and friends—tell me that they clearly understand their drug or alcohol use will hasten their death. They have chosen to pay that price. It's worth it to them. They choose, over and over again, to use one or more addicting substance to bypass the world of authentic struggle, so as to get their highs fast and reliably. Some substance abusers may eventually seek the "easeful death"—a lubricated escape from their wrecked lives—that John Keats, in *Ode to a Nightingale*, acknowledged he was "half in love with."

The addict ultimately creates a chemically induced state of euphoria, a "higher" feeling state that supersedes the boundaries and rewards of everyday, "unmedicated" reality. This escape entails a dedifferentiation—a rounding of the often rough edges of the instrumental world of cause and effect—that is similar to the changes occurring in some maladaptive Meyerian reactions to life events that lead to mental illness. To recall van den Berg (1972), the heavy drinker's protracted inebriated state is one type of "different existence."

By repeatedly choosing to use a mind-altering substance, a person simultaneously chooses to alter his fundamental stance toward the world. In the process of habitually stimulating the brain's pleasure centers, he changes the fundamental nature of his being and mode of interaction with others. This transformation is inauthentic and pathological because it deforms and distorts the authentic instrumental world of cause and effect, what Meyer called the setting for consensually validated common sense.

Unlike defenses of the 1st and 2nd domains, which are psychodynamic alterations of mental life that cause *correlative* changes in brain structure and function, drugs and alcohol act *directly* at the biological pole of the psychobiological unity of the self as active agent. These are 3rd domain defenses: willed, self-gratifying, self-destructive behaviors, which occur more frequently in those having 2nd domain deficits of personality development and temperament.

Assigning alcohol abuse to the 3rd domain takes this behavior out of consideration as an autonomous 4th domain disease and places it in the realm of a willed, self-gratifying, self-destructive choice. In so doing, the FDMI bucks the medical model of the "disease" that has come to be known as alcoholism, while implicitly acknowledging that alcohol is a bivalent substance: using moderate amounts can be socially and medically beneficial; drinking alcohol heavily over a long period of time can lead to serious social and medical problems, and, ultimately, to death.

Researchers who have tried to make the case that alcoholism is a disease (Jellinek 1960) have encountered the same problem as those who argue that all mental illnesses are brain diseases: the absence of empirical facts that support their claim. Yet, as with mental illness, the belief that all people who abuse alcohol are under the sway of a biological disease persists, though not without significant and mounting opposition.

Herbert Fingarette: Heavy Drinking is Not a Disease, but a Willed Bad Habit

Herbert Fingarette, a professor of philosophy at the University of California, Santa Barbara, who is probably best known for his book *Self-Deception* (1969), took on the medical model of alcohol abuse in *Heavy Drinking: The Myth of Alcoholism as a Disease* (1988). "Almost everything that the American public believes to be the scientific truth about alcoholism is false," he confidently states in the introduction (p. 1). Later, he calls this belief a "convenient fiction" (p. 28). Fingarette begins his argument by substituting "heavy drinking" for "alcoholism," reserving this latter term for citing the research efforts of those who study excessive alcohol use as a disease. He sees the disease model as a "hindrance" to understanding what is really going on in the lives of people who drink too much alcohol, as well as to their clinicians' efforts to help them.

However one views the etiology of heavy drinking, it is generally agreed that when people habitually consume large amounts of alcohol, control over this substance is lost. But how? Is control taken over by a disease, or is it willingly given up by the excessive user to achieve the immediate satisfactions of an intoxicated state? Empirical studies have come down on both sides of this question. No unequivocal data point to a disease process that destroys the ability of a person to choose between taking the next drink, or not.

Fingarette claims that much of the empirical evidence points in the opposite direction:

> Most broadly, in all these experiments the subjects' behavior exemplifies the general principles of human motivation that we all recognize. Given what they perceive as substantial reasons to limit their drinking—money, sociability, privileges, or conveniences—these drinkers do limit their drinking. In these special settings [hospitals, where the studies were done], a drinker's self-control may also be reinforced by the *absence* of situations that prompt drinking at home, such as domestic or social frustrations, social enticements, or job anxieties. But clearly it is each drinker's perception of the pattern of positive and negative motivations, and not an uncontrollable abnormal chemical-physiological reaction, that decisively affects the choice to drink, to abstain, or to drink in moderation (p. 37).

As Fingarette sees it, heavy drinking is just another choice that a (relatively) free person can make to achieve any number of goals—including a state of intoxication where a chemically altered world offers easier going, for a while, anyway, until the bill comes due. He also challenges the supposition that the "craving" experienced by many habitual users of alcohol is principally a biological urge. In the medical model, craving is seen as a desire for alcohol that is so intense and so much a part of the addict's make-up that, prior to treatment, willpower is of no use in resisting or overcoming it. In the medical model, the addict's freedom to stop drinking is short-circuited by his disease. Heavy drinking becomes a "reflexive symptom imposed by a disease" (Fingarette 1988, p. 92).

Some heavy drinkers do resist this urge and choose not to continue to drink heavily. Eventually, they find reasons to reassert control, bringing into play a newly mobilized freedom. Fingarette sees the ultimate fallacy of the disease concept of heavy drinking as a paradox: "[Heavy drinkers] are told that they are the unwilling victims of a disease that destroys their ability to manage their drinking and yet that they must strive to exert absolute self-control, that only abstinence can save them" (p. 92). Even the strongest advocates of the medical model of alcoholism must implicitly concede that freedom is involved in both the creation and remediation of this problem.

Fingarette believes there is no single cause for heavy drinking but many reasons why people drink too much alcohol. He cites the critical response by W. P. Rohan to the diagnostic criteria put forward by the National Council on Alcoholism (N.C.A.). Rohan takes on the question, What is the "disease" that has come to be known as "alcoholism?"

> All attempts to identity and define "alcoholism" have failed because the concept itself is fundamentally flawed. "Alcoholism" exists in our language and in our minds, but not in the objective world around us. . . Like many other attempts to define "alcoholism," the [N.C.A.] criteria and related studies fail because they are based on the erroneous supposition that a unique causal entity exists, which resides within certain alcohol users and somehow motorizes their ingestion behavior. An invisible, underlying factor has been invented and invoked to account for unacceptable drinking. Although this entity remains undiscovered, the observable behavior of drinking and its consequences are interpreted as signs of its existence. This reduces a complex variety of drinking sequences and associated effects to an oversimplified formula which is so widely accepted its denial may seem irresponsible or even absurd. So many words have been written and spoken about "alcoholism" that language alone "confirms" it as a reality (Rohan 1978).

In the simplest language, Rohan eloquently deconstructs the concept of alcoholism as a disease, using much the same argument presented throughout the FDMI to counter the notion that all mental illnesses are brain diseases. Put another way, no single phenomenon could reveal what the "disease" of "alcoholism" is. There are only multiple phenomena that reflect the meaning of each person's heavy drinking.

To those who insist that heavy drinking is sustained by the physical symptoms of dependence and withdrawal, Fingarette points out that not all heavy drinkers have these somatic responses. In other words, dependence and withdrawal are not unique to any entity that can be understood as the "disease" of "alcoholism." Instead, he says, prolonged heavy drinking may become, over time, a *habit*, making it more difficult for heavy users to discontinue this behavior: "Habits, associations, and life circumstances would mitigate against the probability of radical change, all quite independently of any physical symptoms. Rather than being a *cause* of heavy drinking, the physical symptoms may be just one more *consequence* of it" (Fingarette 1988, p. 61).

Habits are learned behavior, patterns we fall into after routinely doing things one way, and not another. Good habits promote our well-being and that of others. Bad habits are destructive to us and others. Heavy drinking is a bad habit that may become psychobiologically embedded—as does any human behavior—causing significant psychological and biological damage. For some, this habit destroys their lives and hastens their death.

The habit of heavy drinking can do this kind of harm without being a disease. In no way does its non-disease status mitigate the enormous toll this behavior often takes. In fact, Fingarette says, "once alcohol abusers themselves realize that they have not been stricken by some unidentifiable physical or psychiatric condition, they may find new cause for hope and for a more realistic self-understanding" (p. 66). This corrective insight amounts to giving the problem of heavy drinking its right name and right meaning.

As a learned behavior, heavy drinking may become the way a person habitually comes to deal with difficult life situations. Meyer called this type of response a maladaptive reaction (choice) to the challenges that living presents. This reaction is a psychodynamic defense, rather than an authentic response where freedom is employed to find an adaptive solution.

Herbert Fingarette's thinking has a strong existential bent. Fingarette understands that heavy drinking involves a person's entire life and its numerous interactions, with others and with situations, which may be self-created or imposed from the outside. Those who drink heavily have a unique relation to alcohol. Using this intoxicating substance comes to be their "central activity" (pp. 100–103), the focus of their lives around which everything else and everyone else takes a secondary place and has a secondary meaning. The life of the heavy drinker is "pervaded by a preoccupation with drinking, shaped and driven by the quest for a drink, drinking situations, and drinking friends" (p. 100). The central activity of heavy drinking can eventually come to eclipse the accomplishments of even those who appear to have had good lives and distinguished careers. "Heavy drinkers are people who have over time made a long and complex series of decisions, judgments, and choices of commission and omission that have coalesced into a central activity" (p. 102).

Over time, the choices and decisions that heavy drinkers make become suffused with the psychobiological effects of alcohol—in a world that has been *transformed at the biological pole* by this mind-altering agent. The heavy drinker's life becomes a succession of bad habits. That these bad habits are difficult to break does not necessarily support the disease theory of heavy drinking, though many researchers would argue otherwise. There is inertia in any habit, an inherent resistance to change. "Like any of us contemplating a major change in a central activity," Fingarette points out, "the heavy drinker cannot simply reshape his or her life at will. Internal and external factors—bodily constitution and age, intellect and education, cultural and ethnic norms, economic and domestic circumstances—limit [or enhance] one's potential for change and one's alternatives" (p. 105). The sum of these factors amounts to what Sartre called *facticity*, the givens in our lives, some constant, others not, which may either enhance or limit our ability to act freely.

Fingarette is eager to see into the psyche of the heavy drinker, to understand the meanings of his acts. "Rarely do people wickedly choose a destructive or self-destructive way of life. On the contrary, we shape our lives day by day, crisis by crisis, often only in retrospect able to see the pattern that was evolving. We each share the propensity to choose opportunistically [to our own presumed advantage] when under stress. So, on a series of occasions, a drinker chooses what seems the lesser evil, the temporarily easier compromise, without a clear appreciation of the long-range implications" (pp. 111–112). All that is left out of this incisive and sympathetic take on the heavy drinker's being-in-the-world (Heidegger) is the judgment that, while he is choosing the "lesser evil," he is simultaneously deceiving himself about the significant evil he is capitulating to.

The Disease Model of Heavy Drinking

Most research dollars that are invested in the effort to understand alcohol abuse and its treatment go to researchers who are guided by the notion that alcoholism is a biological disease. Most advertising aimed at those who abuse alcohol and other addictive drugs advises them to seek treatment at facilities that follow the medical model. A good deal of money is made all around from the proposition that those who use debilitating amounts of addictive substances do so because of the genes they received and the way their brains are "wired." The same pitch that goes out to people with mental illnesses of the 1st and 2nd domains is made to those who succumb to the siren call of heavy drinking, an illness of the 3rd domain.

Consumers of mental health and addiction services also have reasons to accept the medical model. The disease concept puts most of the weight for aberrant behavior on the biological pole of our psychobiological unity. This allows people to deny and escape the central—often burdensome—reality of their lives: that, within the restrictions of their facticity, they are (relatively) free to choose their own fate and are responsible for the choices they make that constitute that fate. Here is Sartre, once again, on the ultimate meaning of most mental illnesses: "I regard mental illness as the 'way out' that the free organism, in its total [psychological and biological] unity, invents in order to be able to live through an intolerable situation" (Laing & Cooper 1964, p. 6).

Herbert Fingarette is convinced that heavy drinking is not a biological disease. George Vaillant, a professor of psychiatry at Harvard Medical School, on the other hand, seriously considers this possibility. To Vaillant, the disease of alcoholism lies at the end of a continuum of social drinking, heavy drinking and out-of-control drinking, where a person appears to have lost the *ability* to stop drinking. Implied in this definition is the belief that only a disease could kill someone's willpower to this extent.

No one, including George Vaillant, in spite of his considerable epidemiological and statistical research, can nail down just what the pathological process of a disease called alcoholism might be. It seems that the "disease model" of alcoholism is a disease without a model, and a model without a disease. On the first page of his classic text *The Natural History of Alcoholism Revisited* (1995), Vaillant acknowledges that "our lack of knowledge about alcoholism is astounding."

"Alcoholism," according to Vaillant, "becomes a disease when loss of voluntary control over alcohol consumption becomes a necessary and sufficient cause for much of an individual's social, psychological, and physical morbidity" (p. 45). But this criterion for designating alcoholism as a disease relies only on behavior, specifically on how bad the behavior becomes, what Meyer would call the *degree* of maladaptation. Vaillant's definition seems mostly to chase its own tail. So too does the one provided by the National Council on Alcoholism, which Vaillant cites and strongly endorses: "The person with alcoholism cannot consistently predict on any drinking occasion the duration of the episode or the quantity that will be consumed" (p. 45). Many years ago, during a psychiatry department seminar at the University of Maryland School of Medicine, I heard the presenter speak these lapidary words: "The alcoholic is someone who cannot promise you tomorrow."

Though Vaillant provides a good deal of clinical and research information about alcoholism, including data from his own empirical studies, and offers his inimitable wisdom on the subject, his argument that out-of-control heavy drinking at the far end of the continuum of alcohol consumption is a disease does not convince me. Overall, Fingarette's premise that all heavy drinking is willed behavior and the consequence of acquired bad habits fits well with the existential and Meyerian understanding of aberrant human behavior.

"Science, at best," Vaillant admits, "is only an approximation of reality" (p. 47). When it comes to probing the contents and meaning of human behavior a more direct, intuitive approach can often put the investigator in closer touch with the reality of what is being studied.

An Exemplar of the Phenomenon of the Heavy Drinker

If heavy drinking is not the disease that the medical model calls alcoholism, we need to look to the life of problematic drinkers to uncover the meaning of the bad habits that eventually culminate in this condition.

Bill was a gifted chemist who worked for several drug companies that are household names. His biggest success may have been his contribution to the development of the antiallergenic drug Claritin. He also taught chemistry for a time at several universities and community colleges. Bill had an excellent grasp of the finer points of physical organic chemistry and was a good and enthusiastic experimentalist. But he was not an "empire builder," with the kind of sustained vision and drive required for a major career in academic research.

Bill had serious interests outside of chemistry. He was a ranked squash player in the adult league and, later, a referee in that league. He was a good sailor, had a small boat of his own and sailed the larger boats of his better-heeled friends. Calling him avid doesn't begin to do justice to his interest in lacrosse. He attended all the Johns Hopkins home games and most of their away games, sometimes driving, sometimes taking the band bus. Bill was dyslexic and did not read much, but he kept up with current events on national public radio (NPR), saw many first-release films and went to plays at local theaters. Bill lived his life. He was married twice, divorced twice and had four children.

I don't know when Bill's problem with alcohol began. He did drink when we were in school together, but at that time I saw no sign he was drinking heavily. Because he spent most of his career several states away from where I lived, I did not see him for many years and then only when he returned to Baltimore after separating from his second wife.

When we went out in the evening there was always alcohol. Bill preferred scotch, Johnny Walker Black, cut with water. I would have my customary one drink, and Bill would have many more. Just how many more I do not know. I never realized how much he was drinking until this former squash player, who still worked out regularly at one gym or another, would, on social occasions, lose his balance and fall to the ground. However much he was drinking at that time, he was covering it up well, until he couldn't any longer. When I confronted him, he acknowledged being an alcoholic and not being able to stop or even limit his drinking. Shortly after we spoke about this, he joined AA and was sponsored by a close friend who had been sober for many years. Neither his parents nor any of his three siblings abused alcohol.

Shortly after returning to Baltimore, Bill was hit with some serious health issues. Arthritis had plagued him for years but became more fulminant. His knees were bad, and his hand joints would flare, swell and become excruciatingly painful. Several years earlier, while playing squash, he had a seizure. An egg-sized, non-malignant meningioma was surgically removed from his brain. He recovered completely. He also had a malignant melanoma cut out of his back, the result, he said, of sailing as a teenager without a shirt or sunscreen.

While dealing with these medical challenges and teaching chemistry at a community college, Bill continued to drink heavily. In October 2012 he was arrested for DUI and given jail time. His license was revoked and his car impounded. He was released from jail during the day so he could meet his classes. I cringe imagining what it must have taken for him to keep going under these circumstances. He had to take a bus from the jail, and then walk the remaining way to the college on knees that were becoming weaker and more painful all the time. His girlfriend was finding it more difficult to deal with his drinking. She told me that the only time Bill didn't drink was when he was at AA meetings.

And then things went from bad to worse. In June 2013, while having a cataract removed, he developed an arrhythmia induced by the anesthetic propofol. An arteriogram showed major blockage in several coronary arteries and a myocardial infarction in one artery, a condition that required immediate quadruple coronary bypass surgery. He recovered well from the operation, pushing and enjoying himself during the rigorous physical rehab that followed.

Fortunately, Bill had no recurrence of the arrhythmia that struck him during cataract surgery. But his knees were becoming increasingly dysfunctional and painful. His high tolerance for pain was one reason that he did not have this condition attended to sooner—in fact, until all the cartilage was gone and the knee joints were, as the surgeon said, "bone against bone."

The first knee replacement went well, though Bill did develop a deep vein thrombosis (DVT) sometime after the surgery. Following the second knee operation, several months later, a complication developed in a muscle in the inner thigh that caused him excruciating pain. He was taking more OxyContin than after the first knee operation, and I had the impression that he was using more than was prescribed. This and other factors led to conflicts with his doctors and the hospital staff. A relationship that was once collegial turned contentious.

Continuing to drink heavily through all this medical treatment, which at one point included 14 medications, Bill became increasingly estranged from his older brother, who was chauffeuring him to and from medical appointments and helping to arrange for disability benefits, and his twin sister, who had opened her house to him when he returned to Baltimore after the humiliating end of his second marriage. Bill was losing control, becoming angry (though not at me) and burning bridges. His girlfriend broke off their relationship. She told me that she "couldn't take any more." Bill pushed for them to stay "friends," but she demurred, and he was angry and resentful over her refusal.

By this time, Bill had only two friends left, a woman with whom he had a platonic relationship for some time, and me. He and this woman celebrated New Year's Eve quietly at a restaurant. Not quite two weeks later, I received a call from Bill's brother. A neighbor in Bill's apartment building noticed that his door was partly open. He was found on the floor of his bedroom fully dressed, with two empty vodka bottles close by. A longtime scotch drinker, he had switched to vodka toward the end.

The time of death was estimated to have been two days earlier. Neither the medical examiner nor the family pushed for an autopsy. Bill's doctor told his brother that the cause of death was most likely either a heart attack or a blood clot. There was no funeral, no obituary, only a brief death notice in the local newspaper that ran several weeks after he died. The surviving family members chose not to be named.

My guess is that Bill, emotionally isolated and in increasing physical pain, died from a lethal combination of alcohol and OxyContin. The line between accidental and deliberate death here is thin and indeterminable.

Bill bore the pain of medical illness and disability stoically, never complaining in my presence about how much he was suffering. That stoicism extended to his emotional pain, which, I am certain, he didn't share with anyone. He never said a word about what it meant for him to lose both parents at young ages from heart disease. Or revealed anything about the pain he must have experienced during two difficult marriages, which ended in difficult divorces. He would occasionally talk about both former wives and his children, but always in a lighthearted, ironic way. This had to be a cover-up.

Emotionally, Bill remained a puzzle to himself. While drinking heavily, he didn't need to come to terms with what was going on in his life. Not being able or willing to make a Meyerian adaptive response to his difficult situation in an "unmedicated" state, he repeatedly chose, in a maladaptive Meyerian reaction, to enter and re-enter the heightened state of intoxication. This psychobiological transformation took the hard edges off the reality he was facing, permitting an escape into a "softer" world where pain was dulled by alcohol acting on the brain in such a way that the essential nature of his experience was altered.

Gradually, I came to see an essential difference between the way Bill and I approached and responded to alcohol. I had one drink, which put me in a good place. I did not need more or want more. My instrumental, rational world was still in place, though pleasantly elevated. After one drink, I was ready to leave the bar, restaurant, party, whatever, to resume life in the quickly returning ground state. Bill, on the other hand, did not know what it was to stop at one drink. I never really knew how many drinks he had. Unlike me, he was not eager to go back to his ground state, perhaps because that was not a good place for him to be. He would try to extend the evening and the drinking as long as possible.

I believe that in his ground state, Bill was stuck with many of the painful issues he never adequately dealt with: the early loss of his parents; two divorces; professional reverses; and the estrangement from his children that was, as far as I could tell, at least partly of his own making. I could imagine the pain in all these unresolved emotions being temporarily tamped down by the increasing amounts of alcohol he used. For him, the inebriated state was a better place to be than any non-altered reality he could muster.

As things got worse, he drank more, and as he drank more, things got still worse. When he started using OxyContin excessively after the second knee replacement, and drank increasing amounts of alcohol, he stepped onto a slippery slope that became the downhill course to his end.

Bill would never have cut back on his heavy drinking. He lacked the desire and the willpower—there was too much about his inebriated state that worked for him and not enough in his alcohol-free experience to compensate for abandoning this longtime habit. He was the type of heavy drinker for whom the only healthy alternative would have been to abstain completely, and that was not going to happen. Ultimately, this refusal cost him his life.

Did Bill lose control over his use of alcohol? To me, it seems that he *voluntarily surrendered* control, but only because of what he gained from doing so—a euphoric state where his unresolved conflicts had their edges rounded off and the world seemed good to him again, as it did in the days of his youth and young adulthood. Bill exchanged the rewards of sobriety for what he implicitly took to be a higher purpose: achieving the psychobiologically transformed state of inebriation. This is another way of saying that he *chose* to drink heavily, day after day, even as he continued to attend AA meetings, which he did in part to comply with a court order in the hope of eventually getting his driver's license back.

Bill's years of heavy drinking undoubtedly exacerbated his arthritis and heart disease. The pain and dysfunction caused by these conditions led in turn to his using increasing amounts of alcohol, and later OxyContin, until he went into a downward spiral—that happened so quickly I was unaware of it—which ended in his death. His behavior can be understood as his embracing maladaptive defensive habits that have an identifiable psychodynamic meaning and purpose. Must we presume that any of this was caused by what the medical model of alcoholism calls a disease?

I would bet anything that Bill would approve of my telling the story of his endgame. Always generous—a more loyal friend I never had—he would be pleased if this cautionary tale allowed others who arrive at a similar crossroads to fare better than he did. Let this narrative be his epitaph.

Drug Abuse

We live in a culture that is saturated with drugs: drugs sanctioned by law and prescribed by medical providers, and those proscribed by law that are sold and bought illegally. To people who do not consider their lives to be psychologically and biologically optimal—just about everyone—our culture signals that this shortfall can be surmounted by ingesting one drug or another.

Like alcohol, the recreational drugs marijuana, amphetamines, heroin and cocaine all have a euphoriant effect. Each binds to a different receptor in the brain, changing the neural tone of the electrical circuit that is subserved by the neurotransmitter associated with that receptor. In this process, which is activated at the biological pole of a person's psychobiological unity, the essence of that person's world is fundamentally altered. This alteration of consciousness figures strongly in the motivation for using these drugs, and in the meaning of the abuser's repeated choice of one or more mind-altering substance.

The arguments that Fingarette presents in *Heavy Drinking* against the medical model of alcoholism are equally applicable to understanding why people use and abuse drugs. Similar dynamics are in play. Each drug offers its unique kind and intensity of heightened state.

As with alcohol, people use illicit drugs in amounts that fall along a continuum. Their usage reflects whatever control they have, or do not have, over a drug they may have developed a *habit* of using. This continuum encompasses the capacity to take or leave a drug at the low end and to depend on it at the high end.

Those who use drugs heavily are soon caught in a dilemma. First, they freely choose to take one drug or another, in increasing amounts. Then, because of the heightened state they achieve, they find themselves at an oblique angle to the instrumental world of cause and effect. In this condition, their range of rational and authentic choices narrows relative to what it was in the drug-free state. From that point on, their freedom is plied in a different psychobiological domain (the FDMI's 3rd domain). Their existence is a "different existence," as van den Berg characterized it. And their freedom is a different, and restricted, freedom.

Some who arrive at this state surrender to drugs because they believe, implicitly or explicitly, that taking one drug or another is the way to regulate their lives. In this process, the dialectic with the world becomes increasingly attenuated. Eventually that interaction may cease altogether, and the heavy user, in a psychobiologically transformed and inauthentic state, may himself become the only center he acknowledges. Drugs are relied on to go up emotionally, to come down, to level out, to function. For the heaviest users, the input of others and the world of cause and effect may in time count for little or nothing. Their freedom and involvement in this world is limited to choosing, securing and taking one drug or another into their bodies.

Jordan Belfort, the character played by Leonardo DiCaprio in *The Wolf of Wall Street*, uses cocaine, Quaaludes and other drugs, washed down with staggering amounts of alcohol, to sustain a hypomanic edge (Gartner 2005) that fuels his amoral and illegal pursuit of millions. He functions brilliantly as a stockbroker but is blinded to the consequences of his behavior—until the FBI catches up with him and he loses everything, including his stunning wife. Before being brought down by the law, while living without inhibitions as a narcissist and a drug addict, Jordan Belfort had no understanding of limits. This is a man for whom everything is not enough.

Anorexia Nervosa

In sustaining life, feeding is second in importance only to breathing. This necessity is first provided for us by our primary caretakers. Gradually, we assume the responsibility ourselves. For some, feeding is anything but straightforward. Obesity, which has become a national epidemic, threatens every organ and every organ system. In spite of warnings from the media and elsewhere, people continue to abuse food by eating too much, and eating too much of the wrong food. This behavior, in combination with not getting enough exercise, leads to dangerously large bodies.

How do we understand the overeating that leads to obesity, which seems to be the most common and straightforward way people abuse food? A certain carelessness is at play here and a kind of impulsivity. This lack of discipline allows someone to grab for the most available liquid or solid fare that satisfies the need to be filled up, calmed down, comforted or distracted. The bad habit of eating and drinking too much often begins in early childhood and continues through the adult years. This habit is reinforced by a culture that simultaneously tells people that they should eat moderate amounts of healthful food, and then advertises and makes readily available high-calorie food and drink that contains too much salt, sugar and fat, which are known to be harmful in these amounts.

Though the person who becomes obese makes deliberate, repeated, specific choices to become and remain obese, the meaning of this kind of overeating is usually limited to satisfying immediate, discernible needs. Not so the meanings behind the behavior that leads to anorexia nervosa and bulimia nervosa. These pathologies involve a more profound deformation of a person's being. *Anorexia* derives from the Greek and means "without appetite." "Nervosa" indicates that the condition is a mental illness, and not due to one of many medical conditions that can impair appetite.

Our approach in the FDMI to understanding and remediating the willed, self-gratifying and ultimately self-destructive acts of the 3rd domain follows the behavior modification protocol advocated by McHugh and Slavney (1998) in *The Perspectives of Psychiatry*. First and foremost, this involves *challenging and interrupting the uncontrolled behavior* while helping patients to understand that they have *chosen* to misuse alcohol, drugs, food, etc.; that they are *responsible* for the consequences to themselves and others of their overindulgence; and that they need to re-choose *not* to continue this behavior. They need to understand that no one forced these destructive acts on them in the first place.

Only after patients have regained some control over their uncontrolled behavior can their "underlying" issues be addressed with an expectation of therapeutic success:

> With behavior, we identity activities *drawn* by a goal. Alcoholics drink to get drunk; anorexics starve to get thin. An explanation for behavior is therefore found in its goal-directed presentations and rewards. Looking into the behavior's manifestations as though they were "symptoms" forged by some *specific* mechanism rather than looking "out" at the goal and at the readiness or unreadiness of the patient to abandon that goal will misdirect the therapy. Indeed, the major disappointments in psychiatric treatment of alcoholism, anorexia, and so forth, derived from the assumption that addressing all the demoralizing life conflicts of these patients would lead to the melting away of the behavior, just as symptoms melt away when pathology is cured. The shift of psychiatric attention to the behavior itself, to the readiness of the patient to change, and to efforts at interrupting it (if "only for a day") increased therapeutic success by revealing self-sustaining features of behavior as a critical aspect of its explanation and intractability" (McHugh and Slavney 1998, p. 210).

This tack is in line with a directive often given to substance abusers who rationalize their continued use of drugs and alcohol with the inauthentic excuse that they cannot stop using, or will not stop using, until they "solve" the problems that "caused" them to start using in the first place: "Do better before you feel better." Even more to the point would be the instruction: Stop using *now* even though you don't *feel* like stopping now.

While working with patients' behavior we also need to get some wider sense of what is going on in their lives. The familiar ways of understanding aberrant eating behavior include the desire for someone who has lost control to regain it. Many people find themselves overwhelmed by life events. Their identity comes into question, and with this unwanted ambiguity comes a related anxiety of not knowing who they are. Finding themselves in this uncomfortable position, some will take defensive action, through what Meyer called a maladaptive reaction. A subset of these people may deal with their anxiety by overcontrolling their eating behavior. If you have no idea who you are, it is better to have what Erik Erikson called a negative identity than no identity at all. This kind of defensive reaction probably underlies a good deal of 3rd domain pathology.

One could imagine that some people who find themselves with a shaky identity would resort to the restrictive feeding behavior that has come to be known as anorexia nervosa. Once again we encounter the fascinating and perhaps unanswerable question of why some patients choose one pathological reaction, while others take a different defensive path altogether. Freud struggled with this idea, which he formalized as the choice of neurosis.

Those whose loss of identity leads them to feel powerless may seek attention from others as part of their defensive response. Think of those cases covered by the media that feature a young woman (95% of anorexics are estimated to be women) with a long history of anorexia who has been through many treatment protocols and hospitalized repeatedly. She looks like a skeleton and is experiencing the physical breakdown of her body which, in the absence of receiving external nourishment, is metabolizing itself. The family grinds to a halt in the attempt, seemingly futile, to bring this black sheep back into the fold. Who ever had more raw control over her family than this woman? Some anorexics who come to this extreme state are, no doubt, attempting to punish one family member or another for some real or imagined slight.

Like all defensive reactions, anorexia can have an ironic outcome. What begins as an effort to gain control often ends with a total loss of control over oneself, which ultimately can turn into a game of chess with death. Self-starvation *is* a disease state, not of the brain, as the medical model claims for anorexia itself, but of the entire self-metabolizing body. Some anorexics, in their maladaptive attempt to avoid the issue that has stolen their identity and triggered their extreme anxiety, reach the point where this is the only endgame they are willing or able to pursue.

Another explanation often heard for the behavior of anorexics points to a culture that idealizes a slim, hard body. Seeing images of this "perfection" in photographs and advertisements that saturate the media, a person who is struggling with a collapsing identity may, for reasons that remain opaque, decide that the way out of her identity vacuum is to attempt to become what that image promises. This maladaptive reaction may begin innocently enough by limiting food intake and exercising. But then something goes haywire.

Many people respond within normal limits to the siren call of the slim, toned body. But for the person who becomes anorexic, dieting, exercise and weight loss do not have an instrumental, realistic meaning or goal. Something else, which is elusive and poorly understood, motivates a person to go beyond the normal limits imposed by reason in this venture. If the task were really to have a "perfect body"—and to merge with the segment of the culture that espouses this ideal of bodily perfection—the dieting/exercising/weight-losing person would stop at a point consistent with that goal. In pushing further, then much further in this project, she subverts the goal, producing a body that is the antithesis of the ideal body. It is often heard that the anorexic is hallucinating her body image, seeing in the mirror what does not exist outside her own mind, and that she is delusional in her understanding of the meaning of her situation. What kind of self-deception allows an anorexic to believe that, at 75 pounds, she is still overweight?

Perhaps it is the kind of self-deceiving lie that permits her to reduce her body, as closely as possible, to the skeleton that supports her flesh and blood and mind and brain. In the process of losing so much weight, a large part of an anorexic's humanness is incrementally shed along with it. What remains could be a rudimentary self that replaces the far more complex person whom she once was, but can no longer tolerate being. The meaning of this seemingly incomprehensible behavior is that, in living skeletally, sometimes within an inch of death, anorexics are trying to rid themselves of their connections to this world that have become unbearably burdensome. Their goal is to straddle the line between a minimal life and death. To an anorexic who has reached this state, any flesh on her skeleton is too much because it keeps her too close to the real world, which she is trying to free herself from.

There is no one explanation for why someone becomes anorexic, only reasons to be uncovered why a particular person chooses to deal with an existential crisis by manipulating food intake instead of abusing alcohol or drugs, or stealing, or cutting themselves, or pulling their hair out by the roots, or . . . .

Clinicians need to stop believing that a "broken brain part" is responsible for this kind of behavior. Once the patient's misbehavior is under some control, they should extract the Meyerian *facts* from her story and discern the Meyerian *reactions* that have led to her bizarre, often ironic behavior. Frequently, those with anorexia also display pathology from the 1st and 2nd domains as well, especially anxiety, depression and pathological personality styles.

The diagnostic criteria for anorexia nervosa are relatively straightforward. Paraphrasing the DSM-5 (2013, pp. 338–339): 1) restriction of food intake with the intention of achieving a body weight that is significantly below the standard for someone of the same sex and age; 2) persistent fear of gaining weight or becoming fat, and offsetting weight gain with self-induced vomiting, laxatives and diuretics, and deliberately pursuing calorie-burning exercise; 3) not seeing her body as others do and failing to recognize the damage she has done, which can lead to serious morbidity and, not infrequently, death.

We need to keep in mind that anorexia can be caused by a number of medical conditions, including endocrine imbalances, and malignant tumors that produce chemical substances which override the normal mechanism of satiety. With cancer patients, anorexia can lead to cachexia, a drastic wasting of the body due to loss of weight and muscle mass. These organic anorexias originate in disease states and are pathologies of the 4th domain.

Bulimia Nervosa

The food that is rebuffed by anorexics is pursued by bulimics with an avidity that is equal to the anorexics' rejection. Like anorexia, bulimia is a loss of control of eating behavior. Anorexics reject food and starve themselves, with the intention of getting thin and staying thin. Bulimics gorge themselves and then use countermeasures—induced vomiting, laxatives, diuretics—to offset their overindulgence, in the hope of maintaining a more or less normal weight and shape. Many practicing bulimics appear normal, and keep their eating and purging under wraps. Unlike anorexics, they also continue to menstruate, stay sexually active and, occasionally, become pregnant.

The pathology of anorexia and bulimia has in common the medium of food, but the anorexic and bulimic have opposite goals as they manipulate what they eat and drink, each according to their own needs. In the purest forms, these maladaptive reactions have different meanings and are different, though related, phenomena. A pathological concern with their body size—expressed as the fear of becoming fat—is the most significant common ground they share.

Bulimia derives from the Greek, and translates as "ravenous hunger." Like anorexics, most of those who develop this illness are women (80%–90% in one estimate). Many bulimics, like many anorexics, experience anxiety and depression, have pathological personality styles and manifest other pathology of the 1st and 2nd domains. Bulimia, like anorexia, can have a number of organic causes. In many instances, for one reason or another, the endocrine-based satiety circuit fails to send a "stop eating" signal after sufficient food has been ingested. These bulimias are biological conditions of the 4th domain.

Anorexia nervosa was identified in the 19th century, but bulimia nervosa was not characterized as a mental illness until 1979 when Gerald Russell, a British psychiatrist, published an article in *Psychological Medicine* titled "Bulimia Nervosa: An Ominous Variant of Anorexia Nervosa" (Russell 1979). Thirty patients (28 women and 2 men) took part in a prospective study. In spite of having a morbid fear of getting fat, they had an irresistible urge to overeat, then induced vomiting or purging.

Bulimics like to eat. They eat too much and often quickly, hence the descriptive word bingeing. At one sitting, a bulimic may ingest up to 7 pounds of food. When not eating, bulimics are preoccupied with food, sometimes to the point where this obsession interferes with work and social activities.

Along with coveting and overindulging in food, bulimics also want to maintain what they see as an ideal weight and shape. To do this, they "undo" their bingeing by forced vomiting, usually by sticking one or more fingers down their throat to trigger a gag reflex. They also use laxatives to slow absorption of nutrients through the gut and take diuretics to eliminate water from their body. Overall, this ploy can be thought of as choosing a second defense (purging) to offset the initial defense (bingeing). The double defense allows someone to overeat *and* retain a weight that is acceptable.

These strategies to lose or maintain weight can devastate the body. The most acute danger is electrolyte imbalance, especially the depletion of ionic potassium, a certain amount of which is required for the heart's myocytes to fire properly. Many bulimics have dangerously low serum potassium levels. Prolonged hypokalemia can lead to reduced glomerular filtration rates, urinary tract infections, renal insufficiency and even renal failure. Many other organs and organ systems can be affected as well.

Russell reported that most patients in his study felt that their "urge to overeat differed from sensations of true hunger." "It is not hunger," one female patient volunteered. "Hunger is a feeling of a gap inside you. You eat something small to stop that feeling. I go on eating after I've satisfied that hunger. I want to keep on eating until I feel full—it's the final limit—you can then eat no more." This woman is telling us that bulimics eat in a way that overrides the satiety mechanism.

Because the majority of the patients in Russell's study had experienced an episode of anorexia prior to the study, he feels that bulimia may emerge as a chronic "ominous variant" of anorexia. The factor that ultimately distinguishes the two illnesses is that while anorexics are capable of starving themselves, bulimics can only go so far down this road before reversing course and counteracting their loss of weight with an episode of overeating. They do not want to die of starvation.

The three criteria for diagnosing bulimia nervosa suggested by Russell in 1979 have stood the test of time: "(1) the patients suffer from powerful and intractable urges to overeat; (2) they seek to avoid the 'fattening' effects of food by inducing vomiting or abusing purgatives or both; (3) they have a morbid fear of becoming fat."

The DSM-5 criteria (2013, p. 345) are virtually identical except for the specification in Criterion A (1) of the amount of food consumed during a bingeing event and the time over which this food is consumed; and for Criterion C: "The binge eating and inappropriate behaviors both occur, on average, at least once a week for 3 months." Bulimia nervosa first appeared in the *Diagnostic and Statistical Manual of Mental Disorders* in the DSM-III-R, published in 1987. It would appear that Russell correctly assessed this phenomenon on his first try.

Abnormal Sexual Behavior

Human sexuality is a problematic gift and a multi-edged sword. Sexual intercourse may involve acquiring or passing on a sexually transmitted disease. The sexual drive virtually guarantees the perpetuation of the species, but in many parts of the world, procreation leads to a strangulating overpopulation. For many, guilt attaches to the pleasure derived from sex. Historically, church and state have taken the lead in making laws about what may and may not be expressed sexually, which specify where the sometimes thin line falls between what is allowed and what is forbidden.

In the secular arena, the task of identifying sexual behaviors that are to be considered abnormal has fallen to psychiatry. The declaration of sexual abnormality is a culture-bound and time-bound notion. In 1973, under pressure from gay activists, the DSM-2 (1968) expunged homosexuality from its cache of mental disorders. This "disorder" did not reappear in the DSM-III (1980), or in any subsequent edition of the DSM. Later, many states legalized same-sex marriage even as federal laws against these unions stayed on the books. In 2015 the Supreme Court ruled that gay marriage is a constitutional right. The American Psychiatric Association no longer regards the gay and lesbian expression of sexuality as a mental disorder.

Abnormal sexual behavior has come to be known as paraphilia, a condition that is marked by recurrent deviant sexual urges (Cohen 2003, pp. 420–422). Almost all those who have these proclivities are men. Some paraphiliacs can only become aroused in this unconventional way, while others have conventional sexual desires as well. To some people, their unconventional urges and practices are acceptable while others feel shame. Many are believed to have paraphilic fantasies and desires they keep under wraps. Stress can loosen self-control to the point where latent paraphilic tendencies are expressed as behavior.

The concept of abnormal sexual behavior has multiple layers and multiple meanings. "Abnormal" implies a difference from the norm, in this instance, sexual acts that most people do not engage in, and many disapprove of.

The DSM-5 (2013, p. 685) names eight distinct types of paraphiliacs: *voyeurs* (who spy on others while they are in vulnerable or intimate situations); *exhibitionists* (who expose their genitals to others out of context); *frotteurs* (who rub against or touch others as a way of becoming sexually aroused); *sexual masochists* (who invite and endure humiliation and bondage); *sexual sadists* (who administer humiliation and bondage, usually to sexual masochists); *pedophiles* (who look to children for sexual gratification); *fetishists* (who find sexual satisfaction in inanimate objects or isolated, nongenital body parts); and *transvestites* (who derive sexual pleasure from dressing as someone of the opposite sex).

The intent of *voyeurs* is usually limited to self-gratification, which limits the damage they do to the object of their interest. This act is an unwanted invasion of privacy, but the voyeur usually keeps his distance. He does not need more from the object than he can *see*.

The closest that *exhibitionists* get to having sexual contact with another person is to *show* their genital organs. Again, this perversion is limited to the shock experienced by the target. Exhibitionists seem more pathetic than anything else.

Frotteurs do make contact with the object of their sexual interest, but only briefly and obliquely. The stimulation they derive from this contact satisfies their sexual urge.

Sexual masochists have the urge and need to be humiliated and hurt at the hands of their partner. They invite this counterintuitive response, no doubt for a variety of reasons.

Some individuals are sexually gratified only by inflicting physical pain on their partners. This was the case with Christian Grey, a *sexual sadist*, in the film *Fifty Shades of Grey*. His girlfriend, Ana Steele, a college student, submitted to his need because she was infatuated with this sophisticated, financially successful older man. Eventually, after unsuccessfully attempting to make Christian sexually conventional, Ana's conventionality won out, and she broke off their relationship (she was never a sexual masochist). (In Chapter 10, Christian Grey was used as an exemplar of the phenomenon of schizoid personality style. Clearly, he could also have been cited as an exemplar of sexual sadism.)

Of the abnormal sexual behaviors, *pedophilia* is the most common, receives the most media attention and causes the most damage to its victims. This is an evil that destroys lives. The damage done to those who are sexually abused, usually at an early age, often persists through a lifetime. The principal dynamic in this emotional trauma is an especially nasty type of betrayal, usually by an older person, that shatters what Erik Erikson called basic trust: the feeling and belief that the world is at least a minimally safe and decent place. Distrust of the world to this degree breeds a seething, transformative anger that can undermine every facet of a person's life.

Many of the cases of sexual abuse that we learn about through the media are initiated by teachers, athletic coaches and clergymen, adults who spend considerable time with children and adolescents and hold positions of authority. Their unique betrayal comes from abusing their power over those they are sworn to teach and lead. Unlike most other paraphiliacs, pedophiles break the law. Their forced removal from the community and remand to a setting that offers the chance of rehabilitation serves both the interests of the community and the abuser.

Some abnormal sexual acts override the centrality of the genital interaction characteristic of conventional sex in favor of oversexualizing a single body part. In *fetishes*, this reduction amounts to taking a part for the whole. In a foot fetish, this body part is the sole source of the fetishist's sexual stimulation. It is easy to see how this abnormality could cause considerable frustration and pain to a conventional partner, especially in a conventional marriage.

Transvestites become sexually aroused by dressing in the clothes of the opposite sex. To someone who is predominantly heterosexual, and especially to someone who is married, this urge can cause conflict and provoke shame. Some transvestites have urges to cross-dress, but otherwise function well as heterosexuals.

For other transvestites, cross-dressing is an element of what has come to be called *gender identity disorder*, which amounts to a pervasive dissatisfaction with the gender of the body one was born with. People feel they are living in a body that does not represent their actual gender, and as if nature had made a mistake. Males who are gender dysphoric may feel they have been females all along, and vice versa. Those with the strongest transgender urges may consider gender reassignment through surgery and hormonal replacement.

Though there is no lack of theories, no one knows why people become paraphiliacs—there are probably as many reasons as there are paraphiliacs. But we do know that some of those who become perversely aroused give in to their urges and *choose* to behave in ways that damage themselves and the objects of their desires, in many instances breaking one law or another in the process. Paraphilic *urges* are not chosen, but the *behaviors* that satisfy these urges are.

Most therapeutic efforts to counter 3rd domain pathologies involve interrupting the unconventional behavior, helping patients understand why they should stop behaving in these ways (CBT has produced some good results) and using medication that either "damps down" a deviant urge or generally bolsters mental capability so that the affected person's efforts to change can become more effective.

Self-Cutting

During the ten years that I did psychiatric evaluations in the emergency room, I saw hundreds of patients who overdosed on medications of all kinds. Perhaps a half-dozen took pills that had the capacity to end their lives. Most ingested nonlethal or low lethality drugs with the intention of dramatizing some difficulty they did not know how to resolve. They "overdosed" to get the attention and support of a parent, spouse, significant other or psychotherapist, or to punish one or more of them.

During that decade, I also saw perhaps two dozen patients who had cut themselves, usually on the arm, leg or torso, seriously enough to require sutures. To help gage the seriousness of their intention, I always asked them to show me their cuts, even if this meant unwrapping the dressing the ER staff had already applied; no one ever objected or refused. It occurred to me that these patients saw this display as a further dramatization of their act. Often, along with the fresh wounds, there were older, healed cuts as well. Many cutters repeatedly employ this maladaptive, defensive way of dealing with their desperation. A bleeding cut focuses attention on the body and away from the chaos inside (Favazza 2011).

Those with borderline personality style, especially girls and young women, often cut themselves, sometimes repeatedly. Their identity diffusion and the emotional numbness that ensues from their uncertainty about who they are and who others are have been widely credited as the ground for this action. While cutting, bleeding and being attended to in the ER, these patients assume the temporary identity of a person who is cut, bleeding and being attended to. The tawdry scene they create is intended as a stopgap. Their action is a maladaptive attempt to briefly reconnect with a world they find uncongenial. Some may discover a sense of community with others who act similarly. Patients with dissociative illnesses, mostly women, also cut themselves in a misguided effort to reestablish some semblance of the identity that is diffused through this defense.

The following allocutions from self-cutters were cited in an article by Jane E. Brody (2008) for *The New York Times* titled "The Growing Wave of Teenage Self-injury":

> I feel relieved and less anxious after I cut. The emotional pain slowly slips away into the physical pain.
>
> It's a way to have control over my body because I can't control anything else in my life.
>
> It expresses emotional pain or feelings that I'm unable to put into words.
>
> I usually feel like I have a black hole in the pit of my stomach. At least if I feel pain it's better than nothing.

We are offered here access to some of the meanings of self-cutting: emotional pain is buffered with physical pain; those who have no control over their lives can at least alter the surfaces of their bodies; those who are unwilling or unable to express their feelings in words can do so through a destructive act that everyone can see and be horrified by; physical pain is easier to bear, at least temporarily, than feeling nothing at all.

Cutting is usually done with a razor blade, glass shard or knife, though other implements of varying degrees of sharpness are also used. This mutilating act is not meant to end a life, but to patch a life that is running low on air. Nonetheless, those who use this strategy, because of their underlying 1st and 2nd domain illnesses, are more likely to eventually attempt suicide. Rarely, cutters unintentionally cut too deep, or in the wrong place, and bleed to death.

Cutters see the lines on their skin, the healed ones and the fresh ones, as a kind of map of their lives. Some cutters fear their cut-lines will disappear over time, as if this loss would destroy landmarks in a life created, in part, by making these lines.

An Exemplar of the Phenomenon of Self-Cutting

In her memoir, *Skin Game*, Caroline Kettlewell shows us how her self-cutting grew out of the challenges she faced during her early years and the choices she made in response to these challenges. She reveals what amount to the psychodynamic defenses—Meyerian maladaptive reactions—she used to counter the anxiety she experienced growing up in a family where facing the truth was avoided as a matter of course.

The story of the Kettlewell family that Caroline tells embodies elements from both the American Dream and its well-characterized dark side, the American Nightmare. Caroline's father was an Episcopal priest who left his pastoral job in a Chicago suburb to become chaplain of an all-boys school in rural Virginia, near Charlottesville, where he also taught English. Caroline's mother kept a splendid, if threadbare, house and enthusiastically entertained her husband's colleagues and superiors. Caroline had one sister, who was two years older.

In many ways, Caroline's parents pursued an inauthentic life. Father and mother played their roles, and lived from the outside in. They expected Caroline and her sister to do the same. "My mother felt formless and groundless in this household, where her family's only identity was a rigorous nonidentity, where they marked themselves only by who they weren't, leaving unanswered the question of who they were" (Kettlewell 1999, p. 17). For Caroline, life at home was a charade waiting to be unmasked. Everyone in this family faced the world with the kind of persona that R. D. Laing described in *The Divided Self* (1965), as each "real self" withered underneath its own mask (Muller 1987, Chapter 6).

Caroline's parents had not so much lost themselves as avoided ever becoming themselves. They had developed and honed the *habit* of self-deception. "What I am trying to say is that my family has a history of living lives of fabrication, and after a while it comes to seem natural to edit freely. And if you could pick and choose, wouldn't it be tempting simply to elide what is least pleasant? In my family, we had so profoundly lost the language for anger or unhappiness or despair, for the awkward and the uncomfortable and the unpleasant, that we didn't even know that something was missing" (p. 20). This family talked a lot, but strategically avoided speaking the truth about themselves and each other.

Caroline's lack of selfhood reached the point where she thought of herself in the third person, as another person and not herself. "Now the manner of regarding my life from a distance, as though I were a character in a performance, had begun to pervade my every transaction with the world. Every word and gesture, even sometimes when I was alone, started to feel more like a theatrical enterprise than anything real. I no longer experienced things so much as I experienced them *as* experiences, a step removed" (p. 54). This description of a persona dissociated from its real self seems straight out of Laing's *The Divided Self*.

Caroline first cut herself when she was twelve, in the seventh grade, in a bathroom at the all-girl's school she attended. She continued to cut, on and off, for another 20 years.

Caroline's sister was in the ninth grade, and only two years ahead of her, but socially she was a world away. The sisters talked, but they did not connect. To say the least, Caroline was unhappy. She felt unrooted in the world of "fabrication" that her parents had inclined her toward, and she felt anxious because of the academic and social demands of a new school. Of course, no one saw any of this unhappiness because Caroline was good at covering it up, as she had been taught to do at home. Outside, Caroline functioned well. Inside, she was screaming. In addition to cutting herself, particularly at times of extreme stress, she also developed anorexia nervosa.

This much turmoil can be covered up for just so long. “I cut because something has to give. I cut because the alternatives were worse” (p. 60):

> I needed to kill something *in* me, this awful feeling like worms tunneling along my nerves. So when I discovered the razor blade, cutting, if you'll believe me, was my gesture of hope. That first time, when I was twelve, was like some kind of miracle, a revelation. The blade slipped easily, painlessly through my skin, like a hot knife through butter. As swift and pure as a stroke of lightning, it wrought an absolute and pristine division between before and after. All the chaos, the sound and the fury, the uncertainty and confusion and despair—all of it evaporated in an instant, and I was for that moment grounded, coherent, whole (p. 57).

Caroline understands what she has done as her “gesture of hope,” presumably the hope that is buffering her “uncertainty and confusion and despair.” She created what she calls an “absolute” division between her life before and after making the first cut. She was better in some ways after cutting because she suffered *differently* as a result. In a life that previously consisted almost exclusively of what others wanted from her and expected of her, Caroline now had something that was *wholly her own creation*, as well as vigorously opposed by everyone she had previously catered to. Caroline's self-cutting is an act of *defiance* and assertion against the people who abetted her failure to become autonomous.

Momentarily, Caroline says, while cutting, she was “grounded, coherent, whole.” In some ways, her cutting could be credited as an authentic, if maladaptive act. *She* decided to make the cuts on her skin. It was *her* idea and done to please only her. Now Caroline has an identity, even if a transient one: *I* am the one who is cutting; *I* am making this happen.

When Caroline says “I . . . marked my body as mine,” we must understand this assertion in the context of her total lack of “mineness” before she cut herself the first time. Now her “flesh and its blood” is under *her* “command.” To us, as observers, she seems to command little through this gesture. But we must keep in mind that before making the first cut, she commanded nothing at all.

Caroline gives this description of how cutting momentarily relieved the sting of her overwhelming anxiety. “If you can imagine fighting your way through a howling gale and then stepping into a soundproof room and shutting the door, then I can begin to describe the transition wrought by the stroke of a razor. One moment chaos; the next, a rich, exquisite silence. The blood was the essence, the structure of this silence. The size of the cut mattered less than the volume of the blood” (p. 101).

Always a good student, Caroline worked hard and derived the little identity she had from her academic achievements. She was accepted by Williams College, which fulfilled her dream of attending a “prestigious” school. At Williams, she earned a high GPA while denying herself the satisfactions of learning or achieving personal growth. Her GPA became her identity. With her friends and boyfriends, she mostly went through the motions.

And she continued to cut: "I cut because it worked. When I cut, I felt better for a while. When I cut, my life no longer overwhelmed me. I felt too keenly the threat of chaos, of how things can get away from you in a thousand ways" (p. 176). But then, in her early thirties, long-divorced from her first husband whom she had married one year after graduating from Williams, Caroline decided to stop. "I stopped cutting because I always could have stopped cutting; that's the plain and inelegant truth. No matter how compelling the urge, the act itself was always a choice" (p. 177).

Caroline never lost her sense of agency as she chose one maladaptive defensive behavior after another. She had good insight throughout the ordeal that became her life. Regrettably, she does not tell us how much of this insight came out of her own struggle and what help she received from the psychotherapists she acknowledges working with. Eventually, she earned a master's degree in writing from George Mason University. At the time her book was published, she was living with her second husband and their son in Virginia.

Though cutting the skin is the most common deliberate self-injury, other self-destructive acts are not uncommon. Strategies aimed at other body parts, which are driven by similar psychodynamics and have similar meanings, satisfy the same urge to physically buffer severe anxiety. "I can tell you that there are cutters and biters, pickers and pokers, bangers and breakers and burners and pullers and prickers" (p. 59). It is as if the desperate people who choose to act in these self-destructive ways have decided that their only hope is to damage some part of themselves. Why they choose one part of their body over another for this mutilation remains a mystery.

Uncontrolled Gambling

Gambling for small or moderate stakes is universal. Churches sponsor Bingo; retirement homes charter buses to transport residents to casinos for a day of betting; many buy lottery tickets and stocks; all kinds of people flock to race tracks. And all of this is legal. Most people handle the risk well, which is to say they adhere to limits in these ventures. The most astute limit their betting to what they can afford to lose.

But some people do not have a brake to slow their gambling train and continue to drive with a hand on the throttle, consequences be damned. Control is ceded to a seemingly endless urge to risk more, even in the face of continuing loss and looming ruin. No internal voice is strong enough to say stop.

Searching for an adjective to designate the gambling that leads to hardship and heartbreak, "compulsive," "impulsive" and "pathological" were considered and rejected. These adjectives, previously used by many clinicians and researchers, imply that an autonomous force underlies this behavior, without giving a satisfying explanation for what constitutes this force. Uncontrolled gambling shows every sign of being a deliberate, repetitive choice to relinquish control as the condition of pursuing higher stakes and higher rewards. What we have here is a Meyerian bad habit of the 3rd domain. So, "uncontrolled gambling" it will be. With this concrete, unambiguous adjective, we can stay closer to the Meyerian facts that are discerned in the stories of uncontrolled gamblers, as well as the phenomenon of this destructive behavior.

The consequences of uncontrolled gambling have been widely reported by the media and examined, from different points of view, in the psychiatric literature (George & Murali 2005). Typically, control is relinquished in pursuit of higher stakes and a higher level of gratification than is possible when gambling is under control. As stakes rise, so do adrenalin, dopamine and serotonin levels and, most likely, levels of endogenous brain endorphins as well. Mind and body both partake of the gratification that drives the high-risk taker.

Those who claim that uncontrolled gambling is an addiction and a brain disease cite these changes in brain function as proof of a biological cause. Meyerian psychobiology, on the other hand, sees uncontrolled gambling as a psychogenic bad habit that is inseparably tied to these *correlative* alterations in brain function that reinforce this bad habit, without being the *cause* of the habit.

What we call uncontrolled gambling in the FDMI is labeled gambling disorder in the DSM-5 and is described as "Persistent and recurrent gambling behavior leading to clinically significant impairment or distress . . ." (2013, p. 585). There are nine behavioral criteria. Any four of these nine criteria manifested during a 12-month period are sufficient to make the diagnosis. Severity is determined by the total number of criteria met (mild: 4–5; moderate: 6–7; severe: 8–9). Gambling occurring during a manic episode is not counted as gambling disorder.

In the DSM-5, gambling disorder appears in the Substance-Related and Addictive Disorders section, with this justification: "Although some behavioral conditions that do not involve ingestion of substances have similarities to substance-related disorders, only one disorder—gambling disorder—has sufficient data to be included in this section" (2013, p. 586). The nine criteria for gambling disorder are similar in form to criteria for alcohol and drug addiction, and the DSM-5 speaks briefly and generally about genetic and physiological factors.

As in other mental disorders, the DSM-5 takes gambling to be a disease entity that invades a life and which, in its severest forms, takes control of that life. In contrast, in the FDMI, we see uncontrolled gambling as a willed, maladaptive, self-destructive choice, with a meaning that can usually be discerned. And while we recognize that, in some ways, uncontrolled gambling is similar in form to obsession and its corresponding compulsion, we believe that this behavior is a different phenomenon.

An Exemplar of the Phenomenon of Uncontrolled Gambling

The idea that uncontrolled gambling is a willed, maladaptive, self-destructive choice, driven in part by the desire to achieve the psychobiologically heightened state that comes with playing for high stakes, is borne out by the title character in the film *Owning Mahowny*, played by Philip Seymour Hoffman.

The fictional Dan Mahowny is modeled after Brian Molony, the very real Canadian Imperial Bank of Commerce clerk who embezzled more than $10 million dollars from his bank. That his theft of this enormous sum occurred over just 18 months—from 1980 to 1982—is a good indication of how uncontrolled

Molony's habit was. The screenplay for *Owning Mahowny* was based on the book *Stung: The Incredible Obsession of Brian Molony* (2002) by the Canadian journalist Gary R. Ross.

The film opens with Dan Mahowny being named the bank's assistant manager. In some ways, he appears an unlikely candidate for this position. He is introverted, messily overweight, barely social and focused on his work to the exclusion of everything else, including his girlfriend whom he mostly ignores. His suit fits so poorly that a customer offers to buy him a new one. His car is an old Plymouth, which he has no interest in replacing. Unlike most bankers, Mahowny is largely indifferent to the material world that surrounds him. He seems to live in his own world.

Gradually, we come to understand that world. While moving seamlessly through his day job—at which he excels—his real passion is for betting increasing amounts of money with a Toronto bookie, mostly on college and professional sports. His first trouble comes when this bookie presses him to cover his losses. That jam sends Mahowny to Atlantic City regularly, in search of higher stakes and greater winnings. Nobody knows about these trips, which he can only make on weekends. He loses badly, then very badly. We sense his interior turmoil and his seemingly doomed determination to win it all back. Mahowny has hit the skids and does not reach for the brake.

To cover his losses and generate more money for gambling—at increasingly higher stakes—Mahowny skims from his accounts at the bank. In his most creative scheme, he has a non-existent person apply for a loan. He approves the loan, then endorses the check to himself. He robs Peter to pay Paul but can't get enough from Peter to pay what he owes. Through all this manipulation, he stays one step ahead of his bosses and colleagues at the bank, ducking bullets that seem sure to strike him. He even survives an audit. Step by step, he embezzles millions of dollars. He has every intention of winning back and replacing all the money he stole before anyone realizes it is gone. Mahowny is not a sociopath but a gambler with a bad habit, born of self-deception, who has relinquished all control over his habit.

In one night at an Atlantic City casino, Mahowny, with money embezzled from his bank, bets 70 thousand dollars a hand. He wins 9 million dollars before losing it all. He could have settled for the 9 million, gone back to Toronto, replaced all the money he stole and kept the rest for himself. But for reasons we don't understand he chose not to do this.

With time running out, Mahowny heads to Las Vegas, where he hopes to change his luck and, presumably, how he handles whatever luck comes his way. He bets large and wins large, one round after another, until he gets to 10 million dollars. He stops, and walks away. It is said that the kind of story you get depends on where you *stop* the story. If we stop here, we could imagine a happy ending. But that's not how it was, not for Dan Mahowny and certainly not for Brian Molony, the real protagonist in this story.

As viewers of the film already know, federal agents have been tapping the phone of Dan Mahowny's bookie, which, of course, puts Mahowny on their radar. Two agents follow his big win that night in Las Vegas over a surveillance hookup to their car. When they realize how much money he started with, they conclude that he had to be stealing from his bank. They follow him back to Toronto and arrest him.

An interrogator tells Mahowny that he has a "gambling problem." "No," Mahowny replies, "I have a financial problem. A shortfall." This is the thinking of the uncontrolled gambler, who will not acknowledge, to himself or anyone else that the *way* he gambles *is* the problem. To him, only the result is wrong—he is in prison now. That he understands his problem as "financial' rather than uncontrolled gambling—which constitutes an act of self-deception—does nothing to diminish the fact that he has been misusing his freedom in choosing, over and over, to indulge and strengthen this Meyerian bad habit.

Near the end of the film, a psychologist asks Mahowny to rate, on a scale of 1 to 100, the thrill he felt while gambling. One hundred, Mahowny quickly replies. And how would he rate his next biggest thrill? Twenty, Mahowny responds, without naming that experience. "How do you feel about living the rest of your life at twenty?" the psychologist wants to know. Mahowny's answer: "Twenty's OK."

Convicted of embezzlement and imprisoned, Mahowny is *forced* to acknowledge the bad habit that brought him down. He is willing to consider that an 80% reduction in "thrill" could still leave room for an acceptable, if more conventional life. Accepting this kind of compromise is a major step in overcoming many Meyerian bad habits.

The title of this story, *Owning Mahowny*, cuts two ways: first, Mahowny's bad habit owns him; then, under duress, he makes the choice to own it.

Kleptomania

If the goal appears rational, a person who steals, whether for survival or to satisfy the desire for a luxury item, is considered a thief. In the American Wild West, horse thieves were often hanged. In Victor Hugo's early 19th-century novel *Les Misérables*, Jean Valjean, a peasant who stole a loaf of bread to feed his starving sister's child, was imprisoned for 19 years—and that was just the beginning of his troubles with the French criminal justice system and French society.

Stealing when there is no apparent need or gain merits the label *kleptomania*, a behavior that has been considered a mental illness since the early nineteenth century. The word derives from the Greek: the prefix points to a thief; the suffix indicates madness. By this reckoning, kleptomania is a condition that requires understanding and treatment rather than imprisonment.

Ordinary theft—shoplifting—is common. Kleptomania, according to the DSM-5, is very rare, estimated to involve only 0.3%–0.6% of the general population, though other estimates put that figure much higher. Many more women than men are inclined to steal items they do not need or could afford to buy.

The DSM-5 attributes kleptomania to the "Recurrent failure to resist impulses to steal objects that are not needed for personal use or for their monetary value" (2013, p. 478), while not specifying either the origin of this "impulse" or its possible dynamic meanings. Nonetheless, most clinicians and theoreticians believe that kleptomania is born of an uncontrolled impulse to steal (McElroy, Hudson et al., 1991).

We reject this notion for the same reason we reject the attribution of any mental illness to a loss of impulse control: it is an essentially non-probative idea, spun from Freud's "drive theory," a blunt instrument for understanding human behavior. Freud would have us believe that some unspecified force—perhaps emerging from what he called the "unconscious"—"drives" someone into one pathological state or another.

In the FDMI, no Meyerian reaction is *attributed* to poor impulse control, though it is obvious that many patients do have problems controlling their impulses. Ultimately, our objection to the "impulse" explanation of psychic pathology is that by ascribing such power to this "drive," the role of freedom, will and choice in creating responses to the challenges people face is diluted, if not ignored altogether. As with any pathological reaction, we must look to the *meaning* of why kleptomaniacs steal. To me, as a Meyerian and an existentialist, what is expressed by the word *impulse* in the psychiatric literature is a wrongly conceived and ultimately failed attempt to identify this meaning.

We need to ask, If kleptomaniacs do not steal out of need or for profit, then for what? Why take this risk? Why break the law and expose oneself to detection, embarrassment and legal action? No doubt, Meyerian reactions that lead to kleptomania have multiple meanings.

For kleptomaniacs, simply possessing the stolen items is not the ultimate goal of this bad habit. The impetus may be the act of stealing itself and, in some instances, the desire to be caught in the act and exposed. Teenage girls, especially those with 2nd domain conditions who become kleptomaniacs, may be punishing their parents for real or imagined slights. Wives who feel trapped in conflicted or dead marriages sometimes strike back at their husbands by pilfering an item from a store, fully aware that they could be caught, which would create a scene that is embarrassing for the husband—major payback to be sure. For some kleptomaniacs, their ultimate satisfaction is the "high" they experience, the thrill that comes with "lifting" expensive items from exclusive stores. For others, especially those with sociopathic traits who tend to act out, accumulating their booty over a period of time and basking in the satisfaction of having "liberated" their "collection" may be satisfaction enough.

The DSM-5 does not specify the number of thefts or the period of time within which these thefts must occur to satisfy the criteria for kleptomania. The only reference to time in the DSM is of a "*recurrent* failure to resist impulses to steal" (emphasis added). In considering kleptomania as a Meyerian reaction, it seems fruitful to look to the multiple *meanings* of any act of theft that is suspected of being kleptomania. The principal focus in making the diagnosis should be whether someone steals within the meanings that define this illness, whether the theft occurs just once or repeatedly. After this kind of intention is established, the phenomenon can be further characterized as to its frequency and effect on the kleptomaniac's life and the lives of others who are peripherally caught up in this pathological behavior.

Neuroscience has added its conjecture to the impulse control and psychodynamic explanations for kleptomania. In the DSM-5, only one vague sentence connects kleptomania to a possible brain abnormality: "Neurotransmitter pathways associated with behavioral addictions, including those associated with serotonin, dopamine, and opioid systems, appear to play a role in kleptomania as well" (2013, p. 478). Carefully phrased, these words bypass any convincing argument for a biological cause. It should come as no surprise that there are conflicting reports in the literature about the effectiveness of SSRIs, mood stabilizers and opioid receptor antagonists (which reduce the rush connected with stealing) in treating patients diagnosed with kleptomania.

Cognitive behavioral therapy (CBT) has helped some kleptomaniacs, many of whom also have illnesses of the 1st and 2nd domains, and other 3rd domain illnesses. In a study of 20 cases of kleptomania, McElroy, Pope et al. (1991) found that all the patients studied had lifetime diagnoses of major mood disorders, 16 had lifetime diagnoses of anxiety disorders and 12 had lifetime diagnoses of eating disorders. It is not unexpected that improvement in any of these 1st and 2nd domain conditions would favor a reduction of the kleptomaniac's urge to steal.

The Fourth Domain

Chapter 12 Altered Mental States Induced by a Medical Condition or Medical Disease

Before diagnosing a psychiatric illness of the 4th domain, medical conditions that can cause psychotic symptoms must be considered, and, when possible, ruled out. The most common conditions of this type are due to *metabolic*, *electrolyte* and *toxological* derangements. Patients with these (real) chemical imbalances often experience delirium, a condition of significantly altered consciousness that clouds the sensorium and sometimes produces delusions, hallucinations and other psychotic symptoms.

Delirium

Delirium is the hydra-headed endpoint of many physiological derangements and disease processes that perturb consciousness. Psychosis due to delirium must be distinguished from other types of psychosis such as 1st domain psychotic reactions and 4th domain schizophrenia—different phenomena that cause distortions of reality which, unlike delirium, occur in a clear sensorium. The manifestations of delirium often wax and wane, and resolve once the chemical imbalance or disease process responsible is remediated.

Metabolic Causes

The most frequently encountered metabolic imbalances that cause delirium are hypoglycemia and hyperglycemia, hyperthyroidism and hypothyroidism, vitamin deficiencies (D, B12, folate, nicotinic acid, thiamine), excess of vitamin A and D, Addison's disease and Cushing's syndrome.

Electrolyte Causes

The most common delirium-inducing electrolyte imbalances are dehydration and hyponatremic water intoxication, acidosis and alkalosis, and a deficiency or excess of ionic calcium, potassium, sodium and magnesium. These (real) chemical imbalances can be identified with blood tests that are ordered for every patient who comes to the emergency room, or has a medical work-up elsewhere.

In some instances, laboratory tests can help to confirm or rule out toxic reactions to prescribed and prohibited drugs, overdoses of these drugs and drug-drug interactions. Symptoms of metabolic, electrolyte and toxological derangements, unlike those associated with primary psychiatric illnesses, derive from known changes in brain chemistry, and can be *explained* in the Jasperian sense. The mechanism, however, for how these chemical imbalances alter the products of consciousness is not known.

Toxological Causes

Environmental toxins are notorious for producing psychiatric symptoms, including those associated with delirium and psychosis. Carbon monoxide poisoning—CO is the product of incomplete oxidation of hydrocarbon fuels—causes changes in mental status ranging from mild to dramatic and in sufficient concentrations can quickly lead to death.

Lead-based paint can flake off aging surfaces and be inhaled as small particles or dust by infants and children whose brains are still developing. Lead is a potent neurotoxin, but, unlike carbon monoxide, its toxic effect, even in high concentrations, is insidious: symptoms of lead poisoning can take years to develop. Cognitive damage, resulting in a lower IQ and an array of psychiatric symptoms, especially derangements in mood and behavior, and psychosis, are the commonest consequences. Lead poisoning is a brain disease of the 4th domain that can predispose a person to pathological reactions in the other three domains.

Other heavy metals, organic solvents, insecticides, inhalants such as ether, gasoline and glue, and poisons from plants and fungi can also produce delirium.

Arrested Psychobiological Development of the Brain: Autism, Low IQ, Learning Disabilities, Dyslexia

Autism

Autism is a condition of arrested psychobiological development making this disorder a possible candidate for the 2nd domain (Kanner 1972). But deviant biology seems to be more of a factor here than in other 2nd domain illnesses (Shapin 2016), with symptoms impinging on, rather than emerging from, the lives of its young victims, to cite Meyer's distinction (Kanner 1943; Harris & Piven 2016). Until there is evidence to the contrary, autism is probably best assigned to the 4th domain—though in clinical work with patients, what we have learned about 2nd domain pathology should influence our approach (Levin 2014).

Low IQ

A person's intelligence, as measured by IQ, is a fundamental property of the self. Those with low IQ are at a disadvantage that inclines them toward developing 1st domain reactions because of the additional frustrations they encounter while trying to make their way in the world. Intelligence is partially inherited but depends also on subsequent biological, psychological and social development as well as physical environment, which includes the air one breathes. For those who are mentally subnormal (low IQ), the developmental tasks and stages achieved are different than in persons with normal or superior intelligence, making the cognitively challenged more likely, in some instances, to react maladaptively to the difficult life situations they encounter and to developing illnesses of the first three domains.

Learning Disabilities (Dyslexia)

Learning disabilities, the most common being dyslexia, also effect psychological development and can hinder someone academically and professionally. Some people with these deficits, which are not necessarily tied to intelligence, make extraordinary efforts to find ways around their shortfall, succeeding through what Nietzsche would have called "heroic overcoming."

Neurodegenerative Brain Diseases With Psychiatric Symptoms

Nietzsche, a champion of free will, famously volunteered, "What doesn't kill me makes me stronger." But Nietzsche, who so forcefully extolled the will to power and the need to overcome whatever adversity comes one's way, was, in the end, brought low by tertiary syphilis, a disease that destroyed his brain and his mind, leaving him to die in a psychotic state. Such is the power of a brain disease over our will to power.

Alzheimer's, Pick's, Huntington's, Parkinson's disease, and tertiary syphilis (called the "great pretender" because of the wide range of neurological and neuropsychiatric symptoms it spawns) are 4th domain diseases, each having a well-understood pathophysiology. These medical conditions, and others, including dementia, with its multiple causes and manifestations, are better characterized as *neurodegenerative diseases with psychiatric symptoms* than as primary psychiatric diseases, whose causes for the most part remain unknown.

Those who believe that all alterations in mental life are the product of brain diseases downplay this distinction. Yet it was recognized over a century ago that the psychosis produced by neurodegenerative diseases differed from that seen in schizophrenia, which was then known as dementia praecox:

> [T]he dementia in the plainly organic disorders is different from that of dementia praecox. In the former we find that the dementia represents a diffuse disorder of activisation of memories—and hence gives rise to a diffuse defect of elaboration, retention, memory, orientation, etc. In dementia praecox it shows itself essentially in the sphere of interest in the environment, and in a peculiar distortion of the train of thought. . . . [I]n the organic disorders we find that the content of the psychosis is of secondary importance, while in dementia praecox the content seems to stand in the very foreground of the clinical picture; the content is, moreover, apt to be peculiarly limited, so that in patients who are accessible to analysis we find the existence of special trends which account for the entire content. There is something which these cases of dementia praecox have in common with disorders such as hysteria, certain simple paranoic states and some psychoses of degenerates [criminals], that is,

conditions in which the psychogenic nature of the symptoms is now scarcely questioned by anyone (Hoch 1910).

Of course, by *psychogenic*, August Hoch (1868–1919), a contemporary of Meyer (though he died well before him) meant *psychobiological*, indicating the inseparability of what Meyer called "bad habits" of living from the alterations in brain structure and function that accompany these habits.

Tardive dyskinesia, a neurological disorder that affects many patients who take neuroleptics, as well as other drugs, also has a place in the 4th domain. TD, as it is called, causes disfiguring and debilitating movements throughout the body and, in moderate to severe cases, psychological pain as well.

A virtual anthology of the medical causes of delirium can be found in Phillip R. Slavney's *Psychiatric Dimensions of Medical Practice* (1998, pp. 9–62). The preceding discussion was based on Slavney's Table 3, "Organic Causes of Delirium" (pp. 21–24). The delirious conditions included in the FDMI's 4th domain are listed in tabular form in the Map of the Four Domains.

Physiologically Induced Anxiety

The γ-aminobutyric-acid (GABA) receptor is the primary inhibitory neurotransmitter in the central nervous system. This neural circuit is amenable to enhancement by a number of pharmaceutical agents that bind to the transmembrane GABA receptor protein complex at the benzodiazepine site, which is different from the site that binds the GABA neurotransmitter itself. Benzodiazepines potentiate the GABA signal by further opening the receptor's chloride ion channel.

Without question, benzodiazepines, as well as other agents that bind to different subunits of the GABA receptor, are effective in reducing the symptoms of many different pathological phenomena that involve the primordial emotion of anxiety. But an anxiolytic response to a drug does not signify that "underactive" inhibitory GABA neurons *cause* anxiety in the first place, or constitute the underlying phenomenon of anxiety itself.

From the perspective of Meyer's psychobiology and the FDMI, 1st domain anxiety (Chapter 6) originates in a lack of mutuality and harmony between a person and that person's world. Enhancing the inhibitory tone of the GABA neuronal system with a drug does not eliminate the cause of this anxiety—which is a fundamental lack of trust in the environment one inhabits, leading to a certain *unrootedness* there—but puts a temporary, compensatory, biological "brake" on the exaggerated emotional and affective expressions of this significant disrelationship with the world.

This is why we include anxiety in the 1st, rather than the 4th, domain and why we do not consider anxiety to be a primary psychiatric *disease* with a biological *cause* but rather a *pathological reaction*, which, like all products of consciousness, has an associated biological substrate. As noted earlier, *reaction* simultaneously designates a response to a stimulus—in this case a significant disrelationship with the world—and the psychobiological state resulting from that response.

That said, a number of medical conditions can directly *cause* anxiety. Anxiety is a primary symptom in Graves' disease, an autoimmune disorder that leads to enlargement of the thyroid gland and the overproduction of the thyroid hormones T4 and T3, which are essential to metabolism. Anxiety brought on by a medical condition is caused by an altered biological substrate and is thus considered a 4th domain condition. So, too, are anxiety and panic that are induced by the inhalation of carbon dioxide and the intravenous infusion of lactate solution (Maddock 2001). It has been pretty well established that some individuals, and their close relatives, are more susceptible to these exogenous agents than others, and it is possible that such susceptibility may be at least partially biological and genetic.

The fact that anxiety, as well as panic attack, tends to "run in families" does not mean that biology and molecular genetics always have the upper hand in these conditions. Anxiety and panic can be learned behaviors, which many patients first experience at home from anxious parents then internalize and project onto their encounters with others and the world.

Physiologically Induced Depression

It is known that some medical conditions can cause depression by a direct physiological action on the brain, though the mechanism of this body-mind interaction is not well understood. The occlusion of coronary arteries that leads to coronary heart disease (CHD) can be a systemic illness that affects the entire vasculature, including brain arteries. A diminished blood flow to the structures of the brain that underlie mood is believed to decreases the capacity of these structures to modulate emotion. This kind of vascular compromise may be at least partly responsible for the high rate of depression in those with diabetes.

Depression is well documented in patients who have had a brain stroke. Patients with hypothyroidism often experience severe depression, which remits once their thyroid function returns to normal. Patients with Alzheimer's, Huntington's and Parkinson's disease, and those having some types of malignant tumors, can become depressed as part of the pathological process that overtakes their brain. In some instances, depression appears prior to the diagnosis of the medical condition itself.

On the other hand, as Slavney (1998, pp. 63–75) points out, it is possible to misread fatigue, anorexia, insomnia and other symptoms as manifestations of a medical condition rather than as symptoms of a 1st domain depressive reaction. Depression in a medically ill patient may be the patient's *demoralization* in the face of major somatic compromise, which sometimes carries the threat of physical annihilation. This demoralization is best treated with psychotherapy, at least initially, since giving an antidepressant, mood stabilizer or antipsychotic drug to a body wracked by illness, and already altered by the drugs used to treat the illness, may further compromise the patient, often by inducing delirium.

Many prescribed medications can induce depression by acting directly on the brain. Corticosteroids are notorious for causing depression, paranoia and psychosis. Any patient who presents with what appears to be depression should be questioned about what prescribed or over-the-counter medications are being taken or have recently been discontinued. The acne drug Accutane has been implicated in depression which, in some instances, has led to suicide.

Drugs used to treat depression can also *cause* depression through the brain "chemical imbalance" these agents surely induce. The so-called antidepressant discontinuation syndrome is a rebound effect that occurs in some patients when they stop an antidepressant suddenly, though this effect is sometimes seen even when the drug is tapered. Depression roars back, sometimes stronger than originally experienced. Doctor and patient often ascribe the "relapse" to the drug's former efficacy when, in fact, the drug was masking the neuronal imbalance it created (possibly through a compensatory reduction in post synaptic receptors) while temporarily boosting the patient's mood, acting as a stimulant.

Attention needs to be paid to the possible interaction among drugs, since one drug can increase or decrease the metabolism of others, changing the amount of active drug available to every part of the body, sometimes inducing depression, sometimes delirium. Clinical depression should not be definitively diagnosed until a suspected prescribed drug, or combination of drugs, can be ruled out as the cause of the mood change.

Just about any drug of abuse can leave users with mood changes. After the "high" of cocaine or amphetamine wears off, depression sets in as the body craves another dose of the drug, in part to be rid of this unpleasant feeling. Marijuana, depending on the quality of the product and the amount smoked, can depress mood. When alcohol is abused, this drug, too, acts as a depressant. It can take many months after some drugs are discontinued for depression to resolve. Some drugs cause permanent changes in brain structure and function that result in permanent mood pathology.

Chapter 13 Schizophrenia

Psychosis takes many forms and has many origins. The mode of onset of a patient's psychotic illness—its content and course—usually provide the clinician with a key to the meaning and origin of these altered states.

Adolf Meyer's Psychobiology of Schizophrenia

Paranoia, delusions, auditory hallucinations and visual hallucinations, occurring with normal, elevated or depressed mood, can *emerge* (Meyer's term) from dynamic defenses against anxiety and are considered reactions of the 1st domain. These same pathological manifestations, though usually more intense and longer lasting, can *impinge* (also Meyer's term) on a person because of a structurally and functionally altered brain substrate. Some types of schizophrenia and manic-depression are believed to originate in this way and are taken to be primary, 4th domain brain diseases in the FDMI.

Biological psychiatry's *assumption* that schizophrenia has an organic etiology (there are no incontrovertible empirical facts to back this up) ineluctably casts the mind as a subsidiary function of the brain, as Nancy C. Andreasen insists in *The Broken Brain*:

> The relationship between neuroscience and mental illness . . . is a revolution not so much in terms of what we know as in how we perceive what we know. This shift in perception suggests that we need not look to theoretical constructs of the "mind" or to influences from the external environment in order to understand how people feel, why they behave as they do, or what becomes disturbed when people develop mental illness. Instead, we can look directly to the brain and try to understand both normal behavior and mental illness in terms of how the brain works and how the brain breaks down. The new mode of perception has created the exciting feeling that we can understand the causes of mental illness in terms of basic biological mechanisms. If we can understand how those mechanisms have "broken," we will understand the cause and perhaps develop better forms of treatment (1984, p. 138).

Meyer, in his psychobiological approach, eschewed the single arrow pointing from brain to mind that signifies cause. He substituted a double arrow denoting a dialectical interaction between mind and brain. "Mind," he says, "like every other function, can demoralize and undermine itself and its organ" (Meyer 1906), the brain. Over a century ago, Meyer foresaw what modern epigenetics would demonstrate empirically.

With the freedom he saw inhering in the condition of human consciousness, Meyer concluded that certain choices people make about how they live their lives—developing into what he called "bad habits"—can underlie symptoms that lead to a diagnosis of schizophrenia. The brain's neural substrate can be pathologically altered by this behavior so as to cause what he called "an autonomous disease of the brain." *Dementia praecox*, which is Latin for *premature mental deterioration*, is a term Kraepelin coined for his nosology of psychiatric illness. Eugen Bleuler later introduced the name *schizophrenia*, which derives from the Greek and means *split mind*. This appellation is obviously closer than Kraepelin's to what we are designating here as the phenomenon of schizophrenia.

Meyer proposed that mind pathology could cause brain pathology in 1906 when the pathophysiology of schizophrenia had already been a hot topic of study for some time. He thought of schizophrenia as a "reaction type." Since then, epigenetic studies in animals and humans have established that life experience, both positive and negative, can influence brain neuronal structure and function, which can in turn influence behavior and further development. But in spite of well-funded research that has generated numerous hypotheses, the biological substrate of schizophrenia remains elusive. The two most often cited abnormalities found in the brains of schizophrenics are enlarged brain ventricles and anomalous ocular reactions to a controlled beam of light. Neither finding explains this disease in the Jasperian sense.

The implications of the etiologic heterogeneity of schizophrenia that Eugen Bleuler and Adolf Meyer recognized long ago have not been fully embraced by modern psychiatry. (Bleuler, who was one of the first psychiatrists to approach schizophrenia dynamically, titled his classic text *Dementia Praecox, or the Group of Schizophrenias*.) The invalidity of the DSM-5 criteria for schizophrenia—which include a definitional expansion that encompasses illnesses ranging from those dynamically induced to primary brain diseases—has made it all but impossible for clinicians and researchers to identify where patients fit in the spectrum of psychotic illness. This failure could also account for the failure of extensive research efforts to identify the pathophysiology of schizophrenia.

While the heterogeneity issue goes unresolved, the search for a biological substrate continues and a Jasperian *explanation* for the phenomenon of schizophrenia still eludes us, we owe it to our patients to try to *understand* (in the Jasperian sense) what has gone wrong in their lives. Unlike the DSM-5, Meyer directs us to consider the "facts" that emerge from the life story of someone who we are diagnosing with a mental illness, and to be skeptical of any system that promotes the accumulation and enumeration of what he called "symptoms of disease entities" (Lief 1948, p. 412).

In this kind of symptom-oriented diagnostic system, the patient takes second place to the diagnosis, setting the scene for a *wrong* diagnosis. The DSM-5's meaningless symptoms do not permit the "facts" of a patient's life-story to be properly considered and understood. Patients with 1st domain illnesses, who have a dynamic etiology, are often not differentiated from those having illnesses of the 4th domain, which, by definition, involves a higher degree of brain pathology. Consequently, patients with character pathology (personality disorders in the DSM-5, pathological personality styles in the FDMI) are often misdiagnosed with schizophrenia spectrum illnesses. Apparently this was as true in Meyer's time as it is in our own:

> Certainly the number of those is increasing who agree with me that the bulk of the manifestations subsumed under the caption of dementia praecox [schizophrenia] may be most practically expressed as the inevitable and natural development from a deterioration of habits [into bad habits], partly due to developmental defects of the mental endowment, but in part at least to the clashing of instincts and to progressively faulty modes of meeting difficulties . . . (Lief 1948, p. 236).

Meyer realized that when certain people encounter these difficulties

> trivial and harmless *subterfuges* or *substitutions* . . . become harmful and uncontrollable, [and] tend to assure types of definite anomalous mechanisms, unintelligible and crazy if viewed apart, but more or less intelligible as a string of actions substituting for, and often missing, an efficient adjustment to concrete and actual difficulties (Lief 1948, p. 252).

Let's look carefully at what Meyer is saying here in what may be one of his least lovely sentences. At first, the subterfuges (strategies to escape the terror of acute ontological insecurity) and the substitutions (of bad habits for good ones) may be trivial and harmless. We all try to avoid what we don't like about our lives, fleeing that unpleasantness to a degree. Eventually most of us make the kind of adaptation to our situation that keeps us within the bounds of reality. But some people come to rely more and more on subterfuge and substitution, progressively molding their experience to a template of self-deception. They become more inauthentic and disorganized until eventually their thoughts, words and actions seem "unintelligible and crazy."

This state is what psychiatry calls psychosis. Someone with a psychotic illness lives in what can be thought of as a parallel universe which becomes intelligible only after the meanings of the subterfuges and substitutions are uncovered and understood as symbolic ways of *not* adapting to concrete and actual difficulties.

Under the pressure of situations that the incipient schizophrenic cannot or will not deal with in an instrumental way—by accepting that the self as active agent is responsible for the outcome of what is done or not done, a healthy habit according to Meyer—a self-deceiving transformation occurs that diminishes the person's grip on the world of cause and effect:

> Thus there is developed an ever-widening cleavage between mere thought life and the life of actual application as would bring with it the corrections found

> in concrete experience. Then, under some strain which a normal person would be prepared for, a sufficiently weakened and sensitive individual will react with manifestations which constitute the mental disorders constituting the "deterioration process" or dementia praecox. Unfinished or chronically subefficient action, a life lived apart from the wholesome influence of companionship and concrete test, and finally a progressive incongruity in meeting the inevitably complex demands of the higher instincts—this is practically the formula of the deterioration process (Lief 1948, p. 241).

What Meyer proposes here is a psychogenic mechanism for schizophrenia. In this formulation, the self as active agent exceeds and ultimately breaks the cognitive, emotional and behavioral frame that most people live within, though sometimes with great difficulty, while rejecting the collection of meanings agreed to by these "normal" people.

According to Meyer, emotional conflicts generated by unsuccessful attempts to resolve incompatible elements that occur in a life upset the previous psychobiological integration and promote a dis-integration of mind and body: "There develops an insidious tendency to substitute for an efficient way of meeting the difficulties, a superficial moralizing and self-deception, and an uncanny tendency to drift into so many varieties of shallow mysticism and metaphysical ponderings, or into fantastic ideas which cannot possibly be put to the test of action" (Meyer, Jelliffe & Hoch 1911, p. 46). The premorbid personality of those who eventually go on to develop schizophrenia was further characterized by August Hoch (1868–1919), a strong proponent of Meyer's psychobiological approach. Hoch used the term "shut-in personality" to describe a turning away from the world and a replacement of that environment by an inward-looking, self-referential state:

> . . . the traits upon which we would lay most stress in the shut-in personality, the lack of contact with the environment, the satisfaction with fancies instead of objective interests, the lack of constructive aims and aggressiveness, must have dangers in them which would be difficult to exclude as dynamic factors in the development of these disorders [dementia praecox, schizophrenia], and we must agree with Adolf Meyer when he has again and again insisted upon the importance of faulty psycho-biological habits in connection with dementia praecox (Hoch 1910).

The shut-in person has already turned away from the world, often incrementally over a period of many years, before becoming manifestly psychotic.

Meyer said repeatedly that what happens in the mind can alter the brain, or as Jelliffe saw it, "the organic understructure of the personality" (Meyer, Jellife & Hoch 1911, p. 47). This same premise is at the heart of Gregory Bateson's theory of the double bind that leads to psychosis, which will be considered shortly.

Cocaine, amphetamine, marijuana and other drugs can precipitate temporary, and in some instances chronic psychotic states. This change may occur because a "portal" to a psychotic domain, which has already been partially opened dynamically, is "biologically widened" by these mind-altering drugs. With pharmacological assistance, a dynamically predisposed person may find the path to an alternative reality.

R. D. Laing's False Self, Gregory Bateson's Double Bind

Meyer's account of the etiology of psychosis is strikingly similar to the description that R. D. Laing offers in *The Divided Self* of how people come to be schizophrenic (Laing never mentions Meyer in his book). Laing was a Scottish psychiatrist who also trained in an analytic institute that did not countenance Continental existential phenomenology (Burston 1996). He first read Heidegger at the suggestion of a teacher and later took up Sartre and Merleau-Ponty. Laing's goal in *The Divided Self* was to characterize what it meant for a person to be normal, and then, from that baseline, to show how someone comes to be psychotic.

Like Meyer, Laing developed a philosophical anthropology of normal life (a notion of what it means to be a human being). Unlike Meyer, he drew his concept directly from existential phenomenology. Laing began with what he called "ontological security," where "ontological" is used as an adjective for Being itself, rather than to denote the *structure* of being. According to Laing, an ontologically secure person is "real, alive, whole, and, in a temporal sense, a continuous person. As such, he can live out into the world and meet others: a world and others experienced as equally real, alive, whole, and continuous" (Laing 1965, p. 39). Meyer would have said that such a person had developed the habits of good mental hygiene.

Some people, however, never achieve even a minimal sense of solidity about themselves, most likely because of pernicious influences from heredity, environment and development. Those who are ontologically insecure do not experience the world and others as real, alive, whole and continuous. To protect themselves from the anxiety that comes with this condition, they act inauthentically—in ways that do not constitute a *real self*—by assuming a mask (persona) through which they function. They hide behind the mask, which keeps them from the pain of authentic human interaction but also deprives them of the sustenance that comes with living in an authentic world. Laing calls this stratagem the *false self*.

The degree to which a false self can sustain life for an ontologically insecure person depends on the degree of separation between this person's real self—genuine desires and needs involving others and the world—and how much sustenance that false self can extract from its inauthentic activities. The label *schizoid* is used to describe a person who is relatively functional, if pained, by this kind of accommodation made to ontological insecurity. *Psychosis* describes the process and the result of what happens when the false self collapses under the pressure of reality, which forces its way through the fragile persona.

Two line drawings in Laing's *The Divided Self* let us see how the real self and the false self relate to others and the wider world created by others. The circle in Figure 13.1a depicts the ontologically secure person (the embodied real self) in a dialectical interaction (as signified by the solid overlapping circle and solid ellipse) with its environment: perception is real and action is meaningful.

In Figure 13.1b, the circle formerly representing the real self has shrunk, the "inner" (false) self having retreated, under pressure, from others and the wider

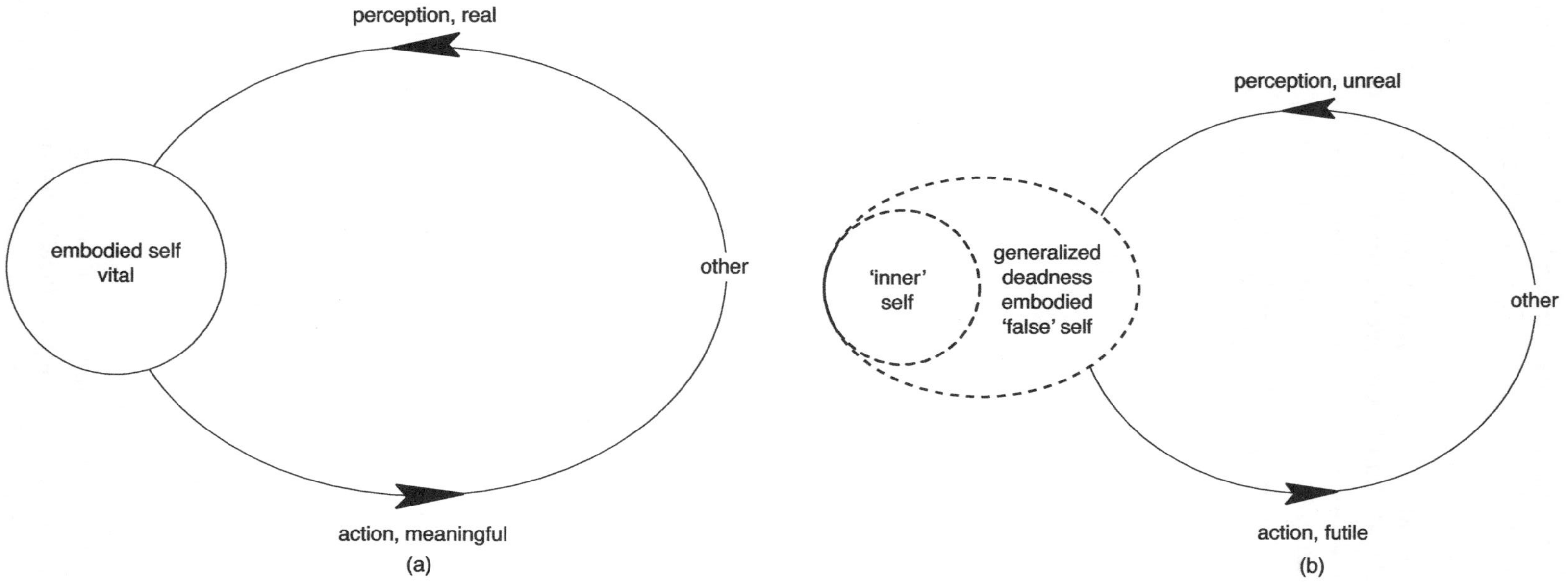

Figure 13.1 The "real self," vital and living dialectically with others in the "real world" of cause and effect. Perception is real, action is meaningful (a); The "false self," having retreated in anxiety from the "real world" of cause and effect, living non-dialectically in a defensively transformed, self-referential world. Perception is unreal, action is futile (b)

Source: Laing, *The Divided Self* (1965), Reprinted with permission

world. The embodied false self, with its "generalized deadness," interacts non-dialectically (as signified by the broken circle and broken ellipse): perception is unreal and action is futile.

While retreating from the disintegrating world outside, an escape hatch—a psychic portal—may open to an interior, largely self-crafted, self-referential world (psychosis), with its lesser demands and eventually even its own language. This letting go of reality is a reaction to *terror* that an ontologically secure person could not even imagine as an amplification of his own worst anxiety.

In severe psychosis, what is left of the *real self* (the "inner" self in Figure 13.1b) becomes a different entity—van den Berg's "different existence"—that is isolated from the real world, as indicated by the broken line that signifies its separation from reality. This *false self* lives in a state of "generalized deadness" because it cannot draw sustenance from the real world, which is the venue of authentic existence. As an unstable entity, the false self eventually fragments. Laing identifies the components of this process of disintegration as *engulfment* (the threat posed by any person or external event), *implosion* (the collapse of the real self under the realization of this threat) and *petrification* (the feeling, as the implosion occurs, of life "hardening" into a less-than-human existence). This pathological transformation of the self is explicated more fully in the author's *The Marginal Self* (Muller 1987, pp. 103–132).

The psychiatrist and psychoanalyst Karl Menninger saw the behavior of his patients who had retreated into Laing's "inner" world—with actions that biological psychiatry reduces to meaningless psychotic symptoms—as having probative meaning:

> An individual having unusual difficulties in coping with his environment struggles and kicks up the dust, as it were. I have used the figure of a fish caught on a hook: his gyrations must look peculiar to other fish that don't understand the circumstances; but his splashes are not his affliction, they are his effort to get rid of his affliction and as every fisherman knows these efforts may succeed (Spandler 2006, p. 55).

Especially, that is, if the "fish" sees himself in an existential struggle with a world from which he is now alienated—out of water, so to speak—with a chance to gyrate off that hook back into his viable aquatic world. Menninger's often-cited metaphor of the hooked fish exemplifies his hope that at least some of his patients could face their true "affliction," and work their way back to the "real" world they had abandoned in terror. Clinicians who understand the meaning of schizophrenic patients' "gyrations" can offer insight and encouragement and assist in this process.

Gregory Bateson

In the mid-1950s, a psychogenic mechanism for *understanding* (in the Jasperian sense) the kind of situations that set an ontologically insecure person on a course to schizophrenia was proposed by Gregory Bateson, an anthropologist who was not a clinician, and his colleagues, some of whom were clinicians. Studying families with a schizophrenic member, Bateson found patterns of disordered, non-logical thinking and communication that put the incipient schizophrenic—the "target" of the family dynamic—in what he called a *double bind* (Bateson et al., 1956).

The double bind is a far more potent stressor than quotidian dilemmas or cognitive dissonance. The concept originated in learning theory, which defines logical types (categories) and their opposites. The pairs include: singular vs. universal; abstract vs. concrete; literal vs. metaphoric; and love vs. hate. Four conditions are essential to create a double bind:

1. The target receives contradictory instructions or emotional messages of different logical types. A mother tells a child that she loves him, then turns away in disgust when he shows affection. Her body language contradicts her words as the messages sent by the two communications clash. In the 1950s and 1960s, the label *schizophrenogenic mother* was attached to mothers who acted in this way. The notion lost most of its appeal once schizophrenia came to be seen as the upshot of a compromised brain neural substrate.
2. No metacommunication is possible. The child is not able to ask which of the two messages is valid or grasp that the communication makes no sense. He does not have the mental maturity to sort this dilemma out on his own.
3. The victim cannot leave the communication field. The world of the child is usually the world as mediated to him by the parents. Most children will not be able to break out of this frame without outside help.
4. Failing to fulfill the contradictory injunctions, the child is punished by the mother, who withholds her love. No matter what he does or doesn't do, the child cannot win.

The young, whose minds and brains have not yet reached a certain point in psychobiological development, are particularly vulnerable to the dilemmas forced on them by this dynamic. Not all young brains are equally vulnerable. An ontologically insecure child with an impaired nervous system, whether due to genetics or epigenetic modification, will be less able to cope with and overcome the psychological onslaught of a double bind.

Bleuler reminds us that we all participate in constructing our own course: "Cares and conflicts, experience and thought-content depend not only on objective experience of the outside world, but more especially on the way each individual experiences the outside world according to his personal scale" (Séchehaye 1956, pp. 78–79). In double bind situations, psychobiological constitution, the severity of the psychological trauma, how often one is subjected to it and the adaptation made to the accompanying psychobiological stress will be key factors in the outcome. Most children who find themselves in these situations will not become schizophrenic.

In fairness to the mother designated as schizophrenogenic, some children are vulnerable to schizophrenia for reasons largely unknown. Some children are notoriously difficult to "mother," and their behavior may limit the best a woman has to offer a child. Also, a time-limited negative experience of her own may influence the way a mother interacts with one child but not another. Of course, there are women whose psychic pathology would destroy the life of any son or daughter (see the case of Renée in Chapter 14). The schizophrenogenic mother is the antithesis of Donald Winnicott's "good enough" mother, who can be thought of as being "bad enough" to foster an environment that makes a psychotic alternative to reality seem attractive.

The contradictory messages sent by the mother (or father, or other authority figure) to the ontologically insecure and vulnerable child thwart a healthy development of the child (or adolescent, or, in some instances, adult), who will, as a result, become even more anxious, insecure and disoriented. Experiencing the psychobiological torsion of being continuously embroiled in a double bind, an individual may try to escape this perverted version of reality for a world of fantasy where the rough edges are rounded off and where an easier time of things can be had, at least temporarily.

The "reality" that "normal" people experience and share, in what is generally referred to as the world of consensual validation—Meyer called it "consensual common sense"—must be understood as a relative reality because no one is entirely "real." To avoid the full hit of what is collectively known as our experience, we all, no matter how "normal" we may seem to ourselves or to others, use stratagems that involve self-deception, which may rise to the level of dynamic defenses. In the *Four Quartets*, T. S. Eliot conceded that "Humankind cannot bear very much reality" (Ricks & McCue 2015, p. 180).

One could imagine some ontological faculty, in ways analogous to the infant's capacity to acquire language, beckoning certain constitutionally and psychologically vulnerable people to enter the "escape hatch" on the other side of which they may live psychotically, out of reach of an "intolerable situation" (Sartre), and of reality as we know it. The resulting "inner" (false) self, which is cut off from reality, is portrayed in Figure 13.1b.

Much of what a person who has succumbed to a double bind says and does will seem bizarre, even incomprehensible. But some of it may be funny, too. This is because the patterns of confused thinking and speaking that are learned from the mother result from the same kind of conflation of logical types that drives the humor of professional comedians, as well as the jokes that even amateurs can momentarily jolt the rational world with. The emanations of both conflations have the same outward form but are clearly different phenomena (demonstrating, once again, why human behavior should not be interpreted until its meaning has been established). Of course, the psychotic is not "in" on his own "joke."

Bateson and his colleagues originally conceived the double bind as a strictly psychogenic path to schizophrenia. But if one considers the degree of psychobiological stress that undoubtedly accompanies the "twisting" of the psyche in this kind of trauma, one can imagine the target's entire *psychobiological substrate* being permanently altered. In such a transformation, psyche (mind) and brain are no longer distinguishable. According to Meyer:

> Failing with what is frequently impossible and undesirable anyhow, these persons [who succumb to mental illness] develop emotional attitudes and habits and tendencies to fumble or to brood or to puzzle or to be apprehensive, until what students of the functional diseases of the heart call "a break in

> compensation" occurs, a break of nature's system of maintaining the balance, with a more or less sudden slump and implication of collateral [brain, physiological] functions (Lief 1948, p. 539).

What Meyer and Laing discovered working with their patients, and what Bateson theorized based on his intuition and the work of his clinical colleagues brings us face to face with the *phenomenon* of schizophrenia. While we, to some degree, *understand* this illness (which may or may not be a brain disease, depending in part on one's definition of a brain disease), we still can't *explain* it in the Jasperian sense. Even if an aberrant neural substrate were never found for schizophrenia, and, after exhaustive empirical study, the quest for the "Holy Grail" were abandoned, we would still *understand* this illness well enough to correctly diagnose patients and offer them a way to deal with their malady.

In making a diagnosis using the FDMI, the emphasis is on identifying *the phenomenon that is the patient's illness*. To do this, we must focus on the facts of each patient's *experience*, how things came to be that way, on what went wrong and why. The phenomenon that emerges from this process is then matched as closely as possible to the phenomena characterized in the FDMI. If it is not possible to make this match, a detailed written description of the patient's life-story should be undertaken. In existential phenomenology, it is a rule of thumb that if something is described well enough, it will be understood.

Meyer would have undoubtedly agreed. Otto Marx, one of his residents, wrote that Meyer "began to feel that if you talked to patients and elicited their history, the reason why they were psychotic often seemed to become very clear and that one should stop looking for what Meyer said was 'something else'" (Marx 1993).

John C. Whitehorn

In 1941 John C. Whitehorn succeeded Adolf Meyer as chief of psychiatry at Johns Hopkins and held that position until 1960. Whitehorn greatly admired Meyer's psychobiological approach and followed his diagnostic and therapeutic lead. Like Meyer, who had studied the neuropathology of schizophrenia early in his career, he also had investigated the "organic" side of this illness, mostly as a biochemist. And, as Meyer had, Whitehorn eventually came to believe that it would be more fruitful for him to study the psychodynamics of schizophrenia than continue with his laboratory work.

This epiphany came to Whitehorn while he was conducting a study in which he administered glucose and sodium acid phosphate to schizophrenic patients who had low energy, hoping to increase their energy. What he found was that the patients in a control group who did not receive the chemical supplement but were engaged in conversation by those doing the study showed the greatest improvement. This unexpected result led Whitehorn to investigate the nature of the interaction between clinicians and patients. He was able to identify some elements in this process that led to good outcomes, as well as other therapeutic attitudes and styles that did not work (Whitehorn, YouTube video).

In spite of heading the Johns Hopkins department of psychiatry for almost two decades, serving as president of the American Psychiatric Association (1950–1951), and taking on other important leadership positions during a time when psychiatry was wracked by internal turmoil, Whitehorn is unheralded today—even at Johns Hopkins, where psychiatric residents do not know his name. He is not mentioned in *The Perspectives of Psychiatry* (1998), the text by Paul R. McHugh and Phillip R. Slavney that brought Meyer's psychobiology into the latter half of the 20th century. And in Jerome D. Frank's and Julia B. Frank's *Persuasion and Healing*, a psychotherapy text rooted in Meyer's psychobiology, Whitehorn's name appears only once in the index, directing the reader to this single sentence: "Psychiatric training at the Johns Hopkins Hospital under Adolf Meyer and John C. Whitehorn instilled a nondogmatic outlook, a respect for facts, and a conviction that systematic observation of individuals in their social context could yield worthwhile insights into human functioning" (Frank & Frank 1991, p. 296). Without pointing to Whitehorn as an example, Paul McHugh, who was a successor to Meyer and Whitehorn as director of Johns Hopkins psychiatry from 1975 to 2001, likes to remind people that it can be a short hop from *Who's Who* to who's he?

Like Meyer, and unlike Freud, Whitehorn believed that many people who act psychotically are candidates for psychotherapy (Young 2012). Whitehorn saw many psychotic patients and was more optimistic than Meyer about the outcome of their therapy. He taught his residents that someone's diagnosis is not the most important factor in the outcome of treatment—what the patient had accomplished *before* becoming mentally ill, and the influence this life experience had on his psychobiological development, for better or worse, was the key factor (Barbara Young, MD, private communication).

Whitehorn came to realize that what ultimately sets schizophrenics apart from those who live in the real world is the way the terror they feel restricts their freedom: "the schizophrenic is characteristically 'independent' in a special sense; he has special resistances against being coerced by conventionality, special antipathies toward being influenced or 'victimized' to serve another's ends—even a very generalized reaction-against-influence. He is therefore rather resistive to authoritarian or rationalistic efforts at psychotherapy" (Whitehorn 1950). Picture someone in a psychotic state, occupying an "inner" world that is sequestered from the "outer" world of reality, someone who retreated there in terror under the influence of an environment that was experienced as crushingly threatening. What Whitehorn calls independence in this sequestered world is not an active *freedom to*, but a passive *freedom from*, which inevitably inclines the patient toward pathological choices and constructs.

This ironic independence is a refusal to bear the "social harness" (Whitehorn's metaphor) that anyone who lives in the real world implicitly accepts. Whitehorn adopted Meyer's designation *schizophrenic reaction* to signify the agency of self that is behind the creation and continuance of some schizophrenias, abetted as these illnesses may be by deficits in biology and development.

Clinicians hoping to literally talk patients back from psychosis into communion with the real world would do well to heed this advice from Whitehorn: "To every patient, his illness is a personal experience, not a category in a catalogue, and if one wishes to establish personal rapport, for the better utilization of psychodynamic influences, one needs to establish liaison through some imaginative appreciation of the patient's attitudes and experience" (Whitehorn 1950). In other words, the clinician must find a portal into the schizophrenic's inner, sequestered world, allowing a therapeutic intervention to be made that empowers patients to part with the ironic way they are being independent in that world. A passive, pathological *freedom from* the need to act may then become a *freedom to* act as an authentic agent in the real world.

Like Meyer, Whitehorn preferred to stick to the *facts* emerging from a patient's story rather than attempt to interpret the abundance of unconscious and repressed material that often comes up during psychosis. In his experience, interpretation of this material did not lead to abreaction, or have a therapeutic effect: "The author has found it a great advantage to approach the study of schizophrenic patients rather more broadly from the viewpoint of the psychodynamics of ordinary life. Fair success has attended attempts to comprehend the significant issues by direct dealings with such patients rather than by interpreting into another idiom" (Whitehorn 1950). Whitehorn was, no doubt, distinguishing his approach from Freud's.

Whitehorn did not spell out an explicit technique for working with schizophrenic patients, insisting that "successful therapy is not necessarily specific therapy" (Whitehorn 1950). Two years after his death in 1973, a compilation of journal articles written by Whitehorn and his Hopkins psychiatric colleague Barbara J. Betz was published under the title *Effective Psychotherapy with Schizophrenic Patients* (Whitehorn & Betz 1975). Betz's contribution spells out *her* therapeutic strategy, which, she makes clear, evolved from collaborating with Whitehorn.

Speaking for them both, she urged clinicians, when working with withdrawn patients, "to permit the patient, as represented by his own moment-to-moment attitudes and reactions, to be the pivotal point around which the therapeutic relationship develops. To do this the therapist needs deliberately to avoid assuming the pivotal role as represented by his professional status or his clinical 'insight,' however accurate, and leaving the burden of mobility and adaptation to the patient. . . . When the therapist approaches the patient in this way, with the attempt simply to be an understanding person, he does not seem to be felt as coercive or a threatening 'influence.'" (Whitehorn & Betz, p. 33). Whitehorn found that therapists who were less directive and didactic got the best results (Whitehorn, YouTube video).

Betz explains why the prospect of being influenced by an outside source—especially a psychotherapist—is so terrifying to a schizophrenic patient: "A therapeutically workable, dynamic issue underlying the schizophrenic illness has been found to lie in the patient's particular orientation toward authority as a power belonging to and imposed by others, rather than a power arising within himself. . . . Many schizophrenic patients refer to themselves by a third-person pronoun, by a collective 'we,' or by avoiding all pronounal self-reliance. . . . [They] do not function in a self-governing manner, yet direction from others is feared and resented" (Whitehorn & Betz 1975, p. 70). While Whitehorn and Betz understood their schizophrenic patients dynamically, their treatment approach was purposely restricted to supportive interventions, at least initially.

Starting in the 1950s, as the new paradigm of biological psychiatry took hold, the psychiatrist's role of facilitator in the psychodynamic reorganization of a person who had undergone a psychotic reaction inevitably took a back seat to pharmacological intervention. While drug-induced changes in brain function often quiet some psychotic symptoms, this intervention does not cure their underlying illness. Dynamic psychotherapy, on the other hand, has empowered many patients diagnosed with schizophrenia to return to the world of reality and be productive there (Saks 2007). Even when treatment was only partially successful, many patients were able to make the most of their seemingly intractable compromise with reality.

The etiology of the mental illness that we call schizophrenia, which is widely acknowledged to exist in different phenotypes, is still unknown. We cannot readily distinguish schizophrenic patients who may have a psychogenic illness from those who may have a primary brain disease—though schizophrenic patients can be distinguished from those with medical conditions and medical diseases that sometimes cause similar psychotic symptoms (Chapter 12).

What we can do is identify the Meyerian *facts* that make up the stories our patients tell us and try to figure out how their psychotic symptoms *emerge* from these facts. In some instances, doing so will allow us to establish the meaning of their symptoms and see how defenses drive patients to enter the orb of psychosis and remain there. With a valid psychodynamic understanding of a psychotic illness in hand, we can say with some confidence that the illness is at least in part psychogenic—with the stipulation that a psychobiological deficit, as well as other biological factors, may have contributed to, and ultimately become part of, the biological substrate of the illness.

We should also acknowledge the possibility that a psychodynamically induced psychotic experience may alter brain structure and function, as Meyer believed. "Mind," he said, "like every other function, can demoralize and undermine itself and its organ" (Meyer 1906), by which Meyer meant the brain.

Until we can specify the etiology and meaning of each psychotic person's illness, we should not assume that every patient we diagnose with schizophrenia has a primary brain disease, and remember that Whitehorn, Meyer and others restored at least some of their schizophrenic patients to health with dynamic psychotherapy.

Chapter 14 Four Schizophrenic Patients, Four Different Schizophrenias

When psychosis occurs as a primary psychiatric illness, patients withdraw partially or fully from the shared experience of the common world that we agree to call reality and undergo a deterioration of intellectual and social functioning. By telling the story of Elyn, a young woman of exceptional promise who was able to realize that promise in spite of her illness; the stories of Renée and Kim, who showed the classic symptoms and course of schizophrenia; and the story of John Nash, who had a spectacular career as a mathematician before developing a debilitating psychosis, we hope to see beyond their symptoms to the *phenomenon* of their illnesses. It should become clear why a valid diagnosis depends on identifying this phenomenon and why a valid diagnosis cannot be made by assessing symptoms alone. Elyn, Reneé, Kim and John Nash embody four very different phenotypes of schizophrenia.

Elyn Saks

Elyn R. Saks is a lawyer and a professor at the University of Southern California Gould School of Law (Muller 2012). In a book aptly titled *The Center Cannot Hold* (2007), Saks tells how she managed to achieve this goal in spite of a chronic mental illness that was diagnosed, at different times, as paranoid schizophrenia and schizoaffective disorder, depressive type.

Elyn grew up in Miami, Florida, graduated from Vanderbilt, received a B. Phil. from Oxford and a law degree from Yale—all with the highest distinction. This in spite of her struggle with a hydra-headed psychosis that came and went but never went away and a "center" that disintegrated again and again after being temporarily restored with the help of therapy, friendship, work and psychotropic medication.

The first indications that Elyn might be heading for a difficult psychological life came while she was an undergraduate at Vanderbilt. Away from home, faced with new challenges and new expectations, she began to "unravel." She describes herself as "frantic during the day, sleepless during the night" (p. 46). This daughter of fastidious professional parents let her hygiene slip even as she realized that her body "stank."

Elyn found it hard to concentrate and to think clearly. Her anxiety was constant, though less while doing academic work, from which she drew most of her identity:

"The task of setting and achieving goals operated as a sort of adhesive; I needed it to hold myself together" (p. 199). Sex with her considerate boyfriend was often "terrifying," as she feared losing herself psychically and physically while merging in the act. This is the *engulfment* that Laing identified in the ontologically insecure person who was heading, under a perceived threat, toward a psychotic break. In Elyn's psychic tug of war, substance abuse was not a contributing factor. Unlike so many people who begin to show signs of a major mental illness at her age, she did not abuse drugs or alcohol.

"My best guess," Elyn says of that time, "is that my illness was beginning to poke through the shell (for lack of a better word) that helped me, indeed helps all of us, maintain a separation between what is real and what is not. For the next few years, that's where things would precariously balance—me unwittingly trying to keep the shell strong, and my illness trying equally hard to break through" (p. 40). In spite of a psyche that was increasingly blurring the boundaries between fantasy and reality, Elyn graduated from Vanderbilt with a perfect academic record, was named class valedictorian and won a Marshall scholarship to study ancient philosophy at Oxford—where her life really began to fall apart. There were trips to the emergency room, stays in psychiatric hospitals, psychiatrists and psychoanalysts, psychotropic medications.

At Oxford Elyn continued to excel academically even as reality became a tougher slog, and she retreated further into her fantasy world. She did not feel herself to be real, live and continuous, as Laing characterized the grounding of the ontologically secure person. Nor did she experience others as real, live and continuous. It was as if she lived behind a wall of glass—Silvia Plath's bell jar comes to mind—that cut her off from what was going on around her. Elyn became frustrated and angry in her isolation and turned that anger against others, seeing ulterior motives where there were none. In fact, she had a coterie of loyal friends, teachers and colleagues.

In her dreams, Elyn killed her friends, teachers and colleagues because she was able to trick herself into believing that they wanted to kill her. This "killing" was how she feigned control when in fact she had ceded control to her illness, or her illness had taken it from her (most likely, it worked both ways). Elyn was self-deceived, depressed, paranoid and psychotic much of the time:

> Psychosis is like an insidious infection that nevertheless leaves some of your faculties intact; in a psychiatric hospital, for example, even the most debilitated schizophrenic patients show up on time for meals, and they evacuate the ward when the fire alarm goes off. So it was for me. Completely delusional, I still understood essential aspects of how the world worked. For example, I was getting my schoolwork done, and I vaguely understood the rule that in a social setting, even with the people I most trusted, I could not ramble on about my psychotic thoughts. To talk about killing children, burning whole worlds, or being able to destroy cities with my mind was not part of polite conversation.
>
> At times, though, I was so psychotic that I could barely contain myself. The delusions expanded into full-blown hallucinations, in which I could clearly hear people whispering. I could hear my name being called when no one was

physically around—in a corner of the library, or late at night, in my bedroom where I slept alone (pp. 98–99).

While at Oxford, Elyn became the patient of a Kleinian psychoanalyst—"Mrs. Jones"—with whom she formed a strong therapeutic alliance, and whom Elyn credits with being the "glue" that held her together, if precariously: "I was falling apart, flying apart, exploding—and [Mrs. Jones] gathered my pieces and held them for me" (p. 98). After three years of intense psychoanalytic work and finishing her B. Phil., again with high distinction, Elyn considered staying in England to continue therapy. But Mrs. Jones encouraged her to return home. As expected with someone of Elyn's psychic fragility, the prospect of losing this alliance induced great anxiety, and led to regression:

> *I go to my session. I threaten Mrs. Jones with a knife. I am very psychotic and out of control. Mrs. Jones is kind and gentle. She asks me for the knife and I give it to her. I start screaming. I throw myself against the wall. Mrs. Jones and her husband restrain me. The ambulance arrives and takes me to the hospital. I become out of control again and am subdued. I am crying and sobbing that I will be leaving Mrs. Jones* (ERS's italics).
>
> With psychosis, the wall that separates fantasy from reality dissolves; inside my head, the fantasies were real, and everything was actually happening. The images I saw, the actions I took, were all real, and it made me frantic. Mrs. Jones had been the glue that held me together. With that glue soon to be gone, would I not shatter into a thousand pieces? The anxiety was overwhelming, and our sessions became more intense and hallucinatory:
>
> *Elyn*: "You can't leave. I won't let you. Plupenitenary issues must be addressed. That's a dress. Come home with me, please?"
>
> *Mrs. Jones*: "I think, you see, that you make yourself confused because you want to avoid the pain of separation. It's upsetting to think I have a life of my own, apart from you. You are trying to live inside me."
>
> *(Elyn has fused with Mrs. Jones by obliterating the boundaries that normally separate two people, which non-psychotic persons observe, usually without realizing it. She has crossed a line here in attempting to become the person who has provided the "glue" that allowed her to have a fledgling, brittle center of self. Note the neologism plupenitentary and the clang association addressed/dress, which are indications of formal thought disorder—an upshot of the psychotic mind's need to create different words and different links between words.)*
>
> *Elyn*: "I *am* inside you! Your organs are slimy, just like you are. You think you own me, but I own you. My every command is your wish. You don't exist."
>
> *Mrs. Jones*: "You would rather kill me off than think I am separate from you."

(Desperate to avoid what she feels is the imminent implosion of her brittle self, Elyn maintains that she is controlling Mrs. Jones as a way to deny that she has lost all control over herself and her situation. This is a 180-degree reversal of the truth. Elyn is living in a fantasy world because, as she sees it, the world of reality is too hostile, and is threatening to annihilate her.)

Elyn: "I see truth. You see lies. In my mind I'm going to Carolina."
Mrs. Jones: "You are so upset about leaving because it disrupts your fantasy that you own me. You have had the fantasy that I was totally under your control. Your possessiveness then spoils me. But I must remain under your control at all costs."

(Elyn's fusion with Mrs. Jones goes beyond possessiveness to the imaginary desire, driven by anger, to destroy what she cannot possess. Actually killing Mrs. Jones would, of course, leave Elyn totally bereft.)

Elyn: "You *are* under my control! You go where I go. There will be no separation. I have killed people before and I will kill them again. I give life and I take it away. You have no choice. I am God. Nothing comes from nothing. Nothing. God. Taken away."
Mrs. Jones: "Your fantasies help you avoid the pain of separation."
Elyn, raising her voice: "They are not fantasies! It's real. I am God. I am the One. One. Two. It's a mess."

(Feeling more and more that she has no power in the real world, Elyn insists that she has absolute power, over herself, Mrs. Jones and everything else in her fantasy world. This is accomplished by an imaginary fusion with God, who is posited as the summum bonum ("I give life and I take it away"; "I am the One"). Imploding, lacking even the most elementary control over herself in the rational world, Elyn nonetheless convinces herself that she is the Prime Mover in her fantasy world! The thousands of people she claims to have killed, here and elsewhere in the book, are killed only in her pathologically transformed mind.)

(The parenthetical italicized comments on the dialogue between Elyn and Mrs. Jones (Saks 2007, pp. 110–111) are those of this author.)

While psychotic, Elyn was mostly lost to the world of reality and had impaired insight. She recovered from the incident just described, and inexplicably, in spite of recurring episodes of psychosis, managed to excel academically. After graduation, Elyn left Oxford and Mrs. Jones, returned to Miami and stayed with her parents until fall when she moved to New Haven to begin law school at Yale where she continued her pattern of academic excellence and periodic emotional collapse. Her psychotic episodes became more severe and bizarre, requiring physical restraint and, eventually, her first antipsychotic medication, which she strenuously resisted verbally and physically. During the next few years, this drug (unnamed in the book), was replaced in turn by Trilafon, Navane, Zyprexa and clozapine, as eventual inefficacy and side effects demanded a change.

No drug completely erased Elyn's psychotic symptoms, but each, for a time, lessened these symptoms and their impact, allowing her to finish law school, though not without taking a year off to deal with her illness. After Yale and several short-term jobs, Elyn was hired to teach at the University of Southern California Gould School of Law where she was promoted to professor and given tenure. She married her longtime boyfriend, Will, who was as dedicated to serving her needs as any man could possibly have been.

As Elyn lived with and against her illness, she became increasingly analytical and insightful as we can see in this *cri de coeur*: "I needed to understand what lay behind my terrible thoughts and feelings and how my psychosis served to protect me" (p. 334). We might ask, How did she come to have these "terrible thoughts and feelings" in the first place? Whom or what did she need to be protected *from?*

Elyn gives little space in her book to her parents, but what she does say about them seems probative. Both parents were emotionally distant from their daughter: "[T]here was a wall of appropriateness between us at all times; in fact, we'd spent years carefully constructing it, I on one side with my particular set of tools, they on theirs, with the tools they'd chosen" (p. 118).

Had Elyn's mother been "good enough," in the Winnicott sense? And her father? At all stages of Elyn's life, they seem to have been such vague presences, as if they were there, but not there for her. A family therapist noted that the parents had "made light of [her] illness and didn't seem willing to accept its seriousness" (p. 163). Elyn admits to being complicit in this cover-up: "I always did everything I could to hide seriousness. I cracked jokes, and laughed, and was gratified when they did the same. It was our way of handling it. It was our habit—and every family has its habits. The levity and irreverence made it possible for us to be together without everyone falling completely apart" (p. 163). Laing might have said that Elyn and her parents had denied their being to save their being *collectively, as a family.*

It eventually occurred to Elyn that a double trickery had ruled her life:

> The illness—the entity—is always just off to the side, just barely out of my sight. But I know it's there. And it tries to trick me into believing this isn't the real Will, and this isn't the real Steve, that reality isn't reality, that I can kill thousands of people with my thoughts, or that I'm profoundly evil and unworthy [this is Capgras syndrome, a delusion where she came to believe that her husband and closest friend were imposters].
>
> At the same time, I'm trying to trick the people around me. I'm OK. I'm functional, I'm fine. And maybe, sometimes, this determined effort to trick them tricks the illness itself. It's like one big con. Steve says he's never seen anyone who fights as I do. I don't consider myself a fighter (and I certainly don't come across as ferocious). But if he's right, then perhaps in my childhood, and in this push-pull with my parents, one can see not only the beginnings of my illness, but the seeds of my health and strength as well. If I'm a fighter, perhaps it's because that's who they taught me to be (p. 327).

Without directly saying that her parents had a role in the development of her psychosis, Elyn, perhaps influenced by Laing and Bateson, whose work she cites earlier in the book, considers that possibility. The "push/pull" with her parents sounds like the kind of mixed discourse, comprising two incompatible and emotionally conflicting signals, that Bateson characterized as a double bind. Bateson believed that such a conflict, in a psychobiologically vulnerable child, can, through a "twisting" of the psyche, lead the child to fragment reality and create the kind of psychotic thought, behavior and discourse that Elyn lapsed into.

One can imagine Elyn as a child being in what Laing calls a state of ontological insecurity—profound anxiety about who she was and how she was to live—putting on a false self—"I'm fine, I'm strong; I don't need you"—and the parents, caught up in their own self-absorption and blindness, wanting to believe her pose, responding with the same emotional coldness that they appear to have shown throughout Elyn's life. This non-response to Elyn's needs may have deprived her of the nurture necessary to sufficiently trust the world in order to take on the challenges of each new developmental milestone, leaving her mind and brain primed for developing a chronic mental illness.

(I have tried to imagine the degree of *terror* that an ontologically insecure child must feel in order for a psyche to "twist" sufficiently, from the pressure of a double bind situation, to cause psychosis. Having experienced anxiety under stress as an adult, I am unable to backwardly extrapolate this feeling to an emotional state in my own ontologically secure childhood that might have put me so far out of harmony with the world, at any time in my life, that I would, in Elyn's words, "cross the line between what is real and what is not." I attempt this imaginary variation hoping to show just *how* different what van den Berg calls the "different existence" of someone with a serious mental illness can actually be.)

Elyn knew that she would most likely never be entirely free of her illness. But during a hospitalization at the Yale Psychiatric Institute, when she was initially floridly psychotic ("People are controlling me, putting thoughts into my head") (p. 132), and on a high dose of antipsychotic medication, she began to see that she could do something significant to help herself. After weeks of miserable and contentious confinement, her psychosis began to lift, and Elyn had an epiphany:

> And then something threw a switch in my head, and I got it. I *got* it. The only barrier between me and the door out [of YPI] was me. I simply had to *stop* it. Stop voicing the hallucinations and delusions, even when they were there. Stop babbling incoherently, even if those were the only words that came to my lips; no, no, it was better to be quiet. Stop resisting; just behave. *Being in a psychiatric hospital is nonsense*, I thought. *I am a law student, not a mental patient. I want my life back, damn it! And if I have to bite my tongue until it bleeds, I'm going to get it back* (pp. 175–176).

By being "quiet" Elyn meant not just putting on an act but making an effort to at least mute her psychotic constructions until she could face the world more realistically without them: "Maybe I couldn't keep the thoughts from coming into my head, but I could organize them, and keep them from getting out. *OK, here I go*" (p. 176). For the first time, it seems, Elyn was asserting herself as an active agent against the illness itself, realizing that she had some complicity in the situation she found herself in. She accepted the fact that her psychotic illness was most likely chronic—what Jaspers called an "ultimate situation," or "boundary situation"—and that it would not go away. She could either continue to deal with her condition half-heartedly, as she had done for so long, or encounter it full on. This would amount to, as she says, finding "the wellness within the illness" (Saks 2013).

Elyn's life, and the story she tells about that life, challenge us to think harder and deeper about the meaning of her "different existence," as van den Berg described the course of someone with a serious mental illness. How did she come to develop this illness, and by what name should we call it? Near the end of the book, Elyn gives credit to "Dr. Freed," a psychoanalyst, who, she says, "helps me to understand how I sometimes use my psychotic thoughts to avoid the ordinary bad feelings that everyone experiences—sadness, rage, garden-variety disappointment . . . he tries to understand my psychotic thoughts as unconsciously motivated and meaningful (which of course they are)" (p. 325).

The fact that "antipsychotic" medication kept Elyn out of the hospital, and functioning as a law professor and legal scholar, does not mean that she has a primary brain disease that drugs remediate (as Synthroid "corrects" hypothyroidism) and may mean that these drugs are acting as tranquilizers that allow her to control her thoughts and emotions so she can meet the challenges of her life less defensively and more realistically. Elyn, who has two brothers, says nothing about any family member ever being diagnosed with a mental illness.

As the book ends, Elyn is still taking clozapine and is told by her psychopharmacologist that she will most likely have to take some antipsychotic medication for the rest of her life. She credits both psychoanalysis and psychopharmacology for the progress she has made. "While medication had kept me alive," she acknowledges, "it had been psychoanalysis that had helped me find a life worth living" (p. 298). For someone so long and so tightly in the grip of a psychotically transformed world as Elyn has been, the challenge of breaking that defensive structure is probably in some ways akin to breaking an addiction to a chemical substance.

Elyn's descriptions of her psychotic (and normal) experiences are taken here to be primary data, in the way that numbers, and the statistical elaboration of these numbers are considered data in the empirical approach to studying psychic pathology. After hermeneutic analysis, what Elyn tells us about her fall into psychosis and her efforts to have a career and a life—her *story*—reveals the phenomenon of *one* of the phenotypes of the heterogeneous illness we call schizophrenia. Her narrative draws us into the inner world of the psychotic person, territory that few clinicians attempt to access or assess.

Renée

Before R. D. Laing characterized *engulfment*, *implosion* and *petrification* as steps in the process of moving from reality to psychosis in *The Divided Self*, the Swiss psychoanalyst Marguerite Séchehaye (1887–1964) charted the contours, surfaces and textures of her schizophrenic patients' interior experience. She designated the dynamic mechanisms used by these patients to attain and sustain what she saw as their purposely diminished state, which was ultimately a way out of a world of reality that was too terrifying and too difficult for them.

In a slim volume titled *A New Psychotherapy in Schizophrenia*, Séchehaye interprets the seemingly inexplicable thought, emotion and behavior of schizophrenic patients, often making clear the meaning of a life that, to the uninitiated, appears meaningless. Séchehaye freely acknowledges her sources. Psychoanalyst that she is, she cites Freud, but also subscribes to the paradigm of existential psychiatry that took its philosophical anthropology from Heidegger and Sartre, producing prodigious figures that included Ludwig Binswanger, Medard Boss, Karl Jaspers and Eugene Minkowski. Laing, too, drew heavily from these masters for *The Divided Self*, which he published in 1960 (three of Séchehaye's books appear in his bibliography).

The clinical material in Séchehaye's book comes mostly from her patient Renée, a young girl whose mother withheld breast milk from her nursing daughter, frustrating an instinctual need. At around age 6, under pressure from the mother's physical and emotional abuse, Renée began to take leave of reality and was subsequently diagnosed with schizophrenia. Séchehaye worked intensively with her for many years, using "symbolic realization," a technique that she originated. This was a dynamic therapy intended to provide the "*satisfaction* (in symbolic form) of fundamental instinctual thwarted needs" (Séchehaye 1956, p. 52). In Renée's case, that need was to be biologically and psychologically nurtured by her mother through feeding, an essential maternal obligation that this woman inexplicably spurned.

Séchehaye describes Renée's mother as ostensibly "sweet and benign" so long as mother and daughter were in the presence of other people. But the situation was quite different when they were alone, as the mother reveals here:

> I have an absolute right over you; if I wanted to, I could kill you; I could make you steal or make you do any wicked thing without the right of anyone to interfere. . . . I know everything you are thinking; it is my right to know, even what you dream. And at night in my room, I know if you are moving in your bed; your body, your mind, your soul are mine; you have absolutely nothing (1956, p. 88).

This stunning admission elicited the following commentary from Séchehaye:

> These words did Renée more harm than the generous scuffing she received. To defend herself from this domination, Renée, at the age of six, struggled to formulate in her mind exactly the opposite of what she was thinking in order to protect herself and to withdraw some part of her privacy from her mother's prophetic power (1956, p. 88).

If Renée's situation does not satisfy the four conditions of Bateson's double bind, one may ask whose situation does?

1. There was a total disconnect between the way the mother acted with Renée when they were alone and when they were with other people. Attempting to adapt

to what amounted to two opposing messages from the sole authority figure in her life, Renée altered her thinking to conform to the mother's expectations of who she should be. She created a false self to hide her real feelings and thoughts. The psychic trauma that such a ploy must have caused this young girl, who had already been constitutionally compromised by the mother's failure to feed and nurture her as an infant, can only be imagined by someone who was not in Renée's shoes.

2. Renée had no way to integrate the opposing messages the mother was sending her: nice and validating in public; destructively shrewish when they were alone. The mother would not have tolerated any attempt by her daughter to authentically grasp and mitigate the conflict created by this mixed message.

3. Renée's mother was her whole world (the father is absent from this story). There was no one to show Renée how abnormal her mother's behavior was or to tell her that this was not the way other mothers behaved.

4. None of Renée's efforts to accommodate the mother satisfied this woman. Renée could not win, no matter what she did or did not do. She was continuous grist for the mother's destructive mill.

Such is the double bind. Renée's mother appears to be the epitome of the schizophrenogenic mother. No wonder Renée sought—and found—an exit to the horrific version of reality to which her mother had subjected her. No wonder she made a strategic retreat into the knotty world of psychosis.

Like so many clinicians who have worked with schizophrenics and thought about how their patients' illnesses came to be, Séchehaye believed that a trauma occurred early in their lives (possibly in the form of a Bateson double bind): one that never healed over, but led to what she called a lasting *frustration*. And, like Adolf Meyer, she sees this trauma as being both psychological and biological: "at birth the psychic existence is completely bound up with the organic [and] it is readily understood that need constitutes the perfect intermediary between physical and psychologic structures" (Séchehaye 1956, p. 52).

Throughout life, the striving for satisfaction involves mind and body inseparably. So does the traumatic frustration of that satisfaction. According to Séchehaye, "At a given moment in the evolution of the illness, in all likelihood at the time of the earliest crises, the schizophrenic suffered an acute, agonizing sense of his very being about to founder into nothingness" (Séchehaye 1956, p. 45). Such an experience of nothingness—the very extinction of being itself—would trigger what Laing called *ontological insecurity*.

Laing saw this condition of extreme emotional trepidation as making psychosis seem, to certain recipients of severe emotional trauma, an attractive alternative to reality. Whether or not someone in this situation will be able to resist the tendency to retreat into the netherworld of psychosis depends on his psychobiological constitution, the nature and severity of the trauma experienced and the age when the trauma occurred. It is generally agreed that the earlier the trauma, the worse the frustration and damage.

Séchehaye takes exception to the commonly held notion that schizophrenia dries up the wellsprings of a formerly vibrant life. While never doubting that the schizophrenic's world is pathological (Laing doubted this), she insists that psychotic thought is "invested with all the libidinal energy withdrawn from reality, alive, dynamic, rich in possibilities and extending its roots into the very heart of instinctual needs" (p. 133). This formulation of the psychotic experience at least partially undercuts the current disease concept of schizophrenia, which postulates that a change in the brain's neural substrate *causes* the schizophrenic's delusions, hallucinations, thought disorder, regression, etc.

As Séchehaye sees it, the "life spark" does not so much go out of the schizophrenic as turn in a different direction, and to a different purpose. In Husserl's parlance, intentionality—the natural leaning of the person *outward* toward the rational world and its possibilities—is directed *inward* toward a mostly self-contained world that answers only to itself. No doubt some patients have had their lives cored by schizophrenia—particularly those with persistent negative symptoms that lead to the deficit syndrome—though no brain lesion has been identified as an incontrovertible cause. This dearth of knowledge exists side by side with detailed pathophysiological explanations for a number of neuropsychiatric diseases, including tertiary syphilis, which is caused by the effect of the spirochete bacterium Treponea on the brain.

For those, like Renée and Elyn, who are caught in a double bind, the world of reality can feel hostile and destructive. A person in this situation may feel bereft and lost and, driven by a paralyzing anxiety, let go of reality, as Séchehaye describes:

> As he enters his psychosis, the schizophrenic lives through an original, altogether novel experience on the phenomenologic [experiential] level, dissociated from his past experiences . . . a gloomy experience [overtakes him], indescribably fraught with presentements [*sic*] of imminent catastrophe and intense anxiety. When the affective charge becomes intolerable, the delirium [not the condition of medical delirium, but a psychotic collapse of rationality] is crystallized and the patient feels relieved; the oppressive sense of strangeness, of unreality, of loss of life contact, finds a form of original verbal expression . . . (1956, p. 61).

On the face of it, schizophrenic verbal productions seem bizarre because they do not relate—and are not intended to relate—to the world of reality, but to a world where feelings of internal catastrophe involving anxiety, terror, anger, aggression, hostility, excessive affectivity or no affectivity, guilt, dissociation, fragmentation, disintegration, mutism, etc. are projected onto the image of what the patient still retains of the real world, and of normality.

The psychotic person's alternative world has its own language and grammar. To those who inhabit the world of reality, such verbal productions—dubbed "schizophrenese"—are unintelligible until they crack the psychotic's "self-preserving" code. Séchehaye came to understand Renée's reconstructed world and then learned the language of her psychosis:

> Everything is in parts, divided, torn, a piece here, a piece there. The world is an immense puzzle, a mosaic; each part is independent and has nothing to do with the rest (62).

(Renée is projecting here her own psychic fragmentation by seeing the world of reality in fragments that have no relation to each other, do not cohere and have no meaning.)

Cold permeates the world; everything is frozen, encased in ice; icy waters are rising to push back the earth's warmth. The sun is no more (62).

(Renée is projecting onto the outside world her own inability to feel or express genuine emotion. She senses no warmth in her reduced state and consequently sees reality as frozen and incapable of supporting life. The sun, the source of energy for life on earth, has gone out.)

Whole cities are crashing, avalanches of rock come tumbling down with a noise like thunder. Only crumbling, yawning holes, chaos and destruction remain. It is my fault, I am the cause of this destruction. I am destruction itself (62).

(Renée is projecting her own psychic disintegration and its catastrophic effect on her life onto the natural world by imagining the literal destruction of this world, piece by piece. Cities tumble into holes, crashing thunderously. She believes that what has happened to her interior world is happening in the world outside her as well. This is Armageddon, and she is responsible.)

In projecting her feelings and thoughts onto what remains of the real world she once knew, Renée is expressing both anxiety and guilt about the trashed world she finds herself in: both that world and the external world are crumbling, and it is *her* fault. This is not, as it first seems, nonsense, but a meaningful expression of a pathologically reduced affectivity and cognition. It is her way of being a psychotic person, of resigning from reality instead of staying resigned to it. Dramatic as Renée's psychotic productions may seem, the accompanying anxiety and guilt are far less than she experienced in the real world. Such is the psychoeconomics of psychosis.

In this state of regression and disintegration, Renée could no longer tell the difference between what was going on in her own mind and what was happening in the world outside her, which she had all but abandoned. As Séchehaye sees it, the schizophrenic "deforms reality, shaping it into something which concerns him instead of adapting himself to it. Intellectual realism might then be defined as supremacy of thinking over the real, thinking that stamps, modifies and deforms the outer world" (p. 135).

To someone rooted in reality, Renée's psychotic verbal productions seem like the ultimate human catastrophe. But not to the schizophrenic, who has to some degree *chosen* this alternative world to escape an intolerable reality, in what can be thought of as a *compromise solution*, as Renée makes crystal clear in *Autobiography of a Schizophrenic Girl* (Séchehaye 1970). Renée wrote this brief text to make sense of her psychotic life once she had returned to reality, and Séchehaye added an "analytic interpretation."

The purpose of the psychotically constructed world is to *protect* the schizophrenic from reality, to *keep reality out*. Eventually, to Renée, reality came to mean a "consuming Fear," which, she said, "I should prefer to escape into madness to avoid" (Séchehaye 1970, p. 32):

> For me, madness was definitely not a condition of illness; I did not believe that I was ill. It was rather a country, opposed to Reality, where reigned an implacable light, blinding, leaving no place for shadow; an immense space without boundary, limitless, flat; a mineral, lunar country, cold as the wastes of the North Pole. In this stretching emptiness, all is unchangeable, immobile, congealed, crystallized. Objects are strange trappings, placed here and there, geometric cubes without meaning (Séchehaye 1970, p. 33).

Renée's fear, with a capital F, derives, no doubt, from what Laing would have seen as her ontological insecurity. By this time, what she called Reality, with a capital R, did not exist for her. She inhabited instead what she called "a country, opposed to Reality," which had a vastly different ontic structure.

Very soon after Renée began analysis with Séchehaye, she came to understand that the "Fear" she was feeling was "a cover for guilt, a guilt infinite and awful"—which she had no doubt acquired from a mother who had repeatedly heaped scorn on her and blamed her for everything:

> During the early sessions, masturbation and the hostility I harbored toward everyone seemed to lie at the bottom. I literally hated people, without knowing why. In dreams and frequently in waking I constructed an electric machine to blow up the earth and everyone with it. But what was really worse, with the machine I would rob all men of their brains, thus creating robots obedient to my will alone. This was my greatest, most terrible revenge" (Séchehaye 1970, p. 35).

In her fantasies, Renée did to others what her mother had done to her. Feeling helpless in the real world, she attempted to compensate by becoming omnipotent in her imaginary world. (Elyn Saks made similar projections: "I have killed people and I will kill them again. I give life and I take it away.") Sometime later, Renée came to believe that the overwhelming guilt that tormented her came from what she called the "System," which was essentially a conspiracy of everyone and everything against her (Séchehaye 1970, pp. 35–36). In fact, the System was a projection of Renée's anger, especially toward her mother, and the feelings of destructiveness that were embedded in that anger and displaced onto others and the world.

This delusion was not just paranoia but psychotic paranoia, which becomes possible when the boundaries between fantasy and reality vanish so that *anything can mean anything the schizophrenic needs it to mean*. These defenses preserve what Séchehaye called the reverie of the "enchanted circle" (Séchehaye 1956, p. 51) of psychosis in which the schizophrenic is immured from the reality that threatens annihilation. Most of what the schizophrenic thinks, feels, says and does can be understood as one defense or another against that threat. Séchehaye offers this explanation for a hebephrenic woman becoming enraged after seeing a cup of black coffee: "Why does this innocuous thing provoke such anger and anxiety? Because the patient sees the coffee, not as the object it is, but in relation to the meaning she attributes to it: its blackness is the devil, come to tempt and poison her" (Séchehaye 1956, p. 135). Clearly this woman had some "devil" of her own that she could not handle.

Renée felt that the System did not want her to tend to her own hygiene or even feed herself. But it was her dis-integrated, severely regressed ego wanting to remain safe in the "enchanted circle" of psychosis and acting through an elaboration of her delusion about the System that discouraged her from taking on this responsibility (see Figure 13.1b, Chapter 13). The active compensation created here indicates that, even when psychotic, the self as active agent is not entirely arrested, and Nietzsche's will to power not entirely extinguished. The voices that Renée hears are anthropomorphized feelings of anxiety, anger, aggression and guilt. Through projection and displacement, these feelings, which are intolerable to her, *become the voices of others*, and, through this defensive ploy, lose some of their sting.

Séchehaye believed that delusions, hallucinations and other defenses that schizophrenics indulge themselves in are ultimately *compensations* for early *frustrations* they could not achieve in the world of reality, having tried and failed at this task. (How could Renée, at age 6, be expected to assert her authentic will against a world-class monster-mom?) Such failures could explain why so many schizophrenics *do not want to relate to the real world*, which is considered by those who live there to be their main defect. This "defect" is therefore meaningful and purposeful. Many patients resist, sometimes violently, the attempts of their providers to coax them back from their parallel universe because they wish to preserve the relative safety and peace they have found there.

To understand the *meaning* of Renée's psychotic productions, Séchehaye looked to the rising stars of existential psychiatry in Europe (this was the 1930s and 1940s), especially Boss, Jaspers and Minkowski. These psychiatrists were strongly influenced by Heidegger's ontology—the study of the structure of being—as explicated in *Being and Time*, as well as by Sartre.

Using Freud's psychoanalytic mechanisms—drives, symbolization, projection, introjection and displacement—and the existentialists' insights about the patient's interior world, Séchehaye came to see that psychotic symptoms "lose their incoherent, hermetic and illogical aspect. It is apparent that beneath a show of disintegration and psychic dissolution, there exists a well defined structure where the patient's images and expressions define a true function, a power of organization and equilibrium . . ." (Séchehaye 1956, p. 4). Sartre would call this organization the schizophrenic's "project," the arc people trace through the world that defines who they want to be and what they want to do with their lives:

> After I gave up looking for a psychoanalytic meaning in Renée's "experienced worlds," in her "world of cold and ice," the "desert world," the "world of implacable light without shadow," she was greatly relieved, and a point of contact was established when, in the existential way, I understood these images represented her manner of living in the world. Renée felt lost in a "universe of

> loneliness and ice"; it was the only "mode of experiencing the universe" left to her altered consciousness (Séchehaye 1956, p. 106).

Séchehaye was able to make contact with Renée once she understood that her verbal productions were *descriptions of the psychotic world she lived in* and not symbols of something else, as the Freudians would have it.

To enter the world of her severely regressed patient, Séchehaye first used pieces of apples (whole apples were too close in form to the breasts that her mother had denied her, and too threatening), as well as dolls and toy animals. By taking this approach, she offered Renée the chance to internalize a mother-object *symbolically*, without employing a *realistic* analytical dialogue, since the slightest attempt to be realistic with Renée led to serious and sometimes violent regressions. Séchehaye cuddled, fed and bathed Renée, like the baby she was at the time her mother first failed her. During the early stage of their work, the therapeutic venue was more crib than couch. Later, as reality became less terrifying to her patient, Séchehaye was able to take a more conventional approach.

Renée titles the final section of her *Autobiography* "I Become Firmly Established in Wonderful Reality." It is not entirely clear from her account how much of a recovery she made and how that recovery was maintained and built upon. With Renée, we do not have a summary of several decades of the detailed description that make Elyn's story so satisfying. At the end of her brief text, Renée is still a rather vague figure. But we do know that she was adopted by Mrs. Séchehaye and eventually became a psychoanalyst.

"Progressively reality was reconstituted and I became more peaceful and free," Renée writes with apparent confidence. "I was particularly relaxed amidst nature, in the woods, at the seashore, far from the stares of people. Subsequently I began to enjoy city pleasures, the large stores, the vivacity, the tearooms" (Séchehaye 1970, p. 86).

At first, Renée's "wonderful reality" depended totally on her mother's support and approval, a continuation of their symbiotic attachment: "[Mama] was the wellspring, the source of normal reality perception. She had only to alter her attitude toward me for living reality to be metamorphosed into a stage setting of arid desert" (Séchehaye 1970, p. 87). Even while reaching beyond her psychotic world, toward reality, Renée was still fused with her mother:

> Sometimes I did not know clearly whether it was she or I who needed something. For instance if I asked for another cup of tea and Mama answered teasingly, "But why do you want more tea; don't you see that I have just finished my cup and so you don't need any?" Then I replied, "Yes, that's true, I don't need any more," confusing her with myself. But at bottom I did desire a second cup of tea and I said, "But I still want some more tea," and suddenly, in a flash, I realized the fact that Mama's satiety did not make me sated too. And I was ashamed to let myself be thus trapped by Mama and to watch her laugh at my discomfiture (Séchehaye 1970, pp. 87–88).

Whatever progress Renée was making at this point, it is certain that "Mama" made no progress whatsoever—she was still the same monstrous, schizophrenogenic mother who had withheld her breast from her infant daughter and, later, abused the child verbally and physically, precipitating her break with reality.

Renée took a significant step toward reality when she learned how not to dissociate herself from the physical pain she experienced in her body. She tells of having a toothache and her mother prompting her to respond in an inauthentic, magical way, leading to the kind of dissociation that had become second nature to Renée. Realizing that the toothache was a part of *her body*, for which *she* was responsible, Renée took ownership of the pain: "Little by little, meanwhile, I began to see the pain as a natural phenomenon belonging to reality and no longer deriving from a magical origin. *And the oneness of my body and myself was conclusively accomplished*" (italics added) (Séchehaye 1970, p. 88).

Renée's disembodied, psychotic self was on the way to becoming embodied in reality!

> I succeeded in strengthening myself to such a point that at the end of two years [of therapy with Mrs. Séchehaye] I was able to oppose Mama and even—something unheard of—to defend myself when she chose to be annoyed with me. And without losing reality! In the matter of stable and valid perception, I had become independent (Séchehaye 1970, p. 87).

Before coming to this point in her recovery, whenever Renée's mother withdrew her approval (which she did whimsically, manipulatively and sadistically), Renée would regress further into her psychotic world. The fact that she could stand up to the mother and not regress meant that she was creating a boundary with this woman, beginning to differentiate herself and take root in the real world.

Renée's reclamation of reality was slow and came in small increments. When she first wanted to grasp an object that was some distance away, she motioned to it as if the invitation itself would bring the object to her. "There followed a long learning period until I began to understand that it was I who had to do the moving" (Séchehaye 1970, p. 87). She also had to learn that her body functions were centered in and controlled by her. "When I urinated and it was raining torrents outside, I was not at all certain whether it was not my own urine bedewing the world, and I was gripped by fear" (Séchehaye 1970, p. 87). These self-reports show us where Renée had to start from, and how hard she had to struggle before staking her claim in reality. As Lewis B. Hill (1955) put it, she had to stay psychotic until she could afford not to be.

Though we would like to know more about the life Renée eventually had, we will have to settle for these closing words from her *Autobiography*:

> If I can put it that way, reality became more real, more rich, and I more social and independent. Now I can accept Mrs. Séchehaye in her own right. I love her for herself and I am eternally grateful to her for the priceless treasure she has granted me in restoring reality and contact with Life.
>
> Only those who have lost reality and lived for years in the Land of cruel, inhuman Enlightenment can truly taste the joy in living and prize the transcendent significant of being a part of humanity (Séchehaye 1970, p. 89).

As if to show us that the psychotic world Renée created to escape the terror foisted on her by her undoubtedly schizophrenogenic mother, Séchehaye relays this self-report by Marie, a schizophrenic who had been a patient of the French existential psychiatrist Eugène Minkowski (1885–1972). Marie's compensated psychotic world included elements of imagination, escape, reverie and mutism. We see here the meaning and purpose of her living in a self-enclosed, self-referential sphere specifically created to exclude reality, the making of which could be seen as Marie's Sartrean project (at least at that time): "I was as though enchanted, living in a dream. I was in an imaginary world, living several lives, and in all these lives, I was the principal character. Once I was married to a good-looking American, who wore gold spectacles. We had a large mansion and we each had our own rooms. What parties I gave. Another time I was living with cave men" (Séchehaye 1956, p. 70). Marie makes it sound as if her life was wonderfully satisfying. But consider how this all appeared to someone who lived in the real world. During the time she was compensating for her frustration with a vivid fantasy life, Marie was difficult and aggressive, often catatonic, and she usually resisted the efforts of anyone who tried to make contact with her. She spent her time in bed, on her back, her head covered with blankets. If anyone persisted in trying to reach her, she would respond violently.

The account Marie gave to Minkowski of her rich inner life is an element of what had been preserved in this regressed patient and what she could still experience when she wanted to. "The revery seems, then," Minkowski says, "to comprise the very warp and woof of Marie's psychotic development and all other symptoms are subordinate and flow from it in direct line" (Séchehaye 1956, p. 71). The self as active agent is very much in evidence here—it is just a different kind of self, and a different kind of activity (Urfer 2001).

The loss of differentiation between the schizophrenic's interior world and the outer world of reality, which allows psychotic projections and displacements to morph into the kind of delusions and hallucinations experienced by Renée and Marie, alter not only the *content* of thought, but its *form* as well. This upshot is known as formal thought disorder, which includes pressured speech, circumstantiality, tangentiality, derailment, ideas of reference, incoherence ("schizophrenese"), neologisms, clanging, perseveration and blocking (Andreasen 1979). In the story that comes next, Kim's thinking is marked by major distortions of both content and form.

Kim

Diagnosing someone with schizophrenia can be a difficult call. But there is no question about the diagnosis with Kim, who was brought to the ER late one evening in October 1995 by the police on emergency petition.

Several weeks earlier, the house Kim lived in and owned was damaged by a fire caused by an electrical short. Though it was fall, she was living in the house without electricity, heat, hot water or phone service. Earlier that evening, a neighbor who knew of Kim's chronic mental illness and had observed her during periods of relapse, noticed a candle burning in a darkened window. Thinking that the open flame might lead to another fire, the neighbor called the police.

Kim, 38, was born in the United States to Chinese parents who returned to Taiwan after her father finished his medical training. Kim and her siblings remained in the United States. She graduated from a prestigious women's college and earned a master's degree in human development. Her marriage to an Asian man ended in divorce. There were no children. She had not been employed for some time.

Kim was first hospitalized at age 26 with what was then diagnosed as a psychotic mood disorder. It is not clear when the diagnosis of schizophrenia was made. The records available to us did not provide any information about her early course but noted hospitalizations in 1992 and 1994, as well as admissions in May and August of 1995.

When I entered the room to begin the evaluation, Kim was sitting on a gurney with a sheet pulled up around her. Her appearance belied what she was soon to reveal about herself. She was short, with a well-developed body, and had dark, shoulder-length hair that was well cared for. This attractive young woman was in no apparent distress and would have stood out in a crowd only for being attractive.

Kim knew who she was, where she was and the date. Asked about her mood, she replied that she felt "fine" and denied being depressed. She also denied having any intention or plan to hurt herself. The chart records did not allude to any past suicide attempt. Kim had no significant medical history or any current medical problems. She did not abuse drugs or alcohol.

Kim told me she had stopped taking her medication because she had died in the recent fire that damaged her house, had been reborn with a new body and a new head, and so no longer needed to take the medication that her former body required (she was not injured in the fire). Kim told me that God spoke to her directly, but she did not offer any further details. "I can see Europe," she said. "I have very different eyes." Her answers to even the simplest questions revealed strong underlying psychotic processes. "I am an Oriental woman. I eat and I shit. I don't know about American women." I cannot recall what question I might have asked to elicit that response.

I contacted the psychiatrist who had been following Kim for some time. He pointed out that her behavior in the ER was not very different from her recent baseline behavior. None of the neuroleptic and atypical antipsychotic medications tried—including Prolixin, Trilafon, Orap, Risperdal and clozapine—had benefited her significantly. Lithium was added to some of these neuroleptics and atypicals but with little effect. After her recent hospitalizations, Kim had been quick to go off whatever medication she had started. The reason she gave me for doing so this last time was clearly delusional.

Kim had not noticeably responded to individual psychotherapy or benefited from the therapeutic opportunities offered by her most recent hospital stays. She seemed to have been drawn into a fragmented world that none of the interventions attempted had the power to draw her out of. In spite of her obvious psychotic state, Kim's psychiatrist felt it was doubtful she would benefit from being admitted now. (She had come to the ER solely on a neighbor's assumption that a lighted candle in a house without electricity portended danger.) The psychiatrist felt that she could be discharged and agreed to see her the next morning. He planned to restart her medication.

Three weeks after I discharged Kim from the ER, she was hospitalized on the inpatient psychiatric unit. She was admitted again five weeks later, and eight weeks after that, and 12 weeks after that. Following each discharge from the hospital, she would stop taking the medication that had been prescribed.

The records showed that Kim was more grossly psychotic during these hospital stays than when I evaluated her in the ER. More withdrawn. More disorganized. More thought-disordered. More delusional. More hallucinatory. The following delusional statements, recorded in the chart, were attributed to Kim during her four admissions to the inpatient psychiatric unit that followed in close order after my ER evaluation: "I'm so superior to everyone"; "George Bush keeps running into my house"; "God was downstairs in my house"; "I am a Jew" (her chart notes she is Asian and Presbyterian); "The Virgin Mary doesn't need electricity, heat or phone service because she lives on a higher plane"; and "I am the Virgin Mary." After this last statement she added, "The one thing I really enjoy is sex." The records noted that, on one admission to the psychiatric unit, Kim had a positive pregnancy test and had an abortion shortly after.

While hospitalized, Kim also reported these hallucinations: "God touched me in my sleep"; "Jesus told me I'm his mother"; and "I have communications with Joseph, and he tells me I'm his wife."

It was clear that Kim could no longer take care of herself—she had been seen begging her neighbors for food. Adult Protective Services was called to investigate, and the inpatient unit asked them to look into what they suspected might be an exploitive relationship between Kim and her "boyfriend." Other instances of Kim's disorganized behavior included her planting flowers in her neighbors' yards and running nude through the alleys of her neighborhood.

During her last admission, Kim was restarted on clozapine. She remained grossly psychotic, delusional and thought disordered. The staff felt she needed intensive, long-term inpatient care, and she was transferred to a state mental hospital.

No reasonable clinician would question the diagnosis of Kim's schizophrenia. The skeletal DSM-5 criteria, comprising symptoms shorn of provenance, are met cleanly and fully: delusions, hallucinations, disorganized speech, grossly disorganized or catatonic behavior, negative symptoms. Only two are required for the diagnosis. Kim had them all except for catatonia. Her chronic course more than satisfied the six-month time requirement. Her deterioration was precipitous and nearly total. She had no medical condition or pharmacological issue that could account for her condition.

Kim embodied the phenomenon of schizophrenia, though unlike Elyn and Renée, we do not have enough information about Kim to understand why and how her psychotic illness came to be. We know nothing about her interior world and can see only the external manifestations of that world.

John Nash

John Nash is considered to be one of the great mathematical minds of the 20th century. A Princeton PhD at age 21, he is best known for developing the mathematics of game theory that was later used to plan military and economic strategy.

During the 1950s, while he was still doing what was considered brilliant work, his thinking, feeling and behavior became unaccountably bizarre, and he was eventually diagnosed with paranoid schizophrenia. Nash angrily resigned his positions at Princeton and M.I.T., making bitter accusations against his stunned colleagues. His wife was not spared from his paranoid rage, and after standing by him for many years, she divorced him (they later remarried). He floundered badly, could not do any sustained mathematical work, or teach, and lost the ability to function socially.

Nash had paranoid and grandiose delusions and auditory hallucinations. He came to believe that extraterrestrials were sending him messages and that the course of his life was being determined by certain sequences and patterns of numbers. He showed a partial response to Thorazine and Stelazine but refused to take antipsychotic drugs after 1970. In the mid-1980s, after struggling for three decades with a serious mental illness that required many hospitalizations, Nash mysteriously got over the worst of that illness and reclaimed a part of his life and his career. He was awarded the Nobel prize in economics in 1994 for work he had done before he became ill.

In 1998 Sylvia Nasar published a widely praised biography of Nash, *A Beautiful Mind*. She carefully parsed every phase of Nash's life, showcasing his brilliance, nobility and tragedy. It is clear from Nasar's book that, during the prodromal phase of his illness, Nash was anxious and overwhelmed by the pressures of work and marriage as well as by the conflict he seems to have felt about his homoerotic attachments.

Nash had always been considered aloof and eccentric, and he may well have been schizoid or schizotypal before his decompensation. These personality traits are not unusual in persons who breathe the rarefied air of mathematics and theoretical physics where the abstract is prized over the concrete and the hard edges of everyday reality can be avoided as a matter of course. Leonard Mlodinow (2012), a physicist, acknowledges that "one of the advantages of theoretical physics is that you can wander in different realities, and yet you're not considered mentally ill." Until, that is, a different reality becomes so "real" that it has one living what van den Berg called a "different existence."

Under pressure, Nash may have found it relatively easy to blur the boundary between a world that was becoming increasingly difficult for him and a more palatable world of fantasy. The weight of the evidence in Nasar's book is consistent with the notion that he dealt with his anxiety by creating a world where he was all but omnipotent and everyone was against him. This scenario fits Laing's take on schizophrenia as a strategy invented to live through an intolerable situation.

In the spring of 2002, PBS aired a TV program on Nash titled *A Brilliant Madness*. Nash provided some insightful sound bites, including this one: "To some extent sanity is a form of conformity. People are always selling the idea that people with mental illness are suffering. I think madness can be an escape. If things are not so good, you maybe want to imagine something better. In madness, I thought I was the most important person in the world" (Kennedy 2002). Nash seems to be saying here that he rejected the rational world after it became too painful for him to live there and embraced what van den Berg called the "different existence" of psychosis. The delusional ideas he developed seemed real, he said, because they came to him in the same way that his mathematical ideas came to him. To Nash, this grandiosity and paranoia, the hallmarks of his psychosis, probably felt like good trade-offs for what Laing would have called his "unlivable situation."

Once he had shrugged off the worst of his illness, Nash could acknowledge: "I thought I was a Messianic godlike figure with secret ideas. I became a person of delusionally influenced thinking but of relatively moderate behavior and thus tended to avoid hospitalization and the direct attention of psychiatrists" (Nasar 1998, p. 335). Nash seems to be saying here that by this time he could distinguish the rational world from the strongly psychotic one he was emerging from. To a considerable degree, he could pick and choose the parts of each world that suited him best.

Nash claims that he partially willed his illness into being and then willed his recovery as well. Of the voices that directed his life while he was seriously ill he said, "I began rejecting them and decided not to listen" (James 2002). His language is direct and strong here, and his words are those of someone who feels he is in control—*he* rejected, *he* decided (very much as Elyn did, it seems). In 1996 he recalled, "I emerged from irrational thinking ultimately, without medicine other than the natural hormonal changes of aging" (Nasar 1998, p. 353). To hear Nash tell it, what the existentialists call the self as active agent appears to have been calling the shots all along—though, for a long period of time, in the domain of a "different existence."

Nash's decision to return to "normalcy" was not a one-time thing but, as Nasar points out, a day-to-day recommitment to the consensually validated world: "Nash has compared rationality to dieting, implying a constant, conscious struggle. It is a matter of policing one's thoughts, he has said, trying to recognize paranoid ideas and rejecting them, just the way someone who wants to lose weight has to decide consciously to avoid fats or sweets" (Nasar 1998, p. 351). Nash's relatively good outcome again reminds us of how heterogeneous the mental illness we call schizophrenia really is. Among other, mostly unknowable factors, an act of Nash's will brought him back from a psychosis that he had (at least partly) willed himself into in the first place.

Psychosis: 1st Domain vs. 4th Domain

Taken at face value, John Nash's story challenges some of biological psychiatry's basic tenets about the provenance of delusions and hallucinations. How could a psychotic illness that lasted decades—one that clearly makes the DSM-5 criteria for paranoid schizophrenia—be willed? Wouldn't a psychosis of that depth and duration have to be a primary brain disease? Some clinicians are so certain of this they insist that if psychotic patients respond to psychotherapy, or recover spontaneously, they never had schizophrenia to begin with.

Though the DSM-5 is silent on the possibility of a willed contribution to psychotic symptoms, the DSM-II (1968) was not fully dismissive of this notion: "Disturbances in thinking are marked by alterations of concept formation which may lead to misinterpretation of reality and sometimes to delusions and hallucinations, which frequently appear psychologically self-protective" (DSM-II 1969, p. 36). We owe it to ourselves as clinicians, and to our patients, to ask, Must we presume a "brain disease" to account for a particular psychotic production? If the patient's narrative of life events suggests psychodynamic defenses that are consistent with the symptoms observed, these defenses may be sufficient to account for the patient's psychotic behavior.

It should not be forgotten that the concept of psychosis was created to capture a way of thinking, feeling and acting that is significantly different from what is understood as normal, or, as it is often said, "consensually validated." If a person can construct a sense of the world within the normal spectrum of consensually validated behavior, who is to say that person is not capable of doing so in the psychotic domain as well?

Because psychotic symptoms can occur with certain electrolyte, endocrine and metabolic derangements, and with the use of some illicit and prescription drugs—all involving real brain "chemical imbalances," and sometimes structural damage to the brain—there is no reason to conclude that all psychotic symptoms are caused in this way. Such a false conflation of the provenance of psychotic symptoms has resulted in many persons who sought help from mental health professionals being diagnosed with mental illnesses they never had.

The American poet Louise Bogan (1897–1970), who experienced her own depressions and mental breakdowns, looked into herself and outward to those she knew and decided that:

> All those odd things [people] do, like falling in love with shoes and sewing buttons on themselves and hearing voices, and thinking themselves Napoleon, are natural: have a place. Madness and aberration are not only parts of the whole tremendous setup, but also (I have come to believe) important parts. Life trying new ways out and around and through (Jefferson 2004).

Poets extend our view of the human enterprise. Bogan's words cut to the heart of what many people who fall prey to a psychotic illness are trying to accomplish by thinking, feeling and acting as they do.

As if not to be outdone by a poet, the psychiatrist Loren R. Mosher imagined a seriously traumatized person explaining a retreat from reality in this way: "Hey folks, I'm out of here. I'm constructing this world as it pleases me, and I don't need to pay attention to that world out there. I'm going to live in this one because that one out there hurts" (Mosher 2004).

All behavior has meaning, and pathological behavior has a *different* meaning that serves a *different purpose*. Eugen Bleuler, Sigmund Freud, Carl Jung, Alfred Adler, Jean-Paul Sartre, R. D. Laing, Gregory Bateson, J. H. van den Berg and many others independently came to this conclusion.

Chapter 15 Diagnosing the Heterogeneous Illness/Disease Known as Schizophrenia

What we learn from Elyn Saks, Renée, Kim and John Nash draws us into the inner world of the psychotic person, territory that very few clinicians access or assess now. The DSM-5 does not bid us enter here.

What Is Schizophrenia?

Though sharing common elements, Elyn's and Kim's illnesses are far from identical phenomena. Kim had no insight, while Elyn's insight, during her more lucid periods, was bountiful even as her illness intermittently waxed to the point where she could no longer function as a person or a professional. Though both had delusions and hallucinations, Kim's distortions of reality were constant, making it impossible for her to participate in the world of reality. Elyn, on the other hand, with the help of her clinicians, friends and antipsychotic medication, repeatedly came back to a baseline, not of normalcy, but of a precariously held reality. Kim had numerous primary enduring negative symptoms, accruing in the *deficit syndrome*, a permanent state of emotional and cognitive attenuation associated with a mental illness. But Elyn was only transiently impaired with negative symptoms, during the worst flares of her illness. Kim's illness seemed to have left her with no "center," while Elyn still had a "center," though, as she realized, one that would not "hold" and continuously needed to be reclaimed.

There is much about Kim's and Elyn's illnesses that remains beyond our grasp. In formulating their diagnoses, this knowledge void needs to be specified as precisely as possible. What we do *not* know about a patient is as important as what we do know or think we know.

Though we have a rather good psychodynamic *understanding* of Elyn's, Renée's and John Nash's psychic pathology, we do not have a biological *explanation* for their "different existences" (we do not have enough information about Kim to even *understand* her illness). In some psychiatric circles, it would be anathema to suggest that what we know now about these three women, or about John Nash, is all we will ever know. Or that mental illness will remain, after all is said and done, largely *mental*—with, of course, *biological correlates* that are unique to each patient.

No one now—not clinicians, not patients, and certainly not managed-care organizations and pharmaceutical companies—want to hear this. But in 10 years, or in 20, if no biological explanation for schizophrenia is in sight, the search for the "something else" that Meyer occasionally alluded to when discussing diagnosis, what remains unexplained after a satisfactory dynamic understanding is in hand, may come to be seen as having been a phantom all along. Meanwhile, we would do well to keep in mind Silvano Arieti's explanation for a schizophrenic patient's olfactory hallucination:

> A patient has an olfactory hallucination; he smells a bad odor emanating from his body. In this symptom a great deal of pathology is encapsulated. The patient feels he has a rotten personality, he stinks as a person. A schizophrenic process of concretization takes place and an olfactory hallucination results. The olfactory hallucination stands for, or summarizes, the whole life history, the whole evaluation of the self, the whole tragedy of the patient. We usually say that the hallucination symbolizes what the patient feels about himself. This is correct, provided we understand that the symbol is a symbol for us, not for the patient. The patient, by virtue of the symptom, stops worrying about his personality and worries only about his stinking body. What we call a symbol actually has a realistic, not a symbolic, value for the patient (Arieti 1974, p. 572).

According to this dynamic explanation, a constitutionally vulnerable person who is experiencing too much terror to continue living in what we call reality creates an alternative reality state—what we call schizophrenia—so as to be able to pull off this kind of "life-saving" transformation.

In the third edition of *Schizophrenia* (2011), edited by Daniel R. Weinberger and Paul Harrison, the argument is made that, while no biological cause has been found for schizophrenia, exciting progress continues to be made, and the momentum going forward promises theoretical and practical knowledge beyond what we have now. In a chapter titled "Neuropathology of Schizophrenia," written by P. J. Harrison, D. A. Lewis and J. E. Kleinman, the aphorism "schizophrenia is the graveyard of psychopathologists"—meaning that the careers of these investigators ultimately do not end well—is claimed to no longer hold. This elegy has been repeatedly cited in articles about the attempts to find a neuroanatomical explanation for schizophrenia (Plum 1972).

The once widely accepted psychogenic theories of schizophrenia advanced by Eugen Bleuler, Adolf Meyer, Frieda Fromm-Reichmann, Harry Stack Sullivan, Karen Horney, R. D. Laing, Gregory Bateson, Heinz Kohut, Silvano Arieti, Theodore Lidz and others were never disproved but simply tossed aside when neuroscience and psychopharmacology replaced psychodynamics as psychiatry's principal paradigm. The efforts of biological psychiatry to construct new explanations for the cause of schizophrenia, which biological psychiatrists hope will replace the flagging dopamine hypothesis, have so far produced a babel of disparate and nonprobative empirical fragments.

These findings are disappointing in their own right, but even more so when compared with the quite satisfying psychobiological-psychodynamic-existential understanding of schizophrenia that prevailed in Europe and America for almost a century. This approach to diagnosis and treatment was the standard before symptoms of unspecified meaning and provenance in the DSM-III, DSM-IV and DSM-5 seized the imagination of psychiatry based on the hope that each mental illness would eventually be shown to have its own biological substrate. What an irony!

If it turns out that at least some phenotypes of the illness we call schizophrenia are psychogenic—and ultimately psychobiological—it would not mean that these illnesses are less serious than schizophrenias that are primary brain diseases, where biology is the initial driving force. Meyer believed that the mind "can demoralize and undermine itself and its organ [the brain]," a notion that annihilates the fictional Cartesian separation of mind and brain.

Through epigenetics—the effect of people's lived experience, often referred to as "environment," on the expression of their genes—what is psychological can *become* biological, and we can imagine schizophrenia being born as a psychobiological phenomenon. This process could account for at least some of the neuropathological anomalies found in the brains of those diagnosed with schizophrenia. Other schizophrenias could be imagined originating as primary brain diseases that induce psychosis, as do a number of well characterized neurodegenerative diseases.

Considering how little we really know about the origin and nature of the mental illnesses that are labeled *schizophrenia*, and the observation of Ho, Andreasen et al. (2011) that antipsychotic medication causes a decrease in brain volume they see as independent of the "disease" process itself, the efforts of those who would medicate young people with antipsychotics, under the guise of arresting their presumed disease at an early stage (McGlashan & Johannessen 1996; McGlashan & Woods 2011) should be reconsidered (McGory 2011; Francis 2011). Before presuming that all manifestations of psychosis, especially in our youngest patients, are the result of a primary brain disease, we need to make every effort to rule out the possibility that these alterations in emotion, thought and behavior derive from 1st domain psychodynamic (Meyerian) reactions to negative or traumatic experience—even when this determination points to the failures or perverse acts of parents, or other adults in a child's life.

Karl Jaspers published the first edition of his *General Psychopathology* in 1913. What he wrote in the introduction seems just as relevant today:

> [T]he principal of this book is to present a psychopathology which, in its concept-building, its methods of investigation and general outlook, is not enslaved to neurology and medicine on the dogmatic grounds that "psychic disorder is cerebral disorder". Our particular scientific contribution is not to imitate neurology and construct a system with constant cross-reference to the brain—this always seems unreal and superficial—but to develop a standpoint from which to investigate the various problems, concepts and relationships within the framework of the psychopathological phenomena themselves. This is the special task of psychopathology, but time and again and at many points we shall of course find ourselves close to associated problems of neurology (e.g. the dependence of particular defects of psychic function on focal brain injury as in aphasia, etc.; the finding that some mental disorders are based upon cerebral disorders as with General Paralysis [syphilis], arteriosclerosis, etc.; the

conjecture that this is also the case with a number of others such as dementia praecox) (Jaspers 1997, pp. 4–5).

Jaspers makes a clear distinction here between the psychosis caused by the damage the *Treponema* bacterium does to the brain (in a primary brain illness with neuropsychiatric sequelae) and the "conjecture" that dementia praecox (schizophrenia) is also a primary brain disease. One-hundred years later, we are still caught up in that conjecture trying to figure this out.

What may ultimately distinguish the phenomenon of a 1st domain psychotic reaction from the phenomenon of schizophrenia (a 4th domain putative brain disease) is the degree of psychobiological disintegration—the "hit" taken by the organism—that occurs when a constitutionally vulnerable person is psychically traumatized to the point of opting out of reality to follow one escape route or another to an "inner" world, to one level or another. Meyer believed that a dynamically driven psychotic experience can alter brain structure and function. Seen in this way, psychoses of the 1st and 4th domains are psychobiological phenomena of different pathological power within what might be thought of as a continuum of psychotic experience.

Mrs. K (Chapter 9) limited her paranoid psychotic reaction to her family. Whatever the origin and nature of the anxiety that spawned her pathological thinking and behavior, it did not require her to be any crazier than that. In his schizophrenic reaction, as Meyer would have called it, John Nash (Chapter 14) needed to psychotically transform his entire world and everyone in it. At its peak, his psychic terror, an emotion that was an order of magnitude more intense and crippling than any anxiety Mrs. K may have felt, demanded an escape from reality itself. If we believe Meyer, Nash's greater psychological transformation caused a greater correlative biological upset as well, putting his illness well into the 4th domain and leaving us to wonder just what kind of reversible "brain disease" Nash actually had!

Diagnosing Provisional Schizophrenia

The time required for the phenomenon of schizophrenia to fully reveal itself as such—or not—can be several months, or several years, depending on a variety of factors unique to each patient. During this period of uncertainty, the diagnosis of provisional schizophrenia may be given to signify that some doubt remains about whether schizophrenia is really present, or when other illnesses have not been fully ruled out.

Missing a patient's schizophrenia can lead to tragedy, but a wrong diagnosis of this illness brings its own tragedy. As things stand, once the word "psychotic" is attached to a person's thinking, emotion and behavior, that person becomes, in the eyes of the mental health profession, a different kind of human being—one whose autonomous brain function has taken over that life, abrogating freedom. In such situations, the self as active agent essentially disappears and is replaced by a robot-like person whose actions have no meaning other than as productions of a compromised biological substrate.

To most clinicians, psychotic symptoms imply the need for neuroleptic or atypical antipsychotic medications, which are known to cause some of the symptoms of the illnesses they are prescribed to remediate. Many clinicians no longer think of neuroleptics and atypical antipsychotics as actual antipsychotic agents, which is to say drugs that correct a "chemical imbalance" that causes psychosis, as was believed for so long. It may well be that these drugs act as major tranquilizers for those who are uncommonly anxious, angry, agitated or muddled.

If psychosis has come about dynamically, the calming, often numbing effect of a tranquilizing drug would be expected to reduce the psychotic productions of someone who is overwrought. In prescribing medication for a mental illness, there is a world of difference between allowing patients to believe that the drug will remodel some chronically malfunctioning brain circuit and telling them that the drug will allow them to deal more effectively with the consequences of bad habits of living they adopted then lost control of. Clearly, in the latter case, a patient is far more likely to pursue a more committed course as an active agent in dealing with his illness.

Anytime a neuroleptic or atypical antipsychotic medication prescribed for psychotic symptoms is stopped, particularly if abruptly, and the symptoms worsen, the *discontinuation syndrome* should be considered as a possible reason for the symptom resurgence. This is not a relapse, or a worsening of the illness per se, but a *rebound* effect, caused by withdrawing the drug.

It is sometimes argued that, if a patient's symptoms are controlled with a medication and the medication is stopped or even reduced and the symptoms return, this means: 1) The patient has the illness for which the medication was prescribed; 2) The medication was controlling the illness; and 3) Withdrawing the medication caused a recrudescence of the illness. None of this is necessarily so. This effect has also been observed when neuroleptics are used, then discontinued, for non-psychiatric conditions, as when Phenergan (promethazine) is given to control nausea, vomiting and other symptoms.

Diagnosing the Phenomenon of Schizophrenia

Meyer noted that when encountering a patient with psychotic symptoms, many clinicians diagnose schizophrenia out of what he saw as "laziness." Laziness is still with us, of course. And, in these litigious times, we might add the fear of reprisal for underdiagnosing to the list of reasons why schizophrenia is so often overdiagnosed.

Typically today a clinician notes the patient's symptoms, lists them, counts them. Using the categorical, neo-Kraepelian DSM-5 diagnostic criteria, an attempt is made to "fit" the patient's aberrations of thought, emotion and behavior to the criteria for schizophrenia, which include the so-called positive symptoms (what patients do that is different from what normal people do) and negative symptoms (what patients no longer do, but once did, that normal people do).

Now what can go wrong here? Quite a lot, as it turns out. First, using the DSM-5, of the five categories of psychotic symptoms listed, *only two* are required to diagnose schizophrenia. Here is symptom counting at its worst, demonstrating the intrinsic fallibility of the DSM's method. How can two—any two—out of five of these symptoms (without known meaning or etiology) *specify the same disease entity and the same phenomenon?* Maybe a better question to ask would be, How many different phenomena does the combination of any two of these symptoms point to? Is it any wonder that so many people have been wrongly diagnosed with schizophrenia? Or that research done with "schizophrenics" so often cannot be validated by other research groups, or that the vast amount of empirical data accumulated so far on schizophrenia do not cohere in a way that points to an *explanation* (in the Jasperian sense) for this illness?

Any clinician attempting to diagnose schizophrenia using the DSM-5 criteria is faced with an essential paradox: It is possible for someone to meet the DSM criteria and *not* be a schizophrenic or have schizophrenia, depending on how one feels about the distinction that some insist on between being mentally ill or having a mental illness. This is because, beyond noting certain aberrations of thought, emotion and behavior, the DSM-5 does not satisfactorily define what it takes to *understand* this illness, much less to *explain* it. Anyone who believes that schizophrenia is a medical disease, like tertiary syphilis or Parkinson's, should heed the implications of this paradox.

The current DSM-5 diagnostic mindset often runs this way: a patient has symptoms that "fulfill" the criteria for schizophrenia; schizophrenia is a brain disease; the patient has the brain disease that we have come to call schizophrenia. When this happens, the diagnosis of schizophrenia falls into a hole of circular reasoning.

The way to diagnose the phenomenon constituting any mental illness is to uncover the psychological meaning of the symptoms a patient presents with. This is accomplished by exploring and characterizing his interior experience to see how trauma and the frustration resulting from it are affecting thought, emotion and behavior, pushing a life toward one pathological condition or another. This was the approach taken here with Elyn, Renée, Kim and John Nash. There are no checklists of symptoms for doing this kind of diagnosis, though symptoms are important in establishing a differential of possible phenomena associated with a patient's dysfunction and suffering.

In psychiatric illnesses of the 4th domain, the biological influence is believed to dominate. In the severest cases of schizophrenia, such as Kim's, we would suspect the greatest contribution from biology, though, as we have emphasized all along, there is no proof that this is so. What we can be sure of is that Kim's pathology comes close to *defining the phenomenon* of the illness that historically has come to be known as schizophrenia. There are robust and bizarre delusions and hallucinations produced through a clear sensorium, which rules out delirium as the cause. Because Kim was neither depressed nor manic, an extreme of mood cannot be invoked as the cause of her psychosis.

Kim no longer lives in the consensually validated world that we have agreed to call reality. Her thinking and emotions are of another world, where the frame of rationality, and of cause and effect, would seem to be irreversibly broken. The only thoughts Kim verbalized were those deriving from her abnormal perceptions and psychotic beliefs.

To us, at first glance anyway, Kim's thinking makes no sense. Neither does her behavior, disorganized as it is. She has no insight, no idea that something is wrong with her. Though we do not know the details of her downward course—her father was a physician, she graduated from college and earned a master's degree, and was formerly employed in ways commensurate with her education—it was certain she could not function anywhere near that level at the time of our interview. Her deterioration featured many primary enduring negative symptoms, which were sufficient in number and severity to qualify her for the *deficit syndrome* (Carpenter et al., 1988).

Even in the severest cases of schizophrenia, not all patients will have Kim's classic features. In the FDMI, the burden of making a diagnosis falls differently, and more heavily, on the shoulders of the clinician than with the DSM-5. One cannot hide behind counting symptoms or take the liberty of "stretching" symptoms to fit a specified number of criteria, since the "criteria" of a phenomenon are not enumerated. Clinicians must consider the Meyerian facts of a patient's pathology, the history as far as it can be established and the reports of those who have witnessed the patient's behavior. From this information the essence of the pathology needs to be culled and the phenomenon identified. As Meyer says, "The picture as a *whole* makes the *diagnosis*. There are no decisively pathognomonic facts" (Meyer 1951, p. 451).

Clinicians should not take patients' claims of "hearing voices" and "seeing things" at face value. Often these reports do not reflect true hallucinations but are heightened recollections of past experiences that can occur in moments of anxiety, anger, stress and need, signifying a dynamic meaning, often wish fulfillment. Those in mourning will often try to "resurrect" the dead by creating a voice or an image of the departed. Schizophrenia is often diagnosed based on such pseudohallucinations. For their own good, patients need to be set straight about what they are really "seeing" and "hearing." Some homeless people, many of whom abuse drugs and alcohol, seek admission to a mental hospital, hoping to receive food and shelter by falsely claiming to be having psychotic experiences and to be suicidal. It takes time to learn how to work authentically and safely with those who would con the mental health system in this way.

Any diagnosis, whether of a mental illness or medical condition, is ultimately a diagnosis of exclusion. This means eliminating from the differential—an array of candidate conditions and illnesses—those that can be clearly ruled out, or, when things are less clear, those that seem less likely. The differential will often include illnesses that are more serious and less serious than the true diagnosis. The clinician must keep in mind the possibility, and the consequences of, overdiagnosing or underdiagnosing *any* patient.

In diagnosing schizophrenia, several lesser psychotic illnesses need to be considered and ruled out, including what we are calling *psychotic mood reaction* (psychosis where a disturbance in mood is the driving factor) and *dynamic psychotic reaction* (psychosis where significant dynamic defenses can be identified). The DSM-5 would consider these to be disorders that are dimensionally related to schizophrenia and to derive from an abnormal biological substrate. In contrast, the FDMI takes these "reactions" to be 1st domain illnesses that originate, one way or another, in maladjustments to life's circumstances that lead to *partial transformations* of a patient's world, making these illnesses a very different kind of phenomenon.

As already noted, certain medical conditions, drugs and alcohol, the withdrawal from these agents and the ingestion of some toxic substances can cause psychotic symptoms. It is important to wait long enough for these effects to clear before diagnosing a primary psychiatric illness. For most patients this resolution happens quickly, but for others it may require many months. In some instances, prescribed medications, drugs of abuse and toxic agents cause permanent damage to the brain neural substrate, and the residual symptoms of psychosis do not clear.

The DSM-5 has rather strict guidelines about how long someone must display the major symptoms of schizophrenia—delusions, hallucinations, formal thought disorder, disorganized or catatonic behavior, negative symptoms—before a diagnosis can be made. For our purpose in the FDMI, the question of duration is redefined as how long it takes a clinician to be convinced that the phenomenon of schizophrenia exists in someone with psychotic symptoms. (For reasons explained in Appendix C, schizoaffective disorder is not considered to be a phenomenon here.) Social and occupational dysfunction, or deterioration, must also be considered, whether permanent, as with Kim, episodic as with Elyn or somewhat temporary as with John Nash. In diagnosing schizophrenia, the main issue is determining if, to what extent and why someone has lost the ability to distinguish between their interior experience and reality.

In significant ways, a child's mind and brain are different from those of an adult. Nonetheless, as more neuroleptic and atypical antipsychotic drugs become available, some clinicians feel the need to use these drugs with an ever-younger population of patients who present with aberrant thoughts, emotions and behaviors. Included in this trend are children who act bizarrely and clash with their parents, who are often pushed to the breaking point by this behavior. The diagnosis of early onset schizophrenia (and early onset bipolar disorder) flourished.

Taking into account that the brains of children are inchoate, which increases their vulnerability to pharmacological stress; that it is normal for children to have active fantasy lives; and that parents may be incompetent or pathological, care should be taken in assessing what may or may not be psychotic behavior and may or may not be early onset schizophrenia. The strongest argument in favor of early intervention, which rests on shaky ground, is that medicating what are taken to be psychotic symptoms will lessen the severity of the "disease" later on. Arguments against this tack include the long-acknowledged difficulty of diagnosing schizophrenia in children; the direct effect of antipsychotic drugs on a developing brain; and the side effects of these drugs, which, in some instances, include metabolic syndrome.

A culture that generally discourages individual responsibility and favors the presumed victim has led clinicians to look away from the connection between disrupted, dysfunctional families and disrupted, dysfunctional children. Instead, they hold no one accountable—not children, and not parents, who can both appear to be victims in these cases—and respond by diagnosing and medicating an often nonexistent psychosis.

Schizophrenia should be diagnosed only after determining that the patient's psychotic symptoms emerge from a *schizophrenically transformed world* as was the case with Elyn, Renée, Kim and John Nash. The identification of that world in a patient—whether the transformation comes about primarily through a traumatically induced psychogenic retreat from reality (Figure 13.1b, Chapter 13), undoubtedly accompanied by a psychobiological alteration of the brain and other organ systems, or, because a pathologically altered neural substrate "splits" the mind—must ultimately rest on identifying the *phenomenon* of schizophrenia. Really, we should speak of the *phenomena* of schizophrenia, since it has been clear for some time that this illness is phenomenologically and etiologically heterogeneous.

Different phenotypes of the illness emerge depending on the defenses employed by the false self, and on how, and to what degree the brain's substrate has been altered. These phenotypes are not the classic putative subtypes of schizophrenia (paranoid, disorganized, catatonic etc.) that are defined by symptoms (not phenomena), and have limited clinical significance (Appendix B).

Chapter 16 Manic-Depression[1]

In Berlin a woman jumped into the polar bear cage just before feeding time and was attacked by two polar bears. A psychiatrist later diagnosed her with bipolar disorder. It takes a split-second to see that this weird tale is a joke, which was told by Jay Leno during his *Tonight Show* monologue on April 13, 2009.

Humor momentarily rips the scab off a truth that is either being passively ignored or actively hidden. During the few seconds we laugh, we touch that truth as some facet of our experience is highlighted and our understanding is broadened. Listening to Leno's joke, I was reminded that, of the 3,000 patients I evaluated in the ER, and the hundreds I saw in other clinical settings who had been diagnosed with bipolar disorder, I was certain that most had been misdiagnosed. They did not have, and never did have this mental illness. Jay Leno's joke momentarily reconnected me to an appalling truth.

How is it that so many patients are misdiagnosed with this illness? The fact is that most clinicians do not have a clear idea of what "bipolar disorder" is. Nonetheless they continue to diagnose, and prescribe medication for a mental condition to which the DSM-5 has confidently given this name.

Before going on to characterize the phenomenon of manic-depression, a case will be made for how common the misdiagnosis of bipolar disorder really is. We begin with the story of an adolescent boy who was brought to the ER by his mother following major changes in his behavior.

The Blatant Bipolar Misdiagnosis of a 13-Year-Old Boy With Paranoid Delusions, Most Likely Due to Amphetamine Psychosis

Unlike many parents who bring their troubled sons and daughters to the ER, John's parents did not insist that he be hospitalized—an irony, since John was the first unambiguously psychotic adolescent I had seen in my 10 years of doing emergency

1 "Bipolar disorder" was introduced in the DSM-III and continued through the DSM-5 as a way of distinguishing unipolar and bipolar depression. The older "manic-depression" is reintroduced in the FDMI to name this 4th domain phenomenon, and to distinguish it from the "unipolar" depressive reaction, a 1st domain phenomenon. Nonetheless "bipolar disorder" (bipolar I, bipolar II) is used here when citing literature employing these terms.

psychiatric evaluations. Earlier that day, after feeling something whiz past his face while walking near the father's house—his parents were separated and the mother had custody—this 13-year-old boy called 911, claiming that his father had tried to shoot him with a gun.

Three months before I evaluated him in the ER, John had been hospitalized after his thinking and behavior took an ominous turn. He became paranoid, acting in ways that would be considered bizarre by any standard and delusional by the standard of the DSM-IV (this was in 2006).

Breaking the law for the first time, John stole a BB gun from a Wal-Mart store. He later explained, "I needed it for protection." Not long after that, while two of his friends were robbing a liquor store, he pulled a knife on the owner. Several days before I saw him, John stole a bottle of cold water from a convenience store. When I asked if he could imagine handling his thirst on that hot summer day differently, he said he could not, in spite of the fact that he lived just two blocks away. To all appearances, John had lost his footing in the rational world.

Two years before his first psychotic episode, John had been diagnosed with depression and attention deficit hyperactivity disorder (ADHD). He was prescribed dextroamphetamine (Dexedrine) and an antidepressant that neither he nor his mother could identify. John stopped the antidepressant on his own but continued the dextroamphetamine until his first hospitalization, when his doctors took him off this drug, possibly out of concern that it had contributed to his psychosis. In the hospital, he was started on risperidone (Risperdal), lithium and diphenhydramine (Benadryl).

The mother insisted that John, though taking all the medication prescribed, was as paranoid on the day I saw him as ever. Shortly before coming to the ER, he told her that he had lost two inches in height. He associated his shrinkage in some vague way with an altercation at school involving a young woman who was not a student there. John told me, with what seemed like total conviction, that someone had removed his left leg and replaced it with a shorter one. "It's no big deal," he insisted, "it's just a leg." He accused his mother and the staff at school of wanting to poison him, and for a time, refused to eat at home or at school.

During our interview, John denied feeling depressed and did not appear to be depressed or anxious. In fact, he was calm and somewhat upbeat, though not hypomanic. There was no hint that he feared for his safety. John was oriented to person, place and time, and showed no signs of delirium. He answered my questions willingly but left out significant parts of his story. He did not mention that he had been diagnosed with and medicated for depression before his first hospitalization, or that he was on probation for the part he played in a recent store holdup (this information came from the mother). Questioned carefully and separately, both John and his mother denied that he had ever been manic or hypomanic.

John told me that his father drank too much alcohol and had problems managing his anger. The mother described the father as "aggressive," and acknowledged that he had probably hit the boy in the past but was not sure if he had done so recently. John claimed that he was afraid of his father, but his mother said the real problem was that John resented the father's efforts to control and discipline him.

It occurred to me that the mother might be tiptoeing around the question of how aggressive the father had been.

Though John clearly preferred living with his mother, she disclosed that he would "cuss her out" at home and refuse to go to school. Sometimes when John's behavior became more than she felt she could handle, as had happened on the day of our interview, she would drop him off at his father's apartment. The father had a child with another woman, and, according to the mother, John resented the attention that was being paid to his 2-year-old half-sister.

John's toxicology screen was negative for alcohol and drugs of abuse, including amphetamines. The lithium level was 0.5 mEq/L. A head CT scan was unremarkable. His sole medical complaint was a chronic cough. The only abnormal lab value was a highly elevated alkaline phosphatase (ALP) (409 U/L; normal range, 25-115 U/L). ALP elevation can reflect a variety of injuries to hepatic cells, including the toxic reaction of hepatocytes with amphetamines.

Though John had been depressed and hyperactive for several years before I saw him in the ER, his paranoia and bizarre behavior had begun only three months earlier—and then only after he drank a "cocktail" (his mother's word) that was made by adding what he thought were ten Percocet tablets (oxycodone + acetaminophen) and nine penicillin tablets to a bottle of soda pop. Two other boys his age drank the same mixture. At the time, according to the mother, John was still taking dextroamphetamine for ADHD.

After reading on the Internet about the effects of Ecstasy—3, 4-methylenedioxymethamphetamine (MDMA)—the mother came to believe that MDMA may have been one of the drugs her son took that night. I asked John if he felt feverish when he woke up the next morning, and he said he did. (Amphetamines interfere with the brain's ability to regulate body temperature.) He also said that he had slept for an extended period of time after taking the drugs. This is an expected effect of the opioid component in the drug mixture he claims to have taken. Amphetamines, especially MDMA, have been associated with the degree of ALP elevation (409 U/L) in John's blood chemistry panel (U.S. National Library of Medicine 2015).

John had not exhibited bizarre or psychotic behavior before his first hospitalization, and there was no family history of psychosis. He denied ever using marijuana, cocaine, heroin, LSD or abusing the prescribed dextroamphetamine. My gut feeling was that John's paranoid delusional behavior was a direct physiological consequence of the drugs in the "cocktail" he ingested, on top of his prescribed dose of dextroamphetamine. I believe this is the most parsimonious answer to the "Why now-What's new" question that I have found so useful in trying to understand ER patients (Muller 2004). I asked the mother if the two boys who allegedly drank the same "cocktail" had any adverse effects, but she did not know and claimed not to have any way of finding out.

Since John was not manic at the time I interviewed him—or, according to both him and his mother, ever—no case can be made for a psychosis induced by elevated mood. One could wonder about a schizophrenia spectrum disorder, but careful questioning of the mother turned up no evidence of any prodromal symptoms or negative symptoms of schizophrenia. She insisted that John was outgoing, sociable and bright. Clearly, he was sufficiently outgoing, sociable and engaged in the world to join his friends in purposely breaking the law. He was in special education classes—getting straight Fs, according to the mother—but was tested and found not to have learning disabilities or to be mentally retarded. The mother reported that he was defiant in school and did not apply himself.

John was transferred from our ER to a private psychiatric hospital. His psychiatrist there, whom I called several days after he was admitted, had switched him from risperidone to aripiprazole (Abilify) and upped the lithium dosage. She reported that John's course had been difficult, and that he had been "bizarre, paranoid and psychotic," though he recently showed some signs of improvement. He was discharged, after 16 days, with the diagnosis of bipolar disorder.

When I told his psychiatrist that both John and his mother had convinced me that he had never been manic or hypomanic, and expressed dismay about her diagnosing John as bipolar, she was not persuaded and made no attempt to justify her diagnosis. That this was happening in one of the highest-rated private psychiatric hospitals in the country did not surprise me. After ten years of doing ER evaluations, I knew that most of the patients I interviewed who had been previously diagnosed as bipolar were not then, or ever had been, bipolar.

I was shocked at this psychiatrist's blatant disregard of the DSM-IV guidelines for making the bipolar diagnosis. John had never been manic or hypomanic, and he acknowledged taking, just prior to the appearance of his symptoms, drugs that are known to cause the type of psychosis he was experiencing.

John had also been diagnosed with bipolar disorder during his first hospitalization three months earlier. Psychiatrists are reluctant to alter a prior diagnosis, especially bipolar disorder or schizophrenia. If anything were to go seriously wrong with a patient following a diagnostic change, legal questions could come up, and legal action could be taken. In an increasingly litigious climate, many psychiatrists have chosen to practice defensively. Countless patients have become victims of this strategy.

The fact is that John's bizarre and psychotic behavior is consistent with *amphetamine psychosis* (Klee 1997). The first report linking amphetamines to psychosis was made in 1938 by Young and Scoville (1938). An Internet search at the time I interviewed John revealed that reports of amphetamine psychosis had recently skyrocketed. Heavy users of amphetamines are more likely to develop this condition, but those who use small amounts of the drug can also be affected in this way. Delusions, particularly paranoid delusions, and anxiety are the main behavioral manifestations. During our interview, John was not ostensibly anxious, but he did have fixed delusions of persecution. Amphetamines are thought to overactivate centers in the brain that modulate the fear response, and this excessive stimulation could have been at least partly responsible for John's symptoms.

Dextroamphetamine, which is metabolized mainly through the CYP2D6 isoenzyme in the liver, is not inhibited by any of the known components of the "cocktail" that John ingested: oxycodone, acetaminophen and penicillin. (The soda pop would have contained sucrose or an artificial sweetener.) It is possible that inhibition of amphetamine metabolism—through some currently unrecognized interaction with one or more of these components, or by some unknown contaminant—may have occurred. Diphenhydramine is a moderate inhibitor of the 2D6 system, but John did not start this drug until he was hospitalized following his first psychotic episode.

After John's mother told me she suspected that her son might have used MDMA on the night his life changed so drastically, my next thought was that the newly ingested MDMA, along with the prescribed dextroamphetamine he was taking, may have additively or exponentially increased the net amphetamine "hit" to his brain, to say nothing of his liver. John's highly elevated ALP could have come from liver damage caused by MDMA. (Hepatic encephalopathy also needs to be considered as a possible explanation for his psychosis.) Though John never acknowledged using this drug, it could have been slipped into his "cocktail" by his companions. This is a common "party trick."

MDMA is made all over the world, sometimes in home chemistry laboratories, and the quality of the product varies greatly. John may have taken MDMA contaminated with a neurotoxic side product, or additive, which caused functional or structural damage to parts of his brain that make it possible for people to live in a consensually validated world.

While we do not know the composition of the "cocktail" that John and his friends ingested, the preponderance of information supplied by him and his mother—along with the timeline for the development of his aberrant behavior—point to one or more amphetamines as the cause of his chronic paranoid psychosis. As an African-American, John was at greater risk for amphetamine toxicosis because members of his race have a higher chance of acquiring a CYP2D6 allele that causes them to be "poor metabolizers" of 2D6 substrates (Wood 2001).

John's case is unusual because of his youth, the fact that he was not a habitual or heavy user of amphetamines and because of how long—three months by the time I interviewed him—he had remained psychotic after ingesting the drug "cocktail." Though the mother said nothing to make me think that John had any premorbid symptoms of a schizophrenia spectrum disorder, this possibility, though unlikely based on the available evidence, could not be excluded at the time I saw him. It is an article of psychopharmacological faith that even a small amount of amphetamine used by someone with a schizophrenia diathesis can set off a full-blown psychosis. The "amphetamine challenge" is known to precipitate psychotic episodes in stable schizophrenic patients.

John's psychosis had an acute, as contrasted with an insidious (slow), onset. This suddenness of deterioration often presages a better outcome than when deterioration occurs gradually. Every attempt should have been made to allow John's psychosis to clear—as even a chronic amphetamine psychosis would be expected to clear—before diagnosing him with bipolar disorder, as had been done during his first hospitalization, just three months before I saw him in the ER, and again when he was hospitalized for a second time after my evaluation.

To me, John's bipolar diagnosis, made on two separate occasions, is indefensible. Even with mania—absent here—the DSM-IV prohibits the diagnosis of bipolar disorder when drugs of abuse cannot be ruled out as the cause of mood or psychotic symptoms. Unfortunately, the DSM is vague about how long clinicians should wait before concluding that these drugs are not the cause of the problem, stating only that most substance-induced psychotic symptoms clear after one month.

Amphetamine psychosis is a 4th domain condition (1st stipulation): *an altered mental state due to known physiological imbalance.* Bipolar disorder (bipolar I, anyway) is also a 4th domain condition (2nd stipulation): *a primary mental disease emerging from a putative altered brain substrate.* These are two very different psychobiological phenomena, requiring very different kinds of therapeutic response.

The *Merck Manual of Diagnosis and Therapy* (2006) offers hope to anyone who has used amphetamines and suffered the kind of consequences that John did: "Recovery from even prolonged amphetamine psychosis is usual. Thoroughly disorganized and paranoid users recover slowly but completely. The more florid symptoms fade within a few days or weeks, but some confusion, memory loss, and delusional ideas commonly persist for months." In the context of John's misdiagnosis and clinical management—which, as far as I am concerned, is clear-cut medical malpractice—the initially humorous story about a woman who was attacked by two polar bears and then diagnosed with bipolar disorder unmasks a tragedy.

Besides making John's psychiatrist aware of my observations and interpretations, there was nothing more I could do for this young man who had briefly been my patient in the ER. Seeing so many patients similarly misdiagnosed with bipolar disorder led me to write *Doing Psychiatry Wrong* and later to undertake the project that became the FDMI. Unfortunately, I had no way of contacting John or his mother to see how he had fared over time.

The Blatant Bipolar Misdiagnosis of a 19-Year-Old Woman With Borderline Personality Style

This next story of diagnostic incompetence and patient betrayal is adapted from a chapter in *Doing Psychiatry Wrong* titled "How Psychiatry Created an Epidemic of Misdiagnosed Bipolar Disorder" (Muller 2008). Only the main points from this rich narrative will be replayed here.

Alicia was brought to the ER by her mother after being contacted by one of her daughter's roommates. Earlier that evening, Alicia, a 19-year-old college sophomore, had been at a party and was spoken to harshly, then pushed by a football player. She became angry and responded with a verbal outburst. Later, at home, she made several superficial cuts to the underside of her left wrist.

Two weeks earlier, Alicia had been diagnosed with bipolar disorder by a psychiatrist, and prescribed Depakote. How a 19-year-old female with mood swings that did not include any of the features of hypomania or mania; who was sexually abused at a young age; who felt abandoned by her father and betrayed by her mother; who lived with chronic feelings of detachment and emptiness; who experienced worsening anger and depression; who showed a general unwillingness to take on the responsibilities of adult life; and who reported a five-year history of self-mutilation, could be diagnosed with and medicated for bipolar disorder is difficult to understand. During our interview, Alicia gave a virtual poster presentation on borderline pathology.

Whenever I interview an ER patient who reports a prior bipolar diagnosis—and that's about one half of the patients I see—I ask the questions from the DSM that would either establish or rule out hypomania or mania. As I put each of these questions to Alicia, she responded wholeheartedly in the negative (interesting, because her answers to most of the other questions were decidedly half-hearted). She vigorously denied ever having been in a heightened, expansive or euphoric mood. Her mood ranged from normal good (when she felt she was accomplishing something special, which, no doubt, distracted her from her base-line feeling of emptiness) to dysthymia (which is how she felt most of the time) to varying degrees of depression (which is how she had been feeling for the last few months). Later, when I interviewed the mother, I went through the same list of questions and got the same negative replies. "That's not my daughter," Alicia's mother insisted.

Alicia met none of the criteria for bipolar disorder and all of the criteria for borderline personality disorder. It was wrong and cruel to label her bipolar and blame what was aberrant in her thinking, emotions and behavior on a brain disease. Perhaps the most awful consequence of this misdiagnosis is that, to the extent that she and her providers accept it, the bipolar label will keep her from addressing what has really gone wrong in her life. This young woman was clearly living with what, in the FDMI, we are calling borderline personality style, a 2nd domain condition. She had not become the target of a 4th domain disease, as her psychiatrist had tried to convince her. The mood swings of many patients—and I believe Alicia was one of them—play out on a middle ground between a 2nd domain pathological style and a 1st domain mood disorder.

Alicia had to be prodded to engage in the interview. She acknowledged that she had been depressed most of her life and never more so than on that night. During the previous five years, she had periodically cut herself on her arms and legs, but never with the intention of ending her life. Alicia always had trouble sleeping and was having more trouble lately. Her appetite was down. Clearly, Alicia was in the grip of a 1st domain depressive reaction, the antecedents of which she would soon reveal.

Hesitantly, Alicia told me that at some point between the age of 3 and 5, she had been forced into a sexual act by the grandson of a babysitter who was about 12 years old at the time. Though she refused to provide further details, Alicia was more forthcoming about the effects of this abuse on her. "Most of my life," she told me, "I have hidden behind a façade," adding that she would often put on a happy face to hide her emptiness and pain. This defensive reaction most likely set the stage for a chronic depression that had recently become acute.

Alicia was an only child, and her father had abandoned the family years earlier. Though Alicia said nothing about this during the interview, the mother told me that she had never forgiven the father for leaving them and that her daughter was more or less chronically angry.

Alicia's anger and depression—each a life-transforming 1st domain reaction—kept her from authentically moving forward in life, ultimately short-circuiting her development as a person. Though Alicia had wanted to be a journalist, she did poorly in school and had withdrawn from all her classes two months earlier. She took driving lessons, but never got her license. The mother offered this insight: "Alicia has problems being an adult. She can't handle the academic pressure of school, or the social pressure, either." This young woman was living a life at loose ends.

Alicia, like so many borderlines, had little insight into how she had fallen into her quandary. She seems to have accepted and settled for her emotional numbness and isolation, with no idea of what to do next. Most of Alicia's trouble seemed traceable to her failure to deal authentically with her sexual abuse and her father's later abandonment. Alicia then became the casualty of a psychiatric paradigm which insists that all mental illnesses are brain diseases and ignores the meaning of the symptoms that constitute these illnesses. Her "mood swings" were the type that borderlines experience (Chapter 10) and were not due to alternating mania and depression, the essential features of the bipolar disorder she had been misdiagnosed with and medicated for.

The Blatant Bipolar Misdiagnosis of a 59-Year-Old Woman With Histrionic Personality Style

Angela's story of betrayal by psychiatry is also taken from *Doing Psychiatry Wrong*. Unlike John and Alicia, whom I evaluated in the ER, Angela was, for several months, my psychotherapy patient.

Angela's insurance carrier had been changed, and she could no longer see the psychiatrist who, ten years earlier, had diagnosed her as manic depressive and prescribed lithium. Married, with an adolescent daughter, Angela was then in her mid-fifties. She had been a nun but left the order when she was in her late 20s. Her chief complaints at the time she started working with me were serious conflicts with her husband and daughter as well as feelings of regret that she had not lived her life well.

Everything Angela said and did felt like drama. She came across as all froth and no substance. She was shallow, self-centered and selfish. Her husband did not make much money, but Angela felt no obligation to contribute to the family finances. She would always find some reason why a job she had was not worthy of her, and quit. She missed no chance to tell me how inadequate her husband was, and that included his inability to satisfy her sexually.

I questioned Angela about her mood. It did not take much prodding to discover that she had never had a manic episode or even any manic symptoms. Nor had she experienced any mood variations that could be stretched to hypomania. Angela's depressions were in the mild to moderate range of severity and never lasted more than a few days. Her mood swings consisted of these down periods, which reverted to a state of euthymic dissatisfaction and frustration, and then went down again, usually after she became more than usually upset about how her life was going. Angela had never had psychotic symptoms or been hospitalized for a mental disorder. She denied ever using illicit drugs or abusing alcohol.

Angela was not, and had never been, manic depressive. Without doubt, she did make the DSM-IV criteria for histrionic personality disorder. She also had some narcissistic features. For ten years, Angela's psychiatrist told her that her problems came from a chemical imbalance in her brain and that the only thing she could do was take lithium, which she did. During that time, Angela lost any chance she might have had to address the real issues that diminished her life and the lives of her long-suffering husband and daughter, who believed Angela had a brain disorder and that she was not responsible for her destructive behavior.

To make sure that I wasn't missing anything, I called the psychiatrist who had granted Angela's "bipolar dispensation," making possible her gratuitous life as a manic depressive. He told me essentially the same story that Angela had told me. He also stuck to his diagnosis, even after I gave him my reasons for believing that it was incorrect. Then he informed me that he had done a part of his psychiatric training at a famous medical institution and was on the committee that set the DSM-III criteria for mood disorders!

I asked the psychiatrist from our group who was managing Angela's medication for another opinion on her diagnosis. He concurred that Angela had never met the criteria for bipolar disorder. As I supported her in our sessions, the lithium was tapered. Angela tolerated the drug reduction fairly well, though her anxiety increased. She did not become manic, hypomanic or depressed, but she began to feel guilty about the pain she had caused her family.

About three months after we started working together, Angela went to another hospital for an outpatient gynecological procedure. She must have put on quite a display of histrionics there because at our next meeting she told me that her gynecologist had said, "I'm not letting you out of here until you see a psychiatrist." An appointment was made with another clinician, and Angela kept it. A few days later, she called to thank me for all I had done for her and informed me that she was continuing her psychiatric treatment at the other hospital.

Repeatedly in our sessions, Angela talked about her "need for approval." As a child she probably did not get sufficient endorsement at home to satisfy her need for acceptance and validation. Angela may have countered this shortfall with histrionic and narcissistic defensive reactions. During a difficult moment in one session she asked me, "Is my makeup messed up?" Angela scored 100 percent for histrionics on the Millon Inventory.

I cannot say I saw my firing coming, but in retrospect Angela's reasons seem transparent. For someone as histrionic and, to a lesser degree, as narcissistic as she was, the work we were doing, though acknowledged by her as helpful, was most likely very difficult for her. By any measure, we seemed to be a good therapeutic match. But what she found out about herself was not flattering, and she struggled to deal with some disquieting feelings. She probably imagined having an easier time with her new clinicians, whom I can only hope had the ability and the will to hold her to the therapeutic task.

Taking away Angela's ten-year diagnosis of bipolar disorder, which had become a significant element of her identity—as well as a justification for the person she was—cannot have been easy on her. If she wasn't a manic-depressive, who was she? With time, I believe, I could have helped her to find different, more authentic ways of being herself.

Many patients who have chaotic lives use their wrong diagnosis to seed the only identity they will ever know. The misdiagnosis of a mental illness in a vulnerable patient can jump-start a life of its own (Sinaikin 2004). This creation exemplifies a broader phenomenon that the Canadian philosopher Ian Hacking (2002, pp. 99–114) calls "dynamic nominalism." Hacking saw that by assigning people a sufficiently resonant label, or name (hence nominalism), some of them will behave accordingly.

Citing Hacking's dynamic nominalism, Joan Acocella (2004) explains what can happen when a patient is given a wrong diagnosis: "[O]nce you invent a category . . . people will sort themselves into it, behave according to the description, and thus contrive new ways of being." Some critics see this process as deterministic, but I understand it as just one of many social cues that people can freely, if inauthentically, choose to follow. In so doing, they are, of course, misusing their freedom.

Many wrongly diagnosed patients, including Angela, have modeled their behavior on the bipolar template, creating for themselves what I have come to see as the "bipolar dispensation": I'm sick, I don't have to follow the rules that apply to others. David Healy, Professor of Psychiatry and director of the North Wales Department of Psychological Medicine at Cardiff University, and author of *Mania: A Short History of Bipolar Disorder*, feels that for some people who buy into their bipolar identity, "Getting the diagnosis confers access to something close to sacramental" (Healy 2008, p. 240). "Bipolarity," according to Joel Paris, "is a diagnosis that explains everything and can be used to excuse everything" (2012, p. 89).

Differentiating Bipolar I/Manic-Depression From Psychodynamic Mood Swings

Nothing in the DSM-IV or DSM-5 actively encourages clinicians to pursue the meanings and origins of mood alterations that are often wrongly diagnosed as bipolar I disorder (a tag that can happily be shortened to bipolarity). Both Alicia and Angela were misdiagnosed because their psychiatrists did not pursue the underlying phenomena of their illnesses, the approach taken in the FDMI. Both had 2nd domain pathological personality styles that are known to include the type of pronounced changes in mood they experienced. Neither ever had a classic manic episode, the principal DSM-5 requirement (Criterion A) for the diagnosis of bipolar I, nor hypomania, which is required for diagnosing the conjectured bipolar II variant.

One may ask, how could this have happened? My answer is two-fold: a false psychiatric paradigm and generally poor residency training for psychiatrists. These factors are dialectically intertwined and have inevitably led to psychiatry's current crisis.

I cannot imagine anyone denying that 4th domain manic-depression (bipolar I) is a real phenomenon, which most likely owes more to biology—in the psychobiological unity that each person is, in sickness and in health—than mood swings that occur in 1st, 2nd and 3rd domain conditions. I have had sufficient experience with patients with borderline and histrionic styles to be able to relate their mood lability to the psychodynamics of their 2nd domain conditions. As palpable phenomena, these shifts in mood are usually distinguishable from the type of shifts that bipolar I patients undergo, which seem to be driven by an autonomous psychobiological process that overrides the conventional dialectic between self and world. This process is not well understood, which is why, in the FDMI, schizophrenia and manic-depression, illnesses of the 2nd stipulation of the 4th domain, are said to emerge from a *putative* altered brain substrate.

Manic depression is often wrongly diagnosed in people with mercurial personalities who display decisive changes in mood but whose behavior is otherwise within the normal range. This diagnosis is also wrongly imposed on those who are living in a more or less chronic state of what was described earlier as *pathological anger* (Chapter 7).

Irritability is an emotion related to anger that some clinicians have developed the habit of substituting for *elevated or expansive mood* in diagnosing bipolar disorder. This substitution is permitted by the DSM-IV and DSM-5's Criterion A, with the justification that elevated or expansive mood *presents* as irritability in some patients who are manic (Winokur & Tsuang 1975). The assumption of this equivalence creates a slippery slope on which many clinicians lose traction. One can be very irritable (or angry) without being manic. *Irritability alone is not the same phenomenon as elevated or expansive mood and should not be "substituted" for these distortions of emotion in the diagnosis of bipolar I.* Only by *not* recognizing the nonidentity of these phenomena could the DSM's "substitution" error have been made in the first place. If it's mania, it has to *manifest* as mania. If it doesn't, it's something else, and only an act of prestidigitation can make it *appear* to be mania. The "substitution" of irritability for elevated or expansive mood has, no doubt, led to many misdiagnoses of bipolar disorder.

"Soft Bipolar" Symptoms: Bipolar II

Moodiness and impulsivity, along with irritability and other negative emotions, have come to be known as "soft bipolar" symptoms. The conflation of these symptoms with mania and hypomania is abetted by the diagnostic imprecision of the DSM-5 but not by the FDMI, which identifies and characterizes the phenomenon that makes each mental illness what it is and not some other mental illness. Irritability, moodiness, impulsivity and other "soft" symptoms may be *properties* of some patients' mania and hypomania but do not constitute or define the phenomena of these elevated mood states. "Soft" symptoms appear, in varying degrees of intensity and duration, in illnesses in all four domains and occur in some people with no pathology. Equating "soft bipolar" symptoms with classic mania and depression is the main reason for the overdiagnosis of bipolar I and for the overmedication of patients who are misdiagnosed in this way.

Ross J. Baldessarini, Professor of Psychiatry at Harvard Medical School, has asked psychiatrists to avoid what he calls a "premature and potentially misleading widening and dilution of the bipolar concept." He notes that "it is hardly surprising that affective instability and fluctuations of mood can be found in many, if not most, other disorders." We have already made the point that wrong diagnosis leads to bad research (Chapter 2), and Baldessarini seems to concur: "Reasons for urging restraint [in making the bipolar I diagnosis] include the strong impression that classic bipolar disorders—an abundance of phenocopies, not withstanding—are about as close to a 'disease' as we have in modern psychiatry. At least, bipolar disorder offers hope of being a coherent and tractable target for genetic, biological, and experimental therapeutic studies. It would be tragic to weaken the [diagnosis of the] disorder just as it is gaining the serious clinical and research attention that it has so long deserved" (Baldessarini 2000). Baldessarini is speaking here of preserving the integrity of what the DSM-5 calls bipolar I disorder and what we are calling manic-depression in the FDMI. The DSM's designation of bipolar II is just one instance of the "dilution" of the bipolar I concept that Baldessarini warns against. It is possible that, without specifically saying so, the psychiatrists who diagnosed Alicia and Angela as bipolar had in mind the bipolar II condition, a so-called milder version of bipolar I, where hypomania is substituted for mania. The DSM-IV and DSM-5 do a poor job of characterizing and differentiating this "weaker" version of the parent condition, mostly by not taking into account the meaning and etiology of the symptoms specified for making this diagnosis.

If bipolar II is a real phenomenon, it should be possible to show that hypomania exists in the absence of any confounding conditions from the 1st, 2nd or 3rd domains. As far as I know, no empirical effort has been dedicated to this issue.

An especially nasty provision in the DSM-5 criteria for bipolar II (Criterion E) opens a hole that, undoubtedly, many patients with 2nd domain conditions have fallen into: "If there are psychotic features, the episode is, by definition, manic" (DSM-5 2013, p. 133). This directive presumes that all psychotic experiences derive from a brain disease, a tenet that is increasingly being challenged by many clinicians and researchers and is addressed here in Chapter 9. Many clinicians do not know how to parse the varieties of "psychotic features," or differentiate the meanings of these aberrant experiences. It is well documented that those with 2nd domain illnesses can act psychotically, though they usually do so only briefly. So, with the DSM-5, true hypomania, or even falsely construed hypomania may be easily "stretched" to mania, and from there to bipolar I.

The mood swings experienced by Alicia and Angela are part and parcel of their pathological personality styles—mostly borderline with Alicia, primarily histrionic and narcissistic with Angela. While these affective changes are *mood components* of their 2nd domain illnesses, they are not *primary mood diseases* of the 4th domain, and not even bipolar II, which would require Alicia and Angela to achieve states of hypomania, which neither ever did. The designation of four domains in the FDMI makes it easier for clinicians to see how mental illnesses have different origins and are different phenomena.

Bipolarity in Children

While few experienced clinicians would reject the idea that some adults can be validly characterized as bipolar I, it is not at all clear that prepubertal children should be described in this way.

Adults are expected to have acquired sufficient control to maintain the behavioral expression of their emotions, within certain boundaries. This capacity is achieved in part through the successful negotiation of developmental challenges that appear at more or less set stages during the life course. Children who have had a "good enough" early life (Winnicott) are usually ready to negotiate the challenges they encounter later—primarily from parents, siblings, members of their extended families, neighbors, friends, school classmates and teachers—while staying within the normal boundaries of mood and behavior. For a variety of reasons many children have not been this fortunate, and their mood and behavior *appear* to be beyond their control. In fact, many of these children, far from being passive victims of some brain disease, are using their freedom to express anxiety, anger, depression and other negative emotions. Often these patients are diagnosed—incorrectly—with bipolar I disorder.

What is really going on with children who are misdiagnosed in this way? A not "good enough" early development plus challenges that come later and are processed as unacceptable and unfair by a child may set the stage for chronic uncontrolled rages that can lead to a bipolar misdiagnosis. During my decade evaluating psychiatric patients in the ER, I saw a number of furious youngsters who were brought in by grandparents, aunts and uncles, older siblings, foster parents and the Department of Social Services (DSS). In many instances it was obvious that these children were being well provided for. But not by their biological parents, who were out of the picture, often because they were drug or alcohol abusers, living their lives on the street, or were incarcerated.

One boy was brought to the ER because he had trashed several rooms in his foster parents' house, refusing to settle for all they had done for him. What he and so many other abandoned children want is their irresponsible, in-the-wind, biological moms or dads back. They can't get beyond their real parents' abandonment which they experience as an all-consuming, all-determining betrayal. They are anxious (Chapter 6), and depressed and angry (Chapter 7). But they are not manic. They do not have a brain disease or need to take medication to "fix" what they are told is wrong with their "broken brain."

These children need to come to terms with what they have lost through their parents' bad behavior and understand the maladaptive reactions they have been making in response to this betrayal. And they need someone to love them, though this may not be possible for a variety of reasons, some of their own making, others beyond their control.

Angry, destructive children from middle- and upper-middle-class families arrive at their uncontrolled emotional states and allied behaviors along a somewhat different path. In most ways, their material needs are provided for. But under a façade of affluence and stability lurks an insecurity and related anxiety that owes a good deal to the instability of a society that once offered certain guarantees but no longer does. For the working class there were opportunities afforded by an industrial economy that required skilled men and women to produce a variety of products. For anyone who was academically talented and willing to do the work necessary to get the degrees and certification required to enter a profession, there were good prospects for doing creative work and advancing regardless of the socioeconomic class they happened to have been born into. This was the good part of the American Dream, which, of course, has always had its dark side. The shadow in front of this once bright promise reaches wider now, darkening the lives of all Americans.

The simple fact is that no one in the United States has it made now. Not the blue-collar worker, not the businessman, not the clergyman, not the lawyer, not the scientist, not the doctor. There is no assurance, as there was from, say, the 1950s to the decade that preceded the turn of the century that anyone prepared and willing to do a job would have one. Or, if they are employed, that there would be a supportive environment in which to do authentic work. Along with the insecurity and anxiety that come with a scarcity of opportunity is the reality that the corporate insistence on profit at all costs has compromised every profession. A once-revered American standard of excellence is fighting for its life in the rearview mirror. The loyalty and long-time commitment that were once hallmarks of American employers and workers are relics of a bygone time. The insistence on the bottom line, which spares no one working now, has led to increased anxiety, pressure, stress, burn-out, and to psychological and medical problems of all kinds. David P. Putnam has identified the sense of isolation that has overtaken Americans because of these and other changes in our culture in his well-titled book *Bowling Alone* (2000).

All of this affects the dynamic between husband and wife that children inevitably become caught up in. Some children handle their situations better than others, and, for a variety of reasons, manage to maintain their emotional responses and behavior within the normal range. Others make maladaptive responses to their situation and are taken by their parents to psychiatrists who lack the ability or the courage (often both) to explain what is really going on. More often than not, the parents' maladaptive responses to the pressure they are feeling will continue to feed their children's maladaptive responses. The psychiatrist, rather than face the challenge of telling the truth—which would mean confronting the parents on points they would rather not concede—and abetted in this evasion by the false paradigm of the medical model of mental illness and the DSM-5 (Muller 2013), will diagnose bipolarity and prescribe medication for this "brain disease." Such is the world we live in now.

Consider who benefits from a bipolar diagnosis. If their child's problems are caused by a brain disease, parents are off the hook. So is the child, because who can blame someone, much less a child, for behavior that is caused by a "broken brain" or "chemical imbalance." Psychiatrists benefit because once this diagnosis has been made, their role is limited to writing prescriptions for drugs that, through one mechanism or another, "stabilize mood." Psychotherapy, which is considered an "adjunct" to psychopharmacology for those with bipolarity, is almost always passed on to a psychologist, social worker or other mental health professional, leaving the psychiatrist to "adjust medication" as needed. With half-hour "med checks," this practice can be lucrative.

I have noticed that the more children (and adults, too) puzzle, annoy and threaten clinicians, the more they are likely to be diagnosed as bipolar, a call that is often made in exasperation as much as anything else, and is at best a clinical "punt." Not infrequently, clinicians put on the spot in this way will deceive themselves about what is really going on as they try to control and punish the child (or adult) with this diagnosis. There are reports of mothers with a combative, overactive child who have unmet psychological needs of their own, who insist that the child be diagnosed as bipolar, in a way that sometimes suggests Munchausen's syndrome by proxy.

Wrongly diagnosed children can also derive satisfaction from their new status as mental patients. If they have been unsuccessfully craving attention, they will have it now. Like adults who are misdiagnosed, children may relish their "bipolar dispensation," which partially relieves them of taking responsibility for their aberrant behavior. Keep in mind how well this worked for my patient Angela who enjoyed the benefits of her bipolar dispensation for over a decade, at the expense of her long-suffering husband and daughter. Kids know how to play this game, too.

The pharmaceutical companies have grown rich from the overdiagnosis of bipolarity, as well as a number of other mental disorders, especially schizophrenia and attention deficit hyperactivity disorder (ADHD). Many multi-million dollar suits and several billion-dollar suits have been won by plaintiffs harmed by using their drugs. Nonetheless the overselling and overprescribing continue because Big Pharma's profits are astronomical, and these companies can afford to settle any claim and still come out ahead (Healy 2012).

Going from the general to the particular brings us to the work of Joseph Biederman, Professor of Psychiatry at Harvard Medical School and Chief of the Clinical and Research Programs in Pediatric Psychopharmacology and Adult ADHD at the Massachusetts General Hospital (Mick et al., 2004). Biederman has received many awards, including those from the American Psychiatric Association, the National Alliance for the Mentally Ill, the Massachusetts Psychiatric Society, the New England Council of Child and Adolescent Psychiatry and Massachusetts General Hospital. According to *Wikipedia* (2015): "In 2007, Biederman was ranked as the second highest producer of high-impact papers in psychiatry overall throughout the world with 235 papers cited a total of 7048 times over the past 10 years as determined by the Institute for Scientific Information (ISI). The same institution ranked Biederman at #1 in terms of total citations to his papers published on ADD/ADHD in the past decade."

The arc of Biederman's rising star began to feel the pull of gravity in 2008 when he became the target of a Congressional investigation, led by Iowa Senator Charles Grassley. Biederman and other psychiatrists who did research on psychotropic drugs had accepted money from the companies that made these drugs, without reporting their income to Harvard as they were required to do under Federal law. Again from *Wikipedia* (2015):

> [The Congressional committee] investigated charges that Biederman earned consulting fees of a least $1.6 million over eight years from pharmaceutical companies, but did not report much of this income to university officials. Johnson & Johnson gave more than $700,000 to a research center that was headed by Biederman from 2002 to 2005, and some of its research was about Risperdal, the company's antipsychotic drug. Biederman responded saying that the money did not influence him and that he did not promote a specific diagnosis or treatment. In 2011, Massachusetts General Hospital and Harvard Medical School disciplined three psychiatrists, including Biederman, for violating conflict of interest policies.

David Healy, in a 2006 article for *PLoS Medicine* titled "The Latest Mania: Selling Bipolar Disorder," made a strong case that the bipolar condition was not only being sold to customers by the mental health profession, but oversold, often to the detriment of its buyers:

> What might once have been thought of as sober institutions such as Massachusetts General Hospital have run trials on Risperdal and Zyprexa on children with a mean age of four years old. Massachusetts General Hospital in fact recruited trial participants by running its own trial adverts [advertisements] featuring clinicians and parents alerting [other] parents to the fact that difficult and aggressive behavior in children aged four and up might stem from bipolar disorder. This does more than recruit patients with a clear disorder; it suggests that everyday behavioral difficulties may be better seen in terms of a disorder. Given that bipolar disorder in children is all but unrecognized outside the US, it seems likely that a significant proportion of these children will not meet conventional DSM criteria for bipolar I disorder. And given that it is all but impossible for a short-term trial of sedative agents in pediatric states characterized by overactivity *not* to show some rating scale changes that can be regarded as beneficial, the outcomes of this research are likely to appear to validate the diagnosis and increase the pressure for treatment (Healy 2006b).

So, it seems, the not-so-sober MGH and Joseph Biederman have conspired to load the deck and rig the game—to create a disease state for its youngest and most vulnerable patients and a need for some of the strongest and most dangerous medications in psychiatry's pharmacopeia (Healy 2007).What we have here is the "triumph" of the medical model of mental illness, the apotheosis of the belief that *all* aberrant behavior, even in prepubertal children, is ascribable to a brain disease. It is the "triumph," too, of the ambition and greed of those who stand to benefit from this misreading of the human condition: psychiatrists who run trials looking for fame and fortune at any cost; universities that employ professors who bring this attention and money to their institutions; and drug companies that have become top profit centers in the U.S. economy.

In the longer *Wikipedia* (2015) citation above, Biederman is quoted as saying that the money he took from drug companies that supported his research and paid him consultant fees "did not influence him and that he did not promote a specific diagnosis or treatment." It is hard to believe that Biederman is not deceiving himself and others here. Would he have been so inclined to think about the conditions of the very young children he diagnosed as bipolar in the absence of the financial and professional incentives offered by drug companies for doing so? Would he have been so ready to ascribe these problems to a 4th domain putative brain disease rather than to conditions of the 1st and 2nd domains?

Considering the boundaries that Biedeman exceeded in diagnosing prepubertal children as bipolar and the harm the drugs he prescribed could cause youngsters whose brains were still developing, it requires an unusually large suspension of disbelief to take him at his word. How could Biederman *not* have been influenced by what the drug companies offered him? That a non-biological, non-disease assessment of these young patients' conditions would have profited him nothing comparable to what he received is surely a strong biasing factor, as it is with other clinicians and researchers working with patients having other mental illnesses. The simple, horrible fact is that in psychiatry now, there is no money to be made and no fame to be gained by pursuing the truth about what is really going on with patients. The payoff comes with treating symptoms of undetermined meaning and unestablished origin with drugs that lessen these symptoms.

American academicians know this and write their grant applications accordingly. The need to keep academic psychiatry departments funded contributes mightily to the continuance of the medical model of mental illness. So does the need for faculty members to stay on good terms with psychiatry departments of other universities that follow the medical model. Every year, professors fill out questionnaires that are used to compile department rankings, which have become all the rage in academia. No one wants to offend anyone now. The mantra followed by politicians—to get along, go along—has been adopted by academic psychiatrists. For a number of reasons, political correctness in psychiatry has trumped the desire to be right (Satel 2000).

Joel Paris offers a precise and compelling critique of the recent trend, particularly in the United States, of diagnosing prepubertal children with bipolar disorder based on equating symptoms of "soft bipolarity" with classic manic-depression (Paris 2012, pp. 65–71). Paris expresses empathy for parents who are forced to bear the brunt of their angry, irritable, impulsive, irascible, hyperactive, moody, disruptive, combative, oppositional, defiant, conduct-disordered, self-destructive children. These emotions and behaviors are components of what has come to be known as "soft bipolarity," which many clinicians "stretch" into bipolar disorder. (What is *not* seen in these children is hypomania or mania.) Parents in this situation are overwhelmed and desperate for any intervention that promises to lessen their suffering and that of their children. They do not understand, or, in some instances care, that the symptoms their child exhibits have been "stretched." Bombarded by the direct advertising of "mood stabilizing" drugs, they are primed to accept a diagnosis of bipolarity, and grateful for a promised pharmacological solution to their child's often frightening behavior.

The rapid swings from one mood to another of these out-of-control children are often misread as ultra-rapid cycling and grandiosity, symptoms of bipolarity. "It is quite a leap," Paris says, "to see such phenomena as bipolarity" (2012, p. 66). Nonetheless, many clinicians take this leap, and for more or less the same reasons they do with adults. This is ground-zero for the misdiagnosis of bipolar disorder.

Paris thinks of the child's assemblage of soft symptoms as *emotional dysregulation* (2012, p. 66), analogous to but less deeply ingrained and enduring than the adult's more trait-like soft symptoms, which he calls *affective instability* (2012, pp. 37–43). Clinicians need some way to name what is really going on in the lives of children who are wrongly tagged with bipolar disorder, and emotional dysregulation seems to capture their experience rather well.

A key issue here is whether prepubertal children with emotional dysregulation go on to become classically bipolar. Paris's survey of the literature reveals that this is not the case. These children continue to be impulsive and unstable and show evidence of emotional dysregulation evidenced by anxiety, substance abuse, unipolar depression and personality disorders. But they do not develop bipolar I or bipolar II conditions as adolescents and adults. "Thus," Paris concludes, "soft bipolarity only predicts soft bipolarity. Any link to classic bipolarity has to be taken on faith . . . one does not see specific treatment responses in these children that resemble what one sees in adult patients with bipolar disorder" (2012, p. 68).

The drugs used for these young patients usually calm them down, but this is due to the nonspecific effect of their tranquilizing action.

Paris offers this overview of the pediatric bipolar "stretch": "Children who are now being diagnosed with 'pediatric bipolar disorder' present with affective instability accompanied by impulsive behaviors—symptoms that are very common among children in community studies (Duffy 2007) and among the most frequent reasons why children are referred to psychiatrists. It is only in the present climate of psychiatry that they have come to be diagnosed as bipolar" (2012, p. 69).

Paris sees the overdiagnosis of bipolarity as a "fad." "Fads," he believes, "are novel ideas that are spread by social contagion and find widespread adherence and enthusiasm. Scientific ideas insufficiently backed up by data can also be fads. No one is immune—not professors, not researchers, and certainly not mental health professionals. Unfortunately, fads lead us to believe things that are neither true nor helpful" (2012, p. 75). Like all fads, this one will most likely run its course.

The United States is the epicenter for the epidemic of misdiagnosed bipolarity in children and adults. It is where this fad got its start and continues to surge, though not without growing, articulate opposition. Both David Healy and Joel Paris work in psychiatry departments outside the United States, where they no doubt feel freer to speak their minds than most American academicians.

Anyone who is making the point that bipolar disorder is overdiagnosed needs to recognize that other researchers have come to the opposite conclusion—that this mental illness is underdiagnosed. Nassir Ghaemi, Director of the Mood Disorders Program in the Department of Psychiatry at Tufts Medical Center, has reported data from a study of 48 patients who were previously diagnosed with unipolar depression where 19 of these patients were re-diagnosed as bipolar I using the DSM-IV criteria (Ghaemi et al. 1999).

My first question is, considering all that has been said here about the "wobble" in the DSM criteria for bipolar I, are the re-diagnoses of these 19 patients true assessments of the bipolar phenomenon? Before relegating these patients to a 4th domain disease state, I would like to see if they could be understood as having conditions of the 1st or 2nd domains—the 2nd domain especially, where narcissistic, histrionic and borderline personality styles include the characteristic shifts in mood that can be, and often have been mistaken for mania.

That said, some people who should have been diagnosed as bipolar I were not. Others, no doubt, had that diagnosis delayed, putting their welfare, and, in some instances, their lives at risk. But a missed bipolar I diagnosis in one patient does not mitigate the unwarranted diagnosis in another patient. I have seen hundreds of patients misdiagnosed as bipolar but not one whose bipolar illness was missed! "The argument that unrecognized bipolarity is rampant in psychiatry," Paris says, "is based more on ideology than on evidence" (2012, p. 47).

Kay Redfield Jamison: An Exemplar of the Phenomenon of Manic-Depression (Bipolar I)

An Unquiet Mind (1995) is Kay Jamison's vivid and poignant memoir of her life with manic-depression (bipolar I), which was evidenced by full-blown mania, alternating with severe, sometimes suicidal, depression. Though the symptoms were classic, her illness went undiagnosed and untreated for many years.

By providing a description of her long struggle with this illness, Jamison, a clinical psychologist and Professor of Psychiatry at the Johns Hopkins University School of Medicine, makes it clear that she thoroughly *understands* (in the Jasperian sense) the pathology that has overtaken her life. But beyond some biological generalities, she cannot *explain* (in the Jasperian sense) the pathophysiology that is presumed to underlie it. Neither can anyone else.

Joel Paris captures this situation starkly: "We just do not know what is and is not bipolarity" (Paris 2012, p. 35). Yet the presumption is that the illness Jamison describes—by any measure an exemplar of some real phenomenon—originates in an aberration of brain structure and function. In the FDMI, we regard Jamison's manic-depression as a putative brain disease of the 4th domain (second stipulation), with the understanding that no definitive empirical proof exists for this claim.

Jamison gives this brief overview of how, almost from the beginning, her life was dominated by emotion and mood: "For as long as I can remember I was frighteningly, although often wonderfully, beholden to moods. Intensely emotional as a child, mercurial as a young girl, first severely as an adolescent, and then unrelentingly caught up in the cycles of manic-depressive illness by the time I began my professional life, I became, both by necessity and intellectual inclination, a student of moods" (1995, pp. 4–5).

Thus Jamison begins her characterization of the phenomenon of classic manic-depression. She becomes "beholden to moods," which is to say her life is driven by her moods, both good and bad, high and low, frightening and wonderful. Eventually she becomes "caught up" in *cycles* of elevated and depressed mood, which distinguishes her condition from other (unipolar) affective illnesses, and suggests an aberrant biological substrate.

"My manias," Jamison tells us, "at least in their early and mild forms, were absolutely intoxicating states that gave rise to great personal pleasure, an incomparable flow of thoughts, and a ceaseless energy that allowed the translation of new ideas into papers and projects" (pp. 5–6). The "high" side of her mood was so agreeable, and so useful in her academic career that she delayed getting any kind of help, even as her alternating mood states became more violent and frightening. For 10 years, she deceived herself about the mental illness that was rapidly overtaking her life, even as she was learning how to diagnose others with this condition. It was only after she was hired as an assistant professor of psychiatry at the University of California, Los Angeles (UCLA) that she sought help and reluctantly began taking the lithium that saved her life.

Jamison grew up in a suburb outside of Washington, D.C.—her father was a test pilot and meteorologist for the Air Force—but moved with her family to San Jose, California, in 1961 when he retired from the military and took a job with the Rand Corporation. A talented student and athlete, Jamison did well at Pacific Palisades High School, thriving in this new environment. But underneath all her success and outward appearance of wellbeing, she began to have the same kind of "black and chaotic moods" that she had recognized for many years in her expansive and charismatic father. These moods and his erratic behavior eventually cost him his job at Rand. "By the time I was sixteen or seventeen," she informs us, "it became clear that my energies and enthusiasms could be exhausting to the people around me, and after long weeks of flying high and sleeping little, my thinking would take a downward turn toward the really dark and brooding side of life" (p. 35). Jamison knew that something was wrong, but she did not know what it was. She was depressed and often thought of killing herself.

By the time she began college at UCLA, Jamison's mercurial moods had evolved into classic manic-depression: mania brought euphoria, increased energy and productivity; a higher level of creativity; a greater awareness and expression of her sexuality; and a need to spend money that she did not have. But then the depression came, which led to reduced energy, interest and productivity, as well as thoughts of dying and hastening her own death.

Jamison describes her college experience as "a terrible struggle, a recurring nightmare of violent and dreadful moods spelled only now and again by weeks, sometimes months, of great fun, passion, high enthusiasms, and long runs of very hard but enjoyable work" (p. 42). We get a close look at how someone who has already proved herself academically is both helped and hindered as manic-depressive illness takes hold of—Meyer would have said "impinges on"—her life: "Much as it did during my senior year in high school, my classwork during these galvanized [hypomanic to early manic] periods seemed very straightforward, and I found examinations, laboratory work, and papers almost absurdly easy during the weeks that the high-flying times would last" (pp. 43–44). She also took up political causes, joined demonstrations and generally felt as if she had power over a world that stretched far beyond her usual life as a student.

"But then as night inevitably goes after the day," Jamison tells us, "my mood would crash, and my mind would grind to a halt. I lost all interest in my schoolwork, friends, reading, wandering, or daydreaming" (p. 44). She woke up each morning not knowing how she would get through the day. What were endless horizons when she was high turned into brick walls after the crash. She had no idea of what was happening to her life.

After completing a doctorate in clinical psychology at UCLA, Jamison became an assistant professor in the psychiatry department there in July 1974. She jumped at the chance to pursue her own research ideas and, as she put it, worked very hard and slept very little, continuing a pattern she had followed in graduate school. Her mood and productivity had been "up" for a long stretch when, at the end of that summer, she "switched" from a productive hypomania to an incapacitating full-blown mania that led to her first hospitalization.

At this point, Kay Jamison found herself beyond her "familiar levels of exuberance and into florid madness," what she calls her "black mania." As so often happens in the natural—unmedicated—state, productive hypomania broke its bounds, lost its traction in the world of cause and effect, and devolved into a useless, manic wheel-spinning. In full-blown mania, common sense, which Meyer saw as the essence of the consensual validation that makes normal life and the social order possible, goes with the wind. Full-blown mania undercuts the reality of *limits*, which are part and parcel of a sane life. Psychotic mania is living proof that the limits sane people observe are elements of the landscape of what we understand as reality and sanity.

Jamison describes how the wheels came off her spending when her "milder manic moods" (productive hypomania) broke their bounds. Credit cards became her best friend. She bought 12 snakebite kits from a pharmacy. Why? Because she believed that God had chosen her and only her to protect herself and her friends from the threat of rattlesnakes in and around Los Angeles (it is not clear that she ever distributed these kits). While in the drugstore, Jamison thought of alerting the *Los Angeles Times* to the rattlesnake threat, but she was too incoherent at the time to follow through with this plan.

On another occasion, within the span of an hour, she bought 3 expensive watches. Later, she bought 20 Penguin books because she thought "it could be nice if the penguins could form a colony." Jamison estimates that she spent more than $30,000 during her two major manic episodes and "God only knows how much more during my frequent milder manias." During some of her agitated black manias, which she describes as "psychotic, seizurelike attacks," she was angry, aggressive, destructive and violent, even with close friends and lovers.

Jamison lists some of the *positive* aspects of her milder manias: "heightened energy and perceptual awareness, increased fluidity and originality of thinking, intense exhilaration of moods and experience, increased sexual desire, expansiveness of vision, and a lengthened grasp of aspiration" (p. 128). She says that she makes it clear to her students that manic-depression can have an upside.

In a chapter titled "The Charnel House," we are introduced to the severe, suicidal and psychotic depression that inevitably came with Jamison's crashes from full-blown mania, which can be counted on to occur when she stops taking lithium. (In her phenotype of manic-depression, mania is the relapse default, which is followed by a long, crippling depression. Her most severe depressions are the kind that Freud and others describe as melancholia). We are told what it was like for her to slide off the cliff of her black mania into this devastating emotional pit:

> Suicidal depression, I decided in the midst of my indescribably awful, eighteen-month bout of it, is God's way of keeping manics in their place. It works. Profound melancholia is a day-in, day-out, night-in, night-out, almost arterial level of agony. It is a pitiless, unrelenting pain that affords no window of hope, no alternative to a grim and brackish existence, and no respite from the cold undercurrents of thought and feeling that dominate the horribly restless nights of despair (p. 114).

Jamison thinks of her manic-depression as a "medical illness." Suffering plagued her body as well as her mind: her agony is "arterial"; she is "bloodless"; she is "bone-weary"; she speaks of her "depleted marrowbone." The life-blood seems to go out of her, compromising vital organs. We are reminded of the antidepressant drug ad that points out, correctly, that "depression hurts." How could it not hurt, considering the psychobiological perturbation of self we know melancholic depression to be?

During the 18 months that Jamison struggled with this melancholia, she seemed to have one foot in the grave. Everything reminded her of the fact that death is everyone's ultimate fate. Worse, she "saw Death everywhere," in every passing moment. She experienced time sluggishly, as a burden. She might as well have been moving through molasses: "Washing my hair took hours to do, and it drained me for hours afterward; filling the ice-cube tray was beyond my capacity, and I occasionally slept in the same clothes I had worn during the day because I was too exhausted to undress" (p. 111). The over-the-top energy of her manic state became no energy at all in her melancholic depression.

Intermittently, Jamison was suicidal, thinking of ways to bring on the death that permeated her thoughts and emotions. She considered jumping from the top of a stairwell at the hospital where she worked. She did not want to be with friends because she felt her constant depression imposed an unfair burden on them. She refused to sign herself into a hospital and knew that, because of how the California laws were written, she could have talked her way out of an involuntary commitment.

Jamison eventually made the decision to kill herself. She took enough lithium to end her life—"handful after handful of pills"—adding an anti-emetic medication to ensure she would not vomit up the lithium. She removed the telephone from her bedroom, but a call came in on the living room phone, and she "instinctively thought to answer it." Curled up in bed, waiting to die, in a near-comatose state now, she "crawled" to the living room and answered the phone. Her brother inferred the meaning of her slurred speech and called her psychiatrist.

Jamison's mother came to stay with her, a doctor friend offered care and comfort, her psychiatrist, whom she greatly admired, stuck it out and friends rallied. She recovered from this episode, returned to work at UCLA and went on to have a significant academic career, while writing about her own illness and advocating for others with manic-depression.

None of these achievements came easily. Jamison makes it clear that her manic-depression is a chronic illness, which cannot be cured, only managed. Lithium was the drug that saved her life and kept her relatively stable, but this pharmacologically aided stability came at a price: nausea, vomiting, occasional toxicity, interference with reading comprehension, blurred vision, impaired concentration, attention span, memory and coordination. To a physically and intellectually active woman like Jamison, these were not trivial perturbations. Using a time-released formulation of lithium and carefully titrating the dose considerably lessened this burden. But lithium is not an easy drug to take indefinitely and, to this day, Jamison still lives with the residual effects of manic-depression. She speaks of her "tidal existence" and of her "struggles to stay sane, stay alive, and to come to terms with my illness" (p. 124).

These Meyerian facts extracted from Jamison's story of her melancholic depression fit the description of the phenomenon of depression given in Chapter 7. Every facet of her depression—and she shows us many facets—can be understood as a consequence of the *dedifferentiation* of her world. The only dissimilarity is that her dedifferentiation occurred to a greater degree than in the 1st domain depression characterized in Chapter 7, and did not appear to derive from a maladaptive Meyerian reaction to negative experience, but from some endogenous source. (She does not mention the possibility of having experienced any psychological trauma or significant loss during her earliest years.) Jamison's depression and mania seem, as Meyer put it, to "impinge" on her life rather than "emerge" from it. In the FDMI, these aberrant mood states are considered manifestations of a putative 4th domain (second stipulation) disease.

We know the kinds of stressors that make life more difficult for Kay Jamison, but we do not know what catapults her into mania, and from there into black mania, or why this mood state eventually devolves into melancholic depression. Mania followed by its collapse into profound depression—in a periodically recurring cycle of these two aberrant mood states—constitutes the phenomenon of manic depression.

The DSM-5 calls Jamison's black mania a "mixed state," where, as is commonly said, *symptoms* of mania and depression occur simultaneously. This is an unfortunate way to name and understand such a condition because "mixed" and "symptoms" somehow imply a side-by-side coexistence of mania and depression, which is counterintuitive, non-phenomenological, non-heuristic and very likely wrong.

Acutely manic patients—and this would include Jamison in her black manic moods—are capable of what Janowsky et al. (1970) call "interpersonal maneuvers" that entail freedom and choice, even as their freedom may be limited by a severely compromised biological substrate. It seems entirely possible that, in a so-called mixed state, a person may reject some aspects of the world—through the dedifferentiation of depression (Chapter 7)—and simultaneously go excitedly overboard for other aspects, through a process of *hyperdifferentiation*, an "interpersonal maneuver" opposite in intent and outcome from dedifferentiation. In this mood state, the self as active agent maniacally attributes to someone or something an importance greatly exceeding anything imaginable by someone who is not manic. In the DSM-5, "mixed state" is merely a metaphor. Dedifferentiation and hyperdifferentiation, on the other hand, signify pathological ontic transformations and transformed states of human being (Chapter 5).

That bipolar I is usually described as consisting of "discrete" *alternating* states of mania and depression does not mean these are always "pure" mood states. The dedifferentiation/hyperdifferentiation theory of mixed states advanced here is borne out in an observation made long ago by John D. Campbell, a psychiatrist who worked with many manic-depressive patients and thought deeply about the phenomenon underlying their illness: "It is not manic *and* depressive psychosis, but manic-depressive [psychosis], indicating an entity with varying mood reactions, one merging into another, not always by sudden reversals or changes in mood, but frequently by gradual transformations, often so slight as to be imperceptible to the casual observer. Likewise, with other emotional reactions in this disease, there is a pathologic *distortion* characterized by a ceaseless undulation" (1953, pp. 83–84). Note Campbell's choice of the words "varying mood reactions," which is consistent with and may owe something to Meyer's psychobiology.

Kay Jamison's manic-depression is so classic that even an instrument as blunt as the DSM can get her diagnosis right—though nothing is said about the origin of the illness and the meaning of its symptoms. As Jamison says, "Although I always think of myself as a manic-depressive, my official DSM-IV diagnosis is 'bipolar I disorder; recurrent; severe with psychotic features; full interepisode recovery'"

(p. 181). It is with the less clear-cut cases of all kinds of mental illness—the cases most clinicians usually see—that the DSM fails so often, and with such destructive consequences.

Robert Lowell's Manic-Depression

The American poet Robert Lowell had an even more fulminant iteration of manic-depression (bipolar I) than Kay Jamison. In *Robert Lowell: Setting the River on Fire*, Jamison praises the active stance Lowell took toward his illness, most fruitfully through his literary creation. In the pages of her layered and convincing text, we see him, time and again, exerting free will in the context of his madness.

Speaking out implicitly for the self as active agent—the possibility of exercising limited freedom even in the midst of the most difficult circumstances—Jamison, pointing to Lowell, concludes that "One gained will by exerting it" (Jamison 2017, p. 19). This existential declaration reminds us of Meyer's belief in the importance of strengthening good habits while attempting to overcome a mental illness. For both Kay Jamison and Robert Lowell, the *choice* to exert that will, most of the time against a contravening biology, made all the difference.

Jamison makes a good case that Lowell, all his life, "struggled to impose his will on forces that were beyond his control" (p. 229). This is a paradox we all face, but Lowell lived it in aces. The general case for this interaction of will and aberrant brain biology had already been stated in the 19th century by Eli Todd, whom Jamison quotes: "The great design of moral management is to bring those faculties which yet remain sound to bear upon those which are diseased, and by their operation to modify, to counteract, or to suspend their morbid actions. This constitutes the process of self-control, the groundwork of cure, the grand tactical principle which is to decide the issue of the contest between reason and sanity" (p. 230). (Adolf Meyer took a page from Eli Todd's book as he set out to create the new psychiatry that would be practiced at the Henry Phipps Clinic at Johns Hopkins Hospital. Meyer's psychobiology became the model for psychiatric practice in North America, until Freud's psychoanalysis pushed it off center stage.)

Lowell had suffered significant early psychic trauma at the hands of his mother. Charlotte Lowell made no effort to hide the fact that she resented her pregnancy. A chart note from Lowell's psychiatrist, written in 1957 when he was forty years old, includes this sentence: "The patient states that when the mother first learned she was pregnant she said she wanted to die." The first psychiatrist who evaluated Lowell, when he was 15, had already noted: "He was an unwanted child" (p. 58).

This knowledge weighed heavily on Lowell. Charlotte Lowell's resentment of her son continued, with only occasional mitigation, for as long as she lived. A difficult child, adolescent and adult, Lowell's relations with both his parents were conflicted and sometimes violent. Jamison speaks of his mother's "grinding disapproval" of him (p. 59). The father, a naval officer, was mostly passive and spent much of his life under his wife's thumb. Unlike his father, Lowell vigorously resisted this woman's efforts to subjugate him. During one hospitalization for mania, the doctor noted that Lowell's basic issue with his mother was that he would "not be mastered by her," a determination that widened to a "general fear of not being mastered by anyone" (p. 59), a major insight into his psychic troubles.

Lowell's fear of being determined by others led him to adopt what Jamison calls a "near-monastic discipline." He came to live more in his mind, through books and ideas, and by writing poetry and prose, than in the environment his parents were imposing on him. Lowell's retreat became a way of being powerful in a world largely of his own making. Psychically speaking, his defensive strategy meant creating an unsustainable, elevated psychic state. In agony and turmoil, he revved his engine and went high, a defense removing him, in many ways, from contention with those he felt constrained by. The result was mania, for which he was hospitalized 20 times, between 1949, at age 31, and 1977, the year he died at age 60 (pp. 112–113).

Jamison offers this powerful insight into how mania worked as a defense for Lowell: "Mania, he told his doctor, allowed him to shatter the control [that others had over him]. Rebellion flared, anger boiled over. When he was manic, he said, he could relive his battles with his mother and win them. It allowed him to vent his rage at being 'fixed in society,' bound to the expectations of his social class; it allowed him to escape the 'dreariness of being a Lowell'" (Jamison 2017, p. 59). Viewed in this way, Lowell's mania had meaning and served a purpose: escaping the circumstances of his life that he found intolerable. He did this by *hyperdifferentiating* (see above) selected aspects of his experience and going overboard in pursuing certain interests. He often related his manic attacks to what he recognized as a "pathological enthusiasm" (p. 190). Jamison sees mania as a "compelling state that confers certainty and power" (p. 229). With Lowell, these feelings often slipped normal bounds and evolved into grandiose delusion. Others were hurt by his disinhibited behavior, predictably those closest to him. Once again, looking at mania as a defense, Jamison observes that, in the manic state, "A moral sense might be compromised in the effort to stay alive; often surviving madness becomes a pragmatic thing" (p. 232).

Lowell precisely and eloquently recounted the story of his life to his doctors, in the process revealing the psychodynamics of his condition, even as the expression of his freedom and will were undoubtedly being attenuated by an altered brain substrate. Whatever biology may have contributed to this severe 4th domain mental illness, choice (through the *misuse* of freedom) and will (Nietzsche's will to power) played a part as well. The case can be made that Thorazine, and later lithium, the medications that helped him most, were acting as tranquilizers, quelling the symptoms of a psychically created mania, driven in part by his "pathological enthusiasms."

Adolf Meyer believed that manic-depression and schizophrenia were, in some instances, brought on by maladaptive reactions that induced changes in the brain which, in turn, led to further psychic deterioration. Meyer's psychobiological theory requires that what we call the mind be dialectically linked to what we call the brain, which is to say what happens in the mind inevitably effects the brain and vice versa. Perhaps Lowell defensively chose and willed his mania, but because his brain was altered in this psychodynamic transformation, he was unable to will out of the terrible, *unintended* sequelae associated with this choice. Like so many with manic-depression, his path from a manic episode back to baseline (an admittedly imprecise designation) ran, as he said, straight through hell. To the degree that Lowell attempted to defensively escape his original state of psychic trauma by creating and perpetuating his manic states, he made a deal with the devil.

The stories of Elyn Saks and John Nash (Chapter 14) leave no doubt that they were as "schizophrenic" as anyone ever diagnosed with this illness. But are their illnesses *caused* by a brain defect, as, say, the psychotic symptoms of tertiary syphilis are caused by a spirochete bacterium (4th domain, 1st iteration)? Elyn Saks had a straight-up schizophrenogenic mother. John Nash makes it clear that pursuing higher mathematics often took his mind out of the consensual, rational world of cause and effect and into a constricted, disembodied interior space. Robert Lowell's mother was a domineering monster, and a case could be made that she, too, had been a schizophrenogenic mother, who created numerous double binds for her son (Bateson, Chapter 13). Though Lowell's chronic illness is best explained as a pathological disregulation of mood, he was often psychotic as well. Maladaptive psychotic reactions often occur in those who experience severe, early psychic trauma.

After recognizing the strong psychodynamic elements in Elyn Saks's, John Nash's and Robert Lowell's illnesses, we could ask: Are we justified in concluding that an altered brain substrate *caused* their major alterations in mental life as the medical model would have us believe? Because I have my doubts about this, I named the 2nd stipulation of the 4th domain, which includes some phenotypes of schizophrenia and manic-depression, primary mental diseases emerging from a *putative* altered brain substrate.

To recall, once again, Karl Jaspers's distinction between *understanding* and *explanation*: we have a good psychological understanding of Saks's, Nash's and Lowell's illnesses but no satisfying biological explanation for them. Having said that, it should be acknowledged that there are different phenotypes of manic-depression (bipolar I), which may have brain substrates that are either biological correlates of psychogenic trauma, or themselves the primary cause of the illness.

Productive Hypomania

Hypomania is defined as a range of emotion bracketed by the high end of normal mood and the earliest signs of mania. For those with bipolar I, hypomania is often experienced as a period of relative stability between their low and high affective extremes. Cognitive and creative processes are accelerated, and everything is seen with greater clarity and felt with greater intensity. Those in the hypomanic state have increased energy and engage more widely and avidly with the world. To someone looking on, it might seem as if an endogenous stimulant drug were sustaining their extended emotional "high."

Kay Jamison delighted in what she called her "mild manias" (hypomanias), and was happiest and most creative while in these moods. We can think of her productive hypomania as an affective zone of near normalcy that is threatened by the extremes of incapacitating depression and mania, which she keeps at bay with the proper dose of lithium and by living sensibly. This ostensibly normal, but pathologically rooted productive mood *state* is not the same phenomenon as the hypomanic (hyperthymic) personality style—a series of *traits*—that John D. Gartner has characterized as the "hypomanic edge" (Chapter 10).

Asked if, given the chance, Jamison would retroactively opt out of her manic-depression, she says she would not—as long as lithium allows her to manage her disease. Even with the torment and paralysis of her worst depressions clearly in mind, she would not be willing to sacrifice her hypomanic experiences. She has come to see her diverse mood states as inseparable, which, at different times have given her the best and worst that life can offer.

The DSM-5 does an especially poor job of delineating what we think of in the FDMI as the phenomenon of hypomania. According to the DSM, the main features that distinguish mania from hypomania are the period of time over which the symptoms of each condition must persist (at least one week for mania; at least four consecutive days for hypomania), and the degree of impairment that each condition causes. For mania (Criterion C): "The mood disturbance is sufficiently severe to cause marked impairment in social or occupational functioning or to necessitate hospitalization to prevent harm to self or others, or there are psychotic features" (p. 124). For hypomania (Criterion E): "The episode is not severe enough to cause marked impairment in social or occupational functioning or to necessitate hospitalization. If there are psychotic features, the episode is, by definition, manic" (p. 125). Arbitrary at best, these distinctions tell us nothing about the origin or meaning of hypomania.

We have already considered the absurdity of the DSM-5's insistence that someone who has been diagnosed as hypomanic must be considered manic if any psychotic symptoms appear. It is no surprise that the atheoretical DSM overlooks the distinction made in the FDMI between 1st and 4th domain psychotic experiences (Chapter 9).

Finally, the DSM-5 specifies identical diagnostic criteria for hypomania whether this mood state occurs in bipolar I or bipolar II patients. This implied equivalency is incongruent with our belief that bipolar I hypomania derives from a 4th domain putative brain disease while bipolar II hypomanias are usually the mood components of 2nd domain maladaptive reactions.

It should be clear that having four domains in the FDMI allows clinicians to distinguish phenomena that may appear to be identical, but are in fact quite different.

Diagnosing the Phenomenon of Manic-Depression (Bipolar I)

The bipolar misdiagnoses of John, Alicia and Angela—three patients who had very different mental illnesses—were no anomaly in my clinical experience. These, and many similar cases, led me to challenge the prevailing psychiatric paradigm, an approach contrived mainly from the DSM, currently in its 5th edition, with its symptoms of unidentified meaning, and the so-called broken-brain part. This approach is also known as the medical model of mental illness.

Having repeatedly pointed to the falsity of the medical model of mental illness, and made the case against the frequent misdiagnosis of bipolar disorder that is a product of this model, we need to look at some of the literature that identifies and characterizes the *real phenomenon* of what we are calling manic-depression in the FDMI. A good way to begin would be with some background on how the concept of this mental illness came to be defined.

We believe that true bipolar I is now—and has always been—a relatively rare condition (Healy 2008, pp. 54, 63, 117, 125). We are convinced that real manic-depression (bipolar I) may be as rare as real PTSD, renamed the post-traumatic stress reaction in the FDMI (Chapter 6). We feel that the rampant *overdiagnosis* of bipolar I disorder, based on the criteria of the DSM-III, DSM-IV and DSM-5, is responsible for the exaggerated estimate of the prevalence of bipolar disorder as 1 percent of the U.S. population, the same figure generally offered for the prevalence of schizophrenia.

In diagnosing mental illness, two camps have emerged, one insisting on narrowly defined categories of the core illness (the "splitters"), the other preferring broader, more inclusive categories (the "lumpers"). Lumpers obviously cast their diagnostic net wider, which leads to a greater number of patients being diagnosed under their rubric.

Users of the 3rd, 4th and 5th editions of the DSM have interpreted the directions for diagnosing bipolarity in different ways. The criteria for bipolar I call for discrete episodes of classic mania in combination with major depression (to the delight of the splitters). But in practice, as noted earlier, anger, irritability and frustration, which are associated with many other mental illnesses, are often misread and misdiagnosed as mania (making the lumpers happy). What purports to stand for a narrow construct of bipolar I, which centers on mania diagnosed with symptoms of unknown meaning and origin, in fact encourages clinicians to downplay the centrality of mania and go broad in making the diagnosis. This inclusive tendency is both the cause and result of an egregious "definitional creep."

A principal reason for this mistake is that the DSM-5 fails to adequately describe what classic mania really *is*, and what it means to *experience* a manic state, from which the symptoms of this aberrant mood have been culled. Put another way, the DSM-5 fails to identify the *phenomenon* of mania. Once the rigor of diagnosing mania was abandoned, the way was opened for diagnosing many varieties of alternating elevated mood and depression as bipolar I. In patients who have 1st, 2nd and 3rd domain illnesses, elevated mood is often followed by a decline in mood. No surprise here, since pathologically driven elevated moods of all kinds are unstable and unsustainable states. Something about a pathologically elevated mood makes a depressive "crash" inevitable.

We believe that while the periodic recurrence of elevated and depressed mood is a necessary component of the phenomenon of manic-depression, a cyclic alteration of mood alone is insufficient to make the diagnosis. There are many reasons why people of all ages can undergo periodic mood swings, including those Healy identifies as "nonspecific overactivity" in the absence of true mania (2008, p. 207). Ascribing all mood swings to biologically driven manic-depression masks the real meaning of these altered—and alternating—emotional states and prevents clinicians from identifying their cause (Khong 2017).

Historically, the diagnosis of manic-depression has often turned on the question of whether *classic mania* should be the focus of the diagnosis, or whether the *periodic recurrence* of mania and depression is the principal criterion. Healy has put together a detailed account of this interesting difference of opinion among Europe's psychiatric thought leaders (2008, pp. 52–88). One can wonder why so many bright clinicians and researchers found it necessary to make this distinction a point of such contention, but that appears to be the way a good deal of academic science works, sometimes to psychiatry's advantage, sometimes not.

We see manic-depression as a unique phenomenon that requires unambiguous, classic mania that is not caused by a 4th domain (1st stipulation) physiological imbalance or a medical disease. We consider mania to be a 4th domain primary mental disease associated with a putative altered brain substrate. We say putative because no satisfactory physiological or neuroanatomical explanation (in the Jasperian sense) has yet been offered for this phenomenon, in spite of investigations that have been ongoing for over 150 years. Evidence of changes in biological function in the brains of those with anxiety, depression and other 1st domain conditions do not necessarily identify the biological *cause* of these conditions. All mood states have biological *correlatives*, and it follows that changes in mood states, whatever the cause, would lead to observable changes in these correlatives.

The FDMI should please the splitters and challenge at least some of the lumpers to re-examine their position. A diagnosis made in accordance with the FDMI requires that a mental illness, to the first approximation anyway, be a discreet phenomenon, which is to say different from other pathological phenomena. This approach is a safeguard against the flagrant "lumping" that has caused psychiatry so much diagnostic heartache.

Like David Healy, Ross Baldessarini and myself, Joel Paris, Professor of Psychiatry at McGill University is a splitter. In his 90-page book, *The Bipolar Spectrum: Diagnosis or Fad?* he offers a stern but fair assessment of the harm that lumpers have done to both patients and the integrity of clinical research by losing sight of what we are calling the real phenomenon of bipolarity. "Spectrum," in Paris's parlance, is a metaphor used to signify the "softer"—less debilitating—symptoms that have come to define a type of bipolarity different from bipolar I. For classic mania, the lumpers substitute irritability, moodiness, impulsivity and other mood variants, and then call the patient "bipolar":

> Bipolar disorder, in its classic form, is a condition that fits the medical model rather well. It was, therefore, rather tempting to redefine a number

> of other conditions that could be seen and treated in the same way. The spectrum concept takes a wide range of complex clinical phenomena and converts them into bipolarity, explained by the popular concept of "chemical imbalance" and treated with the latest psychopharmacological cocktails. Thus, the complexity and mystery of psychopathology is resolved using a dangerously simple algorithm (Paris 2012, pp. 34–35).

To the lumpers, a little of the disease *is* the disease, a leap made possible by assuming that all mental illnesses are brain diseases: a little brain cancer *is* brain cancer, and will unavoidably become more brain cancer. Find it early, treat it early, nip it in the bud is one path through which psychiatric diagnosis has succumbed to the medical model. It was this kind of thinking that led to the "early diagnosis" and "early treatment" of bipolarity in young children.

American academic psychiatrists are disproportionately lumpers, and Paris names some names: Hagop Akiskal (University of California at San Diego); Joseph Biederman (Harvard); Nassir Ghaemi (Tufts); and Dean McKinnon (Johns Hopkins). Frederick Goodwin, coauthor with Kay R. Jamison of *Manic Depressive Illness* (2007), which is often cited as the "standard text" on the subject, is also a strong proponent of the bipolar spectrum. Paris sees the lumpers' approach to diagnosis as "dangerously simple." He recalls H. L. Menken: "[For] every complex problem there is an answer that is clear, simple, and wrong" (Paris 2012, p. 43).

The point has already been made here that unstable mood associated with 1st, 2nd and 3rd domain conditions is a different phenomenon than the mood changes experienced by those with 4th domain bipolar I disorder. Paris, who has devoted a good deal of his career as a psychiatrist to working with patients who have personality disorders, and to thinking and writing about their pathology, parses this difference according to the nature, intensity and duration of these mood changes, as well as their different responses to medication. He cites the work of other clinicians who have made their mark working with this kind of patient: "Unstable and rapidly changing mood has been termed 'affective instability' (Siever & Davis 1991; Koenigsberg 2010), but also has been called emotion dysregulation (Linehan 1993; Gross 2009). Both constructs describe rapid and intense mood changes that fluctuate over the course of a day in response to life events" (Paris 2012, pp. 37–38).

Affective instability in patients with borderline personality disorder (2nd domain) is part and parcel of the psychobiological instability of their borderline state (Chapter 10). Borderlines respond poorly to the pressures of daily life, often with Meyerian maladaptive reactions, each with its own expression of aberrant emotion. As borderlines move through the day, the circumstances they face change, and so do their moods, which are often all over the place. Paris differentiates this kind of mood instability from the less situationally dependent, more endogenous periodic *swings* in mood—up and down—that hypomanics undergo: "[I]n contrast to hypomania, affective instability in

BPD shows a unique pattern. Instead of moving from depression to elation, mood shifts from depression to anger. Moreover, episodes of hypomania are almost never seen in BPD. The key point is that patients with affective disability rarely stay in the same mood more than a few hours. . . . [I]t is a stretch to see these patients as rapid cyclers" (Paris 2012, p. 38). According to the DSM-5, rapid cycling is a type of bipolarity where patients have four or more cycles of mania and depression within one year.

"Stretch" is a key word here, because this is what clinicians do, metaphorically speaking, when they assign patients with affective instability, which can be difficult to diagnose and treat, to the diagnostically more accessible and pharmacologically more "treatable" bipolar spectrum. The ultimate mistake made by these clinicians is ignoring the *phenomenon* of the illness that the patient presents with, which includes the *meaning of his symptoms*. Paris intuitively understands borderline personality disorder as a 2nd domain aberrant personality style and bipolar I disorder as a 4th domain (2nd stipulation) putative brain disease. The failure of clinicians to grasp this distinction—assuming as they do that all mental illnesses are brain diseases—is the main reason why so many borderline patients are wrongly diagnosed as bipolar. Paris cites John Gunderson as saying that it is rare these days to see a borderline patient who has not been diagnosed at some point with bipolar disorder and medicated for it.

Paris writes confidently and incisively about making this differential call (2012, pp. 58–63). To repeat, the main challenge is distinguishing *affective instability* from *mania*, which seems not to depend so much on life stressors as does affective instability, but to come from some other, non-situational (and so far unexplained) source. Meyer, no doubt, would have concluded that borderline personality style *emerges* from a life, whereas bipolarity *impinges* on a life.

What have been called *micropsychotic symptoms* should not lead a clinician to diagnose bipolarity. Like other borderline symptoms, these brief psychotic experiences can appear when patients are under extreme stress and then vanish once the stress is resolved (Zanarini, Gunderson & Frankenburg 1990). This kind of psychotic event belongs in the 1st domain, not in the 4th domain (Chapter 9).

Writing in 2002, Paul Grof, a psychiatrist who had been a major participant in the "revolution" that brought pharmaceutical agents to bear on affective disorders, looked back with dismay as he assessed the full impact of the innovation brought on by the diagnostic lumpers: "Long-term treatments given to virtually no-one thirty years ago are now prescribed for nearly everyone with recurrent affective disorders to the point that the natural course of the illness [including spontaneous recovery] is not known any more. With the use of lithium the concept of affective disorder has dramatically broadened and mood symptoms rather than comprehensively assessed psychopathology have become the center of psychiatric assessment" (Healy 2008, p. 127).

In other words, psychiatrists, succumbing to various pressures, embraced the medical model of mental illness which then devolved into treating symptoms of altered mood as if these symptoms *were* the illness, ignoring in this approach the unique phenomenon of each patient's presentation. This is what happened with John, Alicia and Angela, who had very different illnesses, but were "lumped" together, and diagnosed with and medicated for bipolar disorder. This is the story of many, if not most, of those who have wrongly been called "bipolar."

Chapter 17 Using the FDMI: Diagnosis and Treatment of a Man With 2nd Domain Avoidant Personality Style, and 1st Domain Anxiety, Dysthymia and Pathological Anger

Peter's previous clinical management, based on the medical model of mental illness, included an incorrect DSM-IV diagnosis and improperly prescribed medication. Diagnosis using the FDMI led to a very different understanding and treatment of his condition. The account of our therapeutic work that follows appeared first as an epilogue in the author's Doing Psychiatry Wrong *(2008). The last section of this chapter, "A Meyerian Formulation of Peter's Diagnosis," appears for the first time here.*

Peter was referred by his primary care physician for evaluation of anxiety and possible panic. Always anxious, he had recently become more anxious, and his sleep was down to a few hours each night. His anxiety seemed to keep him from sleeping, and the fact that he could not sleep made him more anxious. In his panic, he was reaching out to friends and relatives. "I'm driving them crazy," he reported, knowing that he could not continue doing so.

Peter

Peter was 57 years old and had been retired for seven years. "Work was too stressful," he said. He lived alone in a house that had been passed on to him after his parents died. His only regular activity was doing volunteer work for a Senior Citizens Center. He had been in the Air Force from age 17 to 19, but was given a general discharge, due to what he called his "bad attitude." Peter earned a bachelor's degree in social science when he was 25, and then took graduate courses in social work part-time while working for the Department of Social Services. He quit that job when he was 30 and received a master's degree in social work the following year. His last employment was a 17-year-stint with a foster care agency where he ultimately became a supervisor. He let it be known that he lasted as long as he did in that job only because his boss had been tolerant of his "short fuse." Peter was nothing if not self-effacing.

At age 19, Peter spent several days in a psychiatric hospital because, as he put it, "I was too argumentative." He took Thorazine during that time but claims that the drug did nothing for him. Later, while in college, he had six months of psychotherapy. He had no further psychiatric care until coming to the private practice group where I worked, more than 30 years later. No one in his family had ever been diagnosed with a mental disorder.

Peter's primary care physician was sufficiently concerned about the headaches Peter reported to order a magnetic resonance imaging (MRI) scan of his brain (no abnormalities were found). Tests for thyroid and liver function, as well as the usual blood work came back normal. Peter was taking Synthroid for hypothyroidism and Xanax at bedtime to alleviate anxiety and to help with sleep. He had been prescribed Seldane for allergies and sporadically took several over-the-counter drugs for hay fever, insomnia and nasal congestion. He had a history of elevated blood pressure and cholesterol, but was not being medicated for either condition during the time I saw him.

Believing that Peter's fast talking and tendency to jump quickly from one topic to another were symptoms of hypomania, the psychiatrist from our group who did the initial evaluation and then referred Peter to me for psychotherapy had diagnosed bipolar II disorder and generalized anxiety disorder. He was started on Tegretol. While the many manifestations of his anxiety were Peter's main psychiatric complaint, dysthymia was also a part of his problem. In fact, dysthymia had been Peter's principal mood during most of his life.

From the psychiatrist's chart notes, it was clear that he originally conceived Peter's problem as a brain disorder—bipolar II is generally regarded as such—that should be addressed primarily with Tegretol. In a chart note from a week before I met with Peter for the first time, the psychiatrist wrote, "Internal referral for psychotherapy made to help patient address dating, etc." In other words, Peter's social isolation, loneliness and inability to connect with women were to be relegated to psychotherapy while the problems caused by his anxiety and mood lability were to be addressed with pharmaceutical agents. The psychiatrist's note from a few days later read, "Explained potential for improvement will not be demonstrated until he has had a therapeutic blood level of Tegretol at least one week."

Readers who are disinclined to pursue a detailed account of Peter's therapeutic course at this time should turn to p. 313, and the section titled "A Meyerian Formulation of Peter's Diagnosis."

Psychotherapy Leading to Structural Change

I started working with Peter on July 18, 1995. We finished 21 months later on April 24, 1997. We met 82 times, weekly, until 3 months before termination, then monthly after that.

It is fair to say that we hit the ground running—Peter was 15 minutes early for his first appointment. We were a good therapeutic match from the start. At a very basic human level, we got along. I believe I was able to quickly convince Peter that I had a handle on what was happening in his life and understood why he was suffering. He always showed up ready to work. Peter put up no resistance to verbally engaging his issues with me—in fact, he spewed them out. For all the anger and verbal outbursts that he reported directing at others, he was never angry at, or in any way abusive to, me. What might be thought of as the "anxious structures" that made up his life were quickly identified and challenged. It was these structures that we chipped away at, week by week. As I hope to show, our work was ultimately judged to be successful by both of us.

After just a few hours of listening to Peter's story, I had no doubt that he was not, and had never been, hypomanic and that the diagnosis of bipolar II disorder was incorrect. (Peter told me that he had always talked fast.) I was also convinced that his mood lability was not due to a primary mood disorder and certainly not to bipolar II disorder, which had previously been diagnosed. The dynamics of his changes in mood were easily traced to an almost constant anger that was rooted in a deep and pervasive anxiety. This angry transformation of his experience kept him from taking the minimal amount of nourishment from the world that is necessary to be a real player there. Peter's ultimate problem was that he was *not* a player and wanted to be one.

In retrospect, the 21-month course of our work can be divided, if somewhat arbitrarily, into two phases. First, the free-fall that brought Peter to therapy was halted. Then a steady improvement began that was discernable to both of us.

1. Stabilization and Initial Improvement (5 months, 23 meetings)

Typically, a mental status examination reports the degree of "distress" a patient appears to be in at the time. At our first meeting, Peter's distress was not acute enough for him to be seen in an emergency room or to be considered as a candidate for hospitalization. But it was clear that he was in deep pain. His face wore the look of distress. He was jittery. He spoke fast and nervously, as if he was trying to save himself from annihilation, with gushes of words that clearly stated what he was feeling. He jumped from topic to topic, but everything he said made sense. Peter was reaching out to me in the hope that I could save him. Like so many people with the kind of problem he was having, Peter had occasional thoughts that he might be better off dead but denied any intent or plan to harm himself. Neither he nor anyone in his family had ever made a suicide attempt.

The only recent change in Peter's life was that, five weeks before he came to our group for help, he had developed insomnia. He had always been able to nap during the day to escape anxiety or boredom and still sleep six to eight hours at night. Now he had trouble getting to sleep at all. When sleep did come, he woke after an hour or two. As this problem worsened, Peter shared his despair with his primary care physician. After seeing that the Xanax he had prescribed would not do the job, this doctor called for a psychiatric consultation.

"When I lost the ability to sleep," Peter told me, "that's when I panicked. I had a good facility for sleeping when I was bored . . . I suppressed the *fear* of falling asleep." There it was, at our first meeting, a significant part of his problem, self-revealed, with minimal prompting from me. This was an authentic cry from the depths. The pressure of what he was hiding from—his dissatisfaction with the life he had made—could no longer be held back by sleep. Peter did not trust the world enough to let go of wakefulness and relinquish himself to the ambiguities of a state where he was required to cede control. "I see it as something I have been suppressing for a long time. I feel a sense of hopelessness. My life stinks . . . lousy . . . nothing to do . . . I have a wonderful facility for keeping things down."

Like so many persons with severe anxiety, Peter had a long list of somatic complaints, which he described to me during our second hour. Bad, nagging headaches topped the list. These headaches had plagued him for years but had become particularly bothersome during the previous five weeks. Other aches and pains, all over his body, were a constant challenge to his mood and his physical strength. A rash and a low-grade temperature came and went and came again, without diagnosis. Four or five times a year he could count on being awakened during the night with chest pains, which were relieved by drinking water. My guess was that most of these symptoms were somatic expressions of anxious feelings that Peter has never been able to deal with and are best understood as attributes of anxiety, not panic.

Peter kept the insight coming. "I see a hard time changing this," he warned me. "I had many chances to do things and didn't take them. I didn't have confidence in myself. I didn't feel I was attractive to women. When I did have a relationship, I was afraid to keep it going. I was afraid of sex. I had little experience with it." No mask here, and no cover-ups for me to challenge. Peter was ready to deal, and he knew how hard this was going to be. He was talking about changing the patterns—and emotional structures—of a lifetime.

When Peter was 21, to his surprise, a woman at a summer camp where he was working pursued him. But when she began telling him about the complex emotional tangle that was her family's life, Peter was overwhelmed by this revelation and quit the relationship. "I was afraid to get involved," he told me. For most of his life, Peter was more or less content to be by himself. Now he feels that his life alone has been wasted and wants to reach out to other people and broaden his horizon. But he does not know how. When he tries to make a connection with someone, the anxiety that invariably comes up leads to conflicts he cannot resolve, and he is paralyzed. Such is Peter's dilemma now.

Part of my job was to encourage Peter to make contacts that would extend his horizon and let him break out of a shell of isolation that he had hidden in for most of his life. At our fourth meeting, he told me that he had joined a Community Center's athletic program and planned to sign up for the singles program as well. "The thought of doing this scares the hell out of me," he said. Peter's anxiety was two-fold: he was afraid of making the moves necessary to overcome his isolation, and he was afraid that, if he did not make these moves, he would be crushed by the worsening anxiety that brought him to therapy. He implicitly grasped his dilemma.

Negativity, impatience, irritability, worry and paranoia are some of the components of Peter's pathological style of living. He knows that these traits have kept him from doing what is necessary to satisfy his needs. Throughout his career as a social worker, his "bad" attitude, as he put it, had caused problems with co-workers and led to his early retirement. "I get too easily irritated. I haven't developed an attitude toward other people that is positive. I want things to happen too fast—part of this is the worry 'I can't do it' or 'I won't be successful.' I get mad when I drive and other drivers don't follow the rules." Peter was acknowledging a low tolerance for conflicted situations. This was a major factor in what he saw as a largely "wasted" life. "Sometimes my worry borders on paranoia. I can't control it. When the situation is over, I know people weren't doing anything to me. But then it starts again. Even when I say 'You're being paranoid,' I would still have the feelings and it would still bother me. It spoils the enjoyment." At times like this, Peter's thinking and emotions were not in sync. He worried constantly about money even though he knows he had, as he put it, "beaucoup money."

Since we began our work, Peter has reported at each meeting the ups and downs in his level of anxiety and mood during the preceding week. At the fifth meeting he volunteered that he had "gone downhill over the weekend." He had more than the usual trouble sleeping, was more anxious and woke up feeling hot and faint. He had a disturbing dream about "a process or procedure that I was not doing right." The dream frightened him and repeated a day or two later. I suspected that the defective "process or procedure" that arose from his subconscious was a dream-work equivalent of his "wasted" life. We were tweaking Peter's defenses when we engaged in our dialogue, and transient flares of increased anxiety were to be expected. "I don't know if I have it in me to do difficult things," was Peter's response to my interpretation. Peter was starting to face issues he has avoided all his life, and this was causing him additional pain but not more pain than he could handle. The dream came again the next week. "This is like starting life all over again," he said.

Peter began our eighth meeting by telling me about what he considered a "slip" in his efforts to get better control of his behavior and achieve greater mutuality with others. On the way from his car to my office, while crossing the street, a woman yelled at him, and he responded with an obscenity. "I give myself a black mark for that," he said. This incident shows how assiduously Peter is pursuing his rehabilitation. He told me that my help with identifying the main features of his neurotic style—negativity, impatience, irritability, worry and paranoia—was allowing him to make specific changes in his behavior as he encounters certain situations. I pointed out that every time he does something to challenge one of these neurotic elements by acting differently than he would have habitually acted, he is internalizing that difference and becoming a little more like the person he aspires to be.

"It will take a year or two to get myself together," Peter told me at the top of our ninth meeting. "This is the situation. I can handle it. I will not fall apart." Peter had already stopped the five-week free-fall that made him seek help. Then, during the next two months, he took another step, projecting what he thought of as the "re-creation of myself." We had the same vision for the task ahead: we were both working for permanent structural change.

Peter brought some written notes to this meeting and he read them to me. "I always say 'no' at first when someone makes a suggestion. I'm stubborn. I only do what I want to do. It has to me *my* idea." For as long as he can remember, Peter has been this way. What he was acknowledging here is ultimately a lack of reciprocity with other people and with the world. There is something deficient—and pathological—about his basic stance toward everyone and everything outside himself. This is a part of his style, and underneath that, the structure of his being. This is what needs to be changed.

During our sixth meeting, Peter made a disclosure that surprised me. "I don't listen well. My mind races on to something else. I pick up the main points, but I don't hear all you say." (I suspect that he was hearing more of what I say than he hears from other people. This kind of attention is necessary for the therapeutic work we are doing.) Somehow, defensively, Peter has learned to turn down the signal of what he hears from others—or perhaps the signal is swamped by the noise that his anxiety has generated between himself and everyone else. The "cocoon" that Peter acknowledges living in for most of his life receives a reduced signal from the outer world.

Peter often reports feeling the knife-edge of heightened anxiety during our meetings. One minute he wonders out loud if he can deal with these uncomfortable feelings. The next minute he assures himself—and me—that he can. Each time he anxiously goes through a situation more daring than those he has been used to and then comes out the other end safely, he becomes more convinced that his anxiety is, ultimately, related to how he chooses to deal with others and the world. For as long as it takes to change a style that never worked well for him, and then stopped working altogether, living on an anxious knife-edge is the only way he will authentically and permanently ever get out of that bad place.

During our next few meetings, Peter continued to brood over what he had made of his life. But his disappointment about how things had turned out was partly balanced by his sense that his life would soon be improving.

"Is this all there is?" he asked as if not expecting an answer. "Am I going to be able to do more? I don't know what to do except keep going. What's the use of brooding? Analyzing it doesn't make it any better." But later, he said: "I've turned a little corner. Nothing that has happened has thrown me. I feel I'm getting something, learning something." The balance in what Peter says here is tipped toward the future; his words imply forward movement. He shows pride at some small accomplishments and acknowledges that there is really no permanent downside to what he is doing. For someone whose style had tipped decidedly toward the past and the negative, this is a step up, and not an easy one: "It's so hard to change. How do you do it? Can I do it?" Peter seems to implicitly understand that the answers to these questions can only be found in his moving forward.

Our 14th meeting came at the end of a week that Peter described as "miserable." He felt "very discouraged and down." He had slept for only four and a half hours the previous night and woke several times with hot flashes. The following story demonstrates how little it takes to throw Peter off his game—and the kind of problem, in one manifestation or another, that has plagued him all his adult life. He had agreed to participate in a registration drive for senior citizens at the Community Center. Then a number of people who had agreed to help did not show up. Peter realized that he would be required to do more work than he had anticipated. He became frightened at the prospect of being overwhelmed by the drive and stayed away from the Center for several days. Looking ahead, these thoughts ran through his mind: "This is going to be too hard for me. I can't do it. Too many things could go wrong. I couldn't handle it."

It took a few days for Peter to resolve this problem, but he did resolve it. He agreed to stay on the registration committee but declined to be the one responsible for the outcome. This was a partial solution, but a solution nonetheless. He smoothed the feathers he had ruffled while this problem was playing its way out.

He had backed off from a chance to take on a higher level of responsibility and commitment than he originally contracted for but ultimately followed through on what he initially agreed to do. Peter's sleep improved and there were no more hot flashes.

But a new traumatic experience reared its head a few days later. Peter has spoken several times about how much he regrets never becoming significantly involved with *any* woman in spite of his chances to do so. At our 15th meeting, this issue came front and center. A friend offered to introduce Peter to a woman he knew. Peter's anxiety soared. Should he, or shouldn't he, go out on this date? "If I don't do it now," he told me, "I'll never have an opportunity to. I don't want to give up on this one." Peter's anxiety over this issue has two parts: first, that his self-imposed cocoon will not be satisfactory to sustain his life, and second, that he is not willing to take the risks necessary to get out of that enclosure. "The possibility of starting the relationship . . . I don't want the stress, the flushes . . . In my mind, I can do it . . . In my gut, I can't." Peter was clearly referring here to the somatic manifestations of his anxiety. When his stress goes up, his body tenses and says, in effect, No to the risk he is considering taking.

Peter is caught between going for it and running from it. "I can't be alone forever," he said. "I've been in this rut so long. It's like an animal that can't change his habits. Every second I want to give up." But he is not giving up. It is interesting that Peter used the analogy of an animal—a species that lacks the range of freedom humans have—when speaking of the rut he is in. In his head, he feels he should be able to make this move, but his (animal-like) gut holds him back.

At our next meeting, Peter reported the following thought about the possibility of taking up his friend's offer to get him a date: "She will want to live with me and marry me." This rumination presumes a good deal. Arrogance aside, Peter reveals himself here as a world-class catastrophizer: put any play in motion and Armageddon will be the inevitable result. I pointed out to Peter that he hadn't even *met* this woman. His reply: "The thought of doing anything to get involved with someone, taking that step . . . the *idea* of dating . . . obsessing about it." Here again is Peter's obsessive loop: I don't have it in me to do it . . . I should give it up . . . I should do it.

I asked Peter if he ever had an experience of doing something that caused him as much pain as the pain he suffers *anticipating* a new situation. No, he said thoughtfully. I pointed out how his negative thoughts led to negative behavior (paralysis of his projected project), along with the somatic concomitants of this paralysis, which, in turn, led to negative outcomes (isolation, disappointment, regret)—a vicious cycle if there ever was one. Peter's response? "I'm trying harder than I ever have before. I'm feeling better than ever." If, through all this pain, Peter is *feeling better than ever*, we must be doing something right.

At the top of our 17th meeting, Peter reported that things had taken a turn for the worse—again: "Miserable. I'm feeling so God-damned down. I'm sick of not being able to sleep and waking up flushed." Peter spoke at length—a monologue, really—about his agitation and what he might do to change things. I pointed out that since we have been meeting, we have been dealing with emotionally charged issues and that he has made a considerable effort outside our meetings—in the real world—to do things he has not previously done, which are also emotionally charged. All of this expressed emotion is making him feel uncomfortable, as the defenses of a lifetime are tweaked, loosened, reinstated (sometimes less tenaciously) and then loosened again. What Peter and I are really doing is titrating the amount of discomfort he can take as he moves forward and out of his cocoon into a life that has a better chance of satisfying him.

It was, no doubt, Peter's complaints about the discomfort he was experiencing that led his psychiatrist to prescribe BuSpar. This anti-anxiety drug was added four months after we started. Problems with sleep have been one of Peter's chief complaints, and Benadryl, to be taken at bedtime, was also prescribed. Up to this point, my efforts to convince the psychiatrist that Peter was not bipolar had been unsuccessful. The Tegretol, which Peter started taking right after the bipolar diagnosis was made, was continued, but gradually tapered.

"It seems like the BuSpar is doing something," were Peter's opening words at our next meeting. "I'm feeling more optimistic. Not feeling down in the morning." (This was one week after the drug was started; generally, BuSpar has an induction period of several weeks, raising the possibility that he was experiencing a placebo effect). We talked about whether BuSpar was responsible for the changes Peter reported. He reiterated his belief that the Tegretol he had been taking for four months did not help him. He doubted that the Benadryl he had just started was doing him any good, either. Why he credited BuSpar and not Benadryl with his improved sleep, he did not say. I explained that the ideal situation would be if, as he tries to reach out for more life, BuSpar were to take enough of the edge off the discomfort he feels to encourage him to continue reaching. I thought I sensed a note of resolve that I had not previously heard when Peter asked, "Where do I go from here?" He made it sound like he definitely wanted to go somewhere. Then he added, "I want to have a couple of weeks feeling good first."

Five months after we started our work, during our 22nd meeting, Peter took his own inventory:

"I have a low tolerance for anything physical or mental that makes me feel uncomfortable."

"I never did see how I could overcome it. I always thought of it as being in my genes."

"I make the same mistakes over and over. I want more out of life, but I don't see how I will ever have it. I don't accept that."

"I can't have a relationship with a woman. I can't even take the stress of thinking about it."

This is mostly familiar stuff, but there are at least two interesting revelations here. This was the first time Peter let it be known that he had thought his anxiety was genetic. What is genetic cannot be changed and is, in the current parlance of brain science, "hardwired." (Peter's male-pattern baldness is genetic.) Has five months of meeting weekly with someone who sees the world as the great champions of human freedom do—Friedrich Nietzsche, Martin Heidegger and Jean-Paul Sartre, among others—somehow convinced Peter that how he feels and what he does have something to do with how he uses *his* freedom to construct his world, however he may have been limited in doing so by snags in his early development?

And then Peter produced these two sentences: "I don't see how I will ever have it [more out of life]. I don't accept that." This admission of a despised and rejected paralysis recalls the last words in Samuel Beckett's novel *The Unnamable*, "I can't go on, I'll go on." Peter the metaphysician: he *can't* do it, but he *will* do it. Is this not a statement of the fundamental human paradox, the starting point of so many of the more difficult and worthwhile things that people do?

During our 23rd meeting, Peter spontaneously issued this declaration: "There has been a definite improvement in how I'm feeling and sleeping. I'm almost back to where I was before this happened." Granting this, Peter feels that he is currently at what he calls a "standstill." After five months, the acute anxiety he felt, along with the portent of his annihilation, is gone. But he is still stuck with the person he has been all his life, and he no longer wants to be that person.

Wondering out loud how this had all happened to him, he talked for the first time in our meetings about his childhood and his mother—it took five months for him to get around to talking about this woman. She was a Russian Jewish immigrant who spoke only fair English. She did not have an active social life. Peter had playmates but he was not particularly popular. He was not very coordinated and "hated" physical education. "I never felt confident about anything from the earliest age," he told me. When he was in the first grade, he wondered if he could put his belt on right.

I asked Peter how he dealt with these feelings of inferiority. "I had a smart mouth. I still can't stop doing this now. I do it over and over. If I didn't do that, I'd be a mute. If you have confidence, you don't need to do this. I can't bring myself to talk to others in a positive way. It feels phony when I do this." At our 24th meeting, these next words came spontaneously from Peter, seeming to originate from some place deep inside him. "It's not the situation. It's the mental uncomfortableness I feel with it. None of these situations [the issues and problems that come up repeatedly during our meetings] were as bad as I thought at first." After hearing this, I asked myself if reality had finally broken through the faulty cognitive and emotional structures that had constituted Peter's neurotic world for so long.

Then came this nugget of wisdom: "You really have to hurt before you can begin to change." Peter has often complained about the pain he has had to endure as a result of the work we are doing. Now he seems to be saying that it was necessary to suffer to get to where he is and that it was worth it. Then Peter said, "It isn't an impossible task." He has often remarked how "hard" this was going to be. His emphasis seems to have shifted from the *difficulty* of crawling out of his cocoon to the *possibility* and the *likelihood* of his being able to make this transition. I pointed out that these changes in his thinking meant real progress toward his goal of living a less anxious and restricted life. To all appearances reluctantly, reflecting his basic negativism and conservatism, Peter agreed with me.

2. Consolidation with Gradual Improvement (16 months, 59 meetings)

At some point—it is not clear just when—I was able to convince Peter's psychiatrist that Peter did not have a primary mood disorder and that his diagnosis of bipolar II was not right. Shortly after that, a Tegretol taper was started. By the time we met for the 26th time, Peter was off Tegretol and on a maintenance dose of BuSpar. He felt this drug helped him to cope better and that it was not causing him any problems. He continued to believe that Tegretol had done him no good and sometimes made him dizzy.

"I don't like the idea that I can't function well without BuSpar," Peter told me, as he extolled the virtues of this drug. Clearly, he is one of those patients who does not want to depend too much on medication, though he seemed willing to let BuSpar be his pharmacological crutch for a while. Peter is feeling better, looking better and looking ahead to a time when he will have changed enough to no longer need any medication. He told me how he had recently overcome several inclinations to go with his habitual negative thinking and how doing this changed a likely bad outcome into a relatively good one. "I want to change peoples' perception of me. I want to change my own self-perception," he said with conviction.

Peter made it clear that his relationship with his mother had been fraught. "Screaming and yelling" were a significant part of their dialogue. He claimed that he "never resolved anything with her." Peter had nursed both his parents to their deaths—his father for two years, and later, his mother for six years. Several days before his mother died, she refused the food her son was trying to spoon into her mouth. Peter, losing his temper, forced the spoon, slightly cutting the inside of her mouth. "I can't forgive myself for what I did," he said of this incident. On the morning she died, her last words to him were "Go to hell." Peter showed little interest in, or apparent need to, rehash the events of his early life. He and I both preferred dealing with the here and now.

Though Peter did not talk much about his mother (and not at all about his father), I infer, with a nod to Donald Winnicott, that this woman was a "bad enough" mother for her son to have had a neurotic development, leading to his neurotic adult life. I doubt that Peter had ever adequately "attached" to either parent, preventing him from making an adequate attachment to others and the world that was unfolding around him. The psychic trauma involved in this failure to connect in these basic ways was, no doubt, imprinted on brain centers that underlie emotion, turning his "emotional idle" up into the range of high anxiety (this is epigenetic imprinting, and not, as Peter believed, genetic inheritance). A pathological life at the level of neurosis was his fate—he had no borderline or psychotic traits—culminating in the episode of the five days of emotional free-fall that brought him into therapy.

At our 28th meeting, as Peter read from a list of concerns he had voiced many times before, I listened for the subtext of his words and took note of his affect. His voice was steadier than I had ever heard it before. His face had a glow, and the frown that had been so prominent before was all but gone. Peter's words told me he was still engaging the issues that he came to therapy with. His body language said things were going better for him.

During our next three meetings, Peter continued to delve into the reasons for his angry outbursts. "I feel like being angry as the first response is me, and anything else is phony," he told me. He readily acknowledged that this kind of retaliation often brings on a counter-retaliation by the object of his anger, which then sends Peter into another cycle of worry and paranoia. He sees this kind of response as a part of what he calls his "internal need." Peter eventually acknowledged that his mother reacted to anything that displeased her with anger (though this distemper dissipated rather quickly), and that she was angry at him most of the time. It seems that Peter learned anger at his mother's knee, then kept on being angry at everyone else he met because he didn't know anything else.

Peter's weakened ego cannot live comfortably with the ambiguity that arises when, as so often happens, someone fails to live up to his expectations. Then Peter attacks what he takes to be another person's "phoniness" with the anti-phoniness club of his anger. With his angry transformation of the event's meaning, he tries to break through the moral ambiguity of these distressing situations by reasserting his challenged sense of self, in the doomed hope of making things the way they *should* be. Using this maneuver, *Peter can momentarily reshape the world through his anger*, defensively dealing with emotions that he cannot deal with without this defense. He knows that most people do not need the defenses he uses. He wants to join their ranks.

I asked Peter what he feels as he goes off on one of his angry transformations: "You SOB. This is the way I feel. If you don't like it, too bad." Then he added: "Why do I have to go into it like that? Why do I get so upset? I would like to think about it in a different way. Is it neurotic to think this way?" Peter feels personally wounded when someone does not meet his standards. He spoke of the "intense need to get back at the person verbally." While doing his volunteer work at the library, a woman lawyer told him that she should not have to pay a fine because she does not finish work until after the library closes, and could not have brought the books back on time. "You want something for nothing," was Peter's response. In Peter's world, the woman is still responsible for paying the fine. Later, he felt ashamed about how he had snapped at her and wished he had said something like, "These are the rules."

Unlike some patients who have varying degrees of belief in the magical power of prescribed drugs, Peter implicitly believes—as I do—that the solution to the array of problems we have been chipping away at for the last eight months depends on his will to overcome the structural deficits of a neurotic development. He does not want any improvement that he has already made, or will make, to come from some pill, because this would seem false. Put another way, Peter does not want to "listen to BuSpar" to feel "better than well," as Peter Kramer's patients "listen to Prozac" and achieve that goal. He has spoken with his psychiatrist about reducing his dosage of BuSpar, and the tapering has begun. He wants to see if he can maintain his current degree of emotional control while taking less of the drug. I see this as a move to take more control of his healing process and as a very positive sign.

By our 36th meeting, Peter had discontinued BuSpar. A week later, he reported no difference in his anxiety level or mood. But the headaches persisted, a dull pain that hit him most when he was not doing anything. Though Peter has put more activity in his life, mostly through his volunteer work, he still has periods of empty time when he feels dragged down by boredom. Shortly after stopping BuSpar, he had his last meeting with his psychiatrist. By that time, all three of us were convinced that medication was not going to fix Peter. Though their parting was amicable, Peter gave no indication of regretting the loss of either his psychiatrist or the drugs he had prescribed. Nor did he appear angry about the misdiagnosis that was made—I was candid with him about this. The forgiveness and generosity Peter showed here surprised me. As is obvious from most of what he says, his stance toward the rest the world was anything but forgiving and generous.

The way I see things now, Peter is continuing to do therapeutic work on a gradually rising plateau. He still struggles with many of the issues he came in with but in a more existential, less neurotic way. He is internalizing the lessons learned during our meetings and growing from this experience. What keeps him moving forward, I believe, is that his life on the plateau he now occupies does not give him the satisfaction he craves. The inertia of his faulty development still holds him back even as he tries to move forward: "I still can't see myself doing certain things. I'm afraid to get into something because of the headaches and flushing that might come." Peter is still fighting anticipatory anxiety. And, he told me again for the hundredth time, the negative thoughts are still with him.

The final sentence of my chart note for our 39th meeting read: "Peter looks better now than at any time since we started nine months ago." I felt that some milestone had been reached. He described the preceding week as "fair, better," and his headaches were down. "Are my worries subsiding or did the headaches become less because I stopped using Becanase?" he asked. (This was a drug he was taking for a stuffy nose.) "I would like to get to the point where, if I have something I can't resolve, I won't worry to excess, and get a headache or a hot flash." Some of Peter's current worries are: his next-door-neighbor is planning to move and he is concerned about who will buy the house; he is having some repair work done on his own house and he wonders if the work will be done right and if he will be overcharged; he is still concerned that if he does not push himself to do more, he will not improve in the way he wants to improve. Peter has gone back to his exercise program at the Community Center, on Monday, Wednesday and Friday. Mostly, he uses the treadmill.

Struggling on his gradually rising plateau, Peter is trying to balance his need to do more with the need not to be overwhelmed by worry and anxiety as he takes on new projects. He points with pride to the small jobs he does around his house and yard. He recently planted 36 small annual plants in his back yard and fixed an aluminum awning. This is in contrast to the paralysis he felt a year ago when he was heading into the crisis that brought him to therapy. "Last year, I didn't get anything accomplished," he told me. "In the back of my mind, I'm still scared that things will slide back, although things are going well." Peter has not complained recently about disturbed sleep, and his outbursts, which have been such a big problem all his life, were not even mentioned today.

"The thoughts go through my mind . . . a semi-boring life . . . I wonder if I might slip back to what got me here in the first place . . . no job . . . not ready to date . . . discouraging . . . this is the rest of my life . . . boring . . . not fulfilling . . . there's more to me than this boring life." As I listened to Peter's stream of consciousness about life on his plateau, with all the limitations and frustrations he brings to the surface here, I believe I heard something closer to an existential cry from the depths than the neurotic productions I had become accustomed to hearing. When I made this interpretation, he appeared to understand.

During out 43rd meeting, ten months after we started, Peter announced that two more months might be the right amount of time to continue our work. Frankly, I was stunned that he was even considering terminating at this point. Some "remaining issues," he said, needed to be discussed. One of these issues was his sexuality, or, as he put it, the lack of his sexuality. "I am as close to being a virgin as a man can be," he told me. It was obvious from the beginning that Peter had a deeply seeded fear of getting involved with a woman; the very *idea* paralyzes him, even now.

When he used the words "fear of homosexuality," I asked him to explain what he was afraid of. "My loneliness . . . Could something happen between a man I like . . . I don't think I could have a physical relationship with a man . . . Kiss a man . . . Have anal sex . . . I don't think I could handle it." He mentioned a man he knew when he was in the Air Force. The man was homosexual and they became friends. One day, the man asked Peter to rub his back. Peter saw this as a sexual overture and declined. He wanted me to understand that he had "no desire" to start a sexual relationship with this man. My initial reaction was that being so sexually inexperienced, Peter could not totally reject the notion that a man might provide him with what he was never bold enough to ask a woman for.

At several of our earlier meetings, Peter talked about the problem he had concentrating on any written text or film that has intellectual or emotional substance. "I'm afraid to look at it, afraid to get into it," he told me during our 45th meeting. Whether it is the real world or the world of fiction, issues involving emotional conflict seem to send out a "stop" signal that paralyzes him. As part of my ongoing effort to prod Peter on to a higher plateau, I recommended that he select a book or film of the type he has trouble with, take it on and let the chips fall where they may. He had previously tried to watch a video of *The Shawshank Redemption*, a movie set mostly in a prison, with a stunning performance and voiceover by Morgan Freeman. He could not see it to the end. He agreed to try again. The next week the report was good: "I liked it. It felt like a triumph that I did it. Got over the hump on it." Peter gave a vivid, detailed and animated account of the story. He enjoyed sharing this victory with me, adding, "Like a lot of things in my life, I wouldn't do something if someone didn't push me to do it." He acknowledged me as his "pusher." Peter's watching this movie entailed the clearing of a blockage—the same kind of blockage, no doubt, that had kept him from going for so many things all his life. "I can't figure out why I do this," he said with what appeared to be genuine wonder. Earlier, Peter had admitted to "tuning out" what others were saying during one-to-one conversations. He has, in fact, tuned out large segments of the world, a practice that has left him isolated and unfulfilled. We have been uncovering the meanings of his refusal of the world. We are challenging the psychological structures that underlie and drive this refusal.

For all of Peter's complaining about how non-ideal life on his plateau is, he has, during the last few months, put together a productive daily schedule. Peter clocks 20 hours a week as a volunteer with senior citizens at the Community Center; he gives 2 hours a week as a volunteer in the pulmonary unit at a local hospital; and he volunteers another 2 hours at a library near his home. He appears to be doing well in this work. It is when Peter is not at one of these venues that time rests heavily on him, that he becomes bored and worried and gets down on himself. He does not enjoy doing anything alone, but is too conflicted about the intentions of others to consistently seek out compatible company. "It's depressing going out by myself," he told me. "Everyone else is with someone else."

At our 51st meeting, just one year after we began, Peter told me he had come to feel that the medication he had been taking may have done him more harm than good. "I don't think I'm the kind of person medicine works on," he said. "I took the medicine because I was so desperate." He recently stopped Seldane for his allergies; the headaches that had plagued him for so long had disappeared. As a somaticizer and a hypochondriac, hoping to find relief from various symptoms, Peter has taken a good deal of medicine. He has a low threshold for physical pain, as well as emotional pain. That Peter is now willing to let go of his pharmacological crutches seems a big step forward. As he discontinues one drug after another, including his psychotropic drugs, he gives no indication of wanting to go back on any of them. Three weeks after stopping Seldane, he has yet to have another significant headache. "It's like night and day," he said.

Two weeks later, Peter gave this progress report. "What the hell am I going to whine about today? I'm on a plateau [he's picked up my metaphor], which isn't so bad. Some time has to pass before anything more happens, before I can do anything better . . . At the back of my mind I think things are not so bad but could be better. I think about the ideal. I would meet a woman and . . . But I don't think about the negative [way things could go]. Maybe right now I'm not ready for this. I'm feeling good now. I don't have many down, negative days now. I guess the right thing is to plunge right in, but I might not be ready. If I think about it, I can get discouraged. If I cope day to day, something good will happen. That's where I am now." These are Peter's most hopeful words yet. Life is not all he would hope it to be, but he is coping with his situation now and looking ahead, if tentatively, to a time when he will have more of what he wants. And he seems willing to work for it.

"I'm almost back to where I was a year ago," Peter let it be known during our next meeting. "But there is a difference. I have a better understanding of how I deal with people. I feel better about a lot of things. But I'm on that plateau. I think of that as a little depressing. I keep plugging, day by day. I can only work on things I am working on now." Peter had only one headache last week, which was quickly resolved with an over-the-counter pain medication. He attributes his improved sleep to the absence of the headaches that have bothered him for so long.

The next month and a half was mostly taken up with a wider and deeper exploration of the joys and sorrows of Peter's life on the plateau. He recently took a bus trip to Atlantic City with a friend. The day went well, and he appeared pleased. This does not seem like much of an accomplishment until it is recalled that, one year earlier, he attempted a similar excursion but was too anxious to even get on the bus. The uneasiness Peter is feeling now, and discusses at length at every meeting, is a prerequisite for his continuing growth. His dilemma hurts him more on some days than on others. Peter is learning to raise the threshold of his emotional pain. He realizes that he cannot get to where he wants to go until this low tolerance is overcome.

This is not easy. The incidents Peter has discussed at our meetings that have caused him pain all have the same form. Some encounter with another person results in his becoming anxious; Peter then fears that his anxiety will increase and that the dreaded somatic symptoms (headache, flushing, disturbed sleep), will reappear; his anxiety increases; he aborts the encounter in hope of discharging the anxiety; he feels regret and frustration at defaulting on the situation. A day or so later, he lets go of these negative feelings, acknowledging to himself and to me that there was never anything to really be anxious about.

Clearly, Peter never learned the art of self-soothing. Most people facing the situations that overwhelm him are able to talk themselves down from the initial anxious feelings that often come with new challenges. Peter cannot do this. Instead, he replays in his head what cognitive therapists call "old tapes" of bad experiences. This projected negativity sends his anxiety into high gear and through the cognitive-behavioral loop just sketched. Peter implicitly understands the pathology of this sequence: "This is a way I'm used to doing things, the way I learned to function." From what Peter has told me about his relationship with his mother, it is not hard to see why.

The following words were spoken by Peter at our 66th meeting: "I'm afraid to believe that I don't let things get me down now as much as I used to. I seem to be better. I don't want to believe it. Nothing positive like that can happen in my life. I'm coping better." If I hear him correctly, Peter is telling me that he fears *not* being as negativistic as he has always been! Even if it is painful, his negative, neurotic life is predictable—he can count on the same anxious pain, and on his identity as the one who is experiencing that pain. But what would a less negativistic life be like for him? What new demands would the world make then? I told Peter that expressing his fear about the improvement he sees in himself is good evidence that he is improving. Peter's next task is to find something positive to replace his negative life with.

The ups and downs of Peter's life continued to be reported and discussed at the meetings that followed. Then, at our 70th meeting came this declaration: "It seems I have gone as far as I can go with therapy. I'm not really making progress the way I want to make it." Despite the fact that Peter continued to struggle with what seemed to be the same issues, it is clear to me that he was struggling more effectively and at a higher level. Acknowledgments such as "Before I started coming here, I did not understand what was going on with me," made with conviction and a sense of gratitude convinced me that our work was having its intended effect. When I asked what the next step should be, he responded, "I can't imagine giving up coming here." I suggested that we meet every other week, instead of weekly, as we have been doing. Peter rejected the idea, saying that he still needs the "support" he gets from our weekly sessions and appreciates the opportunity to "ventilate" his feelings. Though Peter is frustrated with the "stuck" aspect of life on his plateau, he is seeing some forward movement there as well. He still works hard at our meetings. He is not just "feeding," as the psychoanalysts describe the situation where patients come in mostly to have their infantile needs met.

Peter came to our 74th meeting with this extraordinary revelation, which made it easier to understand why his life had been a living death: "I can't stand the anxiety of waiting for the situation to be over. I want all worry taken out of my mind." What Peter is ultimately saying here is that he does not want any ambiguity, uncertainty or risk in his life. I pointed out that he was, in effect, *demanding* that the world not be an ambiguous, uncertain place, where risks must be taken. Put another way, Peter has refused to take life on life's terms. He wanted his own terms! He wanted a "privileged" life where he does not have to play by the same rules as everyone else.

The good news was that Peter is not refusing life on life's terms as doggedly as he had done for most of his life. The following declarations, the first made during our 75th meeting, the second during the meeting that followed, show Peter has come a long way in challenging the psychological structures that have made his life so problematic: "Anything that would really bother me before I am tolerating it better now"; and "I am 100% better than I was two years ago." Clearly, he is not 100% better, but he is slowly raising the level of his plateau.

"I want perfection," Peter told me at our 77th meeting. "I guess that's why I like fantasy stories [and initially had trouble watching *The Shawshank Redemption*] . . . I've always had the expectation that friendships would be forever, perfect . . . A certain level of neuroticism . . . I can't completely overcome it . . . I have to accept life more like it is." These words gave me hope that Peter had internalized the interpretation I made three weeks earlier, as I pointed out why he wants all imperfection removed from his life, so he can have the "perfect" life. He seems to understand that, in making this claim on the world, he is asking for more trouble of the kind he has always had.

Our 79th meeting was our last weekly meeting. A month later, Peter came up with these words that both recalled where we had been and adumbrated where he still hoped to go: "I've been thinking that I won't be coming here any more. Seems like the right time to end. Whatever I haven't resolved that I would like to resolve . . . I've done the best I can . . . I would like to accomplish more, but . . . I may have had an unrealistic idea that I could just go out there and date and be comfortable . . . I don't think I'll be able to push that any further than I have . . . Sometimes you just can't have all the things you want . . . Now I won't have anyone to talk to, I'll just have to do it on my own." These words are a powerful account of Peter's painful efforts to resolve (partially) what has been a life-long agonizing conflict.

Peter had made the decision to end our work at this time. He looked well and seemed in control. I saw little of the agony that was so evident during the last 20 months. I felt Peter had learned enough to be his own therapist now—to keep pushing up to higher plateaus. How much had Peter improved? I would say he was 30%–40% better when he walked out the door for the last time than when he first came through it.

We met once more, a month later. "I now have a doubt . . . Maybe I could understand this better . . . Am I just trying to prolong my therapy because I don't want to quit? . . . Why can't I be the kind of person who doesn't get upset when things aren't the way I feel they should be? . . . Perhaps it's that I don't have a wife to go home to . . . grandchildren." This seemed like the kind of doubt and questioning that would keep Peter honest and moving forward. Looking back, I could only wonder where he had found the ego strength to do the work we did.

I told Peter that, if he wanted to meet again, the door was always open. He never walked through it again. During the years since we finished our work, he has called several times to say he was doing well, continuing with his volunteer work, going places with friends and, yes, becoming involved with a woman or two. I saw him at performances of the local symphony orchestra, usually accompanied by another person. Peter looked good, sounded good and appeared pleased that we had run into each other.

A Meyerian Formulation of Peter's Diagnosis

The psychiatrist who had misdiagnosed Peter with bipolar II disorder made little effort to elicit or understand his life story, or, as Adolf Meyer put it, to formulate a diagnosis based on the facts constituting that story. As happens so often when patients are diagnosed using DSM criteria, Peter's changes in mood were taken to be a primary mood disorder, bipolar II, which clinicians who adhere to the medical model of psychiatric diagnosis see as a brain disease (Chapter 16). Hence, the psychiatrist's prescription of Tegretol, and his belief that the "potential for improvement will not be demonstrated until [Peter] has had a therapeutic blood level of Tegretol [for] at least one week." In other words, Peter had a brain disease, which needed to be addressed with a drug, and psychotherapy was secondary, intended to help with his day-to-day problems.

With Peter's story in hand (step 1), the remaining four steps outlined in Chapter 5 were followed to formulate his diagnosis:

Story → Facts → Bad Habits → Maladaptive Reactions → Pathological Phenomenon(a)

2. The Facts

At the time we began our work, Peter was 57 years old. He was an only child, and both parents were dead. He had retired early from his social work job with a foster care agency seven years before because he couldn't take the stress. Socially isolated, there was no one whom I could contact to check his story. Peter did mention some relatives, but in a way that made me think he would not want me to contact them. I made no effort to get the records from his prior psychiatric treatment and single hospitalization.

Peter's life had hit a wall. Always *anxious*, he was more anxious now, to the point of being emotionally crippled. His sleep was down to a few hours a night, in part due to the increased anxiety, which, in turn, fed his anxiety. To say that he was miserable would be an understatement. He had never been a happy person, but he was more *dysthymic* now. His life was stuck and he wanted my help restarting it. Peter readily told me his story. Though he distrusted most of the people he was encountering at the time, he implicitly trusted me. This confidence and expectation lasted during the 21 months we worked together. It was clear that Peter was *angry* with just about everyone except me. He had a low tolerance for frustration and would lash out at people and situations, sabotaging his already weak hold on everyone and everything he encountered.

3. The Bad Habits

Over time, starting early in life, behavior hardens into habits, good ones that advance our projects and bad ones that get us into trouble. In Meyerian psychiatry, bad habits are seen as poor mental hygiene, habitual ways of acting and reacting that incline a person to adapt poorly to life's challenges. Most bad habits involve self-deception, which allows one to take an easier path, rather than a more authentic one. Meyer believed that bad habits were the royal road to maladaptive reactions and mental illness.

Peter readily acknowledged a number of bad habits, including *negativity, impatience, irritability, worry* and *paranoia*. He took offense easily and responded by being offensive to others. He acknowledged having a "short fuse." Peter saw threats everywhere and reacted by avoiding a good deal of what would have otherwise appealed to him and contributed to his development as a person and a professional. "I had many chances to do things and didn't take them," he told me. "I didn't have confidence in myself. I didn't feel attractive to women. When I did have a relationship, I was afraid to keep it going. I was afraid of sex. I had little experience with it."

Peter joined the Air Force at age 17 only to receive a general discharge two years later because of what he called his "bad attitude." At age 19, he was hospitalized for several days and given Thorazine, because, as he put it, "I was too argumentative." He characterized his interactions with most people as "conflicted." Peter worried a good deal even as he realized that there was no good reason for worrying, in the process acquiring the habit of worry. He often felt "hopeless" and told me that he had "wasted" his life.

Early on, Peter developed a stance toward the world that limited his every action and thwarted his every hope. His pre-pathological bad habits created the ground from which he eventually embraced the defenses that Meyer characterized as maladaptive reactions.

4. The Maladaptive Reactions

It took Peter five months to mention his mother. To say the least, their relationship had been fraught. He spoke of their "screaming and yelling" at each other, and told me that he had "never resolved anything with her." He nursed this woman for six years, during her final illness, and her last words to him were "Go to Hell." This is not Winnicott's "good enough" mother. From both parents, he got the idea that the world was an unsafe and unhappy place.

It is not hard to imagine how Peter became the person he was. As he grew older, he must have carried his parents' limited world view with him. Clearly, he was not sufficiently influenced by his experiences outside the family to alter this fundamentally negative and restrictive stance. He did not develop the basic trust in himself and the world required to thrive and feel good about the person he was. In fact, he reacted maladaptively to much of what he experienced. He developed a 2nd domain avoidant personality style, escaping further into anxiety, dysthymia and anger. (The psychodynamics of the pathological anxiety reaction are parsed in

Chapter 6. The psychodynamic transformations underlying the dysthymic reaction and pathological anger reaction are spelled out in Chapter 7.)

5. The Phenomenon(a)

Sometimes Peter was more anxious, dysthymic and angry than usual, which is to say that his mood varied. By his own admission, he had always been a "fast talker," and when he became agitated he would talk even faster. This feature of Peter's personality style was misread by his DSM-oriented psychiatrist as hypomania, leading him to misdiagnose Peter with bipolar II disorder.

The FDMI approach leads to a very different conclusion. After considering the critical presentation of the "bipolar spectrum" concept in Chapter 16, a clinician could not diagnose bipolar II: Peter was never even hypomanic! Many clinicians who follow the DSM-5 and the medical model of mental illness believe that "mood swings" are due to a biological brain malfunction and are primary mood disorders. The FDMI, in contrast, recognizes that *significant alterations in mood are common in illnesses in the 1st, 2nd and 3rd domains, and that these conditions must be ruled out before a 4th domain bipolar mood disorder can be diagnosed.*

The Map of the Four Domains provides an opportunity to visually gage where a patient resides in the Meyerian domainome. Peter's prior (DSM-IV) bipolar II diagnosis would locate him, incorrectly, in the 4th domain. In fact, Peter lived mostly in the 1st and 2nd domains.

Identifying a phenomenon means demonstrating how one entity is unique and different from other unique entities. We begin the formulation of Peter's diagnosis with a look into the 4th domain, to rule out the likelihood that his foremost psychiatric issues had a biological cause.

The Fourth Domain

Peter had a long list of somatic complaints. Increasing insomnia was one of the issues that brought him to therapy at the time he signed on with me. As already noted, his growing problems with sleep had increased his anxiety, which could be considered his main psychiatric complaint. The frequency and debilitating consequences of Peter's headaches convinced his primary care physician to order a brain MRI scan, which was normal. Peter reported taking Synthroid for hypothyroidism. A medical work-up done just prior to our first meeting included a thyroid panel, liver function tests and the usual blood chemistries. All results were within normal limits. He had a history of elevated blood pressure and high cholesterol but was not taking medication for either condition while he was seeing me. Peter also had allergies for which he was prescribed Seldane, and he took over-the-counter medications for hay fever and nasal congestion.

None of these 4th domain conditions accounted for Peter's psychiatric presentation, though insomnia and headache surely contributed to it. During the time we worked together, Peter maintained a clear sensorium and never showed any sign of delirium or psychosis.

The 1st Domain

The anxiety that Peter developed in his earliest years did not abate as he got older, joined the Air Force, went to college, earned a master's degree in social work, held several jobs and became tentatively involved with women. His anxiety was sufficiently strong and all-encompassing as to limit his success in all of these endeavors. The 1st domain phenomenon that most closely matches his overall pathology is the pervasive anxiety reaction, which is similar in many ways to the DSM-5's generalized anxiety disorder. As Peter's story virtually shouts, he was globally anxious to his core, though he showed no sign of panic in any of its manifestations.

Peter's 1st domain anxiety was a set-up for the 1st domain dysthymic transformation that he made of his experience. How could he have euthymically embraced a world that terrified him so thoroughly? How could he *not* be dysthymic with such a fraught and provisional identity? Some clinicians would have diagnosed depression, but my experience with Peter inclines me to favor dysthymia. The difference between these two phenomena, in the parlance of the FDMI, is the *degree* to which Peter dedifferentiated the instrumental world of cause and effect—the *strength* of the defensive transformation he made in the face of overwhelming anxiety—as he retreated into a flattened, dysthymic world that felt safer to him.

Peter's pathological anger can be imagined as occupying one corner of a triangle where the other two corners represent anxiety and dysthymia. Add arrows to this picture and you get the idea that all three phenomena, though discreet enough, are also interrelated and mutually sustaining. In Peter's world, marked as it is by anxiety, dysthymia and anger, each of these pathological transformations drives the others. On paper, we see three separate phenomena. But in life—existentially—there is only one pathological entity. Meyerian psychobiology and existential phenomenology, which underlie the approach taken in the FDMI, first separate and characterize pathological phenomena, then reunite these phenomena to recover the *person*. That is one reason why in the FDMI we speak of domains and not just of perspectives.

The 2nd Domain

The 2nd domain phenomenon that emerged from a Meyerian formulation of Peter's story was avoidant personality style. No other phenomenon encompasses this and only this set of behaviors. Considering what he revealed about his early life, it is no surprise that Peter developed an avoidant personality.

It must be acknowledged that the DSM-5 behavioral criteria for diagnosing the avoidant person provide good "bones" for identifying the FDMI phenomenon, even if these criteria alone are insufficient to make a valid diagnosis. Paraphrasing the DSM-5, the avoidant person:

1. Avoids work that requires significant interpersonal contact out of fear of criticism, disapproval or rejection;
2. Avoids becoming involved with others for fear of being rejected;

3. Is restrained in potentially intimate relationships because of fear of being shamed or ridiculed;
4. Fears being criticized or rejected in social relations;
5. Feels inadequate in new interpersonal situations and holds back;
6. Feels inferior, unappealing and inept in dealings with others;
7. Is risk-averse. Hesitates to start new relationships and activities.

In the DSM, four of these seven (obviously overlapping) criteria are sufficient to merit a diagnosis of avoidant personality disorder (DSM-5 2013, pp. 672–675). Reading Peter's story should convince anyone that he has *all* of these attributes, and in aces.

Though avoidant personality style predominated, Peter had other 2nd domain pathology. "Sometimes," he told me, "my worry borders on paranoia. I can't control it. When the situation is over, I know people weren't doing anything to me." The key words here are "borders on." People who are really paranoid do not have this insight. Peter's "paranoia" is somewhere between a bad habit and a trait, and not the phenomenon we have characterized in Chapter 10 as the paranoid personality style.

Some clinicians would be tempted to see Peter as having a schizoid personality style, but I do not. Anxiety and fear kept him at arm's length from most of the people he encountered along the way, including all the women he knew. I see his immediate and enduring bonding with me as a point against the schizoid style.

Peter's story is dotted with indications that he is a somaticizer and a hypochondriac, conditions that made life harder for him. Simply put, he transformed some of his mental anguish into physical pain and somatic dysfunction through what Meyer (and others) called psychosomatic reactions, a 2nd domain condition. For many years, Peter had severe, nagging headaches that became significantly worse just before he started working with me. He experienced aches and pains all over his body that affected his mood, demeanor and physical stamina. Rashes came with increased stress, and he had occasional low-grade fevers. Peter volunteered that he was being awakened four or five times a year by chest pains for which no medical cause had be found.

It was undoubtedly in the context of his 2nd domain pathology—spawned by aberrant personality development and temperament—that Peter's 1st domain maladaptive reactions occurred (Chapter 5).

The 3rd Domain

Living the conservative, restrictive and risk-averse life he did, it is not surprising that Peter chose to avoid the self-gratifying, self-destructive behaviors that constitute the 3rd domain. It was simply not in his nature to abuse drugs or alcohol, misuse food, engage in abnormal sexual behavior (he avoided even normal sexual behavior), cut into his body, gamble or steal.

Peter's grit and abiding sense of decency ultimately made it possible for him to sufficiently unwind the maladaptive defenses that he had developed up to age 57 (which were challenged and weakened by our 21 months of hard work) to the point where he could do some of the things he had shunned all this time because of his avoidant fears. Peter marshaled enough of his freedom and willpower to feel better about himself and to enrich the lives of those he allowed into his life, if only to a degree.

Appendix A Edmund Husserl's Phenomenological Method, William James's Pragmatism and the Question of Validity for the FDMI and DSM-5

Existentialism—the philosophy of existence—was first and foremost a revolt against the prevailing analytical philosophy of the West. Plato, Aristotle, Aquinas, Descartes, Hegel and Wittgenstein are a few of the philosophers who thought and wrote in the analytical mode, which focuses on understanding the *essence* of man.

Generally, analytical philosophers ask, and attempt to answer the question, What is man? In the West, this analytical approach was the dominant mode of philosophical inquiry until the mid-19th century when Kierkegaard and Nietzsche appeared and shifted the focus toward understanding man's *existence*. For the most part, existential philosophers ask, What does it mean to live?

Edmund Husserl

Later, Husserl, Heidegger, Merleau-Ponty, Jaspers, Sartre, Camus and others brought existentialism into the 20th century. In creating his version of the philosophy of existence, Edmund Husserl (1859–1938) developed a method—hoping to uncover the *structures of the phenomena he identified*—that was adopted, in idiosyncratic variations by these philosophers, many of whom eventually distanced themselves from this method. Some eventually disavowed the "existentialist" label altogether.

Husserl made possible the discipline of existential-phenomenology—the hyphen signifies the joining of existentialism (the study of what it means to exist) to phenomenology (the determination of the phenomena that comprise this existence). In his formulation of psychobiology, Meyer stayed mostly to the left of the hyphen (Chapter 5). In the FDMI, we are pushing across to the right side so as to include more about the essence of mental illness, without reductively shortchanging the meaning of the (existential) pathological reactions that Meyer identified.

The revolt of existentialism and existential-phenomenology was ultimately against the most prominent of the analytical philosophers, René Descartes (1596–1650), who, in declaring "I think, therefore I am," separated the thinking person from the world that was the object of thought. The *Cogito* allowed Descartes to exert more control over his thinking by removing much of the *doubt* he experienced as he pondered the meanings of the teeming world around him. To create his philosophical system, Descartes had to break the *tie* that binds person and world: his philosophy was not a description of *what the world is*, as the existentialists aim for, but a necessarily *reduced account of the world as reconstructed in his mind*. In this process, the essences he uncovered were stripped of their existence. This was a doubt-free, "safe" philosophy, but one silent about what it means to be a person living in the world with others. Kierkegaard remarked that, for him, reading Hegel, whose analytical thinking owed much to Descartes, was like reading from a cookbook to a starving man (Muller 1987, pp. 3–25, 28).

By the mid-19th century, Descartes's way of understanding the world had deeply colored psychology and psychiatry, relatively new disciplines that adopted a clinical approach to understanding human behavior—especially pathological behavior. By that time, Descartes's *Cogito* had evolved into logical positivism, the conviction that intuition is no match for the messy complexity of human experience and that only the methods of natural science—especially mathematics, biology and chemistry—could render human behavior comprehensible. In this empirical system, knowledge of life was limited to data accumulated through the methods of natural science. The rest, which became the province of the existentialists, was simply left out.

It was the philosophers and psychologists swayed by logical positivism whom Husserl reacted against when he introduced his phenomenological method, with its key intuition of *intentionality*. Intentionality is an acknowledgment of the *inclination toward*, the *link to*, and the *need for* the world and others that every person is born with and cannot escape but *can* pathologically transform (Smith 2008).

Intentionality is Husserl's answer to—and antidote for—Descartes's *Cogito*, which separates mind from world, thought from experience (Husserl 1960; Husserl 1962). Many who come to Husserl for the first time incorrectly take intentionality to indicate a person's capacity for having "intentions," or meaningful interactions with others and the world, which is another, and different, founding assertion of the existentialists. To comprehend and properly make use of existential-phenomenology to understand human behavior, the distinction between intentionality and meaning must be preserved. Recalling the *Webster's Collegiate Dictionary* Latin etymology of intentionality (*in + tenere*), which means to *stretch toward*, will help us to remember that intentionality is the need and proclivity to transcend the solitary self and "stretch toward" others and the world, with its multiple invitations and possibilities.

Both Husserl, who specified a person's natural living space as the *Life-world*, and Meyer, who saw the life of each person as "an experiment in nature" understood that, to live a healthy, authentic life, people must live outside themselves, actively, in a world with others, with an integrated mind, brain and body. It would not be a stretch to say that Husserl and Meyer looked at the world in much the same way.

Because we see Meyer's psychobiological approach as an implicit intuiting of the phenomena of mental illness, Husserl's phenomenological method is Meyer's natural ally. In Husserl's method, a subject under study is first *bracketed*, which is to say isolated from the ongoing flow of the Life-world. This sequestration is brought about through what Husserl called the *epoché*, or *forced halt*. The inevitable preconceptions held by the observers are then identified and sorted through, clearing the air for a perception of the subject where "biases" (points of view, and, yes, perspectives and domains) are acknowledged and expounded. Finally, the phenomenon—what makes an entity uniquely that entity, and different from other phenomena—is characterized by intuiting the *meanings* of its constituent parts as these meanings are revealed to the observer's study (Giorgi 1985).

Many investigators have used variations of Husserl's phenomenological method to identify and characterize phenomena in their own disciplines (Wertz 2011). In the end, with the technical terms set aside, Husserl's method and its variations come down to taking a certain stance toward the world, and, from that stance, *describing the phenomena* that constitute the world we live in and through (Churchill & Wertz, 2014). "It is not so much the procedural steps of soliciting, collating, and 'processing' data that characterize the phenomenological method as it is an orientation or a way of attending to the intentionality of experience" (Churchill 1991, pp. 14–15).

William James's Pragmatism

Truth stipulates that an entity is represented as it is before preconceptions and bias transform what is being apprehended into something else. Ultimately, we need to think about the world in such a way that our own "bias"—no one is without a point of view—tends toward a perspective that can be considered valid because it does not distort what is there.

William James (1842–1910) was an American philosopher and psychologist whose New-World existential thinking—known as pragmatism—significantly influenced Meyer and united him in spirit with the European existentialists. James and Meyer shared the existentialists' view that the truth about others could be intuitively known, a notion that the logical positivists vigorously deny. This denial is a major component of the anthropology that underlies the DSM-III, DSM-IV and DSM-5 and allows the etiology and meaning of symptoms to be ignored. To James, Meyer and the existentialists, such a view of what a person is would preclude a valid understanding of the person's behavior, normal or otherwise.

In his superb rendering of James's life and work, *A Stroll with William James*, Jacques Barzun begins the discussion of pragmatism by citing the need for what he calls a "test of truth." How, he asks, can we know anything substantial about a life that is flux at its core? "If Experience as natively given in consciousness is fleeting, variable, helter-skelter, and if we have the power to work upon it, by attention, by making concepts, by combining images, then we need a way of making sure that the account we give of any experience, the bearing of any connections we discover, is solid, reliable, permanent because [it is] rooted in the nature of things" (Barzun 1983, p. 83). This way of zeroing in on the "truth" is precisely what phenomenologists mean by identifying a phenomenon.

A stick is placed in a transparent container filled with water, one long enough to extend several inches above the surface of the water. Barzun asks us to consider the conundrum of what is observed. At the water line "we see certain lines and colors that makes us think [the stick is] broken—we know from past experience that that is how a broken stick looks. But if we have any doubt, we slide our hand along the stick in the water and feel no break: the idea 'broken stick' is not true;

it disagrees with a subsequent, relevant experience. The pragmatic test is repeated when we pull the stick out of the water, see it whole and lean on it—*not* broken" (Barzun 1983, p. 86)

Ever the concrete thinker, James locates truth close to the ground: "Truth is simply a collective name for verification processes, just as health, wealth, strength, etc. are names for other processes connected with life. Truth is *made*, just as health, wealth, and strength are made, in the course of experience" (James 1907, p. 218).

Pragmatically speaking, truth is what works, and what makes sense in the context of everything we know about the world. Clearly, this "truth" aphorism does not cover all we encounter. James, like Meyer, realized that theories are not absolute transcripts of reality. "Their great use is to summarize old facts and to lead to new ones. They are only a man-made language, a conceptual shorthand, in which we write our reports of nature" (James 1907, pp. 212–213, 57).

Invalidity of the DSM-5

Let us apply James's concept of truth to the claims made by the creators of the 3rd, 4th and 5th editions of the DSM that the mostly behavioral criteria in these texts can be used to diagnose mental illnesses—in spite of their acknowledgment that what was done to increase reliability compromised validity in the process (Bernstein 2011). This trade-off ignores the fact that even if reliability were improved—but how could it be with all the diagnostic "noise" generated by ignoring the etiology and meaning of symptoms?—the sacrifice of validity would render this "reliability" worthless. The DSM-5 fails the pragmatists' test of validity: it does not work; it leads, ineluctably, to many wrong diagnoses. It cannot be fixed because it is not broken—it is just *wrong*.

Every beginning course in natural science belabors the distinction between validity and reliability, and the importance of this distinction in doing research and in interpreting data. But the creators and users of the 3rd, 4th, and 5th editions of the DSM appear to have forgotten their early science training when they created the implicit subtext that as long as clinicians agree, to some extent anyway, on a wrong diagnosis, their agreement trumps the need to get a correct diagnosis. It is hard to imagine what standard of truth and validity is met here. Had Adolf Meyer lived to see the DSM-5, he undoubtedly would have felt that this approach to classifying and diagnosing mental illness lacked "common sense" (Lief 1948)—the signature of his psychobiological approach—and that the DSM-5 was invalid.

Appendix B The Putative Subtypes of Schizophrenia

How the frustration accruing from a schizophrenic's original traumatic wound is compensated, or not compensated, largely determines the phenotype of schizophrenia that will develop. Five subtypes of schizophrenia are characterized in the DSM-IV. The DSM-5 dispenses with these subtypes, as does the FDMI, because we do not consider the phenotypes true phenomena. Nonetheless, we will briefly consider this long-pursued attempt to parse some of the phenotypes of schizophrenia.

Paranoid: The patient is preoccupied with delusions and hallucinations of a persecutory nature. Even if present, disorganized speech, disorganized or catatonic behavior or flat or inappropriate affect are not prominent.

Putting the blame for anxiety and pain on someone else or something else can help hold a fragile psyche together. This compensation has been cited as a reason why paranoid schizophrenics are often more stable than those who do not employ this defense.

Disorganized (formerly hebephrenic): Disorganized speech, disorganized behavior and flat or inappropriate affect are prominent. If delusions and hallucinations are present, these are fragmentary and not organized into a coherent theme. Criteria for the catatonic type are not met.

Catatonic: The core behaviors are prolonged immobility, where unnatural poses are assumed, or repeated "purposeless" activity not associated with external stimuli—in spite of efforts made by others to normalize this behavior. Echolalia (repeating others' words) and echopraxia (repeating others' actions) are considered catatonic responses.

A schizophrenic girl explained her catatonia this way: "I could not move, because if I did, everything changed around me and upset me horribly; so I remained still to hold on to a sense of permanence, weak though it was" (Séchehaye 1956, p. 141). Hoping to survive in her constantly changing, impermanent world, this patient attempted to become a permanent, "frozen" object. Laing might have said that she froze her being in the attempt to preserve her being through this defense.

Undifferentiated: Some combination of delusions, hallucinations, disorganized speech, grossly disorganized or catatonic behavior and negative symptoms, where criteria for the paranoid, disorganized or catatonic type are not met.

Residual: Absence of prominent delusions, hallucinations, disorganized speech and grossly disorganized or catatonic behavior, but with continuing evidence of psychotic disturbance in an attenuated form—including negative symptoms, the deficit syndrome (permanent negative symptoms), odd beliefs and unusual perceptual experiences.

As we leave Elyn, at the end of her book, she would probably be best described as a residual type, with periodic exacerbations. Renée, by creating what she called the "System," became a paranoid type but later largely recovered her stance in reality. Kim seems to be an undifferentiated type. At the height of his illness, John Nash would have certainly made the criteria for paranoid type, but, as he is described at the end of his biography, he would probably be considered a residual type.

In those cases where the designation of a subtype of schizophrenia can be made with a degree of accuracy, this amounts to a refinement of the core phenomenon of the patient's illness. Perhaps what the subtypes reflect most of all are the vastly different dynamics that can be in play in someone who, by dint of genes and environment, and the response made to both, is consigned to a life that is lived, to one degree or another, cut off from the sustenance of the larger world of reality.

For a variety of reasons, the interior experience of schizophrenics changes over time, a fact that limits the concept of subtype. Unless a patient shows a constant pattern of symptoms over a long period of time, it is probably more correct to simply identify the paranoid, hebephrenic, catatonic, etc. *features* of the illness, adjusting this specification if and when symptom patterns do change.

Appendix C Schizoaffective Disorder: An Improbable Phenomenon

Because those who are in the grip of the heterogeneous mental illness/disease that we know as schizophrenia often do not display the extremities of mood—either high or low—we have come to pay special attention to patients with psychosis who do have prominent mood symptoms. These patients appear to be less severely ill and often have a better outcome. With psychotic illnesses, where there is mood, even disordered mood, there is hope, it seems.

Almost two decades before the appearance of the first edition of the DSM in 1952, Jacob Kasanin published an article in the *American Journal of Psychiatry* titled "The Acute Schizoaffactive Psychoses." He reviewed a series of five patients, each of whom had an acute psychotic break and was given an initial diagnosis of dementia praecox. The patients were mostly in their 20s or 30s, and each had what Kasanin called a "specific environmental stress." "The psychosis is characterized by a very sudden onset in a setting of marked emotional turmoil with a distortion of the outside world and presence of false sensory impressions in some cases . . . [which] lasts a few weeks to a few months and is followed by recovery" (Kasanin 1933). Though each patient had been diagnosed with dementia praecox, Kasanin changed the diagnosis to schizoaffective psychosis, reflecting what he called a "blending of schizophrenic and affective symptoms." Clearly Kasanin saw these patients as having an illness different from schizophrenia, Bleuler's term that had replaced Kraepelin's dementia praecox. The "bad end" portended by a schizophrenia diagnosis was not the fate of these patients, who, after relatively short hospital stays, returned to society and to work. (This may be the first use of "schizoaffective" in the psychiatric literature; none of Kasanin's references has a title with that diagnostic tag.)

Considering the acute and easily identifiable stressor in each of these patients, their affective symptoms (most often depression), the brevity of their hospitalizations (several weeks to several months) and the return to their former level of functioning, one could question not only the initial diagnosis of schizophrenia but Kasanin's re-diagnosis of schizoaffective psychosis, which is a DSM-5 schizophrenia spectrum disorder. These decompensations seem better understood as conditions of the FDMI's 1st domain.

Once again, we are reminded that psychosis does not necessarily mean schizophrenia. This distinction is acknowledged in the DSM-5, but is not accompanied by a sufficient consideration of etiology to allow, in many instances, a valid diagnostic call. The makers of the DSM-5 pride themselves on being atheoretical, or agnostic, in these matters.

We are still left with the larger question of whether schizoaffective psychosis, or schizoaffective disorder as the DSM-5 names it, is a real phenomenon or a valid diagnosis in *any* patient. For those who are clearly schizophrenic, like our patient Kim, but who also have significant depression and mania, which Kim did not seem to have, does it make sense to postulate this diagnosis? One way clinicians have been directed to make this call is to determine whether the patient appears more "schizophrenic" or more "affective," and diagnose the former patient schizophrenic and the latter patient schizoaffective. But making this distinction sidesteps the question of validity. "Schizoaffectivity" does not "smell" like a phenomenon.

Perhaps it would be simpler and more valid (Occam's razor) to look for the core 4th domain schizophrenic experience—overall retreat from reality, delusions, hallucinations, thought disorder, which occur over extended periods of time, as well as a deteriorating course and negative symptoms—and call those patients schizophrenic, then add a detailed description of how changes in mood, low or high, figure in these patients' lives. In Chapter 9, the designation of 1st domain psychotic reactions offers the clinician other ways of appraising patients with both psychotic and mood symptoms.

Though schizoaffective disorder is included in the DSM-5, William T. Carpenter, head of the DSM-5 psychotic disorders workgroup, maintains there is insufficient evidence to conclude that the schizoaffective designation is either a valid or a reliable diagnostic concept (Malaspina et al., 2013)—or, as we say in the FDMI, a real phenomenon. So, why retain an invalid and unreliable diagnostic category? Carpenter explains why: "[T]he DSM-5 remains in the tradition of Kraepelin and continues to separate Mood Disorders from Schizophrenia Spectrum Disorders and recognizes the clinical utility in maintaining a diagnosis that is important to clinicians addressing the middle ground." Surely Adolf Meyer, who felt that Emil Kraepelin had relied too heavily on codifying mental illnesses by category, would turn over in his grave if he could read this rational.

We cannot imagine or condone the "separation" of mood and psychosis, which we consider *inseparable* in a mental patient's altered existence. We propose that the "middle ground," which the DSM-5 wants to capture with the designation of schizoaffective disorder, be pursued instead within the 1st domain of the FDMI (Chapter 9) or within the 4th domain mixed states of manic-depression (Chapter 16). In both domains, certain maladaptive reactions to life events are understood to include pathological transformations of mood that are indivisible from the cognitive and perceptual distortions we know as psychosis.

The inclusion of the non-phenomenon of schizoaffective disorder in the DSM-5 is an example of how things can go wrong when mental illness is approached solely from the "top-down," as was done by the psychotic disorders work group. When the "top-down" adherence to theory—in this case Kraepelin's notion that mood and psychotic disorders are separate "entities"—swamps a consideration of the patient's lived experience, which is the "bottom-up" approach followed in the FDMI, a wrong tack ineluctably leads to a wrong result. And so it has gone with so many of the mental disorders that appear in the DSM-III, DSM-IV and DSM-5.

Appendix D Identifying Mass Killers Before They Strike

Even as statisticians insist that violent crime in this country is decreasing, incidents of murder, murder-suicide, suicide by cop and mass murder are occurring with increasing frequency in homes, elementary schools and high schools, colleges and universities, places of work, government buildings, shopping malls, movie theaters and airport terminals.

Repeatedly, we hear that these acts are "incomprehensible" as if something so horrible could not come from humankind. On the contrary, this behavior is human, all too human. To understand how such things can happen, we must probe the outer reaches of what people feel, think and do—and then distinguish between the murderers who act within the boundaries of what we call reality and those who have entered the alternative world we know as psychosis.

Most murders and mass murders are not only rational but meticulously planned. These acts have meanings that emerge from the life story of the perpetrator, in whose eyes a certain goal cannot be accomplished in any other way.

But not all murderers and mass murderers act rationally. People who have retreated from the terror of their lives into a psychotic world, or been forced there by some brain dysfunction, may become paranoid and delusional. Attempting to alter a psychotically construed situation in which they feel they are victims, or to defend against that situation, they may strike out with violent acts that are unfathomable to us, but make sense to them.

During the 10 years I did psychiatric evaluations in the emergency room, I was asked many times by the ER staff to see patients who were suspected of being dangerous to themselves or others. The ultimate call to be made in these situations is not whether a patient is psychotic or not—important as that distinction is—but whether that person is likely to *act* on feelings and thoughts that hold the potential for violence.

Early in my ER career I evaluated a young woman who had been brought in by ambulance after a neighbor observed her behaving strangely and called 911. I remember vividly the lesson I learned from this patient: do not discharge someone who appears potentially dangerous to themselves or others unless you are satisfied that you have their *story*—the sum of the facts that constitute the current state of their mental life—and feel a degree of certitude that a suspected potential for destructive action will not devolve into that action.

The woman reeked of gasoline, which she had poured on herself, and appeared poised to strike a match when the neighbor noticed her and intervened. The discomforting fact is I didn't *have* the woman's story—or, for that matter, a good feel for why she had put herself in this danger, though it was clear she was not psychotic.

I discharged the patient, but she came back to the ER the next day, again by ambulance, after again dousing herself with gasoline. Even during the second interview, she did not tell me what had driven her to act as she had. I have come to recognize this kind of silence as a cardinal indication that a person may be in the deepest trouble and at high risk for harming themselves or others. She readily agreed to a voluntary admission to our psychiatric unit. In retrospect, it seems that her ultimate intention—the meaning of her actions—was to get the help she eventually received. Why she could not, or would not tell me her story and so ask for help directly remains a mystery.

Though there is no reason to believe that this woman ever intended to harm anyone besides herself, the lesson I learned from her may help other clinicians to prevent seemingly at-risk patients from becoming murderers and spare their potential victims from certain death.

Mass murder often comes out of the killer's need to show the world that he (almost all mass killers are males) is not one of life's losers, in spite of being neglected, bullied or betrayed, but the person who is striking back and getting even, ensuring that his name and despicable act will live forever, in history and in infamy. As clinicians, our goal is to get the potential mass murderer's story and detain him before he has the chance to act that story out.

Unfortunately, the imperative of getting a patient's story right is not supported by psychiatry's current paradigm, based as it is on the DSM-5 and its meaningless symptoms, where behavior is parsed into categorically designated illnesses of unknown psychodynamic and biological provenance. Most clinicians trained in this paradigm are not prepared to do the kind of evaluation that is necessary to make an informed call with a potential murderer. That would require gaining access to the thoughts and feelings which will guide his choices and behavior.

This brief essay first appeared as "The Stories Behind Mass Murders," *Hopkins Medicine*, Winter 2014, p. 47. Small alterations were made to the original text.

References

Chapter 1

Belluck, P., Carey, B. (2013). Psychiatry's new guide falls short, experts say. *The New York Times*, May 7, pp. A13–A15.

DSM-5 (2013). *Diagnostic and statistical manual of mental disorders*, 5th ed. Washington, DC: American Psychiatric Association.

Else, L. (2011). Nobel psychologist reveals the error of our ways. *New Scientist*, 2839. www.newscientist.com/article/mg21228390.400-nobel-psychologist-reveals-the-err-of-our-ways.html

Groopman, J. (2007). *How doctors think*. Boston: Houghton Mifflin Company.

Hamilton, J. (2013). Why is psychiatry's new manual so much like the old one? www.npr.org/blogs/health/2013/05/16/184454931

Healy, D. (2012). *Pharmageddon*. Berkeley: University of California Press.

Insel, T., Cuthbert, B., Garvey, M., et al. (2010). Research Domain Criteria (RDoC): Toward a new classification framework for research on mental disorders. *American Journal of Psychiatry*, *167*(7), 748–751.

Insel, T. R., Cuthbert, B. N. (2015). Brain disorders? Precisely. *Science*, *348*(6234), 499–500.

Ioannidis, J. P. A. (2005). Why most published research findings are false. *PLoS Medicine*, *2*(8), 696–701.

Jamison, K. R. (1995). *An unquiet mind: A memoir of moods and madness*. New York: Alfred A. Knopf.

Krugman, P. (2013). The big fail. *The New York Times*, January 7, 2013, A3.

Kupfer, D. J., First, M. B., Regier, D. A. (eds.) (2002). *A research agenda for DSM-V*. Washington, DC: American Psychiatric Association.

Kupfer, D. J., Regier, D. A. (2011). Neuroscience, clinical evidence, and the future of psychiatric classification in DSM-5. *American Journal of Psychiatry*, *168*(7), 672–674.

Lewin, K. (1952). *Field theory in social science: Selected theoretical papers by Kurt Lewin*. London: Tavistock.

Livio, M. (2013). *Brilliant blunders: From Darwin to Einstein—Colossal mistakes by great scientists that changed our understanding of life and the universe*. New York: Simon & Schuster.

Muller, R. J. (2008). *Doing psychiatry wrong: A critical and prescriptive look at a faltering profession*. New York: The Analytic Press/Taylor & Francis Group.

Onitilo, A. A., Engel, J. M, Greenlee, R. T., Mukesh, B. N. (2009). Breast cancer subtypes based on ER/PR and Her2 expression: Comparison of clinicopathologic features and survival. *Clinical Medicine & Research*, 7(1–2), 4–13.

Ross, C. A., Pam, A. (eds.) (1995). *Pseudoscience in biological psychiatry: Blaming the body*. New York: John Wiley.

Chapter 2

Andreasen, N. C. (1984). *The broken brain: The biological revolution in psychiatry*. New York: Harper & Row.

Andreasen, N. C. (2005). *Brave new brain: Conquering mental illness in the era of the genome*. New York: Oxford University Press.

Angell, M. (2011a). The epidemic of mental illness: Why? *The New York Review of Books*, June 23, pp. 20–22.

Angell, M. (2011b). The illusions of psychiatry. *The New York Review of Books*, July 14, pp. 20–22.

Bernstein, C. A. (2011). Meta-structure in DSM-5 process. *Psychiatric News*, March 4, pp. 7–29.

Breggin, P. R. (1991). *Toxic psychiatry: Why therapy, empathy, and love must replace the drugs, electroshock, and biochemical theories of the "new psychiatry."* New York: St. Martin's Press.

Camus, A. (1974). *Resistance, rebellion, and death* (J. O'Brien trans.). New York: Vintage Books.

Carlat, D. (2010). *Unhinged: The trouble with psychiatry—A doctor's revelations about a profession in crisis*. New York: Free Press.

D'Antonio, M. (2013). *Mortal Sins: Sex, crime, and the era of catholic scandal*. New York: St. Martin's Press.

Eisenberg, L., Guttmacher, L. B. (2010). Were we all asleep at the switch? A personal reminiscence of psychiatry from 1940 to 2010. *Acta Psychiatrica Scandinavia*, *122*(2), 89–102.

Frances, A. (2011). The most influential psychiatrist of our time retires undefeated. *Psychiatric Times*, February 2011, p. 41.

Genova, P. (2003). Dump the DSM! *Psychiatric Times*, April 2003, pp. 72–75.

Glenmullen, J. (2000). *Prozac backlash: Overcoming the dangers of Prozac, Zoloft, Paxil, and other antidepressants with safe, effective alternatives*. New York: Simon & Schuster.

Healy, D. (2008). *Mania: A Short history of bipolar disorder*. Baltimore: Johns Hopkins University Press.

Ho, B.-C., Andreasen, N. C., Ziebell, S., Pierson, R., Magnotta, V. (2011). Long-term antipsychotic treatment and brain volumes: A longitudinal study of first-episode schizophrenia. *Archives of General Psychiatry*, *68*(2), 128–137.

Huxtable, A. L. (2008). *On architecture: Collected reflections on a century of change*. New York: Walker & Company.

Kirsch, I. (2010). *The emperor's new drugs: Exploding the antidepressant myth*. New York: Basic Books.

Krugman, P. (2009). How did economists get it so wrong? *The New York Times Magazine*, September 6, pp. 36–43.

Kuhn, R. (1958). The treatment of depressive states with G 22355 (imipramine hydrochloride). *American Journal of Psychiatry*, *115*(5), 459–464.

Kupfer, D. J., Regier, D. A. (2011). Neuroscience, clinical evidence, and the future of psychiatric classification in DSM-5. *American Journal of Psychiatry*, *168*(7), 672–674.

Lacasse, J., Leo, J. (2005). Serotonin and depression: A disconnect between the advertisements and the scientific literature. *PLoS Medicine*, 2(12), 1211–1216.

Lepore, J. (2016). After the fact: In the history of truth, a new chapter begins. *The New Yorker*, March 21, pp. 91–94.
Lieberman, J. (2013). Change, challenge, and opportunity: Psychiatry in age of reform and enlightenment. *Psychiatric News*, September 6, p. 4.
Loomer, H. P., Saunders, J. C., Kline, N. S. (1957). A clinical and pharmacodynamic evaluation of iproniazid as a psychic energizer. *Psychiatric Research Report of the American Psychiatric Association* (Dec.), *8*, 129–141.
Mackay, C. (1980). *Extraordinary popular delusions & the madness of crowds*. New York: Three Rivers Press.
McHugh, P. (2015). The doctor isn't in. Review of Jeffrey A. Lieberman, *Shrinks: The Untold Story of Psychiatry* (2015). New York: Little, Brown and Co. *Commentary*, October, pp. 6–8.
Moran, M. (2013). Lieberman says it's 'our time' for equity and fairness in mental health. *Psychiatric News*, June 21, p. 11.
Paumgarten, N. (2009). The death of kings: Notes from a meltdown. *The New Yorker*, May 18, 2009, pp. 40–57.
Ross, C. A., Pam, A. (eds.) (1995). *Pseudoscience in biological psychiatry: Blaming the body*. New York: John Wiley.
Ruhé, H. G., Mason, N. S., Schene, A. H. (2007). Mood is indirectly related to serotonin, norepinephrine and dopamine levels in humans: A meta-analysis of monoamine depletion studies. *Molecular Psychiatry*, *12*(4), 331–359.
Schildkraut, J. J. (1965). The catecholamine hypothesis of affective disorders: A review of supporting evidence. *American Journal of Psychiatry*, *122*(5), 509–522.
Sinclair, U. (1935). *I, candidate for governor: How I got licked*. Berkeley: University of California Press.
Taylor, R. L. (2014). *Finding the right psychiatrist: A guide for discerning consumers*. New Brunswick, NJ: Rutgers University Press.
Whitaker, R. (2010). *Anatomy of an epidemic: Magic bullets, psychiatric drugs, and the astonishing rise of mental illness in America*. New York: Crown Publishing Group.

Chapter 3

Barrett, W. (1962). *Irrational man. A study in existential philosophy*. New York: Anchor Books.
Barzun, J. (1983). *A stroll with William James*. New York: Harper & Row.
Binswanger, L. (1963). *Being-in-the-world: Selected papers of Ludwig Binswanger* (J. Needleman, ed.). New York: Basic Books.
Boss, M. (1963). *Psychoanalysis and daseinsanalysis* (L. B. Lefebre, trans.). New York: Basic Books.
Churchill, S. D., Wertz, F. J. (2014). An introduction to phenomenological research in psychology: Historical, conceptual, and methodological foundations. In K. J. Schneider, J. F. Pierson & J. F. T. Bugental (eds.) *The handbook of humanistic psychology: Theory, research, and practice*, 2nd ed. (pp. 275–295). Thousand Oaks, CA: SAGE.
Damasio, A. R. (1994). *Descartes' error: Emotion, reason, and the human brain*. New York: Putnam Publishing.
Davidson, D., Strauss, J. S. (1995). Beyond the biopsychosocial model: Integrating disorder, health, and recovery. *Psychiatry*, *58*(1), 44–55.
Dewsbury, D. A. (1991). "Psychobiology." *American Psychologist*, *45*, 198–205.
Double, D. B. (1990). What would Adolf Meyer have thought of the neo-Kraepelian approach? *Psychiatric Bulletin*, *14*, 472–474.

Double, D. B. (2007). Adolf Meyer's psychobiology and the challenge for biomedicine. *Philosophy, Psychiatry, & Psychology*, *14*(4), 331–339.

DSM-I (1952). *Diagnostic and statistical manual: Mental diseases*, 1st ed. Washington, DC: American Psychiatric Association.

DSM-II (1968). *Diagnostic and statistical manual of mental disorders*, 2nd ed. Washington, DC: American Psychiatric Association.

DSM-III (1980). *Diagnostic and statistical manual of mental disorders*, 3rd ed. Washington, DC: American Psychiatric Association.

DSM-IV (1994). *Diagnostic and statistical manual of mental disorders*, 4th ed. Washington, DC: American Psychiatric Association.

DSM-5 (2013). *Diagnostic and statistical manual of mental disorders*, 5th ed. Washington, DC: American Psychiatric Association.

Eisenberg, L. (1995). The social construction of the human brain. *American Journal of Psychiatry*, *152*(11), 1563–1575.

Ellis, R. D. (2006). Phenomenology-friendly neuroscience: The return to Merleau-Ponty as psychologist. *Human Studies*, *29*(1), 33–55.

Engel, G. L. (1977). The need for a new medical model: A challenge for biomedicine. *Science*, *196*(4286), 129–136.

Francis, R. C. (2011). *Epigenetics: The ultimate mystery of inheritance*. New York: W. W. Norton & Co.

Frankl, V. E. (1963). *Man's search for meaning: An introduction to logotherapy*. New York: Pocket Books.

Freedman, A. M. (1995). The biopsychosocial paradigm and the future of psychiatry. *Comprehensive Psychiatry*, *36*(6), 397–406.

Ghaemi, S. N. (2010). *The rise and fall of the biopsychosocial model: Reconciling art and science in psychiatry*. Baltimore: Johns Hopkins University Press.

Giorgi, A. (1970). *Psychology as a human science: A phenomenologically based approach*. Pittsburgh: Duquesne University Press.

Harper, R. (1972). *The existential experience*. Baltimore: Johns Hopkins University Press.

Heidegger, M. (1962). *Being and time* (J. Macquarrie and E. Robinson, trans.). New York: Harper & Row.

James, W. (1907). *Pragmatism: A new name for some old ways of thinking*. New York: Longmans.

James, W. (1920). *Collected essays and reviews*. New York: Longmans.

Jaspers, K. (1997). *General psychopathology, Vol. 1* (J. Hoenig and M. W. Hamilton, trans.). Baltimore: Johns Hopkins University Press.

Kanner, L. (1972). *Child psychiatry*, 4th ed. Springfield, IL: C. C. Thomas.

Laing, R. D. (1965). *The divided self: An existential study in sanity and madness*. Baltimore: Penguin Books.

Laing, R. D., Cooper, D. G. (1964). *Reason and violence: A decade of Sartre's philosophy 1950–1960*. New York: Pantheon Books.

Lamb, S. (2006). Functioning in the Phipps: Theory and practice in Adolf Meyer's psychobiology. Presentation to the Program in the History of Science, Medicine & Technology. The Johns Hopkins University, April 27.

Lamb, S. (2015). Social skills: Adolf Meyer's revision of clinical skill for the new psychiatry of the twentieth century. *Medical History*, *59*(3), 443–464.

Lamb, S. D. (2014). *Pathologist of the mind: Adolf Meyer and the origins of American psychiatry*. Baltimore: Johns Hopkins University Press.

Lidz, T. (1966). Adolf Meyer and the development of American psychiatry. *American Journal of Psychiatry*, *123*(3), 320–332.

Lief, A. (ed.) (1948). *The commonsense psychiatry of Dr. Adolf Meyer: Fifty-two selected papers*. New York: McGraw-Hill.

Malamud, W. (1929). Psychoanalytic mechanisms in clinical psychiatry. *American Journal of Psychiatry, 85*(5), 929–941.

May, R., Angel, E., Ellenberger, H. F. (eds.) (1958). *Existence: A new dimension in psychiatry and psychology*. New York: Basic Books.

McHugh, P. R. (2017). Adolf Meyer: His achievements and legacy. *The Journal of Mental and Nervous Disease, 205*(4), 253–257.

McHugh, P. R., Slavney, P. R. (1998). *The perspectives of psychiatry*, 2nd ed. Baltimore: Johns Hopkins University Press.

Merleau-Ponty, M. (1962). *Phenomenology of perception* (C. Smith, trans.). New York: Humanities Press.

Merleau-Ponty, M. (1967). *The structure of behavior* (A. L. Fisher, trans.). Boston: Beacon Press.

Meyer, A. (1897). A short sketch of the problems of psychiatry. *American Journal of Insanity, 53*, 538–549.

Meyer, A. (1906). Fundamental conceptions of dementia praecox. *British Medical Journal, 2*, 757–759.

Meyer, A. (1915). Objective psychology or psychobiology with subordination of the medically useless construct of mental and physical. *Journal of the American Medical Association, 65*, 860–863.

Meyer, A. (1922). The philosophy of occupation therapy. *Archives of Occupation Therapy, 1*(1), 1–10.

Meyer, A. (1934 [1951]). The psychobiological point of view. In Eunice E. Winters (ed.) *The Collected Papers of Adolf Meyer, Vol. III*. Baltimore: Johns Hopkins University Press.

Meyer, A. (1935). Psychobiology in the first year of medical school. *Journal of the Association of American Medical Colleges, 10*(6), 365–372.

Meyer, A. (1936). A plea for the concept of "sense" as the essence of consciousness, individual and social. In *Proceedings of the Fourth Conference on Psychiatric Education (1938)*, pp. 218–219. New York: The National Committee for Mental Hygiene.

Meyer, A. (1951). The role of the mental factors in psychiatry. In E. E. Winters (ed.) *The Collected Papers of Adolf Meyer, Vol. II* (pp. 581–590). Baltimore: Johns Hopkins University Press.

Meyer, A. (1952). The contributions of psychiatry to the understanding of life problems. In E. E. Winters (ed.) *The Collected Papers of Adolf Meyer, Vol. IV* (pp. 1–14). Baltimore: Johns Hopkins University Press.

Meyer, A., Jelliffe, S. E., Hoch, A. (1911). *Dementia praecox: A monograph*. Boston: The Gorham Press. (A BibiloLife, LLC reprint).

Moran, D., Cohen, J. (2012). *The Husserl dictionary*. New York: Continuum.

Mukherjee, S. (2016). Same but different: Identical twins and the science of epigenetics. *The New Yorker*, May 2, pp. 24–30.

Muller, R. J. (1987). *The marginal self: An existential inquiry into narcissism*. Atlantic Highlands, NJ: Humanities Press International.

Muller, R. J. (2003). To understand depression, think psychobiology, not biopsychiatry. *Psychiatric Times*, August, pp. 41–46.

Muller, R. J. (2008). *Doing psychiatry wrong: A critical and prescriptive look at a faltering profession*. New York: The Analytic Press/Taylor & Francis Group.

Muller, R. J. (2015a). Adolf Meyer (1866–1950). In *Encyclopedia of clinical psychology*, R. L. Cautin & S. O. Lilienfeld (eds.). Hoboken, NJ: John Wiley & Sons, 2015. doi: 10.1002/9781118625392.wbecp068.

Muller, R. J. (2015b). The four domains of mental illness: An alternative to the DSM-5. In

P. Zachar, D. St. Stoyanov, M. Aragona & A. Jablensky (eds.) *Alternative perspectives on psychiatric validation* (pp. 236–252). Oxford, UK: Oxford University Press.

Sartre, J-P. (2007). *Existentialism is a humanism* (C. Macomber, trans.). New Haven: Yale University Press.

Smith, G. P. (2013). Curt Richter and Adolf Meyer: The improbable couple. Lecture given at the Johns Hopkins University School of Medicine, October 16.

Straus, E. (1966). *Phenomenological psychology*. New York: Basic Books.

van den Berg, J. H. (1972). *A different existence: Principles of phenomenological psychopathology*. Pittsburgh: Duquesne University Press.

Chapter 4

Brendel, D. H. (2006). *Healing psychiatry: Bridging the science/humanism divide*. Cambridge, MA: The MIT Press.

Desautels, A. R. (1981). Sartre and the priests at Stalag 12D. *America*, February 14, pp. 114–116.

Eagleman, D. (2013). What our brains can teach us. *The New York Times*, February 23, p. A19.

James, W. (1924). *Memories and Studies*. New York: Longmans, Green.

Jaspers, K. (1997). *General psychopathology, Vol. 1* (J. Hoenig and M. W. Hamilton trans.). Baltimore: Johns Hopkins University Press.

Kettlewell, C. (1999). *Skin game: A cutter's memoir*. New York: St. Martin's Press.

Lehrer, J. (2010). The truth wears off: Is there something wrong with the scientific method? *The New Yorker*, December 13, pp. 52–57.

Lewis, B. (2011). *Narrative psychiatry: How stories can shape clinical practice*. Baltimore: Johns Hopkins University Press.

Mead, R. (2013). Particle follies. *The New Yorker*, January 28, pp. 22–23.

Muller, R. J. (2010). Psychiatric symptoms can be *understood* even when these symptoms cannot be *explained*. *Psychiatric Times*, July 9. www.psychiatrictimes.com/print/article/10168/1604140

Ratner-Rosenhagen, J. (2012). *American Nietzsche: A history of an icon and his ideas*. Chicago: University of Chicago Press.

Sartre, J-P. (1948). *Anti-Semite and Jew: An exploration of the etiology of hate* (G. J. Becker, trans.). New York: Schocken Books Inc.

Sartre, J-P. (1956). *Being and nothingness: An essay on phenomenological ontology* (H. E. Barnes, trans.). New York: Philosophical Library.

Sartre, J-P. (2007). *Existentialism is a humanism* (C. Macomber, trans.). New Haven: Yale University Press.

Chapter 5

Barzun, J. (1983). *A stroll with William James*. New York: Harper & Row, Publishers.

Boss, M. (1963). *Psychoanalysis and daseinanalysis* (L. W. Lefebre, trans.). New York: Basic Books.

Campbell, J. K., O'Rourke, M, Slater, M. H. (eds.) (2012). *Carving nature at its joints: Natural kinds in metaphysics and science*. Cambridge, MA: MIT Press.

Chisolm, M. S., Lyketsos, C. G. (2012). *Systematic psychiatric evaluation: A step-by-step guide to applying "The perspectives of psychiatry."* Baltimore, MD: Johns Hopkins University Press.

Churchill, S. D. (2014). Descriptive and interpretative dimensions of phenomenological research: Complementary or mutually exclusive approaches to human science? Unpublished manuscript based on a paper presented at the 33rd Annual Meeting of the International Human Science Research Conference, St. Francis Xavier University, Antigonish (Nova Scotia), August 12–15.

Craig, E. (2015). The lost language of being: Ontology's perilous destiny in existential psychotherapy. *Philosophy, Psychiatry, & Psychology*, 22(2), 80–92.

DSM-IV (1994). *Diagnostic and statistical manual of mental disorders*, 4th ed. Washington, DC: American Psychiatric Association.

Edmunds, L., Small, L. (2012). The 90-year divide. *Johns Hopkins Magazine*, *64*(3), 51–56.

Erikson, E. H. (1963). *Childhood and society*, 2nd ed. New York: W. W. Norton.

Heidegger, M. (1962). *Being and time* (J. Macquarrie and E. Robinson, trans.). New York: Harper & Row.

Heidegger, M. (2001). *Zollikon seminars: Protocols—Conversations—Letters* (M. Boss, ed.) (Mayr and R. Askay, trans.). Evanston, IL: Northwestern University Press.

Husserl, E. (1976). *Logical investigations* (J. N. Findlay, trans.). London: Routledge & Kegan Paul.

James, W. (1902). *The varieties of religious experience*. New York: Longmans.

James, W. (1904). *The principles of psychology, Vol. 1*. New York; Henry Holt.

Jaspers, K. (1954). *Way to wisdom: An introduction to philosophy* (R. Manheim, trans.). New Haven: Yale University Press.

Jaspers, K. (1970). *Philosophy, Vol. 2* (E. B. Ashton, trans.). Chicago: University of Chicago Press.

Jaspers, K. (1997). *General psychopathology, Vol. 1* (J. Hoenig and M. W. Hamilton, trans.). Baltimore, MD: Johns Hopkins University Press.

Kupfer, D. J., Regier, D. A. (2011). Neuroscience, clinical evidence, and the future of psychiatric classification in DSM-5. *American Journal of Psychiatry*, *168*(7), 672–674.

Lamb, S. D. (2014). *Pathologist of the mind: Adolf Meyer and the origins of American psychiatry*. Baltimore, MD: Johns Hopkins University Press.

McHugh, P. R. (2012). Rendering mental disorders intelligible: Addressing psychiatry's urgent challenge. In K. S. Kendler & J. Parnas (eds.) *Philosophical issues in psychiatry II: Nosology* (pp. 269–279). New York: Oxford University Press.

Menand, L. (2001). *The metaphysical club: A story of ideas in America*. New York: Farrar, Straus, and Giroux.

Meyer, A. (1906a). Fundamental conceptions of dementia praecox. *British Medical Journal*, 2, 757–759.

Meyer, A. (1906b). Principles in grouping facts in psychiatry. In A. Lief (ed.) *The commonsense psychiatry of Dr. Adolf Meyer: Fifty-two selected papers* (pp. 153–168). New York: McGraw-Hill Book Co.

Meyer, A. (1908a). The role of mental factors in psychiatry. *American Journal of Psychiatry*, *65*(1), 39–56.

Meyer, A. (1908b). The problems of mental reaction-types, mental causes and diseases. *Psychological Bulletin*, *5*(8), 245–261.

Meyer, A. (1922). Interrelations of the domain of neuropsychiatry. *Archives of Neurology and Psychiatry*, *8*, 111–121.

Muller, R. J. (2008). *Doing psychiatry wrong: A critical and prescriptive look at a faltering profession*. New York: The Analytic Press/Taylor & Francis Group.

Muller, R. J. (2015a). The four domains of mental illness (FDMI): An alternative to the DSM-5. In P. Zachar, D. St. Stoyanov, M. Aragona & A. Jablensky (eds.) *Alternative*

Perspectives on Psychiatric Validation: DSM, ICD, RDoC, and Beyond, pp. 236–252. Oxford, UK: Oxford University Press.
Muller, R. J. (2015b). Psychotherapy's ontic-ontological divide: Going beyond the hyphen. *Philosophy, Psychiatry, & Psychology*, 22(2), 99–102.
Ortega y Gasset, J. (1956). *The dehumanization of art* (W. R. Trask, trans.). Garden City, NY: Doubleday & Co.
Romanyshyn, R. (2012). The necessity for the humanistic in psychology. *The Humanistic Psychologist*, *40*(3), 234–245.
Séchehaye, M. (1956). *A new psychotherapy in schizophrenia: Relief of frustrations by symbolic realization* (G. Rubin-Babson, trans.). New York: Grune & Stratton.
Sulloway, F. J. (1983). *Freud, biologist of the mind: Beyond the psychoanalytic legend*. New York: Basic Books.
van den Berg, J. H. (1972). *A different existence: Principles of phenomenological psychopathology*. Pittsburgh: Duquesne University Press.
Watson, R. I. (1951). *The clinical method in psychology*. New York: Harper & Brothers.

Chapter 6

Allen, T. E. (2014). *Life of Pi* and the moral wound. *Journal of the American Psychoanalytic Association*, *62*(6), 965–982.
Dobbs, D. (2009). The post-traumatic stress trap. *Scientific American*, April, pp. 64–69.
DSM-5 (2013). *Diagnostic and Statistical Manual of Mental Disorders*, 5th ed. Washington, DC: American Psychiatric Association.
Filkins, D. (2012). Atonement: A troubled Iraq veteran seeks out the family he harmed. *The New Yorker*, October 29 and November 5, pp. 92–103.
Fischer, W. F. (1988). *Theories of anxiety*, 2nd ed. Lanham, MD: University Press of America.
Friend, T. (2014). Nine lives. *The New Yorker*, April 21, pp. 32–34.
Gellene, D. (2014). Sherwin B. Nuland, 'How we die' author, dies at 83. *The New York Times*, March 5, p. B15.
Gornick, V. (2016). Song of inexperience. *The New York Times Book Review*, February 14, p. 29.
Gourevitch, P. (2014). Remembering in Rwanda. *The New Yorker*, April 21, pp. 31–32.
Jaspers, K. (1997). *General psychopathology, Vol. 1* (J. Hoenig and M. W. Hamilton, trans.). Baltimore: Johns Hopkins University Press.
Laing, R. D. (1965). *The divided self: An existential study in sanity and madness*. Baltimore: Penguin Books.
Maddock, R. J. (2001). The lactic acid response to alkalosis in panic disorder: An integrative review. *Journal of Neuropsychiatry and Clinical Neurosciences*, *13*(1), 22–34.
McHugh, P. R., Triesman, G. (2007). PTSD: A problematic diagnostic category. *Journal of Anxiety Disorders*, *21*(2), 211–222.
Muller, R. J. (2003). *Psych ER: Psychiatric patients come to the emergency room*. Hillsdale, NJ: The Analytic Press.
Nuland, S. B. (1994). *How we die: Reflections on life's final chapter*. New York: Alfred A. Knopf.
Nuland, S. B. (2003). *Lost in America: A journey with my father*. New York: Alfred A. Knopf.
Ratey, J. J. (2008). *Spark: The revolutionary new science of exercise and the brain*. New York: Little, Brown and Co.
Salinger, J. D. (2010). *The catcher in the rye*. London, UK: Penguin Books.

Selye, H. (1978). *The stress of life*. New York: The McGraw-Hill Companies.
Tracey, K. J. (2006). *Fatal sequence: The killer within*. New York: Dana Press.

Chapter 7

Beckett, S. (1955). *Three novels by Samuel Beckett: Molloy, Malone dies, The unnamable* (P. Bowles, trans.). New York: Grove Weidenfeld.
Camus, A. (1955). *The myth of Sisyphus* (J. O'Brien, trans.). New York: Alfred A. Knopf.
DSM-5 (2013). *Diagnostic and statistical manual of mental disorders*, 5th ed. Washington, DC: American Psychiatric Association.
Fitzgerald, F. S. (1945). *The crack-up* (E. Wilson, ed). New York: New Directions.
Frank, J. D., Frank, J. B. (1991). *Persuasion and healing: A comparative study of healing*, 3rd ed. Baltimore: Johns Hopkins University Press.
Frankl, V. E. (1963). *Man's search for meaning: An introduction to logotherapy* (I. Lasch, trans.). New York: Pocket Books.
Itzkoff, D. (2014). Robin Williams, 1951–2014. *The New York Times*, August 12, A1, 14.
Jaspers, K. (1997). *General psychopathology, Vol. 1* (J. Hoenig and M. W. Hamilton, trans.). Baltimore: Johns Hopkins University Press.
Lief, A. (ed.) (1948). *The commonsense psychiatry of Dr. Adolf Meyer: Fifty-two selected papers*. New York: McGraw-Hill Book Company.
Meyer, A. (1908). The role of mental factors in psychiatry. *American Journal of Psychiatry, 65*(1), 39–56.
Muller, R. J. (1996). The pathological side of paradise: F. Scott Fitzgerald's decompensated narcissism. A presentation for the series Patients and Fortitude: Authors and Their Illnesses, sponsored by the Office of Cultural Affairs of The Johns Hopkins Medical Institutions, April 11, 1996.
Muller, R. J. (2003). To understand depression, look to psychobiology, not biopsychiatry. *Psychiatric Times*, August, pp. 41–46.
Muller, R. J. (2009). Pathological anger, existentially speaking. *Psychiatric Times*, May 26. www.psychiatrictimes.com/display/article/10168/1416734
Sartre, J-P. (1948). *The emotions: Outline of a theory* (B. Frechtman, trans.). New York: Wisdom Library.
Smith, T. (2013). Stefanie Powers brings Tallulah Bankhead to life in "Looped" at the Hippodrome. *The Baltimore Sun*, March 7.

Chapter 8

Bergman, I. (1989). *The magic lantern: An autobiography* (J. Tate, trans.). New York: Penguin Books.
DSM-IV (1994). *Diagnostic and statistical manual of mental disorders*, 4th ed. Washington, DC: American Psychiatric Association.
DSM-5 (2013). *Diagnostic and statistical manual of mental disorders*, 5th ed. Washington, DC: American Psychiatric Association.
McHugh, P. R. (2008). *Try to remember: Psychiatry's clash over meaning, memory, and mind*. New York: Dana Press.
Ross, C. A. (1989). *Multiple personality disorder: Diagnosis, clinical features, and treatment*. New York: John Wiley & Sons.
Young, B. (2015). *The persona of Ingmar Bergman: Conquering demons through film*. Lanham, MD: Rowman & Littlefield.

Chapter 9

Herbert, W. (1989). Paranoia: Fearful delusions. *The New York Times Magazine*, March 19, pp. 62–64.
Lief, A. (ed.) (1948). *The commonsense psychiatry of Dr. Adolf Meyer: Fifty-two selected papers*. New York: McGraw-Hill Book Company.
Muller, R. J. (2006). Willing paranoid delusions. *Psychiatric Times*, December, pp. 33–35.
Séchehaye, M. (1956). *A new psychotherapy in schizophrenia: Relief of frustrations by symbolic realization* (G. Rubin-Babson, trans.). New York: Grune & Stratton.

Chapter 10

Acocella, J. (2014). Let it go: Are we becoming a nation of hoarders? *The New Yorker*, December 15, pp. 69–73.
Arehart-Treichel, J. (2014). Several therapies show success in treatment of personality disorders. *Psychiatric News*, May 16, p. 31.
Aronson, R. (2004). *Camus and Sartre: The story of a friendship and the quarrel that ended it*. Chicago: University of Chicago Press.
Churchill, S. D., Wertz, F. J. (2014). An introduction to phenomenological research in psychology: Historical, conceptual, and methodological foundations. K. J. Schneider, J. F. Pierson & J. F. T. Bugental (eds.), *The handbook of humanistic psychology: Theory, research, and practice*, 2nd ed. (pp. 275–295). Thousand Oaks, CA: SAGE.
Cleckley, H. M. (1941). *Mask of sanity*. St. Louis, MO: Mosby Co.
Deutsch, H. (1942). Some forms of emotional disturbance and their relationship to schizophrenia. *Psychoanalytic Quarterly*, *11*, 301–321.
DSM-5 (2013). *Diagnostic and statistical manual of mental disorders*, 5th ed. Washington, DC: American Psychiatric Association.
Duffy, J. (2005). Crazy success. *Johns Hopkins Magazine*, June, pp. 35–38.
Erikson, E. H. (1963). *Childhood and society*, 2nd ed. New York: W. W. Norton.
Flynn, G. (2012). *Gone girl*. New York: Crown Publishers.
Freud, S. (1910). The taboo of virginity. *Standard edition of the complete psychological works of Sigmund Freud, Vol. XI*. London: The Hogarth Press, pp. 193–208.
Fromm, E. (1964). *The heart of man*. New York: Harper & Row.
Frost, R. O., Steketee, G. (2010). *Stuff: Compulsive hoarding and the meaning of things*. Boston: Houghton Mifflin Harcourt.
Gartner, J. D. (2005). *The hypomanic edge: The link between (a little) craziness and (a lot of) success in America*. New York: Simon & Schuster.
Glaister, D. (2008). Recordings reveal Nixon's paranoia. *The Guardian*, December 3.
Goleman, D. (2014). Mental muscle vs. A.D.H.D. *The New York Times*, May 13, p. D6.
Goode, E. (2003). Stalin to Saddam: So much for the madman theory. *The New York Times*, Week in Review, May 5, p. 5.
Gopnik, A. (2014). Go Giants: A new survey of the great American novel. *The New Yorker*, April 21, pp. 102–104.
Grotstein, J. S. (1997). *Splitting and projective identification*. Northvale, NJ: Jason Aronson.
Guntrip, H. (1969). *Schizoid phenomena, object-relations, and the self*. New York: International Universities Press.
Hofstadter, R. (1964). The paranoid style in American politics. *Harper's Magazine*, November, pp. 77–86.
Hofstadter, R. (2008). *The paranoid style in American politics*. New York: Vintage Books.

Horney, K. (1950). *Neurosis and human growth: The struggle toward self-realization*. New York: W. W. Norton.

Hughes, K. J. (2007). How paranoid was Nixon? *History News Network*, August 13. http//historynewsnetwork.org/article/41698#STHASH.4CKEKBcA

Jaspers, K. (1997). *General psychopathology, Vol 1* (J. Hoenig and M. W. Hamilton, trans.). Baltimore: Johns Hopkins University Press.

Kernberg, O. (1975). *Borderline conditions and pathological narcissism*. New York: Jason Aronson.

Kernberg, O. F. (1970a). Factors in the psychoanalytic treatment of narcissistic personalities. *Journal of the American Psychoanalytic Association, 18*(1), 51–85.

Kernberg, O. F. (1970b). A psychoanalytic classification of character pathology. *Journal of the American Psychoanalytic Association, 18*(1), 800–822.

Kohut, H. (1971). *The analysis of the self*. New York: International Universities Press.

Kohut, H. (1977). *The analysis of the self: A systematic approach to the psychoanalytic treatment of narcissistic personality disorders*. New York: International Universities Press.

Krog, A. (2015). The transformation of evil. *The New York Times*, Sunday Review, March 15, p. 7.

Kundera, M. (1984). *The unbearable lightness of being* (M. H. Heim, trans.). New York: Harper & Row.

Laing, R. D. (1965). *The divided self: An existential study in sanity and madness*. Baltimore: Penguin.

Lasch, C. (1978). *The culture of narcissism: American life in an age of diminishing expectations*. New York: W. W. Norton & Co.

Leibovich, M. (2015). Donald Trump is not going anywhere. *The New York Times Magazine*, October 4, pp. 28–33, 52.

Lief, A. (ed.) (1948). *The commonsense psychiatry of Dr. Adolf Meyer: Fifty-two selected papers*. New York: McGraw-Hill.

Linehan, M. M. (2015). *DBT skills training manual*, 2nd ed. New York: The Guilford Press.

Lunbeck, E. (2014). *The Americanization of narcissism*. Cambridge, MA: Harvard University Press.

Maccoby, M. (2007). *Narcissistic leaders: Who succeeds and who fails*. New York: Harvard Business School Press.

Mahler, M. S., Pine, F., Bergman, A. (1975). *The psychological birth of the human infant: Symbols and individuation*. New York: Basic Books.

Malthus, T. R. (1986). An essay on the principle of population. In E. A. Wrigley and D. Souden (eds.) *The works of Thomas Robert Malthus, Vol 1*. London, UK: Pickering.

Manfield, P. (1992). *Split self/split object: Understanding and treating borderline, narcissistic, and schizoid disorders*. New York: Jason Aronson.

Masterson, J. F. (1976). *Psychotherapy of the borderline adult*. New York: Brunner/Mazel.

Masterson, J. F., Klein, R. (1995). *Disorders of the self: New therapeutic horizons*. New York: Brunner/Mazel.

Mendes, S. (Director). (2008). *Revolutionary road* [motion picture]. Universal City, CA: Dreamworks.

Miller, A. (2003). *The crucible*. New York: Penguin Books.

Muller, R. J. (1987). *The marginal self: An existential inquiry into narcissism*. Atlantic Highlands, NJ: Humanities Press International.

Muller, R. J. (1992). Is there a neural basis for borderline splitting? *Comprehensive Psychiatry, 33*(2), 92–104.

Muller, R. J. (1993). Karen Horney's "resigned person" heralds DSM-III-R's borderline personality disorder. *Comprehensive Psychiatry*, *34*(4), 264–272.

Muller, R. J. (1994). *Anatomy of a splitting borderline: Description and analysis of a case history*. Westport, CT: Praeger.

Muller, R. J. (2003). *Psych ER: Psychiatric patients come to the emergency room*. New York: The Analytic Press/Taylor & Francis Group.

Muller, R. J. (2008). *Doing psychiatry wrong: A clinical and prescriptive look at a faltering profession*. New York: The Analytic Press/Taylor & Francis Group.

Muller, R. J. (2009). Pathological anger, existentially speaking. *Psychiatric Times*, May 26. www.psychiatrictimes.com/display/article/10168/1416734

Muller, R. J. (2011). Failing narcissistic defenses can turn love toxic. *The Humanistic Psychologist*, *39*(4), 375–378.

Muller, R. J. (2014a). What kind of narcissist are you? *The Humanistic Psychologist*, *42*(2), 215–224.

Muller, R. J. (2014b). Histrionic managers wreak havoc in the workplace: Identifying the phenomenon. *The Humanistic Psychologist*, *42*(4), 402–412.

Muller, R. J. (2016). Can Donald Trump change his spots? *The Baltimore Sun*, November 15, p. 11.

Nigg, J. T. (2006). *What causes ADHD? Understanding what goes wrong and why*. New York: The Guilford Press.

Ovid (1960). *Ovid's metamorphoses* (R. Humphries, trans.). Bloomington: Indiana University Press.

Paris, J. (2012). *The bipolar spectrum: Diagnosis or fad?* New York: Routledge/Taylor & Francis Group.

Reeves, R. (2001). *Richard Nixon: Alone in the White House*. New York: Simon & Schuster.

Reich, W. (1949). *Character Analysis*. New York: Orgone Institute Press.

Ryback, T. W. (2003). Hitler's forgotten library: The man, his books, and his search for God. *The Atlantic Monthly*, May, pp. 76–90.

Sartre, J-P. (1948). *The emotions: Outline of a theory* (B. Frechtman, trans.). New York: Wisdom Library.

Sartre, J-P. (1956). *Being and nothingness: An essay on phenomenological ontology* (H. E. Barnes, trans.). New York: Philosophical Library.

Shapiro, D. (1965). *Neurotic styles*. New York: Basic Books.

Stern, A. (1938). Psychoanalytic investigation of and therapy in the borderline group of neuroses. *Psychoanalytic Quarterly*, 7, 467–489.

Stern, D. N. (1985). *The interpersonal world of the infant: A view from psychoanalysis and developmental psychology*. New York: Basic Books.

Stone, M. H. (1990). *The fate of borderline patients*. New York: The Guilford Press.

Timanus, E., & Brady, E. (2010). Lawyer calls Virginia lacrosse player murder case an 'accident'. *USA Today*, May 4. usatoday.com/sports/college/lacrosse/2010-05-03-virginia-huguely-murder-charge_N.htm

Vaillant, G. E. (1975). Sociopathy as a human process. *Arch Gen Psychiatry*, *32*(2), 178–183.

Vaillant, G. E. (1992). The beginning of wisdom is never calling a patient a borderline; or, The clinical management of immature defenses in the treatment of individuals with personality disorders. *Journal of Psychotherapy Practice and Research*, *1*(2), 117–134.

Vaillant, G. E. (2000). Adaptive mental mechanisms: Their role in a positive psychology. *American Psychologist*, *55*(1), 89–98.

van den Berg, J. H. (1972). *A different existence: Principles of phenomenological psychopathology*. Pittsburgh: Duquesne University Press.
Venter, J. C. (2007). *A life decoded: My genome: My life*. New York: Viking.
Weber, C. (2007). Quoted in tabloid princess, a review of *The Diana chronicles*, T. Brown. New York: Doubleday, 2007. *The New York Times Book Review*, June 10, pp. 1, 10, 11.
Wikipedia (2014). *Monk* (TV series). Much of the factual information about Monk's illness was taken from this entry.
Winnicott, D. W. (1965). *The family and individual development*. London, UK: Tavistock Publications Limited.
Yates, R. (1961). *Revolutionary road*. New York: Vintage Books.
Zweig, P. (1968). *The heresy of self-love: A study of subversive individualism*. Princeton, NJ: Princeton University Press.

Chapter 11

Brody, J. E. (2008). The growing wave of teenage self-injury. *The New York Times*, May 6, p. D7.
Chabon, M. (1988). *The mysteries of Pittsburgh*. New York: William Morrow and Company, Inc.
Cohen, B. J. (2003). *Theory and practice of psychiatry*. New York: Oxford University Press.
Favazza, A. (2011). *Bodies under siege: Self-mutilation, nonsuicidal self-injury, and body modification in culture and psychiatry*, 3rd ed. Baltimore, MD: Johns Hopkins University Press.
Fingarette, H. (1969). *Self-deception*. London, UK: Routledge & Kegan Paul.
Fingarette, H. (1988). *Heavy drinking: The myth of alcoholism as a disease*. Berkeley: University of California Press.
Gartner, J. D. (2005). *The hypomanic edge: The link between (a little) craziness and (a lot of) success in America*. New York: Simon & Schuster.
George, S., Murali, V. (2005). Pathological gambling: An overview of assessment and treatment. *Advances in Psychiatric Treatment*, *11*(6), 450–456.
Jellinek, E. M. (1960). *The disease concept of alcoholism*. New Haven, CT: Hillhouse
Kettlewell, C. (1999). *Skin game: A cutter's memoir*. New York: St. Martin's Press.
Laing, R. D. (1965). *The divided self: An existential study in sanity and madness*. Baltimore: Penguin Books.
Laing, R. D., Cooper, D. G. (1964). *Reason and violence: A decade of Sartre's philosophy 1950–1960*. New York: Pantheon Books.
McElroy, S. L., Hudson, J. I., Pope, H. G., Keck, P. E. (1991). Kleptomania: Clinical characteristics and associated psychopathology. *Psychological Medicine*, *21*(1), 93–108.
McElroy, S. L., Pope, H. G., Hudson, J. I., Keck, P. E., White, K. L. (1991). Kleptomania: A report of 20 cases. *American Journal of Psychiatry*, *148*(5), 652–657.
McHugh, P. R., Slavney, P. R. (1998). *The perspectives of psychiatry*, 2nd ed. Baltimore: Johns Hopkins University Press.
Muller, R. J. (1987). *The marginal self: An existential inquiry into narcissism*. Atlantic Highlands, NJ: Humanities Press International.
Rohan, W. P. (1978). Comment on "The N.C.A. criteria for the diagnosis of alcoholism: An empirical evaluation study." *Journal of Studies on Alcohol*, *39*(1), 211–218.
Ross, G. S. (2002). *Stung: The incredible obsession of Brian Molony*. Toronto, Ontario: McClelland & Stewart LTD.

Russell, G. (1979). Bulimia nervosa: An ominous variant of anorexia nervosa. *Psychological Medicine*, 9(3), 429–448.
Vaillant, G. E. (1995). *The natural history of alcoholism revisited*. Cambridge, MA: Harvard University Press.
van den Berg, J. H. (1972). *A different existence: Principles of phenomenological psychopathology*. Pittsburgh: Duquesne University Press.

Chapter 12

Harris, J., Piven, J. (2016). Correcting the record: Leo Kanner and autism. www.medpagetoday.com/Neurology/Autism/57565?xid=nl_mpt_DHE_¬2016-04-28
Hoch, A. (1910). Constitutional factors in the dementia praecox group. *Review of Neurology and Psychiatry*, 8, 463–474.
Kanner, L. (1943). Autistic disturbances of affective contact. *Nervous Child*, 2, 217–250.
Kanner, L. (1972). *Child Psychiatry*, 4th ed. Springfield, IL: C. C. Thomas.
Levin, A. (2014). When autism entered the lexicon. *Psychiatric News*, May 16, pp. 7, 33.
Maddock, R. J. (2001). The lactic acid response to alkalosis in panic disorder: An integrative review. *Journal of Neuropsychiatry and Clinical Neurosciences*, 13(1), 22–34.
Shapin, S. (2016). Seeing the spectrum: A new history of autism. *The New Yorker*, January 25, pp. 65–69.
Slavney, P. R. (1998). *Psychiatric dimensions of medical practice*. Baltimore: Johns Hopkins University Press.

Chapter 13

Andreasen, N. C. (1984). *The broken brain: The biological revolution in psychiatry*. New York: Harper & Row.
Bateson, G., Jackson, D. D., Haley, J., Weakland, J. (1956). Toward a theory of schizophrenia. *Behavioral Science*, 1(4), 251–264.
Burston, D. (1996). *The wing of madness: The life and work of R. D. Laing*. Cambridge, MA: Harvard University Press.
Frank, J. D., Frank, J. B. (1991). *Persuasion and healing: A comparative study of healing*, 3rd edition. Baltimore: Johns Hopkins University Press.
Hoch, A. (1910). Constitutional factors in the dementia praecox group. *Review of Neurology and Psychiatry*, 8, 463–474.
Laing, R. D. (1965). *The divided self: An existential study in sanity and madness*. Baltimore: Penguin Books.
Lief, A. (ed.) (1948). *The commonsense psychiatry of Dr. Adolf Meyer: Fifty-two selected papers*. New York: McGraw-Hill Book Company.
Marx, O. (1993). Adolf Meyer and psychiatric training at the Phipps Clinic: An interview with Theodore Lidz. *History of Psychiatry*, 4(14), 245–269.
Meyer, A. (1906). Fundamental conceptions of dementia praecox. *British Medical Journal*, 2, 757–759.
Meyer, A., Jelliffe, S. E., Hoch, A. (1911). *Dementia praecox: A monograph*. Boston, MA: The Gorham Press.
Muller, R. J. (1987). *The marginal self: An existential inquiry into narcissism*. Atlantic Highlands, NJ: Humanities Press International.
Ricks, C., McCue, J. (eds.) (2015). *The poems of T. S. Eliot, Vol 5*. Baltimore: Johns Hopkins University Press.

Saks, E. R. (2007). *The center cannot hold: My journey through madness*. New York: Hyperion.
Séchehaye, M. (1956). *A new psychotherapy in schizophrenia: Relief of frustrations by symbolic realization* (G. Rubin-Babson, trans.). New York: Grune & Stratton.
Spandler, H. (2006). *Asylum to action: Paddington Day Hospital, therapeutic communities and beyond*. London, UK: Jessica Kingsley Publishers.
Whitehorn, J. C. (Youtube video). www.youtube.com/user/MedicalArchives/videos?sort=dd&view=0&shelf id=1
Whitehorn, J. C. (1950). Psychodynamic considerations in the treatment of psychotic patients. *University of Western Ontario Medical Journal*, *20*(2), 27–41.
Whitehorn, J. C., Betz, B. J. (1975). *Effective psychotherapy with the schizophrenic patient*. New York: Jason Aronson.
Young, B. (2012). Dr. John C Whitehorn: A wise and gentle man. www.psychiatrictimes.com/blog/psych-history/content/article/10168/2098610

Chapter 14

Andreasen, N. C. (1979). Thought, language, and communication disorders. *Archives of General Psychiatry*, *36*(12), 1315–1321.
DSM-II (1968). *Diagnostic and statistical manual of mental disorders*, 2nd ed. Washington, DC: American Psychiatric Association.
Hill, L. B. (1955). *Psychotherapeutic intervention in schizophrenia*. Chicago: University of Chicago Press.
James, C. (2002). The man, not a legend, of 'A beautiful mind.' *The New York Times*, April 26, p. B28.
Jefferson, M. (2004). I wish I had said that, and I will. *The New York Times Book Review*, April 11, p. 23.
Kennedy, D. (2002). The mind inside the madness. *The New York Times*, April 21, p. AR35, Sec 2.
Mlodinow, L. (2012). Physicist: I studied theories of infinite dimensions—in the university and in Hollywood. *The New York Times*, June 3, p. SR7.
Mosher, L. R. (2004). Obituary. *The New York Times*, July 18, p. 25.
Muller, R. J. (2012). Eliciting the phenomenon of schizophrenia from an autobiographical narrative. *Psychiatric Times*, August 27. www.psychiatrictimes.com/schizophrenia/content/article/10168/2098772
Nasar, S. (1998). *A beautiful mind: The life of mathematical genius and Nobel laureate John Nash*. New York: Simon & Schuster.
Saks, E. R. (2007). *The center cannot hold: My journey through madness*. New York: Hyperion.
Saks, E. R. (2013). Successful and schizophrenic. *The New York Times*, January 27, p. SR5.
Séchehaye, M. (1956). *A New psychotherapy in schizophrenia: Relief of frustrations by symbolic realization* (G. Rubin-Rabson, trans.). New York: Grune & Stratton.
Séchehaye, M. (1970). *Autobiography of a schizophrenic girl* (G. Rubin-Rabson, trans.). New York: Signet.
Urfer, A. (2001). Phenomenology and psychopathology of schizophrenia: The views of Eugene Minkowski. *Philosophy, Psychiatry, & Psychology*, *8*(4), 279–289.

Chapter 15

Arieti, S. (1974). *Interpretation of schizophrenia*, 2nd ed. New York: Basic Books.

Carpenter, W. T., Heinrichs, D. W., Wagman, A. M. (1988). Deficit and nondeficit forms of schizophrenia: The concept. *American Journal of Psychiatry, 145*(5), 578–583.

Francis, A. (2011). Prophet of preventive psychiatry recants: Pulls support for psychosis risk and the use of antipsychotics. *Psychiatric Times*, July, p. 10.

Harrison, P. J., Lewis, D. A., Kleinman, J. E. (2011). Neuropathology in schizophrenia. In D. R. Weinberger & P. Harrison (eds.), *Schizophrenia* (pp. 372–392). Oxford, UK: Wiley-Blackwell.

Ho, B.-C., Andreasen, N. C., Ziebell, S., Pierson, R., Magnotta, V. (2011). Long-term antipsychotic treatment and brain volumes: A longitudinal study of first-episode schizophrenia. *Archives of General Psychiatry, 68*(2), 128–137.

Jaspers, K. (1997). *General Psychopathology, Vol. 1* (J. Hoenig and M. W. Hamilton, trans.). Baltimore: Johns Hopkins University Press.

McGlashan, T. H., Johannessen, J. O. (1996). Early detection and intervention with schizophrenia: Rationale. *Schizophrenia Bulletin*, 22, 201–222.

McGlashan, T. H., Woods, S. (2011). Early antecedents and detection of schizophrenia: Understanding the clinical implications. *Psychiatric Times*, March, pp. 48–53.

McGory, P. (2011). *The Australian*, June 16. www.theaustralian.com.au/news/features/schism-opens-over-ills-of-the-mind/story-e6frg6z6-1226075910650; and communication with Martin Whiteley on June 16, 2011. www.speedupsitstill.com

Meyer, A. (1951). The dynamic interpretation of dementia praecox. In E. E. Winters (ed.) *The Collected Papers of Adolf Meyer, Vol II* (pp. 443–458). Baltimore: Johns Hopkins University Press.

Plum, F. (1972). Prospects for research on schizophrenia. Neuropathological findings. *Neurosciences Research Program Bulletin, 10*(4), 384–388.

Chapter 16

Acocella, J. (2004). Blocked: Why do writers stop writing? *The New Yorker*, June 14 & 21, pp. 110–129.

Baldessarini, R. J. (2000). A plea for integrity of the bipolar concept. *Bipolar Disorders*, 2(1), 3–7.

Campbell, J. D. (1953). *Manic-depressive disease: Clinical and psychiatric significance*. Philadelphia: J. B. Lippincott.

DSM-5 (2013). *Diagnostic and statistical manual of mental disorders*, 5th ed. Washington, DC: American Psychiatric Association.

Duffy, A. (2007). Does bipolar disorder exist in children? A selective review. *Canadian Journal of Psychiatry*, 52(7), 409–417.

Ghaemi, S. N., Sachs, G. S., Chiou, A. M., Pandurangi, A. K., Goodwin, K. (1999). Is bipolar disorder still underdiagnosed? Are antidepressants overutilized? *Journal of Affective Disorders*, 52(1–3), 135–144.

Goodwin, F. K., Jamison, K. R. (2007). *Manic depressive illness*, 2nd ed. New York: Oxford University Press.

Gross, J. (ed.) (2009). *Handbook of emotion regulation*. New York: Guilford.

Hacking, I. (2002). *Historical ontology*. Cambridge, MA: Harvard University Press.

Healy, D. (2006). The latest mania: Selling bipolar disorder. *PLoS Med, 3*(4), p. e185. doi.10.1371/journal.pmed.0030185

Healy, D. (2007). Pediatric bipolar disorder: An object of study in the creation of an illness. *International Journal of Risk & Safety in Medicine*, *19*(4), 209–221.

Healy, D. (2008). *Mania: A short history of bipolar disorder*. Baltimore: Johns Hopkins University Press.

Healy, D. (2012). *Pharmageddon*. Berkeley: University of California Press.

Jamison, K. R. (1995). *An unquiet mind: A memoir of moods and madness*. New York: Alfred A. Knopf.

Jamison, K. R. (2017). *Robert Lowell. Setting the river on fire*. New York: Alfred A. Knopf.

Janowsky, D. S., Leff, M., Epstein, R. S. (1970). Playing the manic game: Interpersonal maneuvers of the acutely manic patient. *Archives of General Psychiatry, 22*, 252–261.

Khong, B.S.C. (2017). Coroner's inquest into an Australian anchorwoman's suicide. Implications for clinical practice and suicide prevention. *The Humanistic Psychologist*, *45*, 23–48.

Klee, H. (1997). *Amphetamine misuse: International perspectives on current trends*. Amsterdam: Harwood Academic Publishers.

Koenigsberg, H. (2010). Affective instability: Toward an integration of neurological and psychological perspectives. *Journal of Personality Disorders*, *24*(1), 60–82.

Linehan, M. M. (1993). *Cognitive behavioral therapy for borderline personality disorder*. New York: Guilford.

Merck (2006). *Merck manual of diagnosis and therapy*, 18th ed. Whitehouse Station, NJ: Merck Research Laboratories, p. 1690.

Mick, E., Biederman, J., Dougherty, M., Aleardi, M. (2004). Open trial of atypical antipsychotics in pre-schoolers with bipolar disorder [Abstract]. *Acta Psychiatrica Scandinavia*, *110*, P51, 29.

Muller, R. J. (2004). In the ER, simple questions yield subtle lessons. *Psychiatric Times*, May, pp. 24–26.

Muller, R. J. (2008). *Doing psychiatry wrong: A critical and prescriptive look at a faltering profession*. New York: The Analytic Press/Taylor & Francis Group.

Muller, R. J. (2013). Biological psychiatry's false paradigm. *The Baltimore Sun*, June 19, p. 19.

Paris, J. (2012). *The bipolar spectrum: Diagnosis or fad?* New York: Routledge/Taylor & Francis Group.

Putnam, D. P. (2000). *Bowling alone: The collapse and revival of American community*. New York: Simon & Schuster.

Satel, S. (2000). *P.C., M.D.: How political correctness is corrupting medicine*. New York: Basic Books.

Siever, L. J., Davis, K. L. (1991). A psychobiological perspective on the personality disorders. *American Journal of Psychiatry*, *148*(12), 1647–1658.

Sinaikin, P. M. (2004). How I learned to stop worrying and love the DSM. *Psychiatric Times*, February, p. 38.

U.S. National Library of Medicine (2015). LiverTox: Clinical and research information on drug-induced liver injury. http://livertox.nih.gov/Amphetamines.htm

Winokur, G., Tsuang, M. (1975). Elation versus irritability in mania. *Comprehensive Psychiatry, 16*(5), 435–436.

Wood, A. J. J. (2001). Racial differences in the response to drugs—Pointers to genetic differences. *New England Journal of Medicine, 344*, 1393–1395.

Young, D., Scoville, W. B. (1938). Paranoid psychosis in narcolepsy and the possible danger of benzedrine treatment. *The Medical Clinics of North America, 22*, 637–646.

Zanarini, M. C., Gunderson, J. G., Frankenburg, F. R. (1990). Cognitive features of borderline personality disorder. *American Journal of Psychiatry, 147*(1), 57–63.

Chapter 17

DSM-5 (2013). *Diagnostic and statistical manual of mental disorders*, 5th ed. Washington, DC: American Psychiatric Association.

Appendix A

Barzun, J. (1983). *A stroll with William James*. New York: Harper & Row, Publishers.

Bernstein, C. A. (2011). Meta-structure in DSM-5 process. *Psychiatric News*, *46*(5), pp. 7–29.

Churchill, S. D., Wertz, F. J. (2014). An introduction to phenomenological research in psychology: Historical, conceptual, and methodological foundations. In K. J. Schneider, J. F. Pierson & J. F. T. Bugental (eds.) *The handbook of humanistic psychology: Theory, research, and practice*, 2nd ed. (pp. 275–295). Thousand Oaks, CA: SAGE.

Churchill, S. D. (1991). *Empathy and intuition: Doing psychology phenomenologically*. Unpublished Manuscript.

Giorgi, A. (1985). *Phenomenology and psychological research*. Pittsburgh: Duquesne University Press.

Husserl, E. (1960). *Cartesian meditations* (D. Cairns, trans.). The Hague, The Netherlands: Martinus Nijhoff.

Husserl, E. (1962). *Ideas* (W. H. B. Gibson, trans.). New York: Collier.

James, W. (1907). *Pragmatism: A new name for some old ways of thinking*. New York: Longmans.

Lief, A. (ed.) (1948). *The commonsense psychiatry of Dr. Adolf Meyer: Fifty-two selected papers*. New York: McGraw-Hill.

Muller, R. J. (1987). *The marginal self: An existential inquiry into narcissism*. Atlantic Highlands, NJ: Humanities Press International.

Smith, D. L. (2008). *Born to see, bound to behold: The history of Duquesne University's Simon Silverman Phenomenology Center*. Pittsburgh: The Simon Silverman Phenomenological Center of Duquesne University.

Wertz, F. (2011). The qualitative revolution and psychology: Science, politics, and ethics. *The Humanistic Psychologist*, 39, 70–104.

Appendix B

Séchehaye, M. (1956). *A new psychotherapy in schizophrenia: Relief of frustrations by symbolic realization* (G. Rubin-Rabson, trans.). New York: Grune & Stratton.

Appendix C

Kasanin, J. (1933). The acute schizoaffective psychoses. *American Journal of Psychiatry*, *90*(1), 97–126.

Malaspina, D., Owen, M. J., Heckers, S., Tandon, R., Bustillo, J., Schultz, S., Barch, D. M., Gaebel, W., Gur, R. E., Tsuang, M., Van Os, J. Carpenter, W. (2013). Schizoaffective disorder in the DSM-5. *Schizophrenia Research*, *150*(1), 21–25.

Index